Praise for *The Billionaire and the Mechanic*

"Splendid . . . Guthrie crisply sketches the complex process that was required for Ellison to establish his own position in the top ranks of yachting and organize the winning team in 2010. A thriller of a tale."

—*Kirkus Reviews*

"From the opening scene in this book—and scene is the appropriate word for its cinematic beginning—the reader is swept along on heart-thumping rides on swift, dueling sailboats, past an assemblage of characters worthy of Dreiser, past the shoals of deceit worthy of Dickens, and coming to rest on the formidable character of billionaire Larry Ellison, who has the will-to-win of his best friend, Steve Jobs, and of a mechanic, who made winning possible. Julian Guthrie writes as if with a magic wand, holding the reader spellbound."

—Ken Auletta

"Surely the most comprehensive book ever written about an America's Cup challenge, *The Billionaire and the Mechanic* will surely be must reading for any yacht-racing aficionado."

—Frank Deford

"Energetically written . . . sure to spark interest among racing fans."

—*Booklist*

"This is one helluva great read. Larry and Norbert—beautiful dreamers both, men with faith in their ability to convert them to reality. This book is fascinating; it informs, educates and entertains about the longest continuously contested trophy in all of sports."   —Bob Fisher, author of
An Absorbing Interest: The America's Cup—A History 1851-2003

"Larry Ellison's America's Cup victory was as improbable as it was inevitable. The same is true of his alliance with radiator repairman Norbert Bajurin. In this absorbing page-turner, Julian Guthrie tells us how they came together to make history."   —G. Bruce Knecht, author of
The Proving Ground: The Inside Story of the 1998 Sydney to Hobart Race

"*The Billionaire and the Mechanic* is pumping with adrenaline and yet full of subtle, surprising details about both sailing and one of the most mysterious, controversial characters on earth. This book is tirelessly reported and Guthrie has a rare writing gift to tie it all together into a work of literary journalism that reads like a thriller."

—Jaimal Yogis, author of *The Fear Project*

"If you're interested in the America's Cup competition, or in sailboat racing generally, you'll love this book. Julian Guthrie's taut and fascinating behind-the-scenes account of the colorful personalities, the risky development of astonishing new boats, and the hair-raising racing tactics of Larry Ellison's long campaign to win the trophy is necessary background reading."
—Derek Lundy, author of *Godforsaken Sea: A True Story of Racing the World's Most Dangerous Waters*

"Julian Guthrie's riveting book takes readers deep into uncharted realms, from the extremes of the ocean to the sublime connection between two singular men. *The Billionaire and the Mechanic* is a wondrously detailed story, beautifully told, by a writer who understands both the intricacies of human nature and the immensity of the natural world."
—Susan Casey, author of *The Wave: In Pursuit of the Rogues, Freaks, and Giants of the Ocean*

"Entertaining." —*Soundings*

"A gripping tale of world-class competition and strategic gamesmanship. . . . It will have enduring value as a great story in its own right." —*Sail World*

THE BILLIONAIRE
AND
THE MECHANIC

Also by Julian Guthrie

The Grace of Everyday Saints:
How a Band of Believers Lost Their Church
and Found Their Faith

THE BILLIONAIRE AND THE MECHANIC

How Larry Ellison and a Car Mechanic Teamed Up to Win Sailing's Greatest Race, the America's Cup, Twice

JULIAN GUTHRIE

Grove Press
New York

Published simultaneously in Canada
Printed in the United States of America

ISBN: 978-0-8021-2136-3
eISBN: 978-0-8021-9331-5

Grove Press
an imprint of Grove/Atlantic, Inc.
154 West 14th Street
New York, NY 10011

Distributed by Publishers Group West

www.groveatlantic.com

17 18 19   5 4 3

Dedicated to Larry and Norbert

Contents

PART III

PART IV

PART I

"All men dream, but not equally."
—T. E. Lawrence

1

The Southern Ocean

Between Australia and Tasmania

December 1998

SLEEK, WHITE, AND BEAUTIFUL, *Sayonara* sailed toward the Southern Ocean, a stretch of sea that circles Antarctica and is home to the world's most treacherous waves. Larry Ellison, at the wheel of his eighty-two-foot, twenty-five-ton maxi yacht, was doing over twenty knots downwind. Feeling the dense air on his face and watching the humidity press against *Sayonara*'s massive mainsail and spinnaker, Larry marveled, "Even *Sayonara* isn't supposed to go *this* fast." His boat began to plane, her bow lifting and the stern skimming the water, an angle the carbon fiber rocket was not designed for and had never done. Something was wrong.

In his red foul-weather gear and gray *Sayonara* cap, Larry looked at Brad Butterworth, a New Zealander with a gentle smile, thick hair, and a cache of major trophies. "*Sayonara* doesn't plane," Larry said incredulously. "It's great to go so fast, but *this* is surreal." They were twelve hours into one of the world's most competitive sailboat races and were sailing so fast they were already ahead of where the race record holder had been in twenty-four hours.

Larry and his team of twenty-two men—a who's who of professional sailors and a smattering of notables, including Lachlan

Murdoch, Rupert Murdoch's son—had left Sydney harbor on the afternoon of Saturday, December 26, in the running of the fifty-fourth annual Sydney-to-Hobart race. It was the height of summer in Australia and the sun shone brilliantly on the hundreds of thousands of people who lined the shore to watch the start. *Sayonara*, with her pristine white spinnaker with the red Japanese sun stamped in the middle—Larry's design—took an early lead in the 628-nautical-mile race due south to the island of Tasmania along the Tasman Sea.

Larry, the fifty-four-year-old cofounder and CEO of Oracle Corporation and a billionaire thirty times over, won the race in 1995 and had driven *Sayonara* to three consecutive maxi yacht world championships since. He wanted to see just how much better a sailor he had become. *It will be an interesting test,* he told himself of his second Sydney-to-Hobart. There was a clarity to be found in sports that couldn't be had in business. At Oracle he still wanted to beat the rivals IBM and Microsoft, but business was a marathon without end; there was always another quarter. In sports, the buzzer sounds and time runs out. Quarterback Joe Montana, with fifty-eight seconds left on the clock, throws a high pass to the back of the end zone and Dwight Clark makes a leaping grab with his fingertips, winning the NFC Championship against the Dallas Cowboys. Muhammad Ali endures seven rounds of pummeling by a younger and stronger George Foreman before knocking Foreman out in the eighth round, regaining the Heavyweight Championship of the World title. Michael Jordan nails his buzzer-beating jump shot against the Utah Jazz to win his sixth championship. Game over. Winner declared.

By early Sunday morning, December 27, the second day of the race, *Sayonara* blazed into the southeast corner of Australia, where the open ocean waves grow bigger and stronger, unimpeded by any mass of land. The wind had built continuously with gusts now approaching forty-five knots (about fifty-two miles per hour) and the sky had grown darker. Before the race the Australian Bureau of Meteorology had issued a gale warning, so sailors knew things could get rough. But Larry and most of the men on board had weathered similar winds in the 1995 race.

Sayonara was getting close to Bass Strait, the waters separating Australia from Tasmania, where the shallow sea bottom kicks up waves like surf and swells hit from all directions. Suddenly, a violent gust of over fifty knots accelerated *Sayonara*, and Larry angled her farther downwind to ease the pressure on her sails and rigging. But it was too late. The huge nylon spinnaker resembling the Japanese flag was shredded like a cotton sheet. With the wind becoming stronger and less predictable, the call was made to hoist the strongest spinnaker—nicknamed "the mini"— they had on board. "That sail is indestructible," Larry said confidently as *Sayonara* sliced through the whitecaps.

Stress focused the billionaire daredevil, who did aerobatics for fun, surfed in storms in Hawaii—he once broke his neck and the injury nearly left him a paraplegic—and had taken Oracle back from the brink of bankruptcy more than once. He was the world's fifth-wealthiest person just two decades after facing foreclosure on his own home and having his water and electricity turned off because he couldn't pay the bills. His hobbies, by his own admission, were a constant search for alternative stress. He had the same feeling now aboard *Sayonara* as when he'd landed his Italian Marchetti jet fighter on the 2,600-foot-long runway of the Bay Area's tiny San Carlos Airport: it concentrated his mind, forcing him into the present; and landing a jet on such a short runway was something his friend Steve Jobs had told him couldn't be done.

Sailing directly south on this Sunday morning, *Sayonara* was pounded by another massive gust and the impossible happened: the indestructible sail broke. The bronze fitting, with heavy threads almost two feet deep in the carbon fiber, had been extruded out of the spinnaker pole and the mini was swinging through the air like loose laundry. Gripping the wheel, Larry wondered, *What kind of force does that?*

Sayonara was now entering Bass Strait, ninety-five miles long and twice as wide and rough as the English Channel. Like the Bermuda Triangle, the Bass Strait had a mythical reputation; nicknamed the Black Hole, it was a place where vessels were lost or shipwrecked, where boats were snapped like twigs.

The gale force winds abruptly dropped, and the wind direction slowly clocked around from behind *Sayonara* to directly in front of her. The storm seemed to vanish as the wind calmed to less than ten knots. Butterworth and Larry, along with *Sayonara's* thirty-four-year-old boat manager Bill Erkelens, debated putting up the big heavy jib. Larry was in favor but Butterworth wanted to wait and sail *Sayonara* through the transition zone, the area where the northerly winds were changing to apparently mild southerlies, with only her mainsail up. They waited for ten minutes, until Larry was convinced they'd passed through the worst of the storm front. He made the call to hoist the jib, turned the wheel over to Butterworth, and headed to the navigation station at the back of the boat. He lowered himself into the hatch and took a seat on the cushioned bench before two adjacent laptops and a panel of communications equipment, warming his hands as he waited for satellite images to appear on-screen. As the first of the pictures filled a screen Larry's eyes grew wide. "Have you ever seen anything like this?" he asked.

Mark Rudiger, *Sayonara's* navigator and a member of the sailing team that had just won the grueling Whitbread Round the World Race, studied the milky images and slowly shook his head.

Looking at the swirling frothy cyclonic cloud with a plus sign in the center, Larry answered his own question: "Well, I have. It was on the Weather Channel and it's called a hurricane. That plus sign is us. We are in the eye of a fucking hurricane."

Back up on deck, Larry heard Butterworth screaming out commands. "It's coming hard guys! Everybody, get that jib down now!" It took about two minutes for the wind to go from under ten knots to back up over thirty. Five minutes later it was a solid fifty knots. Now, the situation was far worse than before. *Sayonara* was sailing at a speed of ten knots *into the wind* rather than going nearly twenty knots with the wind. The apparent wind speed over the deck had increased to sixty knots and the boat was heeling—leaning over—forty degrees. It was suddenly difficult and dangerous to move around on deck.

One by one, the men went below, grabbed their harnesses, and scrambled out of the hatch and back up on deck, where they cabled themselves to the boat to keep from being blown overboard. Moving around on deck involved unclipping one of the two Kevlar cables attached to the harness, then clipping on to a new location, then unclipping the other cable, and so on—slowly, methodically—like a rock climber.

Chris Dickson, who was *Sayonara*'s skipper—in charge of the boat and crew during a race—and one of the world's top sailors but a notoriously difficult boss, yelled at the men. Before leaving the dock in Sydney, the New Zealander had made the team go through rig testing and man-overboard drills. The men grumbled, saying it was a beautiful day, and they resisted, noting that Sydney harbor was full of sharks. Dickson wasn't one for excuses. Men went overboard and every bit of gear was tested and retested. Dickson had been in storms, and he had even sailed in hurricanes, but in boats strong enough to withstand the punishment. Asking *Sayonara* to hold up in a hurricane was like asking a Formula One car to race off-road.

Dickson listened to talk of possibly turning back and abandoning the race. He too wished he were somewhere else. But they were on their own, with no one to help them. Going back would be just as treacherous as sailing forward. With the hurricane upon them, waves like walls pounded *Sayonara*'s sides. Dickson, who had learned to sail as a kid and was the world's match racing champion by the time he was a teenager, started vomiting. Other sailors followed suit.

Larry was sure that there was no turning back and that conditions would worsen as they headed south, going into the latitudes seafarers call the roaring forties. The winds gusted up to sixty-five knots now, with a dissonant, bitter hissing and wailing—far more dangerous than the gale warnings that race officials had issued.

The rain pummeled them in sheets. Larry was somewhere he'd never been before. The sky, the sea, the sounds—everything was off, otherworldly. Trying to lighten the mood he told Butterworth, "This is how I choose to spend my Christmas holiday? It's costing me a lot of money to die here in Bass Strait. How stupid is that!"

Larry's boatbuilder Mark Turner, nicknamed "Tugsy" and "Tugboat," had dropped out of school at age fifteen in New Zealand to learn the craft of boatbuilding. Now he was down below making his way around *Sayonara* with a red marker.

"Tugsy, what the hell are you doing?" Larry asked.

"I'm marking where the carbon fiber is delaminating," Tugsy said calmly, his blue eyes flashing and his cheeks glowing red from being on deck in the wind and rain. "Different layers are snapping and breaking apart. The boat is in pretty bad shape."

"What!" Larry replied in disbelief. "The bow is coming off? That's just fucking great."

Tugsy had been in bad storms before, delivering boats for Larry and others, but he'd never been in a hurricane. Sailors didn't train for hurricanes, because they weren't supposed to *be* in hurricanes. *Sayonara* was being slammed, her parts groaning and wailing under the pressure loads. Tugsy, watchful, laconic, and deeply loyal to the boat and to Larry, was going to do whatever it took to keep *Sayonara* together. From his earliest days he had loved boats, whether images of mangrove rafts or thin-shelled dugouts made from fallen trees and used in man's first voyages on water or the sleek white thoroughbred he was now charged with protecting.

Time slowed, and even blinking felt like a luxury. There was no way off the boat and fear accomplished nothing. The rain stung like needles entering the skin. Larry, usually impervious to motion sickness—he was fond of rolling and looping his jet fighter—started vomiting too. Throwing up repeatedly while trying to steer *Sayonara* through the storm, he heard someone say, "Are you okay, mate?"

Larry thought to himself, *Not really*.

The radios were now down and all communications cut off. They had been shorted out by a water leak early in the race. Larry thought about what would happen if the boat got knocked down or rolled. Sailors could be trapped under the boat; water would rush on board. Losing the rudder or breaking the bow would end things. If they sank they'd have at most thirty minutes of life in the frigid sea. Larry, who lived in homes where every detail was perfect, where shoes were removed before entering to protect fine wood floors and minimize dirt, where cars were kept in temperature-controlled garages, where fresh flower arrangements were works of art, was in a world where money could not buy safety. He scanned the black void—not a single star could be seen and even the bow was hard to make out—and he berated himself again: *What kind of idiot comes out here to be fish food?*

The storm raged through the night and Larry, Butterworth, Erkelens, Robbie Naismith, Joey Allen, and Tony Rae took turns at the wheel, making their way around the yacht clip move by clip move. Mike "Moose" Howard, *Sayonara's* 250-pound grinder, an All-American linebacker at USC and marine combat veteran, had declared it was combat time with the sea.

Larry knew that the longer a hurricane lasts, the bigger the waves get. At the crest of the forty-foot waves, seventy-knot winds struck *Sayonara.* Perched at the top of a steep wave, lashed by the wind, *Sayonara* would free-fall—one, one thousand; two, one thousand; three, one thousand—off the crest and crash-land in a trough as welcoming as asphalt. There, in the relative calm, the wind would drop to forty knots. Then the next wave, another four-story giant, would hit, sending the boat airborne and into the next stomach-turning free fall. Larry watched in awe as Allen and Naismith drilled and patched an aluminum plate to *Sayonara's* main boom, which had bent like a straw in the storm. Their task was like trying to repair a car while riding a roller coaster.

Thirty-six hours into the storm Larry struggled with dehydration and exhaustion. Trying to sleep only made things worse. As the boat went for another free fall so did the men in the narrow carbon fiber bunks, which could be angled into a V with side pulleys to prevent them from falling out. Larry always kept a stash of

Snickers bars and cans of sardines for sailing races, but there was no hope of eating on this voyage. Even a sip of water came back up. In a lighter moment, Larry joked about the perils of trying to go to the bathroom in a hurricane. It was pitch black down below and every time the boat hit a wave he went flying through the air and crashed into a bulkhead. "I could easily have broken my neck," he said. "Now that would have been an embarrassing way to die."

Back on deck, Larry eyed the roiling sea and had an idea. *Sayonara* was on starboard tack, with the waves crashing into her right side. Larry told Rudiger he wanted to switch to port tack.

"It's a better wave angle and I want to get into the lee of Flinders Island," Larry said, aware that it's the waves that kill sailors, not the winds. "The closer we are to the island, the more the waves will be blocked."

"I'm not sure it's the right thing to do for the race," Rudiger said. "I'm going to have to check with Chris."

"Mark," Larry shot back. "Let me be clear. I want to tack the boat. That means we're tacking the boat. Do you think *sinking* is the right thing to do for the race?"

Erkelens agreed that it wasn't the right thing to do for the race—it would put them off course for the finish—but it was the best thing to try to salvage the boat, and save lives.

Tacking the boat shifted their course by sixty degrees. The waves didn't get smaller but *Sayonara* began to take the hits directly on the bow rather than the side of the boat. The pounding was reduced and the ride was less violent. Heading closer to Flinders Island, at the northeastern tip of Tasmania, Larry took inventory: two men had broken bones, a fire had ignited in the navigation station when the electronics got wet and shorted, and his boat was bruised and beaten. But everyone was alive and accounted for. Tacking the boat had made a critical difference.

On the morning of the third day the sun was just coming up as *Sayonara* entered the Derwent River, an estuary leading to the capital of Tasmania. A salmon-pink light cut through the mauve morning sky. The crew of *Sayonara,* the first to reach the Derwent, was welcomed by a small powerboat with a man on board playing Scottish Highland bagpipes, the traditional welcome for the winning boat. On this day, the songs were funereal: "When the Battle Is Over," "O for a Closer Walk with God," "Amazing Grace." The wind was a whisper, blowing at less than eight knots. Larry and his crew were in the river valley, and wildflowers, fern, and towering trees carpeted deep-cut canyons with red dirt ridges. The wildflowers in shades of blue, white, purple, crimson, and heather were bathed in soft pink light. Larry closed his eyes for a moment, listening to the somber sounds of the bagpipe and to the waves gently lapping at the sides of the boat. The air was perfectly calm; the waves like a reassuring heartbeat. The glory of life was theirs.

But it wasn't a joyous victory. Larry looked at Butterworth and said it was like "Disney trying to rewrite the ending of a horror film." The crew had learned upon sailing into the harbor that six sailors had died, five boats had sunk, an estimated fifty-five people had been lifted by helicopter in airborne heroics, and it looked as if only a third of the 115 boats that had started would finish the race. It was already being called the worst maritime disaster in Australian history. *Sayonara* crossed the finish line at 8 a.m. on Tuesday morning, three hours ahead of the next boat, *Brindabella,* which had won the race the year before, and hours ahead of *Ragamuffin,* helmed by an eighteen-year-old Australian named Jimmy Spithill.

Reaching the modest-looking Constitution Dock, the *Sayonara* crew scanned the crowd. A group of women, including Larry's girlfriend, the romance novelist Melanie Craft, had been out partying the night before, drinking margaritas and eating oysters. Although there were reports of a hurricane-force storm in the sailors' path, friends and loved ones had no way of knowing how bad things had been and figured *Sayonara* would be fine with its world-class crew. Expressions changed fast when they saw the looks on the sailors' faces. Nearly three days without food or water. Constant vomiting. A sea that flickered teasingly between beautiful and treacherous. Stepping off the boat, the world's toughest sailors, most of them blue-collar guys, embraced their wives or girlfriends for a long moment; most teared up and a few cried.

Dickson stepped ashore and hugged his wife, Sue. As skipper, Dickson knew enough to let his shoulders drop only after the boat was safely back at the dock and handed over to the shore crew. Standing there Dickson, thirty-seven years old, remembered when he was a teenager waiting in the very same place for his father, Roy Dickson, an accomplished yachtsman, to come in from a race. Other boats were greeted with cheers and fanfare but when his dad arrived on *Inca*—an aluminum forty-five-footer by Olin Stephens, best known for designing winning America's Cup boats—there was silence. One of *Inca*'s sailors had died of a heart attack midway through the race. Emotions on that day, and this one, were a mixture of relief and sadness. They had made it but others weren't so lucky.

On the pier Larry and Melanie embraced. Melanie stepped back to look at her boyfriend's thin face. He was badly shaken.

"I didn't know," she said. "We simply didn't know. We thought you were good."

Larry, dehydrated and fifteen pounds lighter than when he started, was interviewed for local television.

"Did we do everything right?" Larry asked. "Not everything, but we gave ourselves a chance to be lucky. It wasn't Mother Nature's worst. Had it been, she would have killed us. We had a great boat, great crew, and we are lucky to be alive today. Our guys were knocked down over and over again, and they kept getting up and going back to work to do what was needed to keep the boat in one piece and keep all of us alive. I saw heroes out there."

Asked whether he would ever do the race again, Larry, angry at race officials for not accurately predicting the ferocity of the storm, said, "If I live for another thousand years, I'll never do this race again." Then, regaining his sense of humor, he offered a weak smile and said, "No, if I'm around one thousand years from now, in the year 2998, I'll come back and do it again."

Back at Craft's hotel room, Larry peeled off his foul-smelling foul-weather gear. Craft wanted to throw away or burn everything he was wearing. But before jumping into the shower and later taking a hot bath Larry insisted that they hold on to his *Sayonara* jacket. It was something he intended to keep.

Dressed and feeling half human again, Larry headed out with Craft for single scoops of vanilla ice cream. Then they boarded Larry's Gulfstream jet for Antigua, where his family was waiting. Larry slept for eighteen hours straight, not even waking during refueling in Hawaii.

In Antigua, with his family around him, Larry relaxed on the deck of his megayacht *Katana*—named after the samurai sword—and reflected on his pyrrhic victory. Larry told his nephew Jimmy Linn; his daughter, Megan; and his son, David, that he didn't view Sydney-to-Hobart as a win. "There was no sense of triumph, at least for me," Larry said, noting how Ted Turner famously quipped after a serious storm hit the Fastnet race off the southern coast of England, "What storm?" That was not Larry's reaction. "Really great sailors died out there. Beautiful boats, good boats, were sunk. I did get to see how people react in a life-and-death situation, and I got to see how truly heroic some people could be."

Linn, the son of Larry's stepsister Doris, held his hand up and said that the dangerous race was a crazy way to spend his vacation. "What were you thinking?"

Larry deadpanned, "What do you mean? It's one hell of a way to lose weight. Who needs Jenny Craig when you have Sydney-to-Hobart?"

After the laughter died down Larry turned serious. "Why do we do these things? George Mallory said the reason he wanted to climb Everest was because 'it's there.' I don't think so. I think Mallory was wrong. It's not because it's there. It's because *we're* there, and we wonder if we can do it."

2

Radiator Repair Shop in San Francisco

Fall 1999

NORBERT BAJURIN WALKED through the radiator shop with its familiar smells of motor grease and coolant—smells others found repellent but he found reassuring. Taking inventory of two dozen cars, from Chevy pickups to new Jaguars, he listened on the radio to Foreigner's "Love Isn't Always on Time." The tune took him back to more carefree days, when he was single and in the army, when he had three square meals a day, and when there was no one to account for but himself.

In the shop twenty mechanics were at work repairing or recoring radiators, removing the old soldering and giving them new copper and brass centers when surrounding parts held up fine. Increasingly, Norbert's guys were installing radiators with plastic tanks made overseas for a fraction of the old price.

Norbert gave one of his mechanics a pat on the back and asked about his family before talk gravitated to football. Norbert was a die-hard San Francisco 49ers fan, but he was impressed by the come-from-behind story of the St. Louis Rams, a team that had been losing for nearly a decade and was suddenly on fire. The mechanics talked about the chances of the Rams making it to the Super Bowl.

Another mechanic, looking up from under the hood of a car, asked "Norbini" if he'd done any good fishing over the weekend. Norbert, known to love to fish though he hated to sail, said he planned to head out on the bay in coming weeks. During the early summer salmon were caught near the Golden Gate and off the coast of Marin, south of Bolinas. From May through the end of October halibut were to be had in the waters off Crissy Field and along the south side of Angel Island. Rockfish and lingcod were fished from the beginning of June through December and found along the coast and offshore.

Heading toward his office, he took mental note of the wear and tear on different cars and trucks. He could now gauge how close someone lived to the ocean by the level of corrosion. "You're out in the Sunset, right?" he would ask a customer. Or, "You're in the Richmond," knowing those in the one neighborhood were closer than those in the other. Norbert knew he had become a genuine radiator repair guy when he relished the salt air; it was the bread and butter of his trade.

"When one thing goes wrong with the car's air-conditioning, it can cause problems throughout the entire cooling and heating system," Norbert would explain to customers struggling to understand the issues with their cars. "A car's air-conditioning system is like the human body," he liked to say. "The compressor is the heart, the receiver dryer is the liver, the condensers with their filters are the kidneys, the hoses and expansion valves are the veins." Norbert had a friendly manner that customers took to, a habit of leaning into the person he was talking to, an endearing way of flashing a crooked smile. Naturally loquacious, Norbert could marvel at the inner workings of a car engine, recite football stats, banter with the guys, and be silenced for a few seconds as a pretty woman walked by.

Walls of the garage were draped and dotted with bypass hoses and heater hoses, belts, compressors, expansion valves, relays, switches, and automatic control parts for nearly every year, make, and model of car that might roll into the shop. Two massive Magnum lifting systems were next to the intake area. Boxes were filled with radiators and shelves stocked with motor oil and all-weather antifreeze coolant. Norbert, who sold, repaired, and distributed radiators, had begun contracting with a manufacturer in Thailand to make plastic-tank radiators, the latest major convulsion to hit his business. He bought two container loads, which were ten feet wide by forty feet long and held thirteen hundred radiators each. He had explained to his father, Jozo, that they could take a radiator made for a Toyota, which would cost about two hundred dollars to have installed at the dealership, and instead have one made in Thailand that met or exceeded the specifications for the original equipment manufacturing for a quarter of the price. Then they could bring it back to San Francisco and sell it at a 110 percent markup and still come in eighty to ninety dollars cheaper than the dealer.

Jozo (pronounced "Yozo") had arrived that morning at his usual time, nine-thirty, and decamped to his upstairs office, decorated with a midsize marlin and a pinup calendar. He sat at his desk reading the paper and reviewing accounts receivable. For the first time, the shop's records were automated instead of being handwritten in heavy, smudged logs. The issue of electronic accounting had been one of many battles between father and son. Norbert had insisted they invest in computers; Jozo had contended that computers were way too expensive. Norbert finally won, getting his father to agree to a $20,000 investment, and the first day Norbert printed out the accounts receivable his father saw on one page all they were owed. Dad liked what he saw.

The summer before had been especially profitable for Norbert and Jozo Bajurin (pronounced "Byron"), with a prolonged heat wave choking the Bay Area. The crew worked twelve- to fourteen-hour days and every space in the garage was taken up. Norbert said, only half-joking, that he was making Jozo a rich man.

Norbert had joined Alouis Auto Radiator only reluctantly. In doing so, he had to give up a job he enjoyed as a police officer in Rohnert Park, a bedroom community about an hour north of San Francisco, where most of the police work involved daytime break-ins and traffic violations. He had started in Rohnert Park in 1978, at midnight, just six hours after getting out of the military. He was the force's twelfth hire. The Rohnert Park chief, Bob Dennett, was his mentor and confidant and Norbert shared with him the problems he had with his father. Dennett always told him to work things out: "He's the only father you've got."

Standing under the Alouis shop's sign—the A was added decades ago to jump to the start of the Yellow Pages—Norbert looked at his calendar. His dad was now downstairs talking with a customer, one of the old-timers who liked it when the storytelling Jozo was around. He and the old-timer would talk about boats and the best spots for the biggest fish more than they would talk about cars or radiators. Jozo was something of a legend in boating circles, having sailed on a fifty-foot steel hull out of the Golden Gate Bridge to Tahiti and back in 1973.

Jozo, whose formal education had ended in the eighth grade when he started technical school, began in radiator repair in San Francisco in 1959. Frank Glogoshki, a Croatian who ran a business out of his garage in San Francisco's residential Castro District, taught Jozo the trade. Jozo worked at another shop, at Golden Gate Avenue and Fillmore Street, beginning in 1963. He learned the business at a time when air-conditioning systems were first appearing in early Chevrolets and Cadillacs, and radiators were easy. Five models of cars all shared the same type of radiator. Nowadays, one make of car could have five different radiators that worked. In 1967 Jozo became a partner in the shop, and in May 1985 he and his partner moved to the current location on Divisadero Street, where they had 12,500 square feet downstairs and 1,450 square feet upstairs in a building that dated to 1898. Alouis took up half a city block in a gritty part of San Francisco bordering the Western Addition.

Throughout his career Jozo had sent money to his brothers Niksa and Zwonko, and his sisters Franica and Katica, in Croatia. Another brother, Ante, had died at the age of seven, when he was playing in a field and mistook an Italian grenade for a ball. It detonated in his hands. Jozo's siblings in Hodilje, a small fishing village, lived on the equivalent of about eighty dollars a month from the government. To make ends meet they fished and farmed, growing olives, tomatoes, and potatoes and selling oysters and mussels to bring in a few extra dinars or kuna, the local currency.

For the first time in their lives Norbert, who had just turned forty-four, and his father, twenty-two years his senior, were getting along. They had been pulled together by the death of Norbert's mother three years earlier. Gertrude was fifty-nine when she had an asthma attack during the start of a vacation in Europe. After thirty-five years at the Bank of America in San Francisco, where she started as a teller and left as a vice president, Gertrude had retired and gotten a part-time job with a travel agency in Marin County to stay busy. There she had found a $220 round-trip deal to Germany. She was in Amsterdam on her way to Hamburg when she suffered a major asthma attack. She held on long enough for Jozo and Norbert to be at her side when she passed away at a Dutch hospital.

One of the things Norbert and his father had in common was fishing. They also loved stopping in for a drink at the Golden Gate Yacht Club, situated on a quiet, unkempt nook along the San Francisco marina, close to where Jozo moored his boat.

Jozo had lobbied Norbert for years to join his radiator business, where Norbert had worked part-time off and on. In the early 1970s Norbert earned five dollars an hour there and saved enough money to buy his first car, a brown 1973 Ford Pinto.

Norbert joined the radiator shop in 1982. At the time, annual gross revenues were around $1 million. Seventeen years later revenues had climbed to $2.4 million, and a steady year was $1.6 million. As he looked around the garage packed with cars, Norbert took a measure of pride in what he was doing. But it still felt like his father's American dream, not his own.

3

The Island of Antigua

May 2000

CLAD IN KHAKI SHORTS and a *Sayonara* T-shirt, a suntanned Larry Ellison sat down at a campfire with friends and fellow sailors, the sun setting on the clear blue waters and white powder sands of English Harbour in the West Indies island of Antigua.

Larry and his *Sayonara* crew had just won Antigua Sailing Week for the second year in a row. First run in 1967 and known for its gorgeous backdrop and rum-infused après-sailing parties, the race was the Caribbean's most prestigious event. *Sayonara* had bested a fleet of 300 boats, including *Morning Glory,* owned by SAP head Hasso Plattner; and *Boomerang,* owned by the shipping magnate George Coumantaros. In her five years, *Sayonara* had finished first in twenty-five of twenty-seven starts. She also had held up heroically under the near-death battering of the 1998 Sydney-to-Hobart. The win in Antigua gave the Oracle boss his fourth maxi-class world championship and ownership of one of the most successful racing sailboats in history.

Around the campfire, as a Caribbean steel drum band played and a soft breeze blew through the palm trees, Larry sipped water from a plastic bottle. He had abruptly stopped drinking in his early twenties, following an embarrassing incident at a party when he kissed a particularly alluring young woman wearing a diaphanous pink dress. The woman just happened to be engaged to a friend of his. The sailors around the campfire drank beer and talked about the gossip roiling international sailing. The word was that Russell Coutts, the mop-haired Kiwi skipper of Team New Zealand, which had just won the America's Cup, sailing's most coveted prize, had gone to work for a young European billionaire named Ernesto Bertarelli, who was mounting a Swiss challenge for the next Cup, in 2003. The defections by Coutts and four team members—Murray Jones, Simon Daubney, Dean Phipps, and Warwick Fleury—had infuriated New Zealanders and sent shock waves through the legions who followed the sport. Bertarelli had said he simply couldn't live with himself if he passed up such an opportunity. While the Cup had long been dotted with free agents, or mercenary sailors, seeing the successful Coutts and his lieutenants jump ship for another country was akin to watching the United States' top tennis players represent the French in the Davis Cup. For nearly a century and a half, the America's Cup had been fiercely nationalistic. Never had there been such high-profile poaching or defections. And in recent years the Kiwis had become the New York Yankees of sailing, stealing the Cup away from "Mr. America's Cup," Dennis Conner, in San Diego in 1995 and defending it in Auckland, New Zealand, in 2000. Under Coutts, who had earned the moniker "Crash Coutts" for his aggressive tactics, Team New Zealand had not lost a single race.

The news got Larry thinking. He had followed the Cup for decades and was twenty-six when he read the attention-grabbing story of Bill Ficker winning the Cup for the New York Yacht Club. "Ficker Is Quicker" the headline read. Larry liked it that the race had begun a half century before the first modern World Series and nearly two decades before college football was born on the East Coast. The first regatta was held as part of the International Exhibition, or "world's fair," in London, which opened on May Day 1851 and celebrated the latest in industry, arts, and science—from the precursor to the telegraph to the sewing machine.

Among those in attendance at the fair in Hyde Park were Charles Dickens; Samuel Colt; Alfred, Lord Tennyson; and members of the royal family. Paid for by the industrialists who exhibited, the fair was famous for its Crystal Palace made of glass and steel. The vision for the international exhibition came from Queen Victoria's husband, Prince Albert. But the idea for a sailboat race between nations came from a handful of members of the New York Yacht Club, opened in 1844.

America, offered up as the United States' finest display of innovation on the water, was a ninety-five-foot, black gaff-rigged schooner with a concave bow, low freeboard, and cotton sails—said to hold their shape better than the flax sails of the British yachts— and shaped on the lines of a pilot boat. She had set sail from New York City's East River in June and was manned throughout her Atlantic crossing by Captain W. H. Brown—who owned a shipyard at the foot of East 12th Street in New York—and a crew of twelve men. Brown had built *America* for $20,000 in cash. The Marquis of Anglesey, a member of the Royal Yacht Squadron, formed in 1815 and the first club in England granted the "Royal" designation, took one look at *America* and said, "If she is right, we are all wrong." Another Brit remarked that *America* looked like a "hawk among pigeons."

The sailing team aboard *America* was led by John Cox Stevens, the son of a Revolutionary War officer, the first commodore of the New York Yacht Club, and a man known to make a wager or two on sporting events. The crew included James Hamilton, son of the founding father Alexander Hamilton, the first United States secretary of the treasury. The race—fifty-three miles around the Isle of Wight, where Queen Victoria had her summer home, Osborne House—began at 10 a.m. on Friday, August 22, in an eleven-knot breeze and involved one American yacht and fifteen British boats. *America* took an early lead and held on to it, defeating the British yacht *Aurora* by eight minutes. Toward the end of the race, Queen Victoria reportedly asked an attendant to tell her who was in second place. "Ma'am, there is no second," was the reply, a statement that came to embody the Cup.

The victorious American team was handed a bottomless silver ewer weighing 134 ounces and standing 27 inches high, purchased from Robert Garrard, the royal jeweler, in 1848 and presented to the Royal Yacht Squadron. The silver ewer was wrongly inscribed—and remains so today—the "100 Guinea Cup" by the Americans, who confused guineas with pounds (100 guineas would have been £105). It also was mistakenly referred to in the early days as "the Queen's Cup." When the Cup was returned to the New York Yacht Club after the 1851 victory, there was talk of melting it down to make medallions for the winning crew members to wear around their necks. It was saved from that fate and presented to the New York Yacht Club as a perpetual challenge trophy.

The first defense was in August 1870, the year the trophy was renamed the America's Cup, after the New York Yacht Club's winning yacht. More than a dozen American yachts, all racing for the New York Yacht Club, competed against the British ship *Cambria* in New York Bay. *Cambria* finished tenth, the schooner *Magic* won, and *America,* which had been refitted by the U.S. Navy, finished fourth.

From its inception the regatta captivated the public's imagination, for the boats and the races and all that went on around them. It was as much about the innovations and science as about the sailing.

In 1895 an estimated sixty-five thousand people watched the tenth America's Cup from boats off New York City, more than watched what was then called the Temple Cup, the postseason championship series in baseball's National League, that year. The competition had become the biggest sporting event in the world. In the days leading up to the races in New York, steamships arrived from Europe packed with spectators, and trains brought enthusiasts from across America. On race days in England, tens of thousands of people poured into the blocks around Fleet Street, waiting for newspapers to come out with the latest dispatches on the Cup.

The excitement was hardly diminished by the inability of most to actually see the races or understand what transpired out on the course. The sight of the spectacular boats and the massive billowing sails was enough to draw cheers.

At the turn of the century Sir Thomas Lipton, the Irish tea and grocery store magnate, caught "Cup fever" and went after the Cup five times over three decades, from 1899 to 1930, and never won. The scrappy self-made millionaire, who was tall and elegant and an avowed bachelor, got into the Cup competition after befriending avid racers, including the American J. P. Morgan, a competitor for the Cup in 1899 and 1901. Lipton's first boat, *Shamrock,* was imposing, and its hull was painted green. When Lipton arrived in New York for his first Cup challenge, he was welcomed as "Sir Tea" and "Jubilee Lipton" and hailed in the press as a poor-boy-who-made-good. It was a time when automobiles were just beginning to appear, and the United States was brimming with optimism, as the population was close to 78 million and the country was poised to overtake Great Britain as the leader in industrial production. When Lipton arrived in New York, he told the gathered masses, "I am here to win, if possible." At his death at age eighty-one, Lipton—whose popularity grew with each Cup challenge—still dreamed of holding what he termed the "Auld Mug."

Begun as a genteel competition between nations, the Cup quickly evolved into a coalescence of talent and technology, where the battle was fought on land long before it ever reached the sea. Lipton was among the first to see that the American defenders had a huge advantage in that they could build boats to sail in the races only, whereas the challengers needed vessels strong enough to cross the Atlantic before reaching the start of the race.

By the late twentieth century the elite nautical show was considered harder to win than the Olympics. The stories of those who pursued sailing's holy grail were the stuff of lore. The Australian skipper John Bertrand snatched the Cup away from the New York Yacht Club in 1983 in a dramatic, down-to-the-wire victory. The New York club had held the Cup for 132 years, the longest winning streak in international sports. Bertrand described his quest as a "higher calling, a stirring within, something as old as human life." Bill Koch, the billionaire businessman, spent nearly $70 million to win the 1992 campaign with *America³*, also called *America Cubed*. Koch called the race "the most ruthless sporting contest I have ever seen." When Koch won he dived off the bow of his yacht, climbed up to the deck of the San Diego yacht club, and hoisted the trophy above him before the cheering masses. "This is a triumph for American technology and American teamwork," Koch declared. Australian Sir Frank Packer attributed his obsession with the Cup to "alcohol and delusions of grandeur." Others had called it a "rich man's game and a blood sport," and a "gentleman's sport and, because of that, you have to watch everything."

Larry had made a study of boat designs, and he admired and owned the clipper ship paintings of the marine artist Montague Dawson. He marveled at how a race that began with huge schooners weighing 170 tons now involved aerodynamic and hydrodynamic designs and testing by NASA engineers, telemetry, around-the-clock meteorology, and the latest in high-compression carbon fiber. Inexorable innovations in materials science had taken the yachts from timber to aluminum to fiberglass to carbon fiber—a carbon more advanced than that used on a Boeing jetliner. And the classes of boats had also changed dramatically. In the 1930s J-class yachts, which ranged in size from 119 feet overall and 81 feet on the waterline to 136 feet overall and 87 feet on the waterline, were sailed by the world's wealthiest men, including Lipton, Morgan, and Harold "Mike" Vanderbilt, and conceived by the legendary yacht designer Nathanael Greene Herreshoff. During the Great Depression, the America's Cup became the premier international sporting event and lifted downtrodden spirits. Even the boats were given names intended to inspire: *Enterprise* in 1930 and *Rainbow* in 1934. The Cup was interrupted for twenty years by the war, and the races didn't resume until 1958. Money was scarce after World War II, and the America's Cup was an extravagance. When racing resumed in 1958, it was contested in a 12-Meter-class boat (the

"12 meters" had to do with a formula of measurements, not the length of the boat). The international class, sloop-rigged and with masts 85 feet tall, was seen as well suited for match racing. And, more recently, after a controversial legal challenge between New Zealand and Dennis Conner in 1988, it was decided that there would be a new class of boat, the International America's Cup Class (IACC), where boats would be designed to a formula in an effort to level the playing field. These boats first sailed in San Diego in 1992 when Koch defeated Il Moro di Venezia's boat, skippered by San Francisco native Paul Cayard. The same class sailed in the 1995 and 2000 defenses.

With changes to the boats came changes to the crew. The red pants and straw hats of sailors past had been replaced: now, sinewy world-class athletes, who looked like superheroes in their protective vests and tight shirts, wore body monitors to gauge aerobic and anaerobic output, and consulted small electronic displays showing wind speed, sea state, and optimal sail angles. A competition that once drew weekend sailors—often East Coast collegians—and their wealthy patrons now utilized playbooks, sports psychologists, video-based data on opponents' patterns on the water, software showcasing virtual dogfights between the various teams, and live streaming data with pressure loads throughout the boat during races. And while sailors were once paid in room and board—and housed for the summer in Newport mansions—they could now earn tens of thousands of dollars a month or more. The sailors also had gone from having one skill set, simply knowing the boat and reading the conditions, to understanding how the boats were engineered and built and what the physics were behind a boat's drag and propulsion.

Larry's own interest in sailing had been sparked when he was a teenager living in the lower-middle-class South Side of Chicago with his adoptive parents, Lillian and Louis Ellison. He was enthralled by a *National Geographic* cover story about a boy named Robin Lee Graham, the youngest person to solo-circumnavigate the globe. The first installment of the story ran with a picture of a lean, tan, shirtless Graham on his twenty-four-foot sloop *Dove* under the title, "A Teen-Ager Sails the World Alone." Larry read every word of the teen's adventures in his small boat, his navigating to exotic places, and his keeping two kittens and a shortwave radio for company. He envied how Graham's parents supported him on his adventure, as this was the opposite of his own life. Larry's stepfather, a Russian Jew who had come to the United States in 1905 aboard a steamer and had changed his difficult Russian name to Ellison upon reaching Ellis Island, seemed to spend a great deal of time telling young Larry he would never amount to anything, and the two disagreed more than they agreed. Lou Ellison revered authority figures—he was forever grateful to be an American—but Larry found those in charge mostly uninspiring or wrong. When the two debated the virtues of President Eisenhower and his policies, Lou advised Larry, "He's the president. He knows things that we don't know. That information enables the president to make the right decisions, even if we can't understand them." Larry responded, "He looks human to me. I'm sure he makes mistakes like everybody else." Larry never believed in the infallibility of authority figures and was fond of quoting Mark Twain: "What's an expert—just some guy from out of town."

Larry never forgot the "expert" advice he had gotten from authority figures while growing up. As a sophomore at South Shore High School, Larry had been told that if he failed Latin it would "ruin" his life. He looked at his teacher and said, "If I'm paralyzed in a car accident, that might ruin my life, but a grade is just a letter in a rectangle." The teacher was not amused, but Larry studied just enough to get a C. As a junior he had nearly failed biology because he never went to lab, choosing instead to go to basketball practice. His biology teacher, who happened to be the mother of one of his best friends, told him over a family dinner that if she flunked him for skipping all the labs he would lose his eligibility for all sports. Larry countered, "What if I get the highest grade on the final exam and I prove that I know more about biology than anyone else in the class? Will you will still flunk me?" She said, "Yes," and Larry thought, *Cool, so the person who knows more about biology than anyone else in class will be the only one that flunks. That's how the world works.* Uncharacteristically, Larry studied hard and surprised everybody by getting the highest grade on the difficult final exam. The biology teacher relented and gave him a C. In physics class he was equally unpopular with his teacher, as Larry had an obnoxious way of correcting his instructor while he was writing solutions to problems on the board. Larry had what schools in those days labeled a "deportment problem." The story of Graham transported Larry from the regimentation and catechism of high school to the adventure and freedom of the sea. Here was a boy alone at sea for weeks at a stretch; dealing with storms, circling sharks, and broken masts; visiting exotic locales such as Pago Pago and Guadalcanal. Through it all he was his own navigator.

Larry gazed into the Antigua campfire and smiled at the sailors' gossip. Someone announced it was time to head in to change for the night's awards ceremony. A short time later, Larry arrived at the inn wearing khaki pants, a black belt, and a short-sleeved black silk *Sayonara* shirt.

One of the things Larry liked about Antigua was a particular slice of its history. It had been the training ground for one of his heroes, Admiral Horatio Nelson, who as a young lieutenant pursued Caribbean rumrunners from his base on the island. Larry was sure that had he lived in the early nineteenth century he would have joined the Royal Navy. In the army, wealthy aristocrats would pay to outfit and be in charge of a regiment, but the navy was to some degree a meritocracy, where progressing up the ladder was a matter of being skillful at the mathematics of navigation while being lucky enough not to be killed in battle. Horatio Nelson had started in the navy as a powder monkey, one of the kids small enough to carry gunpowder from the magazine in the center of a warship through the small wooden tunnels that led to the cannons on the gun decks. Years later, Nelson commanded the British fleet of twenty-seven ships that defeated thirty-three French and Spanish ships in the famous Battle of Trafalgar in 1805 during the

Napoleonic wars. It was the most decisive British naval victory of the war, and Nelson was victorious—though shot and killed in the battle—thanks to his unorthodox tactical moves. Instead of setting up his fleet in a single line against the enemy, as was the prevailing strategy at the time, he divided his smaller force into two perpendicular lines against the formidable opposing fleet; this configuration left the French confused and, ultimately, defeated.

Larry sat down at a table in the inn. He was still thinking about the defections by superstar Coutts and the Kiwis when Tony Rae, *Sayonara*'s trimmer and a gregarious New Zealander, approached and asked him whether he had thought of taking his sailing team to the next level. He pointed out that Larry already had an impressive crew, with Dickson, Butterworth, Joey Allen, Robbie Naismith, and himself, along with a boat design team led by Kiwi Bruce Farr and the building crew of another Kiwi, Mark "Tugsy" Turner.

"Has anyone ever died in the America's Cup?" Larry jokingly asked. After Sydney-to-Hobart, Larry had sworn off open ocean racing in favor of around-the-buoys regattas. Rae, who went by "Trae," had been a member of Team New Zealand since 1987 and was part of the crew that seized the Cup in 1995 and defended it in March 2000, just two months earlier. He laughed off Larry's question (the answer was yes; a Japanese sailor had died on an America's Cup boat during training) and worked on explaining how a campaign was organized and some of what was required. Forming a syndicate, or team, for the America's Cup was like launching a political campaign. The candidate—team, skipper, and boat—had to be readied and had to win the primary, in this case, the America's Cup qualifying series, the Louis Vuitton Cup, to get to the big dance.

As in politics, the winner, like a gerrymandering legislature, controlled future competitors and ruled until he was unseated. Governing the Cup almost since its inception was the Deed of Gift, first drafted in 1857. At the time, this was a simple 240-word document promising that the race would be "a friendly competition between foreign nations" and that the challenger would travel to the competition "on its own bottom." A provision of the next revision of the Deed of Gift banned teams sailing from any "Great Lakes clubs," and required a challenging yacht club to hold races on an "arm of the sea." Subsequent revisions set forth a whole new series of requirements, from when teams had to give notice of a challenge to the boat specifications and process of registering the boat.

"So why don't you do the America's Cup?" Rae asked, kneeling by the table, with the awards ceremony delayed by more than an hour. Rae assured Larry that Ernesto Bertarelli, with his deep pockets and deeper ambitions, was not the only billionaire who could lure away talented Kiwis. Rae offered to help with the planning and structuring.

Larry mulled over the idea. Team *Sayonara* hadn't lost a buoy regatta since it was launched in 1995. Team New Zealand hadn't lost since 1995. Someone had to lose in 2003. Until now, the Kiwis appeared invincible. Larry hadn't wanted to poach on the team for the same reason he didn't date married women: you don't break up a family.

"Okay, let's do it," Larry said to Rae's surprise. The Oracle boss hadn't asked about costs or sponsorships, questions that typically stalled such decisions, given that a single Cup campaign could run the team owner between $50 million and $100 million and took years of planning before a single race began. Larry reasoned that he could buy the San Francisco 49ers football team and still not play quarterback. Here, he could buy the team and hold the wheel. He had every intention of driving.

Bill Erkelens, *Sayonara*'s manager, was standing about twenty feet away when Robbie Naismith, another member of the Cup-winning Team New Zealand, came over to him and said in a low voice, "You better head over. They're talking about doing the America's Cup, and they're not joking."

Larry told Erkelens that he wanted to do the America's Cup if they could sign up Bruce Farr, who had designed *Sayonara*.

Erkelens looked at Larry and nodded, and the ceremony began. Erkelens knew to expect surprises from his boss. He had been recruited six years earlier to head the building and racing operations of *Sayonara* by Larry's neighbor David Thomson, who raced maxi yachts. The first time Erkelens met Larry was when he went to Larry's Atherton, California, home to present the completed drawings of *Sayonara*. A lifelong sailor and lover of boats, Erkelens had never seen anything like her; *Sayonara* would be spectacular. He and Thomson presented the drawings. Larry took a look and asked one question: "Can she win?" He then proceeded to ask excitedly whether they wanted to see drawings of a new airplane he was building. Erkelens left the meeting with no idea whether the *Sayonara* project was a go, but he understood one thing: he would be dealing with an eccentric.

A week after the Antigua awards ceremony, after delivering *Sayonara* back in South Florida, Erkelens got a call from Larry's office, with Larry on the line.

"Did you hire him?" Larry asked, without saying hello.

"Hire who?" Erkelens asked.

"Bruce Farr."

"You were not kidding about the America's Cup?"

"No, I wasn't kidding."

4

San Francisco Marina

Spring 2000

Norbert closed up his radiator shop on lower Divisadero Street in San Francisco, an area of small, working-class businesses, with public housing close by and a smattering of hip bars, clubs, and cafés. He got into his truck and drove north, climbing the steep part of Divisadero up into Pacific Heights, a neighborhood with some of the priciest real estate anywhere in the world. Reaching Broadway, Norbert paused to look below. Divisadero dropped like a heady roller-coaster ride, with the city and bay a gorgeous pastel tapestry laid out before him. His destination, the Golden Gate Yacht Club, was straight ahead.

Driving into the marina yacht harbor Norbert slowed as he passed the St. Francis Yacht Club, with its Spanish-tile roof and expansive views of the bay. To the right were the slips with yachts belonging to St. Francis members. About 125 yards down the road Norbert passed an old stone lighthouse and the road turned from smooth to bumpy and then, in the final stretch to the Golden Gate clubhouse, to unpaved.

He parked in one of the four spots outside the club and headed down the wooden walkway, through the big door with the porthole for a window, and upstairs to the bar. He had begun spending more time at the Golden Gate and was being lobbied by longtime members to run for commodore. He was apparently just what they were looking for: youngish, had a degree in business, liked good boats and good vino, and had a family attachment to the club through his father. Jozo had joined the Golden Gate Yacht Club in 1996, after Gertrude's death, and Norbert had followed.

Founded on a barge in 1939 by a group of mechanics, carpenters, and fishermen, the Golden Gate was created as the blue-collar antidote to its neighbor the blue-blazer St. Francis, situated between the Marina Green and Crissy Field, a spectacular swath of waterfront land treasured by joggers, bicyclists, windsurfers, and tourists. The two-story clubhouse of the Golden Gate was painted a gray as soft as the fog, its quarters as spare as the St. Francis's were grand. It was home to weekend sailors, 250 members, and a few employees. The club charged a modest initiation fee of $1,000 and a $90 per month members' fee and it was a bring-your-own-booze type of place, with its annual race, the Manuel Fagundes Seaweed Soup regatta, named after its singing bartender. The St. Francis, by contrast, was one of the nation's most venerable, with world-class sailors, 2,500 members, 150 full-time employees, trophy cases and model boats under glass, and an initiation fee of $25,000 and monthly dues of $250. It also had Tinsley, a private island in the California delta, about six to eight hours by sail from the San Francisco marina, or about three to five hours by powerboat. The island was members-only, with docking for one hundred. The Golden Gate was happy with its fish stew potlucks.

Norbert joined a handful of club members at the small bar facing back to the city and down along the eastern shoreline. His wife, Madeleine, who rivaled him in charm and chattiness, was on her way to the club.

Club member Ned Barrett, who lived a few blocks away, was there with his wife, Carole.

Barrett wanted to know if Norbert had said yes to running for commodore. "You better," he said. "They've talked me into running for vice commodore. We'll take this place by storm."

Norbert looked at his new friend and said he was still thinking about it.

Madeline arrived, flustered from her day at work, but happy to see Norbert.

Norbert introduced Madeleine to Barrett, who, he said, was going to be the new vice commodore and was lobbying him to be commodore, making Madeleine the commodoress. Madeleine smiled.

"Never a dull moment," she said, letting Norbert order a glass of white wine for her.

Madeleine had been taken with Norbert from the moment they met. She had worked with his mother at the Bank of America, and when Gertrude suddenly needed to go to Germany for her own mother's funeral Madeleine was asked to house-sit. Madeleine arrived at the house with her son and found the hot water wasn't working, so she called Gertrude's son. Norbert showed up, lit the pilot light, and, as the two liked to say, the rest was history. Their first date was at Benihana, where they talked until the lights were flickering off and the staff waited at the door. They talked about kids, single parenthood, and work. Norbert had two children, Heidi and Nicholas, with his first wife, and both kids were out of the house and off to college. Madeleine's son from her first marriage was also out of the house.

Madeleine found Norbert strong and reliable, but he also was more worldly than she, having spent time in Europe, traveling to Croatia and Germany, often alone even at a young age. In her eyes he was a great guy: he could fix her car, lug her heavy suitcases around airports, and put up with lipstick tubes, frilly curtains, and closets stuffed with clothes he said she didn't need.

From the first day they met she was sure that life with Norbert would be an adventure. He was a rare mix of consistency and reliability while having a daring streak.

It was just before 7 a.m. and San Francisco Bay was a calm slate gray with a few white scribbles, like chalk on a blackboard. The sky was pale blue and there wasn't a trace of fog. The island of Alcatraz was straight ahead, the Bay Bridge to the right and already jammed with cars, and the majestic Golden Gate Bridge to the left, sweeping from the Presidio of San Francisco to the base of the sloping Marin headlands. Norbert and his father headed out from the west harbor of the San Francisco marina in Jozo's boat *Croatia,* a 1978 thirty-foot twin-engine Sea Ray Sundancer with a radar arch. Cheese, salami, bread, wine, and beer were packed in the cooler, along with salmon roe and fresh anchovies to be used as bait for the sturgeon.

"Goddammit, drive straight!" Norbert's father barked. "We're not out sightseeing. With your driving, we'll get there at sunset." Norbert shook his head, his neatly trimmed mustache lifting as he laughed. At least today the weather was cooperating. Norbert remembered the time when he was fourteen and Jozo had insisted they head out past the Golden Gate to fish for striped bass. Norbert drove the flimsy sixteen-foot Runabout with an old Johnson thirty-five-horsepower motor, and soon they were out past the bridge in the turbulent swells and freezing cold, the waves jostling them, and not a thought given to life jackets.

Norbert looked ahead toward the waters of the San Rafael Bridge and then on up to San Pablo Bay, with its rich array of fish, including striped bass, anchovy, topsmelt, flounder, and sturgeon.

Croatia reached San Pablo Bay, a shallow area with a deepwater channel in mid-bay, and the men baited their hooks, setting out higher test lines for the bottom-hugging sturgeon. They removed their jackets and popped open beers. It was a warm day and Norbert knew enough to keep talk to a minimum. *Croatia* was Jozo's haven, his retreat after church to steal a shot of brandy and maybe a nap. In spring through the fall, they fished for salmon and striped bass. The winter months and early spring were good for sturgeon, though reeling in one or two was considered a respectable haul. They loved catching bass to make a vegetable stew laden with chunks of the white fish. During the summer they mooched, trolling and drifting without a motor. The biggest salmon Norbert had caught was a forty-five-pounder. They called the big ones slugs.

Settling in, Norbert understood that the most important thing to fishing was patience, and the silence between them was comfortable. After a while Jozo would share stories in Croatian and tell the occasional off-color joke. There would also be the news of the day: Bill Clinton's impeachment scandal and Senate acquittal a year earlier, in early winter of 1999, continued to perplex Jozo, along with the major conflict in Kosovo, as it hit close to home. From time to time, Norbert's father talked about his days growing up in Yugoslavia under the communist rule of Tito. Jozo's fishing village Hodilje was along the Dalmatian coast of the Adriatic Sea. Hodilje meant "little dogfish" in Croatian and the village was a place where kids learned to scale a fish before they ever set foot in school. At the age of eighteen, on May 22, 1952, after months of anxious planning, Jozo and four friends left Hodilje in the dark of night, walked for miles to a rocky shoreline, and then swam to Olepi, a nearby island where something rare awaited them: a sailboat with an engine, which belonged to a communist doctor. The young men, Jozo, Bendo, Rafo, Dani, and Ante, were fleeing a life of oppression and poverty. Jozo's older brother Zwonko was supposed to have been the one on the communist doctor's boat, but he had stayed back. Zwonko's childhood sweetheart Maria, who would become his wife and mother to their daughter, couldn't leave her family and begged him to stay, so Jozo took Zwonko's spot on the boat. They spent five days in the fourteen-foot wooden sailboat, with no food or water, as packing provisions might have alerted someone. Just weeks before, Jozo's cousin was caught trying a similar escape and thrown into prison. When Jozo and his four friends were picked up by the Italian police off the seaport of Bari, their daring escape from communism made news in Italy—and back home in Hodilje.

From Italy, Jozo and the other young men were sent to the Polish Labor Service in Germany. Jozo met Gertrude at a dance hall in Kaiserslautern in southwestern Germany and the two started to date. Jozo was a romantic and courted Gertrude. She was impressed by his good looks and work ethic. They had relatives in San Francisco who told them that America really was a place where hard work yielded a good life. Jozo and Gertrude Bajurin, with their toddler son, Norbert, arrived in America on February 14, 1957, having sailed from Bremerhaven, Germany, to the United States aboard the USS *General Langfitt,* a U.S. Navy troop transport ship. Norbert and his mother stayed in the cargo hold downstairs and the men roomed upstairs. Jozo and Gertrude met for meals and walks on deck, with Norbert in tow. As the ship made its way into the New York harbor Jozo said a quiet prayer. Boats had been good to the Bajurins. "We came over on a boat," his dad now liked to say, "and with no help, we made it."

Jozo had started out in America digging ditches by day and making pizza at night. He now owned Alouis Auto Radiator repair in San Francisco, and he and Gertrude had purchased a small home for thirty-five-thousand dollars in Marin County in 1965. Jozo repeatedly told his son, "When I was growing up, I walked to school carrying my shoes on my back to save the soles from use." Hodilje was a place where fathers taught their sons the fishing trade using nets as old and treasured as any heirloom, but Norbert had learned to fish from his father's friends. Jozo grew impatient easily and had never been particularly happy with his only son, giving him his trademark silent treatment for days, weeks, or months.

It was odd, Norbert thought now, that he couldn't think of a single day in his life when his father seemed proud of him. He had been a good soccer player as a kid, but Jozo didn't make it to a single game. He had been a dutiful kid, too, coming home from school to an empty house—his parents were always working—and making his bed and theirs, doing the dishes, and setting the table. Even at dinner, when he drank large amounts of milk, his father, in the European tradition, would complain, "When are you going to stop the milk and start drinking wine with dinner?" Whatever he did was wrong.

After lunch on *Croatia,* with still no bites and his father's mood darkening, Norbert said, "Hey, Dad, I've got news I think you'll like."

His father looked his way. Norbert had always thought that if not for the bright blue eyes, Jozo, tall and handsome and with a crooked nose, looked a lot like the actor Robert De Niro.

"I've been elected commodore of the Golden Gate."

Jozo shook his head. "What are you, nuts?"

"Dad, you love that club," Norbert said with surprise.

"Focus on business," his father said angrily, swiveling his seat and turning his back to him. It was the same end-of-conversation response Norbert faced in his senior year of high school, in the spring of 1974. He had turned eighteen in November and his draft registration notice followed a few months later. He went to see a recruiter and liked what the military had to offer. His parents expected him to attend the University of San Francisco, where he had been accepted, and work toward a degree in law or accounting. But Norbert had different plans. He signed up for three years in the army, informing his parents of the decision only after the fact. He talked with his mother first, fearful of his father's reaction, and listened as the two discussed how they might undo what was done. "Can we go to our priest to have it changed?" his mother pleaded with Jozo. It was too late. Norbert left soon afterward to live in a friend's garage and his father stopped speaking to him, but Norbert still graduated with honors.

With two sturgeons caught and one released because it was under the minimum length, Norbert and Jozo packed up and started back in the direction of San Francisco. As they emerged from the protected inlet Norbert eyed the thick fog pouring over the headlands, reaching like a witch's fingers through the dusky cables of the Golden Gate Bridge. The foghorns bellowed their deep resonant sound, with two horns attached to the pier below the south tower, twenty feet above the waterline, and three more suspended from the deck at mid-span. Norbert appreciated that modern technology had not yet replaced the horns, which had been used since the bridge was opened. He knew from his time on the bay that the horns at the pier emit a lower and longer monotone than the mid-span horns, which had two tones. The city from the bay was a beautiful sight, and the approaching fog had changed the powdery blue palette to pearly gray. *Croatia* was going as fast as she could, trying to outrun the fog. Jozo had not said a word since Norbert mentioned the yacht club and his becoming commodore.

When he tried to bring it up again his father gave him a cold stare. "Stick to what you know," Jozo said. "Stick to radiators."

5

Woodside, California

Early Spring 2000

"I'M TALKING ABOUT GREATNESS, about taking a lever to the world and moving it," Larry said, walking the grounds of his new Woodside property with his best friend Steve Jobs. "I'm not talking about moral perfection. I'm talking about people who changed the world the most during their lifetime."

Jobs, who had returned to Apple three years earlier, enjoyed the conversational volleying and placed Leonardo da Vinci and Gandhi as his top choices, with Gandhi in the lead. Leonardo, a great artist and inventor, lived in violent times and was a designer of tanks, battlements, ramparts, and an assortment of other military tools and castle fortifications. Larry joked that had Leonardo not been gay, he would have been "a perfect fit for the Bush administration." Jobs, who had studied in India, cited Gandhi's doctrine of nonviolent revolution as an example of how it was possible to remain morally pure while aggressively pursuing change. Larry's choice for history's greatest person could not have been more different from Gandhi: the Corsican-born military leader Napoleon Bonaparte. "Napoleon overthrew kings and tyrants throughout Europe, created a system of free public schools, and wrote one set of laws that applied to everybody. Napoleon achieved liberal ends through conservative means," Larry argued.

Larry and Steve walked the grounds of Larry's thirty-three-acre estate, Sanbashi, which had taken four years to design and would take a decade to build. When completed in 2004, the estate—an hour south of San Francisco and set in a wooded community with gated horse properties—would have a man-made three-acre lake, six guesthouses, and a main house divided into two zones, one for public entertaining and the other private, with outside walkways connecting the two. The lake was made earthquake-proof by pouring three separate layers of concrete. Thousands of rocks on the property—each handpicked by the Japanese artist Shigeru Namba, a celebrated national treasure in his native land—would be arranged according to Zen principles and look as if they were placed there by the hand of God over millennia. The wooden buildings were being constructed using Japanese mortise and tenon joinery with not a single nail used anywhere. The wood itself came from the Pacific Northwest by way of Japan. Because the best wood grown in North America was almost always acquired by the Japanese, who were willing to pay the highest prices, Larry's designers flew to Japan to bring the best of the best back home. Beams inside the main house would be Douglas fir from British Columbia and the ceilings were to be made of cedar grown in Oregon and Washington state. The floors would be a blond anigre from Africa. And the windows would all be done in museum glass—the glass used for paintings to avoid reflections—something that had never been done before.

Sitting by the lake, in front of a sprawling old oak tree and towering redwoods, Larry repeated his arguments to Steve. "Napoleon invented modern public education, public art museums, and the modern legal system, and ended state-sponsored religious discrimination." As if that weren't enough, he emptied the ghettos and gave the Jews equality in the eyes of the law, Larry said. "Napoleon engaged in war to overthrow kings and tyrants. He had no choice. They couldn't be talked off their thrones."

Steve had heard it all before and would never be convinced. "The Napoleonic wars are named after Napoleon. It's not a good thing to have *lots of wars* named after you," Steve countered, taking long pauses between his sentences, as was his way. "In contrast, Gandhi's methods were moral and his achievements were material. He led India to independence."

"Yes," Larry said. "India got its independence, and along with it a genocidal civil war between Hindus and Muslims. Countless people were slaughtered on both sides." Jobs noted that Gandhi had gone on a hunger strike to stop it. "Yes, and for his selfless efforts Gandhi was shot and martyred just like Lincoln," Larry said. "America's greatest president engaged in a war where over six hundred thousand people lost their lives. He ignored the constitution and suspended habeas corpus, and he instituted a draft to fill the ranks of the Union Army. After the Battle of Gettysburg, Lincoln had to send troops to New York City to put down draft riots. Even the sainted Lincoln was willing to resort to violence to purge the nation of slavery and preserve the Union. He couldn't talk the South out of secession or slavery. The saying 'Violence never solved anything' is nonsense."

Larry and Steve, who had met in technology circles, were friends from their first one-on-one meeting in the mid-1980s. Steve had bought a house in Woodside just up the hill from Larry. His front yard ended where Larry's backyard began. One morning, shortly after Steve moved in, Larry was awakened at dawn by the sound of screaming birds—peacocks. Larry trudged up the hill and knocked on the door, and Steve answered.

"Steve, are those your peacocks?" Larry asked.

"Yeah, they woke me up too. They're really loud, aren't they?" Steve replied. "They were a birthday gift. I don't know what I'm going to do. I hate them."

Larry, an animal lover who funds animal rescue centers around the world, plotted with Steve to relocate his birthday birds. The plan was simple. Steve was to place all the blame on Larry, his nocturnal next-door neighbor, who was complaining about being awakened at sunrise by screaming peacocks. The sleep-deprived neighbor even threatened to look up peacock recipes. The situation was serious and left Steve with no choice. He lived in a neighborhood hostile to peacocks and had to get rid of the birds *for their own safety.*

Steve thought that was a great idea and executed the plan to perfection.

Now that the two men were neighbors—and well rested—they began to spend more time together. They went for walks around Woodside, went on hikes in Castle Rock State Park, which they treasured as their mini Yosemite on the peninsula, and shared family vacations in Kona Village, Hawaii. They'd had this who-is-the-greatest talk before, with Steve offering up Alexandre-Gustave Eiffel, who built the tower; Arthur Rimbaud, the nineteenth-century French poet; Bob Dylan, influenced by Rimbaud; and Socrates, whom Steve said he would trade all of his technology to have an afternoon with. They also debated the role of the founders of great religions, including Christ and Muhammad. Steve liked to say the Beatles were his management model—four guys who kept each other in check and produced something great. Larry liked Galileo and Winston Churchill. "Winston Churchill saved Western civilization," Larry said, knowing his friend didn't approve of Churchill's methods. "Churchill prevented Hitler from invading England. The English people were not enslaved like so many others. Sure, he did it by shooting down lots of German airplanes and sinking the German fleet. Not every problem can be solved by talking."

Steve and Larry had found they had much in common. For starters, they both had adoptive parents. Jobs's birth mother, Joanne Schieble, was a student dating another student, Syrian-born Abdulfattah "John" Jandali, a Muslim. Her parents objected to the relationship, and Steve was put up for adoption at birth. Larry's birth mother, Florence Spellman, was an unmarried seventeen-year-old who had had a fling with a young Italian-American U.S. Army Air Force pilot and learned after he was shipped overseas that she was pregnant. She asked her aunt and uncle Lillian Spellman

Ellison and Louis Ellison, from Chicago, to take Larry in when he was nine months old. Larry met his birth mother when he was forty-eight and never met his father, despite efforts at one point to find him. Jobs was in his twenties when he met his birth mother, and he chose to never meet his father, though he knew who he was. Both considered their adoptive parents their real parents. Both were "OCD," by Larry's admission, and both were antiauthoritarian. They shared a disdain for conventional wisdom and felt people too often equated obedience with intelligence. They never graduated from college, and Steve loved to boast that he'd left Reed College in Portland, Oregon, after just two weeks while it took others, including Larry and their rival Bill Gates, months or even years to drop out. Larry's and Steve's companies, along with Microsoft, had taken shape at the same time, and they had risen and fallen and were both rising again. Both men had started companies with an idea that wasn't their own. In June 1977, Larry founded Software Development Laboratories, Inc., with two men, Bob Miner and Ed Oates. The goal was to create the first broadly used relational database system, which would be faster and better at organizing information than anything else on the market. A handful of academics, led by IBM researchers Ted Codd and Don Chamberlin in San Jose—as well as a group of professors at UC Berkeley—had freely published papers explaining how their relational systems worked. For the first time, data could be manipulated as tables. IBM was in no rush to bring its new idea to the mass market, but Larry was. In a similar way and around the same time, Steve Jobs was invited to the Xerox Palo Alto Research Center to have a look at some of its technology, which included a desktop machine with little pictures, or icons, and something called a mouse that could be clicked. Both Steve and Larry listened to naysayers insisting that the technologies were unsuitable for the commercial market, and then they went ahead and figured out ways to make it work.

The friends also shared a love of laughter. During their combined family vacations in Hawaii, Steve loved to tell funny stories and especially enjoyed making fun of Larry's personal relationships.

Steve would often have trouble finishing his own stories because he'd laugh so hard he couldn't go on. With considerable effort, he'd find his composure and try to finish, invariably failing because he'd start laughing again, even harder. This would happen over and over again until everyone was laughing uncontrollably without having the slightest idea how the story ended.

Looking out at Larry's lake, with the massive bluestone boulders from the Sierras lining the shores, Steve grew silent. A great blue heron landed on a flat rock slightly submerged under the glistening water, sending a family of mallards scattering. Across the lake were more spectacular oak trees and redwoods; in front of them were Japanese maples with a few remaining leaves in autumn hues of garnet and amber. The gentle sounds of water were all around. Gardens were Larry's favorite art form, a collaboration between God and man, a sculpture that never stayed the same.

Finally, Steve, not one to readily give compliments, gestured to the beauty around them and said, "Why do people buy art when they can make their own art?"

Larry thought for a moment and replied, "Well, Steve, not everyone can make his own art. You can. It's a gift."

Larry was a voracious reader who spent a great deal of time studying science and technology, but his favorite subject was history. He learned more about human nature, management, and leadership by reading history than by reading books about business. During a lively discussion over dinner one night, his friend Tony Blair, Great Britain's prime minister, listened in wonder and remarked, "Larry, you read *too* much history." Larry had just finished quoting a section from David Fromkin's *A Peace to End All Peace,* about how the treaty that ended World War I also planted the seeds of strife in the Middle East. Larry, an admirer of Blair's, took the comment as a compliment.

Larry's favorite history book was Will and Ariel Durant's *The Age of Napoleon,* which he had read several times. Like his buddy Steve, and like Larry himself, Napoleon was an outsider who was told he would never amount to anything. When he was ten he was sent from Corsica to military school at Brienne-le-Château in north-central France. His teachers' reports said that he spoke French with a "horrible thick Italian accent" and noted that although the other kids didn't like him he had an exceptionally high opinion of himself. His teachers did mention one positive attribute: he was exceptionally good at math. He was a small-town Italian kid (Corsica used to be under Italian rule) and nothing like the sophisticated Parisians he went to school with. In other words, he was a man with something to prove, an obsessive-compulsive who—while his marshals feasted and drank the night before battles—would work through the night. Larry marveled to Steve: "He'd spread the maps of the area all over the floor of his tent, and then he spent all night planning and dictating detailed orders to each one of his commanders. He'd have roast chicken for dinner because he didn't have to stop working to eat."

"What I'm interested in," Larry continued, "is how can history's greatest general *also* be history's ablest administrator—the creator of the laws, the courts, the schools, the museums, all the institutions that shaped France then and now? How can one human being do all that?"

As he looked at his friend he thought that here was a man who also had that rare combination of talent and will—only Steve's battles were with Microsoft, not England.

Steve and Larry argued about everything, including music and art. When Larry said he thought Paul Simon's lyrics for "The Boxer" were brilliant, Steve laughed and said Larry "didn't know goodness from greatness." "Dylan," Jobs said, "is the genius of our time." It never stopped. No one gave in and they both enjoyed the rallying.

Before Larry and Steve parted ways, Larry mentioned recent regattas he'd won on *Sayonara,* and he talked about the America's Cup race he was readying for. Steve was interested in the materials and the innovations, whether the Mylar used on the sails or the grade of carbon fiber in the hulls. Larry talked about the great time he'd had sailing and racing in the Mediterranean and Caribbean. Part of his job, as he saw it, was to tempt and corrupt his friend with boats and planes so that he would have more fun and more time. Steve was always concerned about his conspicuous consumption; he liked cars and motorcycles but never spent a lot of money. What he loved was designing and redesigning things to make them more useful and more beautiful. Larry was on the Apple board in 2000 when he had the idea that Apple should give Steve—then working for a dollar a year—a $40 million Gulfstream V jet so he could more efficiently take his family to Hawaii for long weekends. (The board also gave Steve ten million shares, with another option grant due in 2001.) Immediately, Steve started designing the interior of his new plane, studying Larry's Gulfstream V and making improvements on Larry's design. When he noticed Larry had one button to open a door and another button to close it, Steve decided on a single toggle switch that would do both on his plane. Steve reversed the placement of the sink and shower in the bathroom on his plane, among other changes. Larry agreed that Steve's redesigns were improvements. Larry, sure he would eventually hook his best friend on the draw of the sea, also lent Steve his boat for family vacations. Steve returned home after ten days aboard *Katana* and enthused, "No one bothers you on the boat. You can read and think and watch the sky change colors at the end of the day." Soon Steve was showing Larry designs for his beautiful new boat, to be named *Aqua*.

As much as they both loved art and design, Larry was convinced that nothing man created would ever rival the splendors of nature. Walking by a clump of two dozen cherry trees in his Woodside garden that would soon come to life again, Larry said, "I don't think that there is anything more beautiful and moving than a forest of cherry trees in bloom." The feelings the blossoms evoked in him were what the Japanese termed *mono no aware,* which roughly translates as "the impermanence of all things."

When pressed, Larry said he considered the prettiest object engineered by man to be a sailboat, but only when it was out in its natural elements of wind and sea.

6

St. Francis Yacht Club

Summer 2000

LARRY SURVEYED THE MEN in club blazers and ties seated in the Northwest room at the St. Francis Yacht Club and looked out at the waters of San Francisco Bay. With him was Bill Erkelens, who had grown up learning to sail at the St. Francis, where his dad was a member. Larry had joined the St. Francis around 1995, when he was told to his dismay—he is not a clubby person—that he couldn't race in major regattas if he didn't belong to a yacht club. Now, in his quest to win the America's Cup, he again was in need of a yacht club.

Under Cup rules *clubs,* not individuals, compete for the oldest trophy in sports. It was widely assumed in sailing circles that the St. Francis would sponsor Larry. A model of *Sayonara,* which had by now won five consecutive maxi world championships, was on display there, along with his gleaming trophies. Larry's daughter, Megan, went to the same school as the daughter of the club's future commodore Charles Hart. In the 2000 America's Cup, the St. Francis had sponsored a team called *AmericaOne,* skippered by Paul Cayard, which had reached the Louis Vuitton finals before losing to the Italian team Prada. Over the summer, the *AmericaOne* assets were sold to Larry for $7 million, including equipment, tenders,

47

storage containers, chase boats, and the two boats that had been sailed by Cayard in the previous Cup. As a part of the deal Cayard would be a member of the Oracle Racing team, and the team would use the boats for practice while the new ones were being built. In buying the assets and talent of *AmericaOne,* from Cayard to the shore crew, Erkelens, negotiating on behalf of Larry, had given the St. Francis first right of refusal. So, like sailing in a steady wind on a warm day, progress between the two parties had been smooth and uneventful. The optimistic assumptions continued through the fall, when the sides agreed to meet.

After pleasantries were exchanged between the men seated at the long table, and drinks were offered—Larry had mineral water—the discussion landed on what Larry planned to name the boat, an issue that had come up in an earlier discussion between Commodore Bruce Munro and Erkelens. Munro had suggested the name *The Spirit of San Francisco.* Larry, who hadn't given the name much thought, replied that he would probably name the boat *Oracle.* To his surprise, he was told the name was "too commercial." He listened as other names were proposed, including *Gold Rush* and *Spirit of '49.* He nodded, all the while cringing at names he considered terrible, and thinking to himself, *Oh, my God, I can't even name the boat!* He also was perplexed by the "too commercial" comment. He knew of regattas and boating clubs where sailing was restricted to amateurs and commercial sponsorships were forbidden. But the America's Cup was no such race—at least it hadn't been in decades. The first hundred years of the America's Cup saw teams backed by wealthy men who were "Corinthian," wealthy hobbyist yachtsmen. But by the mid-1970s a different breed became involved. It was Conner himself who, in the 1980s, stepped away from the Corinthian, amateur model and applied a new regimen of year-round training and testing by professionals and ushered in corporate sponsorships, prompting Ted Turner to complain that he didn't have the same sort of time for such training.

Finally, in a plaintive voice, Larry said, "I don't understand, I can't name my boat?" There was an America's Cup team named after a shoemaker, for God's sake.

Larry was assured that the St. Francis could come up with a name.

Larry and Erkelens shared a look. For a moment, Larry flashed back to the days of his youth, when he was too poor and too Jewish to be allowed into the Chicago Yacht Club. The only way he could've gotten in was to land a job waiting tables or washing dishes.

Clearing their throats and moving on, Erkelens and Larry raised the issue of what would happen if Oracle Racing were to win the Cup and bring it home.* Larry wanted a guarantee that his team would defend the Cup on San Francisco Bay. Under Cup rules, the sponsoring yacht club has the right to pick the defender. Larry was concerned that the St. Francis might choose a different syndicate to defend, one led by favorite-son Cayard, a handsome, charismatic sailor who was the pride of the bay and a distinguished yachtsman. In 1998 Cayard was the first American to win the Whitbread Round the World Race. And Cayard had sailed in a handful of America's Cup teams, in 1983, 1987, 1992, and 1995, and for the St. Francis in 2000.

Larry had sailed with Cayard on *Sayonara*'s first few races, and he was not a fan, telling Erkelens at one point that he never wanted Cayard on his boat again. But Cayard was a part of the package of assets and was one of the team's designated leaders, at least for now.

"Larry, *you* don't win the Cup," said the vice commodore, Steve Taft, who had sailed in two Cup challenges. "The St. Francis wins the Cup. Just like the New York Yacht Club before us, *we* will decide who defends." Taft and others explained to Larry that if they won they would be likely to hold a challenger series, in which Larry's team would be free to compete against others to determine

---

*In a later recollection, Bruce Munro said that the boat name and defense specifics were not discussed in this meeting. My reporting, including interviews with other meeting participants, led me to conclude that these subjects were discussed at this time.

who would defend. Larry knew the New York Yacht Club's selection of a defender could be personal and political, not simply a matter of picking the boat that had the best chance of winning. The New York Yacht Club, which had held the Cup from 1851 to 1983, defending it twenty-five times, treated the regatta as its private property.

Winning the Cup had been the dream of the St. Francis for decades. For some members, it had been an obsession. The club had sponsored two Cup syndicates, in 1987 and 2000. So strong was their Cup lust that St. Francis members had even drawn up a tentative racecourse for the eventual day when the club would bring the Cup race to the bay. Boats would race a triangle starting in front of Fisherman's Wharf, upwind to the Golden Gate Bridge, to a turning mark north of Alcatraz, then back to Fisherman's Wharf.

Since its inception, the America's Cup had been won by the world's most elite yacht clubs, and the St. Francis had long stood in that company. It was a virtual penthouse of San Francisco society. The railroad baron C. Templeton Crocker had been one of its first commodores, and its VIPs of today included Roy Disney, vice chairman of Walt Disney Company; George Gund, owner of the San Jose Sharks; Fritz and Lucy Jewett, longtime Cup backers; and Ray Dolby, billionaire founder of Dolby Laboratories. It had the world-class sailors Jeff Madrigali, Cayard, and Bob Billingham. And its junior program had been a virtual farm team for future champions.

Erkelens, sitting across the table from some of the men he'd grown up sailing with, knew that even if Oracle were to win the Cup for the St. Francis, and then win in a defender series, the St. Francis could later tell Larry to shove off if they didn't get along. There was a saying that had circulated around the New York Yacht Club in the early days: "Britain rules the waves; America waives the rules." One of the first things the New York club did after winning the Cup in 1851 was require all competing teams to submit their boat design specifications to it; this was akin to asking other teams to hand over their playbooks. The St. Francis had its own set of rules. And what one board agreed to, another board down the line could change. The club had two nicknames: "St. Frantic," for its famously fractious membership, and, more recently, "St. Fancy." Erkelens was sure that his boss was not about to spend $100 million of his own money without some guarantees. They needed to carve out rights. Larry explained that he didn't want to control the club's board but that if he won he certainly wanted to defend. He and Erkelens proposed creating a board within the St. Francis's board that would deal only with America's Cup matters. They proposed placing two of their own team members on the club's board; the St. Francis would place two of its members and the foursome would choose a fifth member, giving each side "equal control."

The proposal went over about as well as the name "Oracle" for the boat. St. Francis members were not about to cave in under pressure. It would be like allowing women to join the all-male Bohemian Club.

Larry, clad in a brown suit and black mock turtleneck, was growing more uncomfortable as the meeting progressed. His jacket didn't have brass buttons and he wasn't wearing a tie with flags or ships on it. He wasn't even wearing a tie. He wasn't enjoying sitting there being told how the America's Cup works. The St. Francis board members were courteous but stern, like his grammar school teachers. Whenever he was backed into a corner Larry relished finding an unexpected way out. When he was twelve, his parents, who had regularly taken him to synagogue, expected him to attend Hebrew school so he could be bar mitzvahed. Once Little League practice began, Larry decided to stop going to Hebrew school. One day the rabbi came to their house and told his parents, "If he continues to cut Hebrew classes to play baseball, he's going to be expelled." Larry preferred pitching to studying Hebrew and proudly got himself thrown out of Hebrew school. He was never bar mitzvahed, but he did improve the velocity on his fastball, though not his control.

To the St. Francis side of things, this was Larry Ellison, one of the world's richest people and a man prone to colorful statements and hyperbole, a man who pilots his own Russian jet fighter, skippers his own yachts, and has at least ten high-performance cars, all the same shade of platinum. He was a man accustomed to getting his way, whatever it takes. Larry also was new money; many of the board members represented old. He was learning about yacht clubs; they were born into them.

The future commodore Hart listened to the negotiations. He liked Larry and found him surprisingly gracious. But to the suggestion of a board within the board, he said, "We simply can't do that."

Erkelens could see they were at an impasse. He tried to explain that they didn't want to take over the board; they wanted to place three of five members on a newly created America's Cup board. Taft shook his head. "It would look like Larry bought his way onto the board," he said.

Taft—who had bushy, boomerang-shaped eyebrows, a shaved head, and the wind-chafed face of a lifelong sailor—explained, "The board of directors doesn't have the power to turn the club over. We have bylaws and rules and regulations and we have to follow the laws of the state governing nonprofits. Everything has to be voted on by the members. As one example, we have a bylaw that you have to have been a member of the club for eight years before you can sit on the board. We can't have members on the board who weren't elected."

In Larry's mind, the meeting continued long after it had ended. Larry and Erkelens were stunned that the St. Francis wouldn't budge. Larry said he was not about to go to the St. Francis board to ask permission every time he needed something. He told Erkelens that he didn't dislike the St. Francis people, and he didn't consider their position wholly unreasonable. In the end, though, he didn't like letting them have control. It was the same reason he didn't have a driver, and it was why he liked to pilot his own planes and why he had been married and divorced three times. He didn't like being told what he could and couldn't do.

"This just doesn't work for me," Larry quietly told Erkelens. "If we win, I want a guarantee that we get to defend the Cup."

Still, Hart thought a deal could be worked out. There was no other game in town, he assured himself. But as the men walked out, Taft, who had known Erkelens's father and watched Billy learn to sail, gestured to him and the two found a quiet corner. Taking Erkelens's arm, Taft said, "Son, this dog won't hunt."

Erkelens squinted. "Pardon me?" he said. "What does that mean?"

"This dog won't hunt?" Taft said. "That's a no."

A week later, Taft addressed club members at their regular weekly yachtsmen's luncheon, in the club's elegant grillroom overlooking the bay. Taft and members of the board wanted to explain why they were voting against partnering with Larry Ellison. There were those who supported the board's decision, saying proudly, "The St. Francis is not for sale," like a mantra, yet others thought they were making a whale of a mistake.

Peter Stoneberg, a club board member, listened to the emotional discussion.

"Here you have a guy who is willing to pay for everything and wants a few pretty simple guarantees in return," Stoneberg argued to a mix of boos and applause. "The Cup is getting more and more expensive, and you don't have a billionaire coming through the door every day saying he is willing to pay for literally everything. Just imagine if we were to win!"

Taft, too, was surprised by the level of dissension and was feeling beaten up by the whole thing. It hadn't been an easy decision to make.

Cayard, loyal to the St. Francis but in contract to Oracle Racing, knew enough about Larry to know that he would never get into a deal unless he could run the show. Cayard had been dismayed when he heard club members practically bragging that they had turned down Larry Ellison, saying they weren't about to let some billionaire come in and buy their esteemed club. Commodore Munro had told a local sailing magazine, "Essentially, you're asking to buy our yacht club. We're not for sale." Not all club members wer so resolute. Cayard sent a letter of admonishment to the St. Francis board of directors.

I am writing to express my disappointment in your handling of the Oracle Racing negotiations. I am disappointed for two reasons. First, our Commodore saw fit to discuss the dealings in public forums such as *Scuttlebutt* and *Latitude 38*. Secondly, our Commodore's renditions of the proposal are inaccurate, to put it politely.

I have read the following quotes in *Latitude 38,* "But since St. Francis is a California corporation, the law requires they be elected. So the club could not legally comply with Oracle Racing's request even if it wanted to." This is false. The Oracle Racing proposal specifically acknowledged that board members had to be elected and changes in bylaws required a majority vote of the members and it allowed for that.

Further in the same article and in the Commodore's letter to the membership, he states that Oracle Racing asked the board to guarantee a vote of the membership. This is simply not stated anywhere.

The assertion by the Commodore "But after checking with our lawyers, we found that we couldn't legally do any of these things" is both false and insulting.

Similar stories were pontificated at a recent Yachtsman's lunch where our commodore was the guest speaker.

The fact that the Oracle Racing proposal was not acceptable to the Board of the St. Francis Yacht Club is not good and sufficient reason to misstate the facts to create an alibi in an attempt to justify a decision.

I find this behavior unprofessional and, as a member, embarrassing. Frankly, it is not the type of leadership I remember around our club.

Sincerely,

Paul Cayard

Charles Hart, who had wanted the deal to happen and who'd read Cayard's letter with sadness, said to the board, "It is a very big disappointment for this club." The regret was audible in his voice.

7

The Golden Gate Yacht Club

January 2001

A FEW DOZEN PEOPLE stood in the upstairs dining room of the Golden Gate Yacht Club, opening bottles of wine and beer. A potluck dinner buffet was served and Norbert was sworn in as the club's sixtieth commodore. In years past, commodores had been teachers, administrative assistants, and maître d's, but Norbert was the first radiator repairman. Next to the fireplace sat Ron Matlin, a CPA who had been brought in only weeks before to look at the club's books. As soon as he could get Norbert alone, Matlin pulled the newly minted commodore aside and said in a low voice, "Dude, do you know what you're getting into?" Norbert wasn't expecting this. Matlin said, "There is a huge mess that you are inheriting. It appears to me that the club has been everyone's personal fiefdom."

Norbert studied Matlin, who looked like an extra from *The Godfather*. He had dyed black hair, thick knuckles, gold chains, and a pug nose, and he didn't mince words. Norbert wasn't sure what to make of the club's new accountant, who was from Winnipeg, Canada, and had owned one of the first Budget rental car franchises.

Norbert took a deep breath. "Tonight we party," he said. "Tomorrow we work."

Within days, Matlin's words began to sink in, as Norbert discovered the little club had a big debt. Matlin ticked off some of the more notable problems he'd discovered: the club owed $95,000 in back property taxes to the city and the city was running out of patience; the club had organized as a for-profit entity yet never tracked any profit; the club had a contract with a catering company that took its money but didn't provide food service.

All in all, the 215-member club was close to half a million dollars in debt.

Norbert shook his head. His father had told him that the best days of the club were in the past.

Norbert's response to it all was, "If the ship goes down, we're going with it."

"A few more things," Matlin said, impressed by this undaunted commodore. "Don't know if you know it, but until I came along, their bookkeeper was the cousin of a member who lived on her boat, docked here at the club for years, and never paid a dime in docking fees. They had some bookkeeping files but it was pretty much trash, not even as accurate as a checkbook."

"What did the accounting records look like?" Norbert asked.

"They had a QuickBooks file," Matlin replied, "with no historical value but great hysterical value." Matlin had been backfilling the books as best he could to bring accounts up to date. Basically, Matlin told Norbert, "We are broke, destitute, and hundreds of thousands of dollars in debt."

Matlin, who at one point owned a restaurant on Union Street in San Francisco, had done accounting for a number of bars and restaurants around town.

One of Norbert's and Matlin's first tasks was to fire everyone except the bartender and dishwasher and throw the catering company out on the street. Norbert even fired the cleaning crew, saying he would do it himself. "One of our two remaining employees has gold teeth," Norbert told Madeleine with a sigh. On his daily drive to the radiator shop, Norbert—who had the ruddy tan of a sailor, the easygoing disposition of a mechanic, and the nattiness of a commodore on a budget—would prioritize with Matlin the crises for the day. Matlin quickly came to see Norbert as a guy he wanted on his side in battle. They began to joke that Matlin, sixteen years Norbert's senior, was club consigliere.

"Every purveyor the club has, from Southern Wine and Spirits to Young's Market, will no longer sell to us unless it's COD because we're so far behind on all of our bills," Matlin informed Norbert. "The club's good standing is a thing of the past."

"See what you can offer," Norbert said, driving across the Golden Gate Bridge in his red Nissan truck emblazoned with ALOUIS AUTO RADIATOR. "Buy down the debt. We'll take any dues coming in and plug holes where we can."

The problem was that members were dropping like flies, resigning their memberships. The ones who were left were "cheap," as Matlin put it, or "unsupportive," as Norbert more generously put it. The club had an aged membership, and old-timers like Jozo were convinced the club had no future.

For months, Ned Barrett, newly sworn in as Norbert's vice commodore, would get calls in the middle of the night from the San Francisco police saying the club's front door had been left wide open. Barrett, who lived a few blocks away, across Marina Boulevard, would throw on his bathrobe and head over to lock the doors. "It's a three-ring circus," Barrett said to his wife, Carole, when he climbed back into bed.

Matlin spent hours on the phone with vendors, saying, "If you want to get paid, I can give you a little bit over a long period or a lesser lump sum now. We want you to be our purveyor going forward. Can we start working with you again?"

As Matlin fought off creditors and scrambled to keep the club's insurance going, Norbert and Madeleine formed the club's two-person entertainment committee. They started Thirsty Thursdays, and encouraged members to drop by for good company, drinks, and a potluck dinner and urged them to "bring friends and potential members—renegades welcome." A monthly newsletter, *Changing Tides,* was begun and it featured stories on some of the boats loved by members, including *Mirene,* a tugboat that had recently won the local Festival of the Sea Tugboat race. A Valentine's Day dinner was planned, with Madeleine in charge, along with a "Bunny-by-Boat" Easter brunch, a singles club dinner dance, and a St. Patrick's Day party. In one seventy-three-hour span, Norbert and Madeleine spent thirty-four hours at the club, ordering supplies, taking reservations, making and serving food and drinks, running to the store for more groceries, cleaning up, and dipping into their own pockets to pay for things big and small, from the insurance to coffee.

Arriving back at the club early one morning Norbert headed upstairs. There, passed out by the fireplace, was their employee—the gold-toothed bartender, still drunk from the night before.

When Matlin walked in, Norbert gestured to the snoring bartender and said, "Is there a light at the end of the tunnel?"

"Yes," Matlin replied, "and it's an oncoming train."

The bartender was fired and another stepped in: Madeleine. Tiny and dark-haired, with a wry sense of humor and a deep love for her husband, Madeleine spent the workday at Wells Capital Management, an investment arm of Wells Fargo Bank, where she was a client services representative, and then headed to the club at night to start mixing drinks. What Madeleine didn't know she learned fast—and mistakes were forgiven because of her apologetic smile, cheerfulness, and free-flowing advice. She soon made what regulars were calling the best martini in town, mixing it to perfection.

Norbert, meanwhile, was dialing for dollars, offering the club's dining room and kitchen to local theater groups and cooking schools. He talked with the management of *Tony 'n' Tina's Wedding,* an Italian wedding play and dinner show, about having performances at the club. He talked with the California Culinary Academy about running classes at the Golden Gate. He offered the club's "great views, great kitchen, low price!"

The genesis of the money problem, Matlin had concluded, was that club members had gotten in over their heads with the building of a new clubhouse after the 1989 Loma Prieta earthquake, which had hit the liquefaction zone of the Marina District hard. With the use of federal emergency relief funds, the modest club on the barge had been replaced by a two-story structure at the end of Yacht Road. "Their building was one that the membership could not sustain," Matlin sighed.

By the end of January, Matlin and Norbert were putting pressure on members to settle old bar tabs and pay late dues. They flirted with the idea of getting another small-business loan but were delinquent on the one they had. Matlin watched Norbert spend his mornings trying to save the yacht club, listened to him talk about his day spent at the radiator shop, and heard of his nights back at the Golden Gate. "He doesn't quit, that boy," Matlin told his wife. "You couldn't get a better player on your team."

At the same time Norbert was struggling with the Golden Gate he faced other challenges. His radiator repair shop had seen revenues hit the ground like a broken tailpipe. He listened as President George W. Bush, newly sworn in, blamed the recession on his predecessor. Norbert was scrambling to deal with changing times, as radiator manufacturers were using the Internet to go directly to customers, bypassing distributors such as Alouis. Customers could easily do comparison shopping and buy radiators online.

After another full day at the garage and a long night working at the club, Norbert closed the Golden Gate's door and walked slowly up the creaky wooden plank to the parking lot. He looked back at the building with its chipped paint and big door that welcomed anyone. The club had served members for nearly seventy years, giving the city's working class a place to dine and drink and swap salty tales. He chuckled to himself thinking of the stories he'd heard from two of the club's earliest members, Rene Allemand, who went by "Flip," and his older brother John, who were born in San Francisco to French parents. They had built their first boat, a fourteen-foot sloop, *Taba,* before they were out of high school and for decades operated a boatyard, complete with a small office and a much bigger bar, in Hunters Point, farther south on the bay. The cigar-chomping Rene had joined the Golden Gate Yacht Club a week after it was founded on the barge, and he loved to reminisce about the "wild bunch of guys who would cuss and drink and act pretty rough-and-tumble." The Allemands had been among the last of the region's boatbuilders to work by hand. They favored wood over other materials and embodied San Francisco's seafaring past; from their bayside yard they had seen Chinese shrimpers come and go, and they had helped build navy cargo ships during World War II, watched hilltop parcels of land snatched up for twenty-five dollars, and relaxed at clambakes on the nearby white-sand beaches. Norbert knew, too, how the club had been a blessing to his father after his mother died. For a while, it was a bond he and Jozo shared. Now, the relationship was back on shaky ground, the neglected Golden Gate was facing bankruptcy, and he feared he had been named captain of a sinking ship. He worried that if he didn't do something radical soon, the club's burgee, emblazoned with the image of the Golden Gate Bridge, would be retired and he'd be remembered as the commodore who lowered the flag and closed the doors.

As Norbert sat in his upstairs office at the radiator shop, browsing a sailing magazine, an article about Larry Ellison's surprising falling-out with the mighty St. Francis caught his eye. It wasn't the Ellison name that prompted Norbert to read the story; he was far more intrigued by the St. Francis, situated just up the road from the Golden Gate. A number of his club's regulars serviced boats belonging to St. Francis members. And he drove by the storied club almost daily. The story got Norbert thinking. He knew of Ellison's love of sailing and penchant for winning. In sailing circles, it was major news when the billionaire cofounder and CEO of software giant Oracle had announced his bid for the America's Cup.

But now, for reasons unclear to Norbert, Ellison and the St. Francis were on the rocks. So why, wondered Norbert, couldn't the Golden Gate sponsor Oracle Racing?

Later that day, Norbert sheepishly ran the idea of a deal with Ellison by a few of the club members, including Ned Barrett and Madeleine.

"Oh sure, Norbert, a guy like Larry Ellison is really going to partner with us!" Madeleine said smiling. "I love you, but this idea *is* crazy."

Dave Haskins, a retired Stanford administrator and former sailing coach at Cornell who served as the club's rear commodore, told Norbert that the odds were about as good as asking a group of weekend hikers to scale Everest. Haskins, whose fifty-two-foot sloop was moored in the East Bay, was helping out by sprucing up the club. The Golden Gate had trophies but they were in the closet and looking a little the worse for wear. He had gotten them out, cleaned them, and was having some replated. "The New York Yacht Club has an entire trophy room," he told Norbert.

"And we have a closet," Norbert replied with a smile.

Matlin had a different take on Norbert's idea. He had just read a cover story on Ellison in *Business Week*. Ellison wore dark shades and the headline on the cover was "ORACLE IS COOL AGAIN." The story noted the quadrupling of Oracle's stock price in less than a year, moving the company ahead of IBM in market capitalization. The value of Ellison's stake in his company had surpassed the holdings of Bill Gates in Microsoft ($52.1 billion to $51.5 billion). "Sure it's nuts," Matlin said. "We're crazy. But so what? We certainly have nothing to lose when we're dealing from a position of having nothing. What's the downside?" Matlin asked Norbert if he'd ever seen the movie *The Bad News Bears*, about the team that were the worst and came from behind. "They had the nearsighted pitcher and the overweight catcher, and they made it all the way to the championships!" Matlin said.

"As I recall," Norbert said of the 1976 film, "the Bears didn't actually win." But, he noted, they had one hell of a party. "You can't lose what you don't have."

Matlin added that, from what he'd read, Ellison was a "self-made man, which says a lot. He should appreciate the underdog." More pragmatically, Matlin noted Ellison was also "a very rich man who loves racing" and happens to need a yacht club. "This ain't rocket science. He needs a yacht club and we have one."

Norbert didn't dare mention the idea to his father, who continued to berate him for taking over as commodore. "The club won't be around in a year," Jozo had said one day while he was working on his boat. The latest financial figures seemed to support his prognostication: it remained $453,000 in debt and members were dropping out and taking their $90 monthly dues with them. Some couldn't afford the monthly fee: others said the club had seen better days.

Soon after reading the story, Norbert tracked down an e-mail address for the head of Oracle Racing, Bill Erkelens. In a formal and somewhat timid note sent on the morning of February 7, 2001—the subject line: "Golden Gate Yacht Club Available"— Norbert introduced himself and the Golden Gate. "Rumor has it that Mr. Ellison and Oracle Racing are looking for a new yacht club in San Francisco." While the Golden Gate's facilities are "approximately half the size" of the St. Francis's, Norbert wrote, the view and the marina accessibility are the same "if not better. If negotiations cannot be accomplished with the St. Francis, our club may be your answer."

To Norbert's surprise Erkelens, who was in talks with half a dozen clubs across the state—from the California Yacht Club in Los Angeles to Bay Area groups including the Richmond Yacht Club in the East Bay, the Corinthian in Tiburon, and the San Francisco Yacht Club in Belvedere—responded the next day. "I would love to have a chat," Erkelens said in his e-mail. While succinct, Erkelens's note was more than Norbert expected. *I'm an ex-cop in the automotive business*, he thought. *What do I know?*

One thing that people did know was that should Larry Ellison win the America's Cup in New Zealand in 2003 the entire Bay Area could share in the big win. The victorious team earns the right to pick the place for the next race, so bringing the Auld Mug home would be like handing a city a winning lottery ticket, generating hundreds of millions of dollars for the economy. And for the yacht club sponsoring the home team the event would be a veritable bonanza. The club's newfound prestige would be the envy of the international sailing world. The Golden Gate would be the little engine that could.

8

The Golden Gate Yacht Club

February 2001

STANDING IN THE DOORWAY of the Golden Gate Yacht Club, Norbert smiled broadly and shook hands with the tall, boyish Bill Erkelens. The two shared a laugh over Erkelens's toddler daughter, Ashley, who was missing a shoe.

Erkelens had flown up from Ventura, in Southern California, where Oracle Racing had a temporary base camp and boatbuilding operation to meet the Cup's nationality requirements, which mandated that team members show proof of residency in the United States for six months prior to the competition. Erkelens wanted to meet Norbert in person, and Norbert was anxious to see whether Erkelens was for real.

Walking inside, Norbert showed off the burgee room downstairs, with hardwood floors and pictures of commodores in nautical caps. The two walked up the carpeted stairs and into the bar overlooking the docks.

Snacks and sodas were offered, and Norbert, with Ned Barrett, sat down with Erkelens at the commodore's table in the corner by the window. Ashley toddled around, making Norbert smile and providing much-needed levity. Norbert was nervous, certain he was out of his league. Erkelens found the dining room inviting and spotless, and he was impressed by the views. He immediately liked Norbert and the vice commodore Barrett, who spoke with a Bostonian accent and enthused over his own boat, a 1966 classic Chris-Craft, one of the first fiberglass boats. Erkelens was familiar with the modest club tucked away at the end of the road past the lighthouse. While growing up sailing at the St. Francis, he'd always enjoyed the Golden Gate's midwinter regatta and appreciated the working-class spirit and Friday night "beer can" races, where sailors raced around "cans," or marks, and returned to the club for free beer and barbecue. His father, Bill Erkelens Sr., had quit the St. Francis in 1987 when the club assessed members $5,000 each to help pay for Tom Blackaller's Cup campaign in Australia. Blackaller was a larger-than-life character, an accomplished sailor, avid race car driver, and jokester—whose nickname was Charlie Brown and who had mentored Paul Cayard. "I don't like Tom and I'm not paying him $5,000," Erkelens's father had said, jumping ship for the Richmond Yacht Club, which was not unlike the Golden Gate in that it was founded to promote affordable sailing. Many members there made their own boats and sails, helped construct the clubhouse, and ran their own races.

"A lot of clubs have asked us to pay them cash up front for the sponsorship, and that's not something we are willing to do," Erkelens said, wanting to be honest with Norbert about what Oracle Racing had to offer. "The yacht club in Los Angeles, a private club, wanted one million dollars up front. I had to buy a new suit even to go there and talk. Other clubs have been nervous about the liability."

Barrett said, "We heard that Larry wanted things that the St. Francis couldn't give him." He said it sounded reasonable that Larry would want control, especially of his right to defend. "We would certainly be in favor of that."

"If we can do this deal," Erkelens said, looking at the two men, "the idea that Larry and I have is this. Would it work if Oracle Racing and one hundred team members become dues-paying members of your yacht club?"

Norbert had played his share of poker but was never much good at it. His face gave too much away. "We would be honored to have Oracle Racing as members of the Golden Gate," he stammered. He told Erkelens the dues and membership fee and did a quick calculation, realizing that these alone would bring in more than $200,000.

Norbert added that the club could certainly handle any of Oracle's demands. "I am confident that this can be a win-win for Oracle Racing and for the Golden Gate."

Erkelens got on the phone with the team's attorney, Melinda Erkelens, his wife. She would meet with the Golden Gate's attorney. Erkelens asked Norbert for a short history of the club and the annual regattas, and a list with contact information for club members and board members. His staff needed to do a complete audit of the club's books. Norbert had told Erkelens in one of their first exchanges that the club was heavily in debt. He wanted Erkelens to know about all the bad things but also to be clear the club had "real potential and enthusiasm." Erkelens said he understood and just needed to make sure there were no surprises, financial or otherwise, lying in wait for the team. "After that, after we have a tentative agreement, the next step will be to have the Golden Gate Yacht Club draft a notice of challenge to the Royal New Zealand Yacht Squadron on the Golden Gate Yacht Club letterhead," Erkelens said.

Norbert looked at Barrett. He didn't want to jinx anything but couldn't help wondering if this was all for real. Erkelens said that, assuming everything checked out, he would then arrange for the $300,000 entry fee to be wired to the club's account. As the men talked, their attorneys had already jumped on the line.

Erkelens liked it that the Golden Gate Yacht Club had nothing to lose. And he liked this commodore named Norbert, a radiator repair man who had more natural class than many of the millionaires he had raced for in the past. Norbert walked Erkelens and his daughter out to his jeep, parked between the Golden Gate and the St. Francis. He imagined the reaction of the folks at the St. Francis if they saw him talking with Erkelens. The two shook hands, and Erkelens said it looked as though they had the makings of a deal.

Erkelens knew that Larry liked the idea of the Golden Gate Yacht Club, and he wondered if it had something to do with the fact that it was within shouting distance of the St. Francis and was the shaggy mutt habitually overlooked for the purebred puppy. Erkelens had sailed with Larry for years and knew he believed that the best things happen when the consensus is ignored. He knew his boss revered Galileo for telling the experts of his time that the earth was not the center of the universe.

Norbert walked back inside and took a seat at the bar.

"Pinch me," he said to Barrett. "This has to be a dream and I'm going to wake up and it ain't real."

Norbert picked up the phone and called Matlin and asked him to organize the records Erkelens had requested. Matlin, thrilled with the development, encouraged Norbert to take things one step at a time. He updated Norbert on his own bits of good news, including his recent trip to the San Francisco treasurer's office, where he had cut a deal, negotiating the club's back taxes down significantly. Matlin cautioned Norbert, though, that time was running out on the Golden Gate. "This, my friend, is our Hail Mary pass," he said. "It has to happen."

Within days of sending Erkelens all of the requested paperwork, Norbert received a draft contract from Oracle Racing. The title of the confidential document made him sit back in his chair: "America's Cup XXXI, Challenge and Defense Agreement." It began with the Cup's background and stated, "If the (sponsoring) Yacht Club and Oracle Racing win the Cup in 2003, the Yacht Club will become the trustee of the Cup and responsible for the conduct of subsequent match or matches."

Norbert, who was six-foot-one and on the lean side to begin with, had lost nearly fifteen pounds since taking over as commodore just six weeks earlier. Too busy to sleep, too preoccupied to eat, he juggled the needs of the radiator business and the demands of his father; his home life, which included Madeleine, a cat named

Tatiana, his two grown kids—Heidi, who was twenty-five, and Nicholas, twenty-one—and his twenty-one-year-old stepson, Jason; yacht club business, including all of the bills, collectors, and grumpy members; and fast-paced, ever-changing negotiations with Erkelens on behalf of his billionaire boss, Mr. Ellison.

Making things more difficult at the Golden Gate was a hefty nondisclosure agreement; Norbert was bound by it: he couldn't tell club members what he was working on, even as many were quitting. The club was down to 250 members—seventy-five had not paid their dues in months or years—from a high of more than 350, and more were threatening to resign. Norbert returned to his home in Larkspur, just north of the Golden Gate Bridge, exhausted. "What in the world am I doing?" he asked Madeleine. "We're way too small to try to play with the big boys."

Jozo hadn't changed his tune, warning Norbert to concentrate on radiators. The refrain was becoming as familiar as the I-carried-my-shoes-to-save-the-soles story. Jozo told Norbert he'd worked too hard for too long to have his son take *his* business for granted. Madeleine had her own approach. She wanted to understand what her husband was up against, so she picked up the biography *The Difference Between God and Larry Ellison: God Doesn't Think He's Larry Ellison*. She peppered Norbert with pillow-talk tidbits. "The Oracle Way . . . was simply to win," Madeleine read aloud. "How that goal was achieved was secondary." She went on, "While Ellison demanded absolute loyalty, he did not always return it. The people he liked best were the ones who were doing something for him. The people he hired were all geniuses until the day they resigned, when, in Ellison's view, they became idiots or worse." He never graduated from college, Madeleine marveled, and he had become a billionaire two decades after investing twelve hundred dollars in an upstart named Software Development Laboratories, the precursor to Oracle. Early in his life and even through much of his twenties, everyone around him seemed concerned he would have no idea how to make money. "There's an irony," Madeleine said. Larry's first wife,

Adda Quinn, accustomed to Larry's floundering and bouncing from one computer programming job to another, got fed up and divorced him when he borrowed thousands of dollars to buy a thirty-four-foot sailboat even though they were still making payments on his twenty-four-foot sailboat.

The high-flying billionaire had been married and divorced three times, Madeleine noted. He drove Ferraris, then switched to convertible Bentleys and Acura NSX sports cars. He spent weekends flying with his son, staging mock dogfights over the Pacific Ocean. Norbert tuned out the pillow talk; he told his wife he would reserve judgment until he met the man in person. In Norbert's eyes, Mr. Ellison—as he called him—was a guy who came from nothing and made his life a success. Norbert believed in looking someone in the eye and forming his own opinion.

A month later, in March, Norbert stood in front of the mirror in the bathroom of his Larkspur home and rehearsed the speech he planned to deliver that night. A note had been sent out reminding everyone of the membership meeting, and a handful of volunteers were enlisted for a phone chain to alert people that there would be an "important discussion about the club's future."

Norbert and Madeleine arrived at the Golden Gate early to check the bar inventory and talk with the new part-time general manager, Bill Chow. Only a handful of people knew the importance of the night. As a final test of Norbert and the Golden Gate, Bill Erkelens wanted to see whether club members would support the idea of a partnership with Oracle. If Erkelens sensed hesitation the tentative deal was off. Norbert had no way of knowing how members would react, especially the old-timers.

With about eighty people gathered in the dining room, Norbert said he wanted to give a talk about the "great little club's past, present, and future." He looked at Madeleine, who was seated at the commodore's table, with members of the Coast Guard as guests. He talked about the city's working-class traditions, and of the Italians, Irish, Germans, Croatians, and other immigrants who had come to this "slice of heaven by the sea" to make a better life. The Golden Gate was originally incorporated on September 15, 1939, as the Puerta de Oro Yacht Club, the name Golden Gate having been copyrighted by another club. The name was changed to the Golden Gate two and a half years later, on March 14, 1942, when the other club relinquished the name. According to its early mission statement, it was to be the "workingman's yacht club," Norbert explained. "One of the main reasons people have joined this beautiful club is the views we have of the harbor, the Golden Gate Bridge, and the bay," Norbert continued. "Our membership fees and dues are considered low for the real estate on which we're built. Our Bloody Marys are three dollars and fifty cents. And we know how to have a good time!" He smiled, noticing longtime member Bonny Almeida, a seventy-four-year-old former diesel mechanic and fisherman from Portugal. With him was Primo, a parakeet who sat on his finger and offered kisses on command. "Much has happened to this club since it was started by ten boaters in 1939," Norbert went on. "The increase in operating costs and the continually changing management requirements have altered the landscape for us. We have to make our own future, work together to overcome obstacles, and never lose sight of the vision of those ten founders who came before us, who had the idea of this club."

Norbert could see that everyone was looking at him like, *Here we go, the club is going to close and we're here to lower the flag*. It was time for him to deliver the news. He took a deep breath and said, "To ensure our continued existence a major step has been taken. For the past several weeks we've been negotiating an alliance with Oracle Racing to make a bid for the America's Cup. If we win, we will bring the Cup back to America where it belongs and defend it on the San Francisco Bay."

At first, there was silence. A moment later, the room erupted into cheers.

Finally, as the clapping and whistling died down, Norbert couldn't help cringing when he saw the hand of one member, known to be against everything, pop up. Norbert reluctantly called on him.

"We're on the right path," the man said. "We don't need to turn into a big fancy club. What business do we have in the America's Cup? If that happens, we won't even be able to use our own club!"

Norbert smiled and said, "You don't understand. This is the club's last chance. We are not on the right path. Larry Ellison is saving this club. There is no more Golden Gate Yacht Club unless this deal happens, and unless it happens now. And of course we will be able to use our club. This is the lifeline being thrown to our club. Again, let me be clear. If we don't do it there will be no Golden Gate Yacht Club. It's as simple as that."

Rear commodore Dave Haskins spoke out. "This is history! I heard our neighboring yacht club didn't like what Larry wanted to call his boats. Heck, the Golden Gate wouldn't mind a bit to have the Oracle name on a boat. Our attitude is, call it anything you want. We're not overly sophisticated. We'll be out there waxing the boats if that's what was needed."

The applause rose again. Erkelens smiled at Norbert, and the two men shook hands. Club members encircled Erkelens, offering him handshakes and hugs and ideas on how they could help the team.

Off to the side stood Dave Miller and his wife, Lydia. "Who would believe it?" he asked, his eyes welling with tears. For years Miller, who had built a business selling roofs that open into skylights, was one of the club's silent angels, bailing the Golden Gate out of trouble. If the roof leaked, he paid to have it fixed. If windows needed repair, he got it done. Miller and his wife, both Russian Jews born to missionary parents in China, had come to San Francisco on a boat after World War II. They lived in Daly City, and Dave's pride and joy was a forty-two-foot Viking, which he had spent years restoring.

Matlin found Norbert and said, "Dude, this is the save of a lifetime. We pulled it off! You pulled it off!" The membership agreement alone with Oracle Racing would come close to cutting their debt in half.

Norbert shrugged and laughed. "Yogi Berra said, 'If you come to a fork in the road, take it.' I took it."

Madeleine watched Norbert. "This is phenomenal," she said, giving Norbert a kiss. "Who knows what this will lead to?"

That night, less than three months after Norbert sent off the first e-mail to Erkelens, it became official: the once moribund Golden Gate Yacht Club was named the official sponsor of Oracle Racing.

The Golden Gate Yacht Club had given Larry Ellison precisely what he wanted but couldn't extract from the St. Francis: control of present and future America's Cup operations. Oracle would have three members—Bill Erkelens, Melinda Erkelens, and team CEO Chris Perkins, a well-known sailor (and a longtime member of the St. Francis)—on the Golden Gate's eleven-member board of directors. More important, the club would create a new and separate board to oversee all of the America's Cup challenge and Oracle would have three of its five seats.

Possibly the most titillating provision, though—at least to Norbert and members of the Golden Gate—allowed that if Oracle were to win the ornate silver ewer, the yacht club would have the right to keep it for half the year. For more than 150 years the Cup had been held, guarded, and proudly displayed by the winning yacht club.

In this most unlikely of partnerships, the little club had landed a sugar daddy and the corporate chieftain had snagged a cheerleader. The agreement had perks for both sides. The mechanic turned deal maker had steered the club away from bankruptcy and onto the stage of the world's most elite nautical show. The technology titan had pulled off a quiet coup. He had found a way to set the rules, pick the players, run the show, and be a part of the team. And what a message he was sending.

Larry told Erkelens, "I was never comfortable with the ambiguity in dealing with the St. Francis. I want to understand precisely what the deal is. Uncertainty and indecision drive me insane. Some people think I'm a control freak. They're right."

The plainspoken Erkelens agreed, saying, "The St. Francis would have been a pain in the butt to deal with. *They* need to be in control."

Norbert returned home that night from the Golden Gate well after midnight. A handful of club members had stayed, toasting the deal and raising a glass to the Golden Gate's red, white, and blue burgee, which had received an eleventh-hour reprieve. Looking at the clock, Norbert knew it was time to turn in. On the table next to his bed was the confidential "Challenge and Defense Agreement." It was full of legalese, but it was the most riveting document Norbert had read in a long time. In a formal notice of challenge to the Royal New Zealand Yacht Squadron, Norbert had written:

> This constitutes the notice of challenge by the Golden Gate Yacht Club to the Royal New Zealand Yacht Squadron for the yachting trophy which was initially won by the Yacht America in a race around the Isle of Wight on August 22, 1851, and which is known as the America's Cup.

In another paragraph, sure to raise eyebrows in the yachting community, Norbert wrote:

> Finally, enclosed is a copy of the Deed of Trust for our Sea Weed Soup Perpetual Trophy that, among other GGYC regattas, is held annually on an arm of the Sea—San Francisco Bay. Our yacht club looks forward to participating in the America's Cup XXXI event which you are organizing.

Putting the papers back on his nightstand Norbert knew that at some point he needed to have a heart-to-heart with his father. In the meantime, he was due back at the garage early the next day. There were cars needing help, radiators needing fixing. But on this night, the mechanic wanted to dream about a different type of metal: the Auld Mug.

Before drifting off to sleep, he told Madeleine, "When the Cup went from New Zealand to England for the hundred-and-fiftieth-anniversary events, I read that it was in first class. When we win the Cup and bring it home I think it should ride in coach with us."

PART II

"Most people run a race to see who is fastest.
I run to see who has the most guts."
— Steve Prefontaine

9

The Hills of Santa Barbara

Summer 2001

C HRIS DICKSON, the leader of Larry's America's Cup team, stood in the doorway of a bus, glaring down at Bill Erkelens's secretary, who was on the sidewalk below holding a clipboard.

"Get on the bus, we are leaving," Dickson said.

"We are missing two people, and Bill said we can't leave," the secretary replied.

The 140 men and women of Oracle Racing were hot, tired, and ready to leave the Boy Scout camp they'd rented in the chaparral hills above Santa Barbara for a weekend of team-building exercises. Erkelens, trying not to be exasperated himself, had told the team they needed to wait and was about to join an assistant in the search for the stragglers when suddenly he heard raised voices.

"We need to wait," the secretary insisted.

Dickson walked down the stairs and stopped within inches of the woman, who was six months' pregnant.

"No," Dickson said. Using his index finger, he began to poke the woman's chest, changing his cadence to mark time with his angry words: "We . . . Are . . . Leaving . . . Now."

Nearby, Erkelens stood immobilized. But the woman's husband, a cook for the team, was not. He lunged from the back of the bus and had to be restrained before reaching Dickson.

"Get your fucking hands away from my wife!" the sous-chef yelled from inside the bus.

Erkelens shook his head. *And this was after a weekend of bonding.* He had been trying everything he could think of to build cohesion, holding team barbecues and taking over restaurants on Friday nights—and now a weekend of togetherness with a $50,000 price tag. But instead of unity the tension was heightening between the American sailors and builders who came with *AmericaOne* and the Kiwi sailors and builders who were part of *Sayonara*.

As Dickson saw it, the purchase of the *AmericaOne* assets came with a "poison pill": the people. The *AmericaOne* crew acted superior to the Kiwi-heavy *Sayonara* group and were under the impression it was *their* campaign that Larry was putting his money into. As Erkelens saw it, the New Zealanders were actually better—they worked harder, had more talent, and demanded less. On this point, Dickson and Erkelens agreed. "If a pile of crap needs moving," Dickson said, "the Americans on the team will debate how it should be done and who will do it, while the Kiwis will grab a shovel and move the pile." And within the ranks, each group seemed to consider itself superior to the other: the engineers had the brains but the sailors had the brawn, and the shore team had both, or so the factions liked to think.

The weekend in Santa Barbara included everyone: engineers, builders, managers, secretaries, shore crew, cooks, management, trainers, and sailors. Erkelens had hired a well-known British company called Enabling Visions, whose motto was "The Art of Success." The firm worked with sports teams and large corporations and prided itself on a staff composed of former Royal Marines. Erkelens was learning the ropes of an America's Cup campaign, where team members were uprooted from their homes and asked to live and work together seven days a week, and where races were years out, requiring steady motivation and an ability to adapt to change. As

America's Cup veteran Tom Ehman, who served as Oracle Racing's head of external affairs, had told him, "The America's Cup is three years of meetings, followed by a yacht race." Erkelens's own family life had been shaped around boating operations. Erkelens called his children "*Sayonara* kids," as his son Josh was born in 1998 and was five weeks old when the family moved to the Mediterranean to prepare for the King's Cup, and Ashley was born in New Zealand in 2000. His wife, Melinda, was team attorney.

It was still two years out from the start of racing between the nine challenger teams that wanted to win the right to sail against Team New Zealand in the America's Cup. But team members were already putting in twelve- to sixteen-hour days. There was the management of the old boats and the engineering, designing, and building of two new ones. There was the marketing, corporate hospitality, sponsorships, sales, team branding, media handling, and business administration. There were uniforms to acquire, as well as food, housing, and insurance for more than 140 people of sixteen nationalities. There was the shipping of parts, including sails, hulls, gear, and tenders, and the paperwork for customs, a bureaucratic headache of its own. Operations were costing his boss, Larry, an astonishing $100,000 a day. They were in talks with several major corporations about sponsorships but deals had yet to be finalized.

Erkelens, whose childhood ambitions were to work ski patrol in the winter and design sailboats in the summer, earned his bachelor's degree in design and industry with a focus on manufacturing. He figured he would graduate and go to work for a big company in the manufacturing of goods. During college he worked on sailboats to earn extra money, and one of his clients was David Thomson, the neighbor who had encouraged Larry to get into maxi yacht racing. He was well versed in the lexicon of boatbuilding and boat design, as well as in business administration, but nothing could have prepared him for the inflated egos of superstar athletes, the factions, the tension, and the jockeying for position. Things were far simpler on *Sayonara,* where sailors were hired for a race, arrived for practice, performed during the regatta, and left afterward. Some were hired for the next race; others weren't. The sailors—Dickson included—were independent contractors. And Dickson's role was specific: he was either the helmsman or, when Larry drove, the coach. Brad Butterworth, easygoing and professional, served as *Sayonara*'s tactician, the "eyes on the water," looking for wind changes, plotting their next move, and reporting speed in relation to the competition. *Sayonara*'s full-time staff consisted of Erkelens, his wife, and one or two others.

After four years of racing in venues across the globe *Sayonara* had won four consecutive world championships and had never lost an around-the-buoys regatta, a series of relatively short races made up of upwind and downwind laps around marker buoys. That winning streak almost came to an end in 1999, though, when Larry agreed to let Ted Turner, CNN's founder and chairman of Turner Broadcasting, drive his boat in the Cowes Race Week regatta. Turner, who had won the America's Cup in 1977 with *Courageous* and was named U.S. Sailing's Rolex Yachtsman of the Year four times, did not sail well and finished in back of the fleet in the warm-up races and the first race in the regatta.

That night, Larry had called and asked Erkelens to come to his yacht *Katana*. "I've seen enough," Larry told Erkelens. "Ted's not driving very well. I'm taking my boat back. *Sayonara* has always won around the buoys, and we're not going to start losing now. I'm driving all the Cowes Week races." He said that *Sayonara* would be Turner's for the Fastnet Race. "He can drive as much as he wants," Larry said. "I promise not to come near the wheel."

The next morning Erkelens, who had grown fond of Turner and his wife Jane Fonda, who babysat his kids one night, had to take a tender to Turner's yacht to deliver his message. Erkelens had been impressed by Turner and the way he dealt with the sailors, greeting them by name, leading crew meetings, and at the end of the day thanking them individually for their time and service.

Welcomed aboard as Ted and Jane were having breakfast, Erkelens got right to the point.

"I'm really sorry, Ted, but Larry is taking his boat back," Erkelens said, aware that he was telling an America's Cup champion that he wasn't good enough to drive *Sayonara*.

Turner looked at Erkelens as if he didn't understand what he was saying.

Erkelens apologized and said, "I'm just the messenger."

From the second race on, Larry drove—and *Sayonara* won the Cowes Week regatta. The next day marked the start of Fastnet, a long-distance race that starts at Cowes on the Isle of Wight, heads west through the English Channel and the Irish Sea, turns around Fastnet Rock off the southwest coast of Ireland, and heads back east again and finishes at Plymouth on the south coast of England. With Turner driving, *Sayonara* suffered her worst defeat ever, finishing behind boats she had never lost to before and would never lose to again. Larry spent the entire three-day race sleeping belowdecks, coming up only to eat and find out how far behind the leaders they were. Larry swore he would never again lend his boat to anyone. Later, he told Erkelens, "Sailing today is very different from when Ted was racing. It's no longer the Joes raised at the yacht club. It's the pros who dominate this brave new world of boat racing."

When Turner won the America's Cup, in 1977, the race cost him under $3 million. The figure was now approaching $100 million. The world's best sailors and tacticians were set aboard the most astounding boats engineers could dream up and money could buy, and were placed on an unpredictable aqueous racetrack where speed had no limits. Erkelens was doing his very best to prepare his team.

At the campground in the hills of Santa Barbara, the stragglers had finally been found; everyone, including Dickson, had been calmed down and seated; and the buses could now head back to the team's base of operations in Ventura, about twenty miles away.

As he looked out the window, Erkelens went over the ups and downs of the weekend. It had begun almost as painfully as it ended. They'd spent their first night in a hotel before arriving at the camp. An inspirational speaker named Alan Chambers, who had been the leader of the first successful British team to walk unsupported from

Canada to the North Pole, gave the welcoming talk. Chambers spoke of what it took to plan for and execute peak performance. He described how he had spent five years planning and researching for the walk, had lived with families of Eskimo, and had perilously floated off alone on icebergs during his ten weeks on the ice.

"Tugsy" Turner sat back in his chair and listened, hand to chin. He feared the weekend of bonding would be a bust, and it took time away from working on the boats. He listened and tried to keep an open mind as Chambers went on about how to manage adversity. He began to tune out when the speaker said everyone needed to "work together as a team" and "make it happen." When Chambers said, "The only limits are those of vision!" and went on for what seemed like an hour about floating adrift on icebergs, Tugsy rolled his eyes and Erkelens cringed.

Then, on the first night at the Boy Scout camp, the team had been split into four groups of thirty-five: red, blue, yellow, and green. After putting their bags into their bunkhouses team members were asked to construct a large tent that would be used the next day. The task supposedly got them working as a team from the start. The teams were asked to do a sequence of tasks, with the color groups split into another four teams. When the first exercise of the day required them to "elect" a leader, Tugsy knew they were in for some fun. He stopped himself from laughing aloud as Cayard, the American star, and Dickson elbowed for position, reminding him of two boys going after one new toy. Dickson and Cayard, among others, were in contention for the skipper position, reminiscent of when Steve Young and Joe Montana both wore San Francisco 49ers uniforms. But Dickson and Cayard got along about as well as the basketball stars Shaquille O'Neal and Kobe Bryant or baseball sluggers Barry Bonds and Jeff Kent.

During the bonding exercises Cayard ended up leading his team, and they built bridges and worked to get people across a rope ladder and over rocks. Erkelens had been slightly encouraged when he noticed that designers and sailors were sitting together at the bonfire and playing polo in the pool. But what Erkelens hadn't seen—and was only now beginning to hear about on the bus ride home—were the fights that had broken out, even in the pool.

The bus incident only reinforced Erkelens's worries that there was a different side to Dickson, called "Dicko" by his teammates. As the buses neared Ventura, Erkelens concluded that he needed to have a conversation with Larry about these concerns. Larry had won five maxi world championships with Dickson as his tactician, and Erkelens knew that his boss was interested in performance over personality. Furthermore, Larry certainly would dismiss a team-building event like this as silly. The problem was that Larry had never seen Dickson come unhinged, except during the Sydney-to-Hobart, and in that case all bets had been off, as Dickson was horribly seasick along with everyone else.

Larry hadn't seen what others saw, the near fisticuffs on the boat with his own team members and the berating behavior. Larry had seen only the way he won when Dickson called tactics. Dickson was a great sailor, maybe the best around. When he was twenty-six, in 1987, he was skipper of Team New Zealand's first Cup campaign. Dickson had also skippered one of Japan's two teams in 1992, coming in third in the Louis Vuitton Cup, and he was owner and skipper of a New Zealand–based, TAG Heuer–sponsored campaign in 1995, again coming in third in the challenger series. But Dickson was as tempestuous as he was talented, and he was known in sailing circles as "heavy weather."

The match races between team members off the coast of Ventura inevitably grew heated, and Dickson would lay into the crew: "You're a fucking idiot and you shouldn't be allowed out on a boat" or "You're an imposter" or "How do you even make a living at this?"

Fortunately, from Erkelens's perspective, there was no lack of talent on the team if Dickson had to go. Erkelens had confidence in the other sailors in the running to drive: Cayard; Peter Holmberg, who was from the U.S. Virgin Islands and had been a silver medalist in the 1988 Olympics in Seoul in the men's single-handed

Finn class; and the British-born John Cutler, a bronze medalist in the same class at Seoul.

Erkelens knew that Larry listened to the ideas of others, but also that he had become an almost unrivaled success in the history of business largely by ignoring consensus. Erkelens had seen how Larry could act swiftly and make decisions that took everyone by surprise.

10

Atherton, California

September 2001

"Mr. Ellison, turn on your television right away," said a member of Larry's household staff, rushing into his den.

It was early on the morning of September 11, 2001, and Larry had been up before dawn, working in his study overlooking his Japanese-style garden in Atherton. He tuned in to CNN just in time to see a Boeing 767 smash into the South Tower of the World Trade Center in New York. As a pilot, he knew there was no way this was an accident, as some were speculating. Another jet had hit the North Tower fifteen minutes earlier. Within minutes, a third airplane would dive into the Pentagon and a fourth jetliner, originally heading for San Francisco and identified as United Airlines Flight 93, would crash into a Pennsylvania field.

Larry dialed Safra Catz, his longtime friend and trusted lieutenant at Oracle Corporation. Catz and Larry had met in 1986, when she worked at Donaldson, Lufkin & Jenrette, the investment bank that took his company public. She had been hired at Oracle in 1999 and now served as his assistant, doing as much of the CEO's job as she could.

"Who do we have in the World Trade Center?" Larry asked, still wearing his terry-cloth robe. With more than one hundred thousand employees worldwide, he was sure there would be losses. "We need names and contacts for family members as soon as possible."

After sending off a dozen e-mails Larry had a quick breakfast—sand dabs, rice, a soft-boiled egg, green tea—then got dressed and headed to work. It wasn't long before he learned that Oracle had lost seven employees in the towers, including one man who ran back into the building to try to help others. He learned that Todd Beamer, an Oracle account executive, was on board Flight 93, the doomed jetliner heading from Boston to San Francisco. Beamer, on his way home, appeared to have led a fight in the cabin against the terrorists, stopping them from reaching their intended target. Larry had names and phone numbers for families, and from his eleventh-floor office at Oracle in Redwood Shores he spent hours making calls of condolence.

Over the next few days, with the New York Stock Exchange, the American Stock Exchange, and NASDAQ closed, Larry listened to suggestions from managers and employees, including a prevailing idea that Oracle should also temporarily close out of respect for the fallen.

"Oracle can never close. We're not Macy's, and we're not NASDAQ," Larry said in a conference call. "The army, the navy, the marine corps, the CIA, all rely on our systems working all day, every day. Everyone dealing with this crisis—the police, fire departments, and hospitals—works twenty-four hours a day seven days a week and they expect us to do the same."

After getting its start as Software Development Laboratories in 1977 and landing as its first big client the CIA, Larry's company attracted a range of government agencies interested in collecting massive amounts of information and sorting it in a timely way. Oracle Corporation's earliest clients included the Defense Intelligence Agency and National Security Agency. (The company name was changed from Software Development Laboratories to Relational Software, Inc., in 1979, and to Oracle Systems Corporation in 1982.) Oracle's relational database allowed these agencies to sift and search through vast amounts of collected intelligence information and find the one piece of information they were looking for.

From his home office—distinguished by sixteenth-century samurai armor and artifacts—Larry worked with Catz and others to help relocate some of the U.S. Army's displaced staff from their bombed-out offices in the Pentagon to several Oracle office buildings throughout the Washington, D.C., area. Larry listened to revelations that one of the terrorists had an outstanding arrest warrant in Broward County, Florida, and that the CIA had been looking for others because of their connections to Osama bin Laden. It struck Larry that if the CIA's system had checked IDs of the men, they would have been prevented from getting on planes. Listening to news that Mohamed Atta, the Egyptian-born terrorist and leader, had been trained as a pilot in the United States, Larry pulled his own pilot's license out of his wallet. It was printed on paper flimsier than a teenager's fake ID.

What needed to be done, Larry realized, was to make life tougher for terrorists by combining the nation's myriad databases into a single database that listed all the people known to pose a threat to national security. Along with a single terrorist watch-list database, the country's agencies also needed to make it more difficult to counterfeit existing ID cards, including driver's licenses, pilot's licenses, and passports. In an opinion piece published in the *Wall Street Journal,* Larry called for the creation of a new single database—not fifty different ones—with information that should be shared and better ID cards. "We should take our existing IDs and make them more difficult to forge," he wrote. "And after we do that, we need to have a single database where we keep track of foreigners who come into this country." He said it was time to bring "government databases, such as Social Security and law-enforcement records, together in a single national file." It would be maintained and run by the government. And Oracle would provide the software for free.

Larry had never been busier. In addition to trying to strengthen the nation's security system, he faced the sudden challenge of repairing Oracle, which like many major companies in the aftermath of the terrorist attacks had taken a huge financial hit. When the markets opened on September 17, the longest shutdown since the Great Depression, the Dow Jones Industrial Average fell 684 points, its biggest one-day point loss in history. Oracle stock, taking a beating along with the entire tech sector, dropped to around $10 a share, compared with about $38 a share a year before. Oracle's quarterly earnings report, issued before the markets opened, was succinct, with Oracle recording first-quarter net income of $511 million on revenue of $2.2 billion. Earnings per share had increased to nine cents, compared with eight cents in the first quarter of 2000.

The company's earnings statement read: "In the aftermath of Tuesday's terrorist attack on the United States, Oracle Corporation is announcing its Q1 quarterly results without comment or elaboration. Oracle has seven people missing in the World Trade Center, and one person lost on United Flight 93. Our heart goes out to all of the families who have lost loved ones. We pray more survivors will be found. Our efforts and energies are now focused on helping the agencies of our government—relief, law enforcement, intelligence and military—respond to this national emergency. Our people, computers and facilities are being retasked to help these agencies reestablish systems that have been interrupted by the attack."

Larry flew to Washington for meetings with the nation's top security officials, including the FBI director Robert Mueller and CIA head George Tenet, along with California senator Dianne Feinstein, the ranking member on the Intelligence Committee. The first thing that needed to be done was to upgrade the FBI's ancient computer systems, which paled in comparison with the modern Oracle technology in use at the CIA. In every meeting and interview, Larry made it clear that he wasn't calling for the creation of a new national ID card, though he was suggesting adding biometrics to cards already carried and combining the separate CIA, FBI, INS, and IRS databases into a unified database watch list.

Returning late one night from a trip to the nation's capital, Larry unwound at home by picking up his guitar. Playing didn't relax him; it distracted him. The discipline and the difficulty of getting better appealed to him. He had started out on the guitar with folk music—thinking the guitar was sure to "impress the chicks"—but he had taken up Bach and Mozart and found Mozart far more difficult. He also continued to read voraciously. The books on his nightstand included *Fate Is the Hunter: A Pilot's Memoir,* by Ernest K. Gann; *The Jordan Rules,* by Sam Smith; and William Manchester's multivolume biography of Winston Churchill. After September 11, Larry thought more about what it must have been like living in England in the early 1940s, how the uncertain outcome of the world war made relationships more urgent and the everyday more precious. Having one's country under attack changed everything.

His priorities were clear and the America's Cup would have to be placed on the back burner. It would also mean less time with some new toys that had long been in production: a $35 million Bombardier jet and a 456-foot yacht, the length of one and a half football fields. The new yacht, *Rising Sun,* would have five decks, and a gym, spa, sauna, wine cellar, private cinema, and basketball court. Meanwhile, his new estate, being constructed in Woodside, would cost almost $100 million to finish. Although Larry had no intention of scaling back on these things, he did plan on spending less time playing, as playing seemed frivolous in light of recent events. Things like family vacations to the British Virgin Islands, where he loved to windsurf, would have to wait.

In the weeks following September 11 Larry talked off and on with Bill Erkelens. The Oracle Racing training camp had closed for two days after the attacks. The team was getting ready to move to its permanent base in Auckland, and Erkelens was frustrated that Larry—who had made it clear he wanted to drive in the America's Cup—had been to the training camp in Ventura only once. It was only an hour-long flight to Ventura from the San Carlos Airport, where Larry kept some of his planes. Erkelens wondered how he was ever going to get Larry all the way to New Zealand. When the syndicate was formed, Larry was going to be CEO and Erkelens would serve as COO. Now, Erkelens was doing both jobs, for Larry was simply not around and it was clear that his mind was elsewhere. The events of September 11 had given Larry a new enemy, one that didn't race yachts.

To be sure, whenever Larry felt remotely close to being at risk of failure he couldn't stop working. And now everything—his country, his business—seemed at risk. Like most overachievers, he was driven not so much by the pursuit of success as the fear of failure. He didn't build Oracle so he could be richer than Bill Gates. Instead, it was all about Oracle beating Microsoft. He was part of Team Oracle and he wanted his team to defeat every rival.

One thing that became more important to Larry after September 11, he told Erkelens, was a certain number for his second America's Cup boat. The first, *USA-71,* had already been assigned.

"We need to make sure we get seventy-six for our next boat," Larry said. "I want it to be *USA-76.*" Boat numbers were issued in sequential order, although it was possible for a team to work with the measurer if a certain number was preferred.

Larry also said he wanted the American flag to be put on all team uniforms.

"Can we do that?" Erkelens asked.

"Of course we can," Larry responded. "If Ralph Lauren can put his initials inside the flag and put the flag on his teddy bears, we can certainly put flags on a sports team sailing for the United States."

This conversation was one of the rare moments during the aftermath of the terrorist attack when Erkelens had Larry's full attention, so Erkelens went over some of the team's match racing results off the coast of Ventura. Using the two *AmericaOne* boats, numbered 49 and 61, Erkelens had been trying out different combinations of boats, gear, and sailors, often watching from the umpire boat. The first race was halted by a broken batten and a tear in the mainsail, Erkelens said to Larry. The second race had Cayard as helmsman of boat 61 and Holmberg as tactician. Cutler helmed 49 and Dickson called tactics. Cayard and Holmberg easily won. In race three, Cayard was at the helm of 61 and Cutler was tactician, while Dickson drove 49 and Holmberg called tactics. Cayard and Cutler took an early lead and won decisively. In another series of round-robins designed to see who performed best as helmsman, Holmberg had ten wins and two losses, Cayard had six wins and six losses, Dickson had four wins and eight losses, and Cutler had four wins and eight losses.

Erkelens used the stats as an opportunity to broach his concerns about Dickson. "I understand that you've had a lot of success with Chris as your tactician when you drove *Sayonara*," Erkelens said. "He is a perfectionist and could be the best sailor in the world." The problem was that Dickson couldn't get other people to work with him, Erkelens said. On any given day, he would end up screaming at his own teammates, who had to be restrained from going after him. He was the John McEnroe of the sailing world, talented but trouble.

"Great," Larry said. "I've got Cayard, who's an asshole, and Chris, who's crazy, leading our team. An asshole and a crazy man. Perfect."

"Yes, but you've got a lot of good guys too," Erkelens said.

"Look," Larry said. "I'm not there. I can't assess the situation. I don't know who you are going to have take Chris's place. You do what you think is the right thing."

Larry told Erkelens that there was one caveat. He wanted Cayard off the boat first. After sailing with him in some of *Sayonara*'s early races in 1995, Larry swore he'd never sail with Cayard again. He was one of America's best sailors with great America's Cup experience and a solid track record, but Larry's experiences with him were memorable for all the wrong reasons. During *Sayonara*'s very first race, a winning and record-setting run in the Coastal Cup from San Francisco to Catalina Island, Cayard was up on deck sharing stories with the crew while Larry was driving. One particular story was about Cayard being paid to drive the racing sailboat of a certain captain of industry, while at the same time he was sleeping with *both* of the man's daughters. Larry, who has a daughter, listened to the story and concluded that Cayard was a colossal jerk. Then on the Transpac race from Los Angeles to Hawaii, Larry watched as Cayard spent too much time checking on flights out of Hawaii instead of focusing on winning the race. Rather than sailing the great circle, the shortest route between Los Angeles and Hawaii, *Sayonara* dipped south of the course. Cayard expected to be rewarded with more wind. Instead, they sailed miles out of their way only to find less wind. The gamble cost *Sayonara* the race; they finished second. Larry took the loss badly. He thought Cayard took losing too well.

Erkelens knew that many in the sailing community, particularly those with an allegiance to the St. Francis Yacht Club, speculated that Larry had never intended for Cayard to sail but had him locked in golden handcuffs so he couldn't sail for anyone else. Larry found the rumors ridiculous, telling Erkelens that he never wanted Cayard out of the competition. "I'd have been happy to let Paul sail for another team," Larry said. "Unfortunately Cup rules just don't allow people to change teams during a campaign. It's not like baseball; you can't be traded."

Cayard would continue to receive his full salary, Larry told Erkelens, but he would be relegated to shore duties. "You need to have a meeting with Cayard and tell him that he'll be paid in full but he's off the boat."

In mid-October, just as the team was packed up and headed to New Zealand, Erkelens reluctantly met with Cayard over coffee. He had tried to convince Larry to keep Cayard on the boat. Holding his coffee cup, Erkelens told Cayard of Larry's decision. He could see that Cayard simply didn't understand the sidelining and, with his own sizable ego, refused to accept that he had made mistakes with Larry early on, mistakes that Larry was not one to forget.

Erkelens then met with Dickson to tell him his job was being narrowed. Erkelens had warned him about his erratic behavior off the boat. He explained to Dickson that Larry had decided Cayard would not be coming to New Zealand and that John Cutler would take Cayard's place as sailing operations manager. Erkelens also told Dickson that if he continued to have outbursts he would see his job eliminated. Erkelens laid out Dickson's job description moving forward. He would remain a member of the sailing team and afterguard. He would be one of the team's two primary helmsmen for testing and race training, reporting directly to Cutler. He would have authority over his own boat *while helmsman,* but Cutler would run daily sailing operations for the team and would have full authority over him. Erkelens said emphatically, "You will follow his direction on and off the water."

Dickson had believed for some time that Erkelens had it in for him, but he was not about to be outfoxed in his bid to become the go-to helmsman. He was already planning his strategy to stay on top.

11

San Francisco to New Zealand

Fall 2001

NORBERT STOOD IN the United Airlines terminal of the San Francisco International Airport and dialed his father. It was Friday evening and he knew his dad would be at his cousin's house in South San Francisco.

Speaking above the din, Norbert explained that he was at the airport and heading to New Zealand. He had told Jozo earlier in the week but wanted to remind him. "I'll be back in a few days," he said.

There was silence. "Dad, are you there?"

"So you've got a nice big deal for the Golden Gate Yacht Club?" Jozo shot back. "What about Alouis Radiator? You can save the yacht club but what about the business?"

Norbert shook his head. It was no use saying again that the economic downturn was not his doing, and that the fallout from September 11 was a bit beyond him.

"Dad, I'll be back in the shop, at work, on Tuesday," Norbert said, resigned.

His father added a few choice words and hung up on him. Norbert slowly placed the pay phone back on the receiver.

"Let's get a drink," he said to Madeleine, who could see the hurt on Norbert's face and knew he'd been on the phone with Jozo. She had seen their ups and downs and consoled him through the disappointments. Jozo was hard on Norbert, and Madeleine was tired of it. She had seen Norbert and Jozo develop a closeness after Gertrude's death but she'd also seen Jozo act brusque and downright rude. She remembered how excited Norbert was when his father had invited him to miss a day of work to go fishing. As it turned out, he invited Norbert because he needed a third man on the boat. Madeleine still laughed wryly remembering Jozo's first visit to their home in Larkspur. Madeleine proudly showed off their private patio leading to their own dock and boat slip.

"It's a swamp," Jozo harrumphed. Ever since, Madeleine, who is Sicilian and Spanish but fancies herself French, called it "Le Marais," meaning "the swamp," after the district in Paris. She even had a LE MARAIS sign made for their kitchen—something that appeared to go unnoticed by Jozo.

Norbert and Madeleine were heading to New Zealand on a hospitality mission, to find hotels and activities for members of the Golden Gate Yacht Club during the run-up to the America's Cup.

Race one of the Louis Vuitton Cup was to start on October 1, 2002, only a year away. The French fashion house—founded in 1854 by Louis Vuitton Malletier, who began by selling well-crafted luxury trunks—had first offered a trophy to the winner of the challenger selection series in the summer of 1983 in Newport, Rhode Island. In that first year, seven teams (including three from Australia) competed in 12-Meter class boats. *Victory* from Great Britain, *Australia II, Azzurra* from Italy, and *Canada I* made it to the semifinals. *Australia II* defeated *Victory* four races to one to win the Louis Vuitton Cup, and went on to challenge Dennis Conner's *Liberty* for the America's Cup. *Australia II,* sponsored by the Royal Perth Yacht Club, owned by Alan Bond and skippered by

John Bertrand, defeated Conner in the seventh and deciding race, ending America's long hold on the trophy and changing the history of the race by showing that the Cup was truly up for grabs. Bertrand, a sailmaker in Melbourne, had made his first try for the America's Cup with *Gretel II,* in 1970. He earned a master's degree in naval architecture from MIT, won a bronze medal in the 1976 Olympics in the Finn class, and was a part of Bond's *Southern Cross* in 1974 and *Australia I* in 1980.

The next America's Cup match, in 1987, saw Conner, sailing for the San Diego Yacht Club with *Stars & Stripes,* face *Kookaburra III,* from the defending Royal Perth Yacht Club. Conner easily defeated the Aussies four races to zero, becoming the first sailor to lose the America's Cup and then win it back.

Since 1983 the Louis Vuitton series had been both a selection tournament and a dress rehearsal, determining the best of the challenging teams and giving the challengers an opportunity to hone their skills on the course. The format of the Louis Vuitton Cup finals, and usually the semifinals, emulates—if not replicates—the America's Cup match in course configuration, length, and number of races. There is a round-robin period, with points increasing as teams advance; then there are the semifinals, between the top four boats, and the finals, a best-of-nine series between two teams. (On occasion, owing to time constraints, the Louis Vuitton semifinals have been the first to win four races, or they have been contested on shorter courses of two laps instead of three but over the same leg length.)

Madeleine, seated by the window, was excited about the trip, but Norbert dreaded it, as they had to stay in a different hotel every night. He liked to unpack once and settle in. Madeleine, a keen observer who could spot a fake Louis Vuitton bag from across the room, would assess the hotels and amenities. Norbert expected a stressful trip.

Now, less than two months after the attacks of September 11, the plane was full and Norbert grumbled about being at the very back by the bathrooms. He put his book and magazines away and kept his shoes on. He would order a Scotch or a glass of wine and try to forget his father's words. He replayed a recent visit to his father's house when, for whatever reason, he had come right out and asked his father why he had never told him he loved him. Jozo studied Norbert before swiveling his armchair to the wall. Finally, about thirty minutes later, as Norbert headed out the door, Jozo swiveled his chair back around. "I'm just not that type of guy," Jozo said.

Fourteen hours after takeoff, Norbert and Madeleine stepped off the plane in Auckland, the "City of Sails," with around 1.2 million people, making up about one-third of New Zealand's population. Nearly 90 percent of the country's population lived on the water, and it was only the second nation since 1851 to grab the Cup away from the Americans. In 1995, Team New Zealand, led by Sir Peter Blake in San Diego, had energized the country by taking the Cup from America. In 2000, Team New Zealand—Russell Coutts as skipper—had defeated Italy's Prada Challenge five races to zero. Three former America's Cup class boats, from 1992 and 1995, were in front of the airport to welcome visitors to the home of the Cup.

"I can't wait to get to the hotel and take a shower," Norbert said. One of the first things they did when traveling was to look in the local telephone directory and see whether there were any Bajurins. On this day, after their long flight cramped like sardines in coach, scanning fellow passengers for those who could be possible terrorists, they were met by overly cheerful Air New Zealand representatives and taken straight from the airport to the local cultural center. There, Maori dancers in loincloths did what Norbert labeled the "ooga chooga dance." Over the next three days Norbert and Madeleine packed and unpacked as they moved from hotel to hotel. Madeleine rated the rooms for comfort, cleanliness, bedding, smells, bath amenities, and the chocolates and weather reports left on pillows. They went skeet shooting and visited wineries. They participated in their own team confidence-building camp where they were cabled into small baskets and sent flying through the trees. Warned about the fast-changing weather in New

Zealand, they woke up one day to sun and went to sleep to snow. They shook countless hands and saw the North Island, Auckland, and surrounding areas first and then traveled to Queenstown on New Zealand's South Island.

Everywhere they went they had a driver, which was a first for both. And everywhere they went Norbert was addressed reverentially as "Commodore."

On their first moment free from the scheduled tours, tastings, and team building, they headed to the Oracle base, situated on an American Express barge in the America's Cup "Sailing Village" in Viaduct Basin in downtown Auckland. Swiss billionaire Ernesto Bertarelli's Team Alinghi—named after an imaginary friend that Bertarelli and his younger sister dreamed up as kids—was composed of Coutts, Brad Butterworth, Dean Phipps, Murray Jones, Warwick Fleury, and Simon Daubney. It had been one of the first syndicates to arrive in New Zealand with a new boat and was dubbed by the press the team to beat in the Louis Vuitton Cup.

Walking along Halsey Street, a waterside thoroughfare with chic outdoor cafés and street magicians and performers, Norbert and Madeleine listened to the dazzling array of languages being spoken. The biggest pleasure yachts they'd ever seen were moored along the quay. Flags flew from Italy, Switzerland, France, Sweden, Great Britain, and the United States. The shore bases resembled small cities. Team members in crisp uniforms mixed with Auckland security. Getting into the base camp was like entering a Swiss vault.

"It's like an Olympic village," Norbert said wide-eyed. Looking out at the sparkling Hauraki Gulf, Norbert reminded Madeleine that this was where the previous Cup, in 2000, had been fought and won by Team New Zealand, sailing *Black Magic*. The long *New Zealand Herald* headline had read: "IT'S MAGIC! THE AMERICA'S CUP IS NEW ZEALAND'S CUP! AND WE PLAN TO KEEP IT 25 YEARS!"

"Now, there are death threats against the Kiwis, particularly Russell Coutts, because they went and sailed for the Swiss," Norbert said, shaking his head as he noticed the banners along the streets reading "Loyal"—a message directed at the sailors branded turn-coats by their countrymen.

The Oracle Racing base was situated next to *Prada,* one of two Italian syndicates in the race. Patrizio Bertelli, who with his wife, Miuccia Prada, had taken a small family luggage business and turned it into one of the biggest names in fashion, was an avid weekend sailor for two decades before he got into competing. His two previous Cup campaigns had cost him more than $100 million, and their budget for this effort was $55 million. *Prada* had recently erected a wooden fence between the piles on its water boundary wall, as espionage was rampant. Already, Dennis Conner, head of the American Team *Stars & Stripes,* had accused Seattle's *OneWorld,* financed by Microsoft cofounder Paul Allen and Craig McCaw, founder of McCaw Cellular, of stealing design secrets, including hull drawings and sail and mast data, to create its new yachts. Polo Ralph Lauren was outfitting team OneWorld. McCaw and Allen had jumped into the race, flush with dot-com profits. With their deep pockets they had assembled a promis-ing design and sailing team, including the talented sailor Jimmy Spithill. And because of their almost unlimited finances—and with so many teams in contention—the salaries paid to sailors took the biggest jump in the sport's history. Suddenly, the top sailors were getting six figures a month, and good sailors drew five figures a month.

Conner's team had drawn attention when it signed Pfizer, along with Nautica and the software company Manugistics, as sponsors. The logo for the impotence drug Viagra was painted on the mast of Conner's boat and jokes were made about the "stiff competi-tion." Oracle, for its part, had just signed the German automaker BMW as its title sponsor, with the high-end car company com-ing in with a sponsorship valued at around ten million euros. The team's name was changed to Oracle BMW Racing.

Norbert and Madeleine were greeted by Bill and Melinda Erkel-ens and taken on a tour. Oracle BMW Racing's employees, and forty-five of their children, had been housed. A school was set up, along with restaurants and shops. More like a small town, the camp included its own cooks, trainers, meteorologists, nutritionists, attorneys, and teachers. Larry had opened Core Builders, his own boat design company in the United States, run by Mark Turner and Tim Smyth out of Anacortes, Washington, with boatbuilding operations also set up in Auckland. A computerized design program had been created to allow the Kiwi-born designer Bruce Farr to scroll through hundreds of virtual Cup-class boats and explore every conceivable possibility for the slightest gain in speed or correction in drag. Farr used the program to analyze thousands of hulls, looking at computer representations of stress loads and staging virtual races between the most promising hulls. Velocity-prediction programs, factoring in design variables from the boat length to the sail area, showed how a particular design would perform in a range of weather conditions and swells. The team had its own wind tunnel to test sail shapes and used some of the same methods employed by NASA in building and testing the space shuttle.

Norbert and Madeleine met the Oracle sailing team and the shore crew, which included an impressive collection of veteran New Zealanders. Many of the Kiwi team members had been with Erkelens and Ellison on *Sayonara,* including Dickson, Robbie Nai-smith, Mike Sanderson, and Nicki Eckart. Paul Cayard, Norbert and Madeleine were told, was being paid around $1 million not to sail. At the back of the hospitality area—complete with a pizza oven—was something that brought an even bigger smile to the commodore's face. It was an enormous GOLDEN GATE YACHT CLUB sign.

Madeleine put her arm around Norbert.

"I had no idea how big this whole thing is," Norbert said.

"Even if you're into boating, you really can't have any idea," Madeleine agreed.

The two listened as Erkelens talked about Oracle's full-time meteorology team, led by American Bob Rice, the best-known sailing forecaster in the business. The team collected round-the-clock direction and wind speed data using feeds from half a dozen boats and a weather buoy rented exclusively to Oracle.

The competition schedule was set. The nine teams from six countries would stage 120 races over five months. Oracle had Dickson, Cutler, and Holmberg—though Dickson's place on the boat was tenuous. Alinghi had Russell Coutts, Butterworth, Murray Jones, and Jochen Schuemann. Great Britain's GBR Challenge was skippered by Ian Walker. Le Défi Areva from France had skipper Luc Pillot. Mascalzone Latino was headed by the shipping magnate Vincenzo Onorato and featured an all-Italian crew. One World had Spithill and Peter Gilmour; Prada Challenge had Francesco de Angelis and Rod Davis; Team Dennis Conner had Ken Read at the helm; and Victory Challenge was Sweden's first America's Cup bid since 1992.

As they made their way back to the hotel, Madeleine and Norbert, still awed by the sights, slowed to a stop at the very same time. They looked up, not at falling snow but at the enormous and colorful banners strung across the chic street and featuring the names of the competing yacht clubs from around the world: Société Nautique de Genève, Royal Ocean Racing Club, Union Nationale pour la Course au Large, Reale Yacht Club Canottieri Savoia, Yacht Club Punta Ala, Seattle Yacht Club, New York Yacht Club, Gamla Stans Yacht Sallskap, and—there it was again—the Golden Gate Yacht Club.

Norbert marveled that only a few months earlier the Golden Gate had been heading toward bankruptcy. "Now we're up there with the most prestigious yacht clubs in the world!"

Under their banner, the mechanic and his wife stopped for a kiss.

On the day before they were scheduled to head home, Madeleine and Norbert faced more mandatory sightseeing. It was November 11, Norbert's forty-sixth birthday. After seeing more wineries, more historic buildings, and more Maori dancers, they were told they were being taken to one of New Zealand's finest attractions, its famous glowworm caves on the North Island.

Coming out of the tunnel, where they had seen glowing, oozing worms—giving Madeleine the creeps and making Norbert think of

Indiana Jones's Temple of Doom—they finally, thankfully, reached the end. There in front of them was a table set with cake and champagne, and at the table were members of the Oracle Racing team.

"Happy Birthday, Commodore!" they yelled in unison.

Two months later, back in San Francisco, Norbert was finally going to meet "Mr. Ellison," as he called him.

It was early in the evening of December 3, 2001, and tens of thousands of conventiongoers poured out of Moscone Center in downtown San Francisco after a day at Oracle OpenWorld, the company's annual conference and exhibition, which drew upwards of forty thousand people. Madeleine nudged Norbert, saying, "Look, they're trying to take the beanbags!"

Norbert smiled nervously. He had polished his best pair of dress shoes and made sure his gray slacks, white shirt, and blue blazer were pressed. He had taken off his tie earlier in the day, seeing that ties were a rarity. He repeatedly smoothed his hair and mustache and was distracted as Madeleine told him that conventiongoers apparently tried to exit the hall with anything that wasn't bolted down. The black beanbags, stamped with ORACLE, were a particularly hot item, an Oracle staffer had told her.

"How do you talk to a billionaire?" Norbert asked Madeleine.

The two were standing in the Golden Gate Yacht Club's kiosk on the convention floor, next to the booth for Air New Zealand. Madeleine forced her attention away from the beanbag heists and looked at her husband. She knew he was anxious about finally meeting Larry Ellison. After the deal between the Golden Gate Yacht Club and Oracle Racing was announced, sailing bloggers wrote that Ellison had "bought" the Golden Gate and Norbert had done his best to dispel the rumors. Madeleine, who had recently looked up Oracle's stock price, couldn't believe she was going to meet someone worth *fifty billion dollars*.

"This is a guy who thinks outside the box," Madeleine said, having now gone through two biographies on the businessman.

"I like it that he's still friends with his ex-wife, the mother of his two children. That says a lot. He admits he's a better ex-husband, and I think that's courageous. Some guys just are!"

"I know," Norbert said. "He's sure to be a great guy. But hey, I'm nervous." The closest he'd gotten to anyone with money was on their latest trip to New Zealand, when he saw wealth at a level hard to fathom. And the closest he'd come to the famous was looking at the two signed photos—of John Wayne and Frank Sinatra—that hung on the wall of his bar at home. He'd met Paul Cayard, but Cayard glared at him when he found out Norbert was head of the Golden Gate Yacht Club, which had reaped the benefits of the falling-out with the St. Francis. Norbert had seen Mr. Ellison coming in from races and heading to the St. Francis—he would always smile and wave or give a thumbs-up—and he was inspired by Ellison's humble beginnings and stratospheric success. This was a titan of industry, a dreamer, an innovator, a nerd—Henry Ford meets a Wright brother. He also was a guy who had influenced how people lived their daily lives, in ways most didn't know, whether in booking a flight or using an ATM machine.

The Bajurins, along with several members of the yacht club, were joined at the technology event by members of the sailing team, including Peter Holmberg and Mike Sanderson, the mainsheet trimmer. Their day was spent shaking hands and talking about the Golden Gate Yacht Club and the America's Cup regatta. A model of *USA-76,* built by Turner and Smyth and crew, was behind them.

Norbert felt his palms perspire as lights in parts of the hall were switched off and the last of the conventiongoers were ushered out. Security came in and chairs were set up. There were a small number of invited reporters, along with Norbert and Madeleine, and Ned and Carole Barrett.

"You can tell someone important is going to come in," Madeleine whispered excitedly. "Everyone is rushing around to make sure things are perfect." At that moment, in walked Larry, escorted by Judy Sim, Oracle's chief marketing officer. She whispered a few things to her boss and Larry surveyed the small invited group.

After questions were lobbed about the new Oracle9*i* database software, giving Larry another opportunity to criticize his rivals, saying their software was slower, less secure, and more expensive than Oracle's, Larry was asked a question that made him smile.

"Larry, tell us about the America's Cup and how you feel about partnering with the Golden Gate Yacht Club."

"We've got a great team and a fast boat," Larry said. "So I think we have a chance." Gesturing to Norbert, he said, "I believe the commodore of the Golden Gate is right over there. Why don't you ask him what he thinks?"

Larry urged Norbert to take the seat next to him.

Norbert tried to look confident. Adjusting himself on the tall chair, Norbert said, "To me, it's a dream come true. We are a little boating club, and I was just down in Auckland, New Zealand, and things look great. We have a great team, great boats, and we have Larry Ellison!"

"I love the Golden Gate Yacht Club," Larry offered. "It reminds me of the smaller clubs in New Zealand. In New Zealand there are more sailboats than cars. If you are a seven-year-old girl, and your dad is a cop, you sail. If you're a nine-year-old boy, and your mom's a nurse, you sail. In the USA every kid gets a bike. In New Zealand every kid gets a boat. The kids are out racing their little P-class boats [an inexpensive single-sail dinghy] by the time they're five. Some even sail to school. Most yacht clubs there are open to everybody. In New Zealand, sailing isn't a sport of privilege."

"It's a place where you have a radiator repair man as commodore?" a reporter offered.

"Yeah, sure it is," Larry said, looking at Norbert. "Remember, I was raised in the South Side of Chicago. In my old neighborhood, repairing radiators was a very good job. Norbert has his own shop and owns his own home, which would put him in the first tier of the small-business people I knew growing up. For too long, the America's Cup defenders and challengers have come from a few elite yacht clubs, the most elite being the Royal Yacht Squadron. When the prince of Wales, Queen Victoria's oldest son, was commodore, Sir Thomas Lipton challenged for the America's Cup several times, but he couldn't get in the club. Our list of elite clubs begins with the New York Yacht Club and the St. Francis. I've been a member and raced for the St. Francis for years. I respect the top clubs, but I feel more comfortable at the Golden Gate. I like their inclusive blue-collar membership. It reminds me of my old neighborhood and the small-town clubs in New Zealand."

After the press conference ended, Larry and Norbert stood eye-to-eye and shook hands. Norbert thought of two dogs sizing each other up. They were the same height—both are six-one—and build, and Norbert was surprised by how comfortable he felt with Larry. He watched how Larry charmed Madeleine and spent time talking with the Barretts. He had the politician's skill of making you feel as if you were the only person in the room.

The two stole a few minutes to themselves.

"You know," Norbert said, "this deal with the Golden Gate has changed history."

Larry said, "I like being a part of that. Now we need to make some more history by winning."

Before leaving the room, Larry offered, "You and your wife have to come to dinner on board my boat during the Louis Vuitton Cup."

"We'd love to," Norbert beamed.

Then, Larry said to the commodore, "We've got a lot in common."

"Oh?"

Larry replied, "You run a business, I run a business. It's not so different."

When Larry arrived at his San Francisco house that night, he headed to the living room to look out at the bay. His home—white, modern, and minimalist—is filled with surrealist and cubist paintings and sculpture by Picasso, Giacometti, and Larry's favorite art deco painter, Tamara de Lempicka. But the most beautiful picture was on the other side of his floor-to-ceiling windows, a spectacular panoramic view of the Golden Gate Bridge and beyond. Larry often sailed by the Golden Gate Yacht Club, or passed in a tender on his way back to the St. Francis after a race. It would be late afternoon or sunset and there were always a few men and women out on deck, holding up bottles of beer or Styrofoam cups. They looked as if they were having so much fun. He laughed to himself. Here he was, trying to trade Styrofoam cups for the America's Cup.

12

Oracle Base Camp
Auckland, New Zealand

Winter 2002

ANOTHER DAY OF in-house match racing was planned for the Oracle sailors, and Chris Dickson was pitted against Peter Holmberg to race just outside the Viaduct Harbor in Auckland. The two men took off in their Etchells 22s, fast and stable thirty-foot sloops used for training. The Etchells boats respond with wind and waves in ways similar to but scaled down as compared with the America's Cup boats. Launching an America's Cup boat took ten men, and it was costly and time intensive. By contrast, a fiberglass Etchells could be tossed into the water and sailed by three people.

Dickson and Holmberg, each with a trimmer to shape the sails and a bowman serving as the eyes on the front of the boat and controlling the headsails, practiced their starts and went over rules and tactics. The races were short, typically no more than twenty minutes. Henry Menin, a former attorney, competitive sailor, and respected judge on the water, who worked as Oracle's rules adviser, followed in his boat. The wind was blowing at around eight knots and Holmberg increased his lead. At the same time, something went wrong with Dickson's boat and Menin called a penalty. Dickson came undone and began to scream at his guys, and sailing came to a halt.

Informed of the blowup, Erkelens said to himself, *He's been warned.*

Erkelens looked at his watch and placed a call to Larry. It would be mid-morning in California, as New Zealand was nineteen hours ahead. Reaching Larry, Erkelens hesitated before explaining what had happened on the water.

"Chris lost it again," Erkelens said. "We had this deal with him that if he verbally abused the team he would be gone. I talked to him many times."

After what seemed like a minute of silence, Larry said, "Okay, do what you have to do. I still think Chris is the best sailor we have, but you are there and I'm not. Do what you need to do."

Not long after Dickson and crew had returned to base, Erkelens called Chris into his office. The Kiwi had a habit of acting shy and coy after his fits of anger. Taking a seat, he barely made eye contact with Erkelens, and Erkelens felt equally uncomfortable. He looked at Dickson as an exceptionally talented guy and an intimidating presence.

"We had a rule that you wouldn't abuse your team and you broke that rule," Erkelens began. "I have talked to Larry and, with his approval, I am suspending you with pay. We are sending you home."

Dickson finally looked directly at Erkelens and said he was making a big mistake. "If you've got a problem with me being here," Dickson said, "if you are just happier without me around, I've got better things to do."

Erkelens paused and said, "Yep, I'd rather you weren't here. I believe it's the best thing for the team."

Then, as quickly as he had taken a seat, Dickson stood and smiled and left the office. For months, Dickson had felt the behind-the-scenes politicking. He was the first to admit he was a pain-in-the-ass helmsman. He was deaf to excuses, and many of the sailors blamed him for Cayard's exit. He also knew Erkelens didn't like him and believed Erkelens had for months been trying to build a case against him, to get rid of him without being sued. On a recent day when there was no sailing and everyone was asked to show up to clean the yard and help the shore crew, Erkelens assigned Dickson the job of painting lines in the parking lot. Dickson did his job, buying the paint and painting what he thought were the most beautiful lines ever done in a parking lot anywhere.

As Erkelens watched Dickson go, he guessed that it wouldn't be long before the Kiwi started lobbying Larry from behind the scenes. He had already received a handful of the e-mails Dickson sent to Larry, blaming the team's problems on everyone but himself. They were a few months away from the beginning of the round-robin series and Erkelens was eager to galvanize the team.

The meeting was formalized with a letter in which Erkelens wrote, "The most recent recurrences of inappropriate behavior have left me no choice but to advise you of a change in your responsibilities within the campaign. I truly believe that this is the right thing to do for the team and for our America's Cup challenge effort." Dickson was assigned to consulting duties, effective immediately.

"Your salary will remain unchanged," he wrote. "During this reassignment, your participation within the syndicate will be limited to consultation as described above (when requested) and such duties will be performed from home."

Erkelens offered to set up a meeting with the team's public relations department to "strategize on how to manage the potential publicity from this role change." Then Erkelens called a team meeting to announce the news. "We got rid of the cancer," he said, "and now we can be a team."

13

Redwood Shores, California

Spring 2002

Sitting in his eleventh-floor office in the bayside tidelands of Redwood Shores, south of San Francisco, Larry said to Safra Catz at Oracle, "I was beginning to think I should retire. Everyone has been telling me how great these companies like Pets.com and Webvan are. 'Larry, don't you know?' they said. 'All that matters is eyeball traffic and clicks.' I said, 'Yeah, but what about actually making money? What about that old-school idea of revenue?'"

It was March and Oracle's stock had plummeted to $7.70 a share from $45 a share, wiping out 80 percent of Larry's net worth. Looking at his sixteenth-century Japanese screens depicting the Genpei War, fought between the Genji and the Heiki clans over who would rule the imperial court, he joked to Catz, "Reporters seem to enjoy writing about how I've lost almost all my money. But I'm a man of modest needs. I can still live on the ten billion dollars I have left. Maybe now when I want that omelet with *pommes frites* I'll have to say, just give me the omelet."

Oracle's underlying business was strong—the company made over $800 million in operating profit and had a 35 percent operating margin in its second fiscal quarter—but the markets were crashing and Oracle's stock price was crashing along with them. Nearly half of the Internet companies created since 1995 were gone, casualties of the dot-com bust, which wiped out an estimated $5 trillion in market capitalization. Pets.com began in February 1999 and closed in November 2000, after buying a $1.2 million Super Bowl ad and burning through $300 million in investment capital. Webvan, the Foster City–based grocery home-delivery service created by executives who had no experience in supermarkets—yet attracted funding from companies including Goldman Sachs, Benchmark Capital, Sequioa Capital, and Yahoo—filed for bankruptcy in 2001 after burning through hundreds of millions of dollars to buy a fleet of trucks, build automated warehouses, and expand aggressively nationwide.

"The bubble went on and on and my confidence was beginning to waver," Larry said. He had begun to think perhaps he *was* wrong: Maybe profits didn't mean a thing. Maybe it was all clicks and eyeballs and maybe he should retire. "The companies were saying it was *a new economy,* that making money wasn't the thing," Larry said to Catz. "The bubble was kind of group insanity. I would hear, 'Yes, but don't you love the Webvan idea?' As a customer, sure, I love it. I especially love that John Doerr and Kleiner Perkins are subsidizing my salad, but the company will never make money."

Larry had made his share of mistakes as he built Oracle, and he didn't intend to repeat them. In 1990, three years after yet another market crash and in the midst of the savings-and-loan debacle, the beginning of the Gulf War, and a spike in oil prices, Larry was forced to lay off about 10 percent of the workforce, nearly five hundred people. Oracle had doubled its revenues the previous ten of eleven years and was the fastest-growing company in Silicon Valley. The hard-charging CEO had counted on continued growth and built up expenses, wrongly believing the weak economy could not hobble Oracle. After the layoffs, which had hit him hard personally, he realized he'd made the classic mistake of an inexperienced executive who should have adjusted expenses to the new reality of the recession. Now, older and wiser and having weathered economic ups and downs, he had seen the tech business go through periods of fad and fashion, reminding him of the women's clothing business. He'd say, "Orange is *not* the new pink." The dot-com hype was only the latest fashion in computing. The market would overreact on the upside as the bubble inflated. And it would overreact on the downside after the bubble burst. The market could be wildly wrong for a few years but usually got it right over the long term.

He recounted how in the early 1980s he talked to Michael Dell about the proliferation of PC companies that seemed to pop up out of nowhere and were gone a year later. More recently, in the dot-com heyday and shortly after the AOL–Time Warner merger, he got a call from Farzad Nazem, who used to work at Oracle and was now a top executive at Yahoo. Nazem told Larry, "Disney wants to merge with us. Why would we ever want to do something like that? What have they got?" Larry answered his old friend, "Gee, let me think. They have the most valuable film library in the world, the most valuable TV channels in world, and successful theme parks everywhere. Disney makes tons of money and they're probably the most beloved brand on the planet. Now, what have you got? A Web page with news on it and free e-mail. Has everyone gone crazy?"

With all of Larry's joking and glibness, with all of his high-adrenaline hobbies and pursuits, Catz knew that Oracle was his baby. He could marry and divorce, befriend presidents and prime ministers, devour history books and biographies, and debate about the greatest minds, athletes, cars, planes, suit makers, poets, writers, and musicians. But Oracle was in his marrow.

When he was in his twenties, when everyone around him was concerned he would never make any money, Larry looked at his life as a great success. He'd ride his bike from Berkeley to Yosemite, where he was a rock climbing instructor. He was a guide on rafting trips down the Stanislaus and American rivers. He built his own white-water kayaks and played respectable folk music on his twelve-string Martin guitar. He could wow the

pretty girl at the Palo Alto bookstore by reciting a poem from
A Shropshire Lad, by A. E. Housman, beginning with: "When
I was one-and-twenty I heard a wise man say. . . ." The poem
worked; the girl swooned. When Larry wasn't hiking, cycling,
river rafting, or romancing he found work as a for-hire computer programmer. When Software Development Laboratories
was started, Larry had two goals: to make enough money to have
a nice house, a car, and a family and to be able to do interesting
work with people he liked. He envisioned a company with fifty
people. By 1985 Oracle had sales of $24 million. When it went
public in March 1986—just one day before Microsoft—Oracle
had a market value of $270 million. By 1990 sales were at $916
million. Along the way, though, risks and setbacks were constant.
Early on, when the company was still small and could have closed
any number of times, Larry had his house foreclosed on and
his water and electricity turned off because he couldn't pay the
bills. Living in the Woodside hills, he found out where the water
main was, got a bolt cutter, and turned his water back on. He
learned how to do the same with his electricity. Now, even in
the midst of another economic meltdown, Oracle was in a place
of unimagined dominance. Oracle's databases managed most of
the world's most important information: allowing banks to keep
track of how much money a customer had on deposit; giving
airlines the ability to track what seat a person was in; letting the
navy monitor where enemy fighters were and what threats were
posed; giving the government the ability to keep track of how
much individuals were owed in tax refunds; letting the Defense
Department track up-to-the-moment locations of individual
soldiers and ballistic missile submarines. Oracle had become as
ubiquitous as Microsoft, but in ways less widely known. Every
time a person used a credit card, withdrew cash from an ATM,
bought a plane ticket, or ordered something online, chances were
that an Oracle database was making it possible.

"Here, we are competing at the very highest level—Oracle versus IBM, Oracle versus Microsoft," Larry said to Catz. "The stakes

are high, much higher than in the America's Cup. Beating IBM is a lot more important to me than beating Team New Zealand."

Catz knew that when the company was doing great Larry became interested in other things. Oracle had his full attention now.

Six months later, at the end of September, Larry turned his attention back to the America's Cup. The markets had been rising and falling, and a week earlier, on September 24, NASDAQ plummeted to a six-year low. Larry knew that the markets would eventually stabilize, and he was not taking his eyes off Oracle. At the same time, he needed to be in New Zealand for the start of the Louis Vuitton Cup, which would determine who would go up against defender Team New Zealand for the main event in February.

Larry had not spent much time practicing with the team, but he still planned to be on the race boat and do at least some of the driving. When he arrived in New Zealand he figured the quickest way to knock the rust off was to drive the B boat, *USA-71*, in practice races against Peter Holmberg driving *USA-76* crewed by the A team. After a few days of practice, several things became clear. The team was inflexibly split down the middle between the old *Sayonara* guys and the new hires, and the two sides barely spoke to each other. The *Sayonara* crew had been banished to the B boat, which Larry joined. It was also clear that while Holmberg did a good job starting the boat, he wasn't as good at getting the maximum speed upwind and he was slow through the tacks. In the practice races, Larry consistently did better than Holmberg on the upwind legs, especially if there was a tacking duel. So Larry decided he would have Holmberg do the starts and helm the downwind legs and he would drive the upwind legs. Sailing manager John Cutler and most of the guys on the A boat, who didn't like their billionaire boss parachuting in and changing things, had a different idea. They wanted Holmberg to drive all of the time and Larry to watch the races from the comfort of his megayacht.

The Louis Vuitton Cup begins with two round-robins. Each of the nine challenging teams races each of the others once in the first round-robin and once again in the second round-robin. Oracle BMW Racing started strong in the first round-robin. In the first race, Oracle was up against the Prada-sponsored Italian team, Luna Rossa, which had won the Louis Vuitton Cup in 2000 but had lost in the America's Cup to Team New Zealand. Oracle beat Prada by forty-two seconds and led around every mark on the eighteen-and-a-half-nautical-mile course. In its second race, Oracle continued its winning ways by beating the other Italian team, Mascalzone Latino. Oracle's third race was against Team Dennis Conner's boat, *Stars & Stripes*. Holmberg won the start and earned Oracle a small, half-boat-length lead. When Larry moved to the wheel to drive the first upwind leg, John Cutler physically blocked him from taking the wheel. For an uncomfortable moment, Larry pushed back until Cutler moved aside. Larry steered the boat and extended the small initial lead into a big lead, with Oracle winning the race comfortably. Larry shook his head. The encounter with Cutler would have made for interesting TV—a fistfight onboard *USA-76* between the team owner and his sailing manager.

In race number four, Oracle beat Le Défi Areva, sponsored by and named after the French nuclear power generation company. Rather than a traditional shade of French blue, the Areva boat—nicknamed "Atomic Warrior"—was painted an iridescent greenish yellow, a slight variation of the color used on DANGER RADIOACTIVE signs. On its arrival in New Zealand the Areva boat was met by a flotilla of protest boats from Greenpeace and others that gathered at the entrance to the Viaduct flying antinuclear banners reading "Wind Power Not Nuclear Power." Locals were happy to see the winless French team lose again.

Oracle was one of two unbeaten teams halfway through the first round-robin. Race five was against Alinghi, skippered and driven by Russell Coutts, who had never lost an America's Cup race and had almost as good a record in the Louis Vuitton Cup. Larry had raced against Coutts once before, years earlier in a regatta in the San

Francisco Bay. Larry had been winning every start and every race against a fleet. Coutts was tactician for SAP's Hasso Plattner, driving *Morning Glory*. Plattner complained to Coutts that it was impossible for his boat to beat *Sayonara* in the owner-driver regatta, that *Sayonara* was like the mechanical rabbit, which always led the greyhounds over the finish line. In the next race, Coutts took the wheel to make a point. Larry won the committee boat end of the line and thought *Sayonara* would once again start ahead of the rest of the fleet, until *Morning Glory* crossed the starting line late but with enough speed to roll right over the top of them and take the lead. Larry was stunned. He did a double take and noticed Plattner wasn't driving *Morning Glory*. Larry smiled and shouted, "Hey, Russell, you're not supposed to be driving." Coutts stayed on the wheel for a few minutes to solidify his lead, and then turned the helm back to Plattner, who lost the lead and then the race to *Sayonara*. Larry wanted another chance to race against the great Russell Coutts, the man everyone considered the best in the business. He had no illusions about being in Coutts's league but still he relished the challenge.

Race five against Alinghi began with Coutts so dominating Holmberg during the prestart maneuvering that the race was practically over before it began. Holmberg was seriously outmatched. Larry watched in awe as Coutts drove and Brad Butterworth managed the race and called tactics. The team handled every maneuver and mark rounding perfectly. "They may be a better team," Larry told close friends who had watched the one-sided race, "but we have a faster boat, so we don't have to sail as well as they do to beat them."

After absorbing their first loss, Oracle now came up against the team from Great Britain. Larry was confident they would beat GBR Challenge's boat, *Wight Lightning*. It was the Britons' first Cup bid in fifteen years and they were not on anyone's list of top contenders.

Zipping his jacket and putting on his team cap as he stepped off his yacht *Katana* and onto the tender that would take him to *USA-76,* Larry told his girlfriend Melanie, "The only way we can lose to GBR is if we sink."

Larry was going to be in the afterguard, the "thinking part" of an America's Cup racing yacht that includes the helmsman, tactician, strategist, and navigator. Oracle's afterguard for the GBR race included Holmberg and Larry, along with navigator Ian "Fresh" Burns and tactician Tomasso Chieffi.

The forecast on this day was for strong winds of twenty-five knots, which by the start of the race failed to materialize. As the teams headed out onto the Hauraki Gulf, the breeze blew from 300 degrees at a light eight to ten knots.

After a split tack start, *Wight Lightning,* helmed by Andy Beadsworth, sailed toward the right-hand side of the racecourse while the Oracle boat took the left. As the boats continued to separate farther from each other Larry became uncomfortable. Picking one side of the course and separating is a crapshoot. If the slower GBR boat got more wind or a favorable shift in wind direction, it could get to the first windward mark before Oracle. And that's exactly what happened: there was more wind on the right side and GBR rounded the mark first with a thirteen-second lead.

It is conventional wisdom in match racing that the faster boat should stay close to the slower boat. It's called covering, and it minimizes the impact of different wind speeds and directions on the racecourse. The theory is simple. When the faster boat covers and sails in the same wind conditions as the slower boat, the faster boat wins. Because Oracle chose to split rather than cover, it sailed in less wind and lost the first leg to GBR. But it was still early in the race and the Oracle team had time to recover.

The tactician, not the helmsman, decides when to tack the boat and when to jibe, and also decides when to split and when to cover. Larry thought Chieffi had made a mistake by not covering on the first upwind leg. Oracle was able to pass GBR on the second upwind leg and started the second run downwind with a safe lead—safe, that is, until Chieffi called for a jibe without properly taking into account the position of the trailing GBR boat. By jibing in the wrong place, the Oracle boat had become vulnerable to an attack by GBR. When racing downwind, the leading boat has to be careful not to sail into a position where the trailing boat can block its wind. GBR simply waited for Oracle's next jibe, jibed right with it, blocked Oracle's wind, and passed a helpless *USA-76*. Sailors call it getting rolled. There was no redemption this time; GBR won the race by thirty-six seconds, and this was a race no one had expected the Brits to win.

Right after the fatal jibe, Chieffi went to Larry to apologize. It was clear Chieffi felt terrible about the tactical mistake, and so did Larry. Chieffi was one of the nicest guys on the crew. Larry liked him, and they had sailed together before, when *Sayonara* raced in Italy. But the loss was devastating. "We all make mistakes," Larry said. "The first one I can live with, but not the second. I've seen enough."

"What a fiasco," Larry said as he jumped back into a tender. "Oh my God, this is fucking unbelievable. We have no chance with this afterguard. How did this team get here? How did we make so many bad decisions?"

After the tough loss to the British team Oracle faced a very difficult race number seven. The crew was pitted against an undefeated OneWorld, Craig McCaw and Paul Allen's team from Seattle. OneWorld had a fast boat and a highly regarded crew led by skipper and tactician Peter Gilmour and the youngest driver in the Louis Vuitton Cup, the nineteen-year-old Australian Jimmy Spithill. OneWorld maintained its unblemished record by handing Oracle another defeat.

In the eighth and final race in round-robin one, Oracle managed to end its losing streak by beating the Swedish team Victory Challenge. That gave Oracle five wins and three losses and placed the team third among the nine Louis Vuitton Cup competitors. Larry needed to make some changes.

The mood was solemn and expressions were anxious as Larry walked into the sail loft to face his team. A mandatory morning meeting had been called after the loss of three of their last four races and Bill Erkelens was one of the few who knew what

Larry was about to say. The men stood in a semicircle in the open, sunlit room. Larry knew many by name but the majority were strangers to him.

Larry began, "Right now, we are at best an average team. Half the teams are better, half the teams worse. The way things are, we don't have a prayer of winning this thing."

He saw some of the guys nodding and heard others grumbling.

"Since I got here, I've practiced with you guys, and I've been out on the boat during our races," Larry said. "I've been gathering a lot of data along the way. All of you can see that we made too many mistakes out there on the boat. Those mistakes caused us to lose races we should not have lost. If we keep making serious tactical errors, we are all going to be at home watching the Louis Vuitton finals on TV." He went on, "I think you always learn more from losing than from winning, so I've had the opportunity to learn a lot these past few days. I've learned that we need to make a leadership change in our team's afterguard. I'm done learning through losing."

After a pause, Larry said, "Some of you guys are going to be unhappy about this, but I'm bringing Chris Dickson back as tactician and skipper."

Loud cries of "Oh man!" and "No way!" followed.

Stu Argo, the team's star sail trimmer and an America's Cup veteran who had been a member of Bill Koch's winning team in 1992, said, "There are a lot of people here who will not sail with him. I will quit before I sail with him again."

"You don't have to like him," Larry said. "I'm not asking you to date him. I'm asking you to sail for him. If some people feel they cannot remain on the team, I understand. We will continue with the people who choose to stay with this team, want to stay on the team." After listening to more grumbling and protests, Larry talked about another tempestuous athlete. "Michael Jordan screamed at his teammates. He didn't travel with his teammates. He was aloof. He traveled on his own plane, not on the team plane. He didn't hang around or talk much with his teammates. But he had a burning desire to win—a will to win—and he won."

A frustrated Erkelens listened in silence. He had told Larry before the meeting that he had promised the team Dickson wasn't coming back. "My credibility is now shot to smithereens," he said. "You are going to have to sell the team on this." Erkelens thought that Dickson had been lobbying Larry behind the scenes, which wasn't the case. Dickson had been as surprised as everyone else when Larry called and asked him to rejoin the team.

Argo, a champion wrestler in school who was known for his ability to read the telltales and get the most out of a sail, raised his hand again. "We've voted Chris off the team," he said. "I'm a huge believer in chemistry on a boat. This pill is too large to swallow. I bow out."

A dozen other sailors applauded and said they would leave with Argo. Larry listened as his decision was called "ridiculous" and as he was told he hadn't been around so he had "no sense of the real Chris Dickson" and "no idea what was really going on." Argo likened Larry's decision to hearing that your best friend is marrying his ex-wife for the third time and you are expected to be happy and think it's a great idea.

Tugsy Turner listened as the discussion volleyed back and forth. Larry had not been involved in the campaign, as he was working to stabilize Oracle. He simply had not seen Dickson the way other people did. Tugsy knew Dickson well and knew that he could be both brilliant and brutal. In Tugsy's mind, though, the sailing team was only part of the problem. He'd had an uneasy feeling for months that they had picked the wrong design for the boats *USA-76* and *71*. They both had deep keels, which reduced the sail area, doing fine in breeze and upwind but not sailing well downwind or in light air conditions. Tugsy tuned back in to the discussion. Larry said he would happily talk with any of the sailors individually after the meeting. But he made himself clear. "It's my decision. Chris is coming back to lead this team. He's an exceptionally good tactician, and we need a good tactician. I know he's intense. He's also disciplined and decisive. He is the best sailor on this team. You can't vote our best sailor off the team."

Sidelining Dickson, Larry said, was like the time in the 1980s when the Apple board replaced Steve Jobs with John Sculley. "How dumb was that?"

Erkelens could see the level of dissension and unhappiness. It certainly wasn't the *Braveheart* freedom speech Larry probably wanted, inspring his troops to pick up their swords and prepare for battle.

Then another sailor raised his hand and said, "I thought we were here to have fun." The room went silent. Erkelens smiled to himself. Early on, he had created a team mission statement. The first objective was to win in 2003. But Erkelens had told the team: "If we are going to work long days and have our families and lives uprooted we have to have fun. We aren't just going to suffer every day so Larry can hold up the Cup. Fun *is* important."

Larry looked at the young sailor, one of the team's huge grinders—he didn't know the sailor's name—and narrowed his gaze. "Fun? You think we're here for fun? Do you think losing is fun? I don't. This is professional sports, not a third-grade T-ball game. Is sailing fun? Yes, if you want to sail to Sausalito and sit and do a little fishing or sunbathing out with your family, that can be fun. If you are sailing in the America's Cup, if it's your job, you are supposed to work very hard. We are here to win. Winning, that's my idea of fun."

The young sailor wouldn't back down, insisting that they had been "promised" they would have fun.

Finally, Larry looked at him directly and said, "If you want to have fun, go buy your own fucking boat. Chris Dickson will be the skipper of Oracle BMW Racing until we win the Cup or we're defeated on the water. That's my decision and it's final."

Mike Howard, the six-foot-three, 250-pound grinder who had been aboard *Sayonara* during Sydney-to-Hobart, raised his hand.

"Hey, we need to do our best, to work together now as a team," said Howard, a team leader. "Despite everything that's happened, we need to support this decision and support Chris going forward."

Before inviting sailors to come and talk with him individually, Larry said there was one more point he wanted to make. "Vince

Lombardi's most famous line is 'Winning isn't the most important thing, it's the only thing.' That is not the Lombardi line I love." When Lombardi left the Green Bay Packers, where he'd won all of his championships, and went to an also-ran team, the Redskins, he was loved and feared by players. Larry said, "He came in and made the following short speech: 'Every team in the National Football League has the talent necessary to win the championship. It's simply a matter of what you're willing to give up.' Then Lombardi looked at them and said, 'I expect you to give up everything,' and he left the room. Winning is a habit. Unfortunately, so is losing. Sure, there is the talent, but there also has to be the will. Give me human will and the intense desire to win and it will trump talent every day of the week."

After meeting individually with team members, Larry left the sail loft that morning sure of a few things. The team didn't want him driving. They didn't want him on the boat. And they probably didn't even want him in New Zealand. On the plus side, Dickson was coming back and he would no longer be the most hated guy on the team. That person was now Larry Ellison.

At 9:30 a.m. on a cool December morning, Norbert and Madeleine stepped aboard *Katana,* the most elegant yacht the two had ever seen. They had been invited for lunch and would be meeting Melanie Craft for the first time.

They were greeted by the captain and staff and taken on a tour of the 244-foot boat with seven guest suites built by Blohm & Vass, a German shipyard best known for building high-speed naval vessels equipped with gas turbines. The yacht's former owner was the Mexican mogul Emilio Azcárraga, who had named her *Eco.* Larry immediately redid the boat's interior, from what some of his friends had taken to calling "deco Mex"—a black lacquer, red leather, south of the border interpretation of art deco style—to elegant modern wood furniture, paneling, and upholstery in a palette of cream, sand, and beige.

Norbert swooned over the basketball court and was dazzled when he was invited to sit in the captain's chair. "It's like the starship *Enterprise*," Norbert marveled, looking at the panels of instruments, switches, and screens.

It was the start of the Louis Vuitton semifinals and they would soon be headed out into the Hauraki Gulf to watch the race. Since Dickson's return as skipper and tactician, Oracle BMW Racing had won eleven straight races, losing only once, to Alinghi. Oracle now faced OneWorld, driven by Jimmy Spithill, in a best of seven race series. If Oracle beat OneWorld in the semis, Larry's team would race Alinghi in the Louis Vuitton Cup finals. The new afterguard had Dickson in charge and calling tactics with Holmberg driving. Larry took himself off the boat because he didn't think the team could bear having him and Dickson on board at the same time.

Within a few minutes, Melanie appeared on deck and greeted Norbert and Madeleine warmly.

"So *you're* the commodore," Melanie said.

Norbert was self-conscious, sure that the pretty woman with sandy blond hair and perfect skin was looking at his crooked teeth. She guided them to the back of the boat, where Larry was pacing on deck.

"I wish he'd calm down," Melanie said. "He gets so wound up on race days. There is less stress when he's driving. It's hard for him to be standing on the sidelines watching."

The boat left the dock, and after about twenty minutes at sea *USA-76* reached the starting area for the race, only to learn that it would be delayed by weather. Madeleine, Norbert, and Melanie joined Larry on deck. Looking out at the water from the starboard side, they saw dozens of dolphins swim right up to the boat and then dive under and come up on the other side.

"That's so sweet how they're all following one another," Melanie said.

"Following with a purpose—they're horny," Larry said.

Norbert glanced at Mr. Ellison, who was wearing khaki pants, an Oracle Racing shirt, and the very same Sperry Top-Siders from the Billfish collection that he himself wore. "We've got the same shoes," Norbert said to Madeleine.

Not long after, Norbert watched Ernesto Bertarelli's private yacht, the 150-foot *Vava,* arrive and anchor alongside *Katana.* Bertarelli's Alinghi team had already made it to the Louis Vuitton finals. Bertarelli and his wife, Kirsty, a former beauty queen from England, were out on *Vava's* top deck, scouting the competition.

Norbert whispered to Madeleine that Bertarelli's boat was half the size of Larry's.

He also had heard that Bertarelli's billionaire status had come from the sale of his father's pharmaceutical company to Merck for around $10 billion. "Larry made his money," Norbert said with pride. Bertarelli and Larry talked for a few minutes, laughing and joking.

Norbert said, "Is this the scene where someone asks, 'Do you have any Grey Poupon?'"

When it was time for lunch the small group headed back inside. The chef appeared to present the menu, including the entrée of petrale sole. Wine was offered, and Norbert noticed that Larry was the only one not drinking.

"Hey, Mr. Ellison," Norbert began.

"Call me Larry."

"Okay," Norbert said smiling. "Larry, I got something for you."

Norbert had brought with him a navy blue police sweater with patches, a crest, and a star—the kind worn by club commodores and the kind he wore as head of the Golden Gate Yacht Club. Larry thanked Norbert, stood up, and tried the sweater on.

"You're going to be commodore next," Norbert said smiling.

Larry talked briefly about his decision to bring Chris Dickson back on the boat. "Several guys quit the team when I brought Chris back," Larry said. "They got really angry. That's okay. We were losing and now we're winning. I'm happy. I think the team has finally stabilized."

"You're the team owner," Norbert said. "It's your decision. Not easy. But your decision."

A cartoon had appeared in the *New Zealand Herald* showing Dickson in an Oracle boat and all of his teammates jumping ship, suggesting that Dickson thought he didn't need a team and the team wouldn't follow anyway.

After lunch, the group moved to the living room and Larry asked Norbert about the radiator business and about the yacht club.

"Business is tough," Norbert said, noting that the shop hadn't fully recovered from September 11. He admitted that he sometimes felt "like a fire hydrant. I get pissed on all the time." But he was confident business would bounce back, and he was having a great time in Auckland. Norbert said they'd had an incredible time at the Louis Vuitton ball two nights earlier.

Larry and Melanie had arrived in Auckland too late to attend.

"It was great," Norbert said. He'd had no idea before the event how it all worked. They were invited but no one was told the location. They went to a designated place, where they were then ferried to another location. The party was down a long set of stairs in a basin, and everyone looked gorgeous in black tie. The air was fresh and clean after a day of rain and the food and drinks were amazing, along with the live music. "And there were these cable lines overhead," Norbert said, "with small gondolas. The skipper of each team had his own gondola. There was Chris Dickson! Floating overhead!" Norbert recounted how they had returned to their hotel at around 6 a.m. after having burgers on the street at their new favorite spot, the White Lady.

"Oh, I saw Paul Cayard there," Norbert added.

Larry's expression didn't change. "Oh really?" was all he said. Then, out of the blue, Larry asked, "Did they give you a suit?"

"A suit?" Norbert asked.

"Yes, a Hugo Boss suit. Everyone on the team gets one."

"No," Norbert said, watching Larry stand up and leave the room.

Norbert and Madeleine looked puzzled until Larry returned with a garment bag.

"Here, I have one. I want you to have it," Larry said. "Try it on. Don't worry, I have other suits."

Norbert unzipped the bag. It was a nice, classic-looking navy blue suit. He stood up and tried on the jacket, which was his size, forty-two long.

"Looks great," Larry said. "Go and try the rest on."

Norbert went off to the bathroom and tried on the pants, which were another perfect fit. He returned to show off the suit and thanked Larry. All he could think of to say next was, "Hey, Dad, can I have the keys to the boat too? I promise to get it home by midnight?"

Everyone laughed.

Later, as Madeleine and Melanie visited—Melanie said she was a sailing neophyte and had read *Sailing for Dummies* before coming to the races—Norbert and Larry had time to talk on their own. Larry mentioned his upbringing and said he'd come from the "rough South Side of Chicago." Norbert said, "Well, I came over on the boat." Norbert then shared a story that was one of his first memories. He was crossing the Atlantic with his mom—the two would go back to Germany and Croatia each year—and they were on board a transport ship. One night, gala night on the ship, Norbert was placed in a room with a babysitter and a bunch of kids, all speaking different languages. "I remember just leaving, having to get out of the room," Norbert said. "I was in my pajamas and just walked out. I was maybe four years old." A steward found him on deck as he stood at the rail peering out at the ocean. Smiling, Norbert said, "I think it means I was destined to be commodore!"

The stories continued from both sides. Norbert was amazed at some of the things he was hearing. While Larry was driving Gianni Agnelli's racing sailboat named *Stealth,* Gianni would tell stories about his days as Europe's most famous playboy. The handsome Italian owned Fiat, Ferrari, Maserati, Lancia, and Alfa Romeo and had his own jet-set arsenal of cars, planes, lavish homes, and yachts. Agnelli, who backed his own America's Cup team in 1983, told Larry he had bought the only "two motor yachts he ever wanted to own: *Eco* and *Izanami*." The most memorable Agnelli story was about his affair with Jackie Kennedy when she was first lady, describing how John Kennedy would call up his wife and say, "More Caroline, less Gianni." Larry wondered how the president of the United States, who was having his own affairs, found the time and nerve to complain about his wife's affairs. Larry loved the irony of it all.

In early January 2003, just a month after their last trip to New Zealand, it was time for Norbert to travel again from San Francisco to Auckland, this time for the start of the finals of the Louis Vuitton Cup.

The all-American semifinal series between Oracle and OneWorld proved to be a one-sided affair: the Oracle team won four straight races, knocking the other American team out of the competition. At the press conference following their last race, helmsman Jimmy Spithill said pointedly that the Oracle boat was "faster upwind and faster downwind" than his boat. Larry agreed with Spithill but wondered whether it would be fast enough to beat Coutts and the formidable Kiwi-heavy Alinghi team. With Dickson as skipper, Oracle had charged ahead and made it to the Louis Vuitton finals. Out of nine teams from six countries, only two remained.

British bookies who had taken bets on the outcome were only partially right. Alinghi had been placed as the team to beat, followed by Prada, and then Oracle. Now, Oracle and Alinghi—both with Kiwi skippers and billionaire backers—would fight it out in the best of nine race series for the right to face Team New Zealand for the trophy in February, less than one month away.

It was 5 a.m. when Norbert threw his blue carry-on into the back of his truck and headed south on Highway 101 across the Golden Gate Bridge to the radiator shop. His passport, already stamped six times in New Zealand, would soon get another stamp. He went over all of the things he had to do before picking up Madeleine at her office downtown and boarding a United Airlines flight to Auckland. He had to go over accounts receivable, payroll, and inventory at the shop. What consumed his thoughts, though, was the Oracle BMW Racing team—his team. Norbert had lost, gained, and lost weight; stopped, started, and stopped smoking; and paced so much that he was wearing out his shoes. He had been calling Madeleine with greater frequency, complaining of pains in his stomach. He had gone on a Special K diet, eating cereal for breakfast and lunch, as he was again trying to shed a few pounds.

There was always a price to pay for rewards. When things got too good he braced for a storm. When his mother was finally stepping into her golden years she died on vacation. When he joined the army, a decision that shaped him as a man, his father stopped talking to him. When he landed the deal with Oracle Racing and developed a friendship with Larry he lost friends. People came to him with a stream of requests to be put in touch with Larry, to see whether Larry would come to a charity event, to see whether Larry would be interested in funding a children's hospital or get behind any of a million different causes. Even Norbert's relatives in Croatia bugged him to ask Larry to bring the next America's Cup to the Adriatic Sea, without understanding that there was the small matter of winning the Cup first. Norbert found out that a lot of people considered Larry a crook simply because he had so much money. "No one gets *that* rich without being a crook," a friend told him with certainty. Norbert could understand why Larry insulated himself the way he did. "Who could blame the guy?" Norbert said to Madeleine. Everywhere he goes he is hit up for something.

The fog was thick in the city, and the café near the radiator shop didn't open for an hour. He headed to the small, dimly lit front office and plugged in a space heater. Hours later, fueled by several cups of black coffee, he looked at his TAG Heuer team watch. The morning had flown by and he would barely make it to the airport on time. When he swung by to get Madeleine, she looked at her watch and rolled her eyes.

"I just want to get on that plane and sleep," Norbert said, arriving at the airport. "I'm going to get a pillow, close my eyes, and be off to la-la land." Norbert proceeded to sleep for twelve of the thirteen hours. When he awoke he started talking about the challenge the team faced.

"If you look at Oracle versus Alinghi from a win-lose track record, it looks like Alinghi has the upper hand," Norbert said. "But we've been down before and come right back up. I have a lot of faith." As further proof, Norbert produced a fortune from a cookie a customer had given him before he left. It read: *Your ability to believe has created an upcoming dream that will come true.*

Madeleine smiled. Norbert loved the guys on the team.

Upon arriving in Auckland, Norbert told a bleary-eyed Madeleine that he wanted to drop things at the hotel and then make a special trip up the hill to his favorite local spot. He tapped his jacket pocket, where he kept a small but important glass vial.

Norbert hailed a cab from the Metropolis Hotel, which had apartments for the team and was where they liked to stay. The driver passed familiar sights in one of Auckland's oldest suburbs. There at the corner of Scarborough Terrace was St. John the Baptist Catholic Church, opened in 1861 and said to be the oldest parish in Auckland. Next to the small, simple white timber Gothic Revival church was a cemetery plot enclosed by a white picket fence. Norbert walked inside and made the sign of the cross. He had been raised Catholic and the refrains and rituals were a part of him.

It was early afternoon and Mass was over. Norbert took his seat in a pew and began to pray. It was his routine when he was in Auckland.

"Hey, God," Norbert began. "It's Norbert here. I'm back in New Zealand and our team has a chance to win this thing. You may or may not like billionaires, but they are your children too. Just let us win. We're a little club. You must like underdogs." His sense of pride had grown with each victory. He knew it was Larry's team but Norbert felt it was his too. He also prayed for the safety of members of the Swiss sailing team, including Russell Coutts. And at the last minute he threw in a prayer about his relationship with his father, asking whether it could one day be healed. He said the Lord's Prayer, along with a Hail Mary.

On the way out he lit a candle before heading to the baptismal font. He reached inside his jacket pocket and pulled out the small container, an old glass eye washer. He filled it with holy water. Walking through the charming neighborhood, dotted with cafés and art galleries, Norbert hailed a cab and headed for base camp.

Arriving at the base, Norbert got waves, smiles, hugs, and high fives from the team members.

"Commodore, are you going to bless us today?" asked bowman Geordie Shaver.

Both Alinghi and Oracle were going to sail the same boats they had used since the beginning of the first round-robin. Alinghi would race *SUI-64* against Oracle's *USA-76*.

"I'm straight off the plane, straight from church, and I've got the holy water," Norbert beamed. The engineers could worry about aerodynamics and hydrodynamics, the builders could fixate on the latest in compression carbon fiber, the meteorologists could look at thousands of points of data, and the sailors would have a lifetime of training behind them. Norbert had his talisman. Every time he christened the boats the team won. Walking out to the mooring area, he carefully removed the top and sprinkled the holy water on *USA-76*.

After a lifetime of sailing, years of training, and the on-again, off-again with the team, Dickson, forty-two, was racing his childhood rival and fellow New Zealander Russell Coutts in the finals of the Louis Vuitton Cup. Dickson, from Auckland, had come up short in his three previous America's Cup efforts. Coutts, who was from Wellington, New Zealand, and was a few weeks shy of his forty-first birthday, had not lost a single America's Cup race, having won for Team New Zealand with *Black Magic* in 1995 and *NZL60* in 2000. Alinghi had already defeated Oracle five times in six encounters, losing one race by just four seconds. Both teams said they had made significant improvements to their boats, re-configuring them for better light air performance.

At a press conference, Coutts said, "We are looking for a real battle this time. We have a lot of respect for their team." And Dickson said, "We are a significantly different boat than we were a month ago. We know we have found boat speed in a lot of different areas, and we don't think we have compromised anywhere to get it."

Larry had made the decision before the start of the finals to bring *USA-76*'s keel up as high as possible and add sail area, reducing stability but adding potential speed downwind. "How do you beat a team where you are going to lose every start?" he had said to Dickson. Holmberg was a good driver, but he was not Coutts. Larry was sure that they would lose the starts and that they'd be beaten to the weather mark. The only chance they had, in his mind, was to optimize the boat for downwind and more speed in the light area. (Because of the greatly increased sail area, the Oracle boat was also faster than Alinghi upwind in conditions of under ten knots of breeze.) If the races took place in light air Oracle could win.

After a one-day postponement of the start of the finals—winds had gusted to twenty-five knots—the first race was finally set to begin.

USA-76 drew cheers when it gained a slight lead off the starting line, but the heavy wind conditions favored Alinghi on the upwind legs. Within fifteen minutes Alinghi had a six-boat-length lead around the first mark. Oracle played catch-up downwind, but Alinghi extended its lead of forty-seven seconds to a lead of one minute and twenty-three seconds after the next upwind leg. Oracle gained on the next two legs but lost time on the final run to the finish. Alinghi had taken race one. Crew member Simon Daubney said, "This was one of the more relaxed races we've had so far. In previous races we've won we always had our hearts in our mouths." The second and third days of racing took place in wind conditions unfavorable to Oracle, and Oracle lost both races. Larry's gamble was not paying off.

An enormous front-page picture in the *New Zealand Herald* showed an irate Larry talking to a grim-faced Dickson at the end of another lost race. Larry, in multiple layers of sailing gear and a black

USA-76 baseball cap, gesticulated with his hands wide apart, and Dickson, his lips pursed and sailing gear zipped to his chin, looked away. The headline read: "A $200M QUESTION: CAN ORACLE EVER BEAT ALINGHI?" The story suggested that "the wheels may be falling off the America's Cup bid by Oracle BMW Racing" and went on to say, "The battle of the two Kiwi-skippered teams now firmly favours the Swiss and Russell Coutts, who has beaten rival Chris Dickson six times in a row [including earlier match racing]. . . . Oracle have a day to turn around their fortunes and somehow eclipse Alinghi's upwind power. The boats meet tomorrow with the first team to win five races taking the Louis Vuitton Cup."

On the boat with Dickson after the third loss, Larry was the first to say he was angry. "We agreed on a strategy," he said, exasperated. "We had agreed that we would not split with Alinghi on the downwind legs. We were supposed to cover Alinghi, sail deeper angles, get into a jibing duel, and then try to roll them. Instead you split and played the shifts. We agreed on a strategy. We had a plan. Tell me why you didn't follow the plan."

Dickson said nothing and refused to look Larry's way. Finally, Larry told the team they were heading back to the docks.

Arriving onshore, the team was met by a group of reporters. Dickson remained stone-faced. Asked how he felt about Oracle's chances, he said, "The result that we achieve in this America's Cup will be with all of us for as long as we live."

The next day, the fourth day of racing, Alinghi won the start, took the lead on the first upwind leg, and rounded the first weather mark and headed downwind well in front. The breeze on this day was under nine knots, giving Oracle a speed advantage. Oracle used that speed to attack and pass Alinghi on the first downwind leg. As the conditions stayed light throughout the race, the Oracle boat sailed away from Alinghi, eventually beating the Swiss team by over two minutes. It was Coutts's biggest losing margin in forty Louis Vuitton races dating to 1992. The *New Zealand Herald* ran a front-page picture of Larry smiling and giving the thumbs-up. The paper noted that it was "Coutts' worst loss in a decade."

"It was a thumping," Dickson said happily as he returned to the dock, filled with cheering spectators, who hoped to see the races drawn out and wanted Coutts beaten. "We've been disappointed not to get more points so far," Dickson said. "Now that we've got one, we'll be trying really hard to make it two."

Holmberg, who drove while Dickson called tactics, cautioned, "Don't get too excited; we've got four more to go."

The next day, Friday, Alinghi narrowly defeated Oracle by thirteen seconds to establish a four-to-one lead. The Swiss team needed only one more race to head to the America's Cup and send Oracle packing.

Norbert, who had watched the races from a chartered boat with dozens of members of the Golden Gate Yacht Club, was flying out the afternoon of what felt like the final race. Alinghi needed its final win to eliminate Oracle, and Erkelens invited Norbert to have a talk with the team before racing began. The mood was somber when Norbert walked into the downstairs meeting room, a secure area accessible only to the team. He could see the long faces and feel the mix of tension and resignation. Erkelens asked for everyone's attention and said the commodore would like to say a few words.

Norbert looked at the men who had become his extended family. He had partied with many of them and come to respect and love them. They'd had their share of champagne and Stella Artois beer and stayed up all night dancing and drinking together at the Louis Vuitton ball. They'd hit local bars and ended many a late night at the White Lady. He had gotten to know Peter Holmberg's parents and was touched by the pride they showed in their son.

"I just want to say that I'm proud of everyone here," Norbert said, with Erkelens standing by his side. "It's been fun. I've made a lot of good friends and I feel like we are a family. We've shared great times on the water, and greater times off the water."

He drew some knowing laughter but noticed Dickson was not smiling.

"All I can say is, I've been in situations where you are behind, where you are the underdog, and you can come back," he said. "I believe in Hail Mary passes. I've had a few of my own. Just go out there and do your best. You can win."

One by one, Norbert shook hands or exchanged hugs. Norbert and Madeleine were heading to the airport. They hadn't known how far the team would get, and they'd booked the flights months before. Both needed to return to work. Looking back at the team one more time, Norbert felt it was a final good-bye. He imagined he wouldn't see most of them again.

Erkelens had the same feeling of things winding down. As he looked at it, Alinghi simply had a faster boat and a better team. He had told his wife, Melinda, "If you're fast, you don't have to make hard decisions. When you're slower, you have to pull rabbits out of your hat and do incredible things with the maneuvers, and push the rules so far that you almost cross a line." Erkelens thought Holmberg's starts were good, but the boat just wasn't as fast upwind, so they were never going to get to the weather mark in front of Alinghi. Even if they won the start, they still weren't getting ahead at the weather mark. "Our best move has been to pitch the boat downwind," Erkelens said, "then stay as close to Alinghi as possible after the start and on the first upwind leg, and attack her downwind. It is the only move we have, and I don't think it is good enough." *USA-76* was faster than all the other boats, but slower than Alinghi in most wind conditions. To the ever-pragmatic, straight-talking Erkelens, the fastest boat wins.

Norbert and Madeleine arrived at the Auckland airport and went to Air New Zealand's business-class lounge. They had made the trip so often that they were cashing in frequent-flier rewards.

The one television in the lounge was set to the Louis Vuitton Cup finals and the race was beginning. The problem was that a diminutive brunette wearing a lavender suit—she reminded Norbert of the Queen Mum—stood directly in front of the television, blocking everyone's view.

Finally, someone asked the lady if she could move.

She turned around, and Norbert exclaimed, "Oh my God, it's Ernesto's mother!"

Maria-Iris Bertarelli shrugged, pointed to the television, and said something about her son being out there sailing.

Minutes later, the race was on and the sailors, who wore microphones, could be heard calling each beat. Norbert listened as Dickson screamed at Holmberg, "If you aren't going to get it together now, you'll never get it together." The racing, which had been delayed for nearly two hours owing to light winds, started in an eight-knot breeze, conditions that favored the Oracle boat.

About an hour and a half into the flight the captain made an announcement that Swiss challenger Ernesto Bertarelli's Alinghi team, skippered by Russell Coutts, had won the Louis Vuitton Cup finals by defeating the American challenger Larry Ellison's Oracle BMW Racing, 5–1, "eliminating the United States from the America's Cup competition and winning the right to challenge Team New Zealand for the America's Cup starting in February."

The racing had been close, and on the final downwind leg *USA-76* was able to use her speed advantage to catch Alinghi, race side by side for several exciting minutes, and then roll over the top of the Swiss team and take the lead. But it hadn't been enough. At the start of the race, Coutts had maneuvered Holmberg into a bad position and Oracle Racing was assessed a penalty (and had to do a 360-degree circle before the finish). As the Oracle boat did her penalty turn, Alinghi passed right on by, crossed the finish line, and won the race. The mistake at the start killed the American team.

"I don't think Larry will do it again," Norbert said with a sigh. "But we've had a lot of fun."

Madeleine held Norbert's hand. "We probably would never have made it to New Zealand had it not been for this." They certainly would not have met Larry. And Norbert wouldn't have become pals with the sailors and their families.

Norbert's mood brightened and he said, "Instead of our little club closing, we got to be a part of the America's Cup."

A month later Norbert followed the America's Cup news from his radiator shop. Team Alinghi, with its crew of top New Zealanders, crushed Team New Zealand 5–0 in the thirty-first America's Cup, and the trophy left Auckland with the Swiss on a chartered plane. Arriving in Geneva, the team and the Cup were met by local dignitaries and the Swiss president Pascal Couchepin. A crowd of forty thousand people welcomed them home, and Bertarelli was hailed as a hero for bringing the Cup to Europe—and to landlocked Switzerland—for the first time in the race's 152-year history.

The only news Norbert had heard from Larry was that he had turned his attention to playing competitive tennis, telling his friend the Oracle executive Judy Sim, "Tennis is a lot less expensive than the America's Cup."

Toward the end of the workday at the garage, Norbert was surprised to get a call from Bill Erkelens.

"Hey, would you like to do it again?" Erkelens asked. "Larry is going again, and he wants the Golden Gate Yacht Club to be Challenger of Record for the 2007 Cup." Norbert knew that the Challenger of Record plays a major role, negotiating the rules for the next event with the defender and representing the interests of all eventual challengers.

Norbert chuckled to himself. He had just received a letter from his father, sent to the yacht club. It was Jozo's resignation letter. His dad was ending his membership at the Golden Gate. Not only that, he wanted Norbert to know he was joining the St. Francis.

Norbert brought himself back into the conversation. Erkelens told him that Chris Dickson would be running the next campaign.

"I'm out and Chris Dickson is in," Erkelens said. "There's not room for the two of us."

Before Norbert could respond, Erkelens, who sounded perfectly fine, said that Larry and Bertarelli were "shaking things up" with the America's Cup and had planned a number of races over the next few years in order to make the regatta more accessible.

"The next race is in three months," Erkelens said, "and the Golden Gate is the host."

14

San Francisco Bay

September 2003

I T WAS THE second day of sailing on San Francisco Bay when
Ernesto Bertarelli came off his chase boat and onto the weathered docks of the Golden Gate Yacht Club. Hundreds of spectator boats bobbed in the choppy waters between the Bay Bridge
and the Golden Gate Bridge, out to Alcatraz and over to Angel
Island, and past the charming waterfront tourist town of Sausalito.
Windsurfers zigzagged between boats and thousands of people
filled bleachers and lined the shores and seawalls, from the start
of Crissy Field, along the Marina Green, and out to the base of
the Golden Gate Bridge. Uncharacteristically warm sunshine
and cloudless skies had replaced the fog, and the wind blew at
around twenty knots. Bertarelli had just lost his second consecutive race in the Moët Cup, a rematch between his Alinghi
team and Oracle BMW Racing. In six days of scheduled racing,
Bertarelli and Larry would compete in an owner-driver duel,
and a pro-driver series pitted Oracle's Gavin Brady helming and
Chris Dickson calling tactics against Alinghi's Jochen Schuemann
driving with Brad Butterworth as tactician. During the second in
the series of owner-driver races, Larry won the start for Oracle
and Bertarelli was forced to take the unfavored left side of the

racecourse. The races started at Treasure Island and had two up-wind and downwind laps followed by an upwind finish in front of the parking lot between the St. Francis and the Golden Gate yacht clubs. Larry's *USA-76* came in forty seconds ahead of the Bertarelli-helmed *SUI-64*.

Norbert led Bertarelli from the docks to the clubhouse, which was thronged with sailing fans. Press conferences were held by Bertarelli, Larry, and other members of both crews at the end of the day's races. Hundreds of journalists from across the globe descended on the club, jockeying for position. Both floors of the clubhouse were packed from opening to well past closing time, and Norbert was there each day before 7 a.m.

"I'd love to have a shower," Bertarelli, soaked from his race on the bay, told Norbert.

Norbert looked at him. "Sure. Just a minute," he said. The club had two small bathrooms, each with a shower. He went and checked the bathrooms. No towels.

"Do we have any towels?" Norbert whispered to the club's new manager, Bill Chow.

"I don't think so," Chow replied, working the bar. Norbert's mind raced. He had worked with Erkelens every day for weeks planning the event. Erkelens was in charge of shoreside logistics, but Norbert was tasked with operations at the club. Towels were something he hadn't thought of. He rummaged through a linen closet and came across something white. Tablecloths. *Well, they're clean,* he told himself, sniffing the fabric.

Making his way through the crowd back to Bertarelli, he wondered whether he could really offer the Swiss billionaire, in town with his gorgeous wife, *tablecloths* instead of towels. He could hear Madeleine's admonishments: *You didn't, Norbert.* But what the heck, he thought, *When you reach a fork in the road, take it.*

"Mr. Bertarelli," Norbert said. "We don't have towels but we have this." He offered him a folded tablecloth.

Bertarelli looked at the tablecloth, looked at Norbert, and said, "No problem. I'll just go down the road and have a shower." Down the road, of course, meant the St. Francis, which was benefiting from the Golden Gate's hard work and throwing parties for Alinghi. Norbert shrugged it off. As he saw it, the Golden Gate was the Golden Gate. It had tablecloths instead of terry cloth, hamburgers instead of filet mignon. But it was hosting one of the greatest sailing events ever seen on San Francisco Bay.

As the Swiss billionaire went down the road to the St. Francis, Norbert headed back to the docks. Larry had arrived. Norbert had learned that after the loss in 2003 Larry had briefly considered not trying again. The truth was that the finality of the defeat haunted him. As he looked at it, he had no one to blame but himself; it was his team. He had spent several weeks looking in the mirror and seeing a loser—*but not a quitter*. The Oracle boss decided that the second campaign would be built entirely around Dickson, with the tempestuous Kiwi running the show and handpicking the team.

Larry was mobbed as he stepped off his boat. Reporters wanted a quote. Photographers wanted a picture. Club members wanted to get close to him. Some just wanted to shake his hand or touch his sleeve. Others wanted to share sailing stories. Norbert had gotten good at running interference. Norbert continued to be lobbied by friends, relatives, colleagues, and strangers who wanted something from Larry. Norbert would refer the more legitimate requests to Judy Sim. Norbert also had gotten good at deflecting criticism of Larry. He now asked the person in question if he or she had ever met Larry. No. Norbert asked if the person knew anyone who knew Larry. No. The Larry he knew, Norbert would say, was a "class act."

An hour later Bertarelli was back from the St. Francis and took his place next to Larry at the afternoon press conference. Larry and Bertarelli had announced major changes to the Cup, including relaxing the design and nationality rules. They planned a series of qualifying regattas, leading up to the Louis Vuitton Cup, with teams racing all over the world, from San Francisco to Newport, Hong Kong to Cowes, England. "Cramming all the America's Cup racing into a three-month period once every four years makes it hard to attract and hold on to sponsors and sustain the interest of fans," Larry said. "Holding the races way offshore makes it impossible to watch in person unless you're on a boat. We want to make the America's Cup more like Formula One. We want high-quality TV coverage, and we want to make it easy to understand and exciting and enjoyable to watch, in person and on TV." The men said that for the first time in the history of the Cup racing would be stadium style instead of offshore, so spectators onshore could see the boats up close and feel a part of the action.

Formula One was probably as close to the America's Cup as any other sport, combining the latest in technology and materials science with the best in human performance. Both dealt in high-level aerodynamics, with boats trying for maximum power with the least drag, and F1 cars going for maximum downforce with minimum drag. The sports shared the objective of creating ever-lighter structures while maintaining strength and stiffness.

The America's Cup trophy was on display nearby, having been delivered to the club in an armored car. Also nearby was the new and glistening Moët Cup, in the shape of a champagne bottle, still up for grabs. Larry and Bertarelli were flanked by Oracle Racing's CEO Dickson, Alinghi helmsman Schuemann, and San Francisco's mayor Willie Brown. Bertarelli, his hair still damp under his Alinghi cap, joked with Larry, who, having taken the lead 2–0, was in a great mood. Dickson noted that Oracle's racing team was almost entirely different from the team that had been defeated by Alinghi 5–1 in New Zealand. Dickson was skipper and tactician on the boat and he was also team CEO. Gavin Brady, a Kiwi who worked for the Italian syndicate Prada in the previous campaign, was the new helmsman. And John Kostecki, a Bay Area native, Olympic silver medalist, and recent winner of the grueling Volvo Ocean Race, was the new strategist. Bertarelli said that his Alinghi team was the same as that which had won the America's Cup, with one exception: Schuemann was driving, not Coutts. He gave no explanation for his star skipper's absence, though rumors were circulating of financial problems between the superstar Kiwi sailor and his Swiss boss.

Larry and Bertarelli, who had become friends during the 31st America's Cup, had a shared goal of taking the America's Cup to the people, and the first step was the Moët Cup. The regatta had begun with citywide events including youth sailing, a giant party at Pier 41, and a fireworks display that rivaled any Fourth of July spectacle—all paid for by Larry.

"After Alinghi won the Cup in 2003, Ernesto and I talked about staging a series of regattas all over the world in America's Cup boats," Larry said. "This America's Cup World Series could happen every year during the years leading up to the next America's Cup. It will keep the professional sailors employed and on the water and also give Ernesto and me a chance to take the wheel to drive against each other. We both want to improve the America's Cup and make it more exciting and commercially successful."

One major step in that direction was a new sponsorship deal that Dickson and Oracle's director of external affairs Tom Ehman had negotiated with BMW, their partner for the previous Cup campaign. This time, they had a sponsorship valued at eighty million euros—well over $100 million—plus cars for the team and a unique collaboration with some of BMW's engineers, who would work with Oracle Racing engineers on the design of the new boats. The team's name was no longer Oracle BMW Racing. It was now BMW Oracle Racing.

Toward the end of the press conference Bertarelli was asked how it felt to lose when he was more accustomed to winning. After a pause, he said, "It's very therapeutic for us to not just sit back and think that we are the best and not continue to work hard. But we came here to win."

Larry added, "We have sailed a lot better here this week than we did in New Zealand. We have a stronger team than we did in New Zealand, and we've raised our game to the point where we can compete with the very best sailing team in the world, Alinghi."

A day later, after the final race, Larry returned triumphant to the docks of the Golden Gate. He and the Oracle team had won, though not without a fight from Alinghi. After winning the first two races, Larry had a big lead at the first weather mark of the third race. Then disaster struck. The crew lost the spinnaker pole overboard while bearing away downwind. *USA-76* lost its pole, lost its lead, and lost the race. In race number four Larry got too aggressive and went for a kill at the start; it didn't work. So he tried it again in the final and deciding race and this time it worked perfectly. He prevented Alinghi from starting—closing out *SUI-64* at the committee boat—and gained an insurmountable lead for *USA-76* at the start of the race. After it was all over Larry beat Bertarelli 3–2 in the owner-driver series and Gavin Brady did his part by outmaneuvering Schuemann by a score of 4–3 in the pro-driver series. Larry was pleased. After two weeks of practice his new sailing team had beaten the America's Cup champion—minus Russell Coutts. Larry was aware it wasn't *quite* the same thing.

Hundreds of people again lined the decks of the club and poured onto the walkway and piers below. Norbert was there to congratulate Larry as he stepped off the tender. Melanie stepped off first, and she and Norbert took cover as champagne was sprayed. In the midst of the revelry, Norbert turned his eyes downward. His feet were getting wet. Water was starting to come over the piers, which were weighed down by the crowd. He gently tugged Melanie's elbow and said, "It's time for us to go up." Looking at the water, Melanie said, "Oh, yes it is." Norbert moved Melanie up the pier to higher ground and then motioned to some of his guys to try to calmly—without alerting anyone—start moving other people off the old pier. He had visions of revelers slipping into the bay and a front-page headline that might read *Ellison wins, revelers sink*. Fortunately, Larry soon made his way through the crowd, and the masses followed, with the only soaking coming from more champagne. As the press conference was held inside and the trophy awarded, Norbert stood by himself on the deck. Looking out at the bay, still filled with spectator boats of every kind, he saw the massive America's Cup yachts heading to their mooring in Richmond, looking like giant war machines returning to their base. For the first time, Norbert could see what it would look like to host the

America's Cup in San Francisco Bay. He could picture the stunning, high-tech boats coming close to the shoreline and imagine people lined up along Crissy Field all the way out to the Golden Gate Bridge. It would be the America's Cup for the people, taking sailing from offshore to the natural stadium of San Francisco Bay, from a sense that it was inaccessible to a realization that this was an event anyone could enjoy. Of course, first they would have to win.

Late that night, after the crowds had gone home, after tents and bleachers were removed and the detritus had been cleaned up, Bill Erkelens lingered. The event had gone flawlessly. He had gotten the sponsors, organized the race committee, and commanded a legion of volunteers. And it had been fun, a welcome contrast to his experience running the America's Cup team. This was Erkelens's final job for Oracle Racing. After telling Larry there was no place for him on a team led by Chris Dickson, he had taken a job offer managing a racing team and building its boat in Australia. He would bring with him the hard-earned knowledge of the intricacies of professional sports and the way a million different pieces need to come together for success. As the Aussie sailor John Bertrand, who was helmsman of *Australia II,* which ended the New York Yacht Club's long grip on the America's Cup, wrote in his book *Born to Win*: "The Australians came and won the America's Cup. We came and took it away with brilliant crew work, seamanship, preparation, administration, and a very, very fast boat. And we won it because, in the end, we wanted it the most."

Erkelens knew that winning required seamless teamwork, an elusive banding together to create a "group reflex and reaction at the right moment," as the legendary basketball coach Phil Jackson had put it. "That bond, that unity, is a very fragile thing. It's really almost something holy," Jackson said. Erkelens had watched Dickson step back on the boat before the Louis Vuitton semifinals and begin to win. He knew Larry gave Dickson credit—it validated the decision to bring him back—but Erkelens believed the momentum had been building. He saw Holmberg as a talented driver who was well liked by the team and could have taken the team just as far had Larry believed in him. He thought that giving Dickson credit for the victories was like watching one political party come into office and take credit for what the other had put in place. But Larry dealt in numbers. He had won with Dickson in the past, when he was driving and Dickson called tactics. Dickson's wins *were* impressive on paper. But Erkelens knew that his billionaire boss was not about to grab the trophy he wanted until he understood the almost holy nature of a team.

Not long after winning the Moët Cup and joining forces with Bertarelli, Larry agreed to another merger of sorts. On a grassy knoll next to his man-made lake dotted with lily pads and teeming with fish, under a century-old oak tree and cushioned by the quiet sounds of water, Larry held hands with Melanie Craft, his girlfriend of five years. They had been engaged for years and she had grown tired of the barbed questions: "So how long have you been engaged?" or "Melanie, are you *still* engaged to Larry?" The two were about to head off on a family vacation and Melanie wanted the "family" part to be for real.

The two met at Bix restaurant in San Francisco, a jazz supper club with dim lighting, great martinis, and a sexy vibe, and Larry was taken by the clean-cut blonde with the high cheekbones and blue eyes. Melanie had graduated from Oberlin College and had studied archaeology at American University in Egypt. After college, she worked at a variety of odd jobs, from bartender and pastry chef to house cleaner and safari driver, but she was most interested in writing fiction. She had a boyfriend when she met Larry, and Larry had been married and divorced three times, first to Adda Quinn, for seven years; then to Nancy Wheeler Jenkins, for a year; and then to Barbara Boothe, the mother of his two children, for three years. Larry had never proposed to any of the women, not even Melanie, as he never had any desire to marry, didn't think he was good at marriage, and felt that after three tries he should be banned from ever marrying again. "Three strikes and you're out," he would say, more serious than joking. "The state should make it harder for people to get married, and nobody should be allowed to get married after three divorces. The courts should simply say, 'I'm sorry, Mr. Ellison, you've used up your three-marriage limit, you're done. You can date but you cannot get married.'"

But here he stood on this December day, prepared to wed his fourth wife. He had listened to Melanie, who had written two novels and had a third on the way—this one, called *Man Trouble,* about a romance novelist who seduces a billionaire—talk about the thinly veiled digs, which got to her and came mostly from nipped and tucked society types who seemed to delight in her prolonged engagement. She wanted to become a real family.

"I don't think I'm good at it, and I don't think I should do things I'm not good at," Larry said. "Freud believed there are two important things in life—love and work, and not necessarily in that order." As Larry saw it, work defines a person. Work is ego, work is selfish; love is about others. He was happy being in long-term relationships, as he found the allure of dating lots of women generally overrated, emotionally exhausting, and meaningless. His lack of interest in marriage was not about fidelity but had more to do with problems he had with authority. In marriage, he had to live a good part of his life the way the other person wanted him to live it. Larry wanted to live his life his way. He knew, too, that relationships changed after the tying of the knot. His girlfriends supported his daredevil antics and around-the-clock work schedule. His wives told him he was spending too much time at work, he shouldn't drive so fast, he shouldn't fly his jet into the San Carlos Airport because the runway was too short, he shouldn't do aerobatics or surf in storms or race sailboats in the Southern Ocean.

The idea of being with one person who was made for you—the soul mate argument—struck Larry as ridiculous. A self-described "slave to reason," he scoffed at the odds of meeting that one special person. "There are seven billion people on the planet. The idea that you would meet the one person in the world who's made for you is so statistically unlikely that it would almost never occur," he would say. "However, you can meet someone and eventually become so close, so intimate that she becomes your soul mate."

Real friendships lasted a lifetime, and his relationship with his kids and family were the most important and lasted a lifetime, but marriages ran their course, and a relationship that had worked wonderfully eventually stopped working and both people stopped being happy. He told Melanie, "I know that when you're young, you dream about meeting the right person and living together happily until you're ninety, and then you die. That's a fairy tale. Marriages are complex, they require a lot of hard work and compromise, and they often end badly. At least that's what I've experienced in my life."

Melanie insisted that since they would not be breaking up whether they married or not, it would just be "easier" to get married.

"Okay, I'll do it if it's so important to you," Larry said. It was a familiar refrain, as marriage always seemed important to the woman when he was in a long-term relationship, but it was never important to him.

They were joined by Melanie's sister, Kira Craft; Tom Lantos and his wife, Annette; Larry's son, David, and his daughter, Megan; and friends Laurene Powell Jobs and Steve Jobs, who served as wedding photographer. Lantos, a Holocaust survivor and U.S. congressman who was a national leader in human rights, was there to officiate. Lantos had become like a father to Larry and the two—both Hungarian Jews—had taken trips together to Israel and Hungary. Larry adored Lantos for the same reasons he loved Steve: both men were brilliant and had a strong and clear sense of right and wrong. They were also just great to spend time with.

The groom's wedding ring was borrowed from Steve and it went as far as Larry's knuckle. Larry was fifty-nine; Melanie was thirty-four. Larry loved Melanie dearly, but even as he was saying his vows he remembered a line by Woody Allen: *A relationship is like a shark, either it's constantly moving forward or it dies.*

15

Newport, Rhode Island

June 2004

THE NEXT OF THE WORLD SERIES REGATTAS was under way in Newport, Rhode Island, and Larry and Bertarelli were once again competing on the water and spending time together after the races. They were having dinner on Bertarelli's yacht *Vava* when Bertarelli, who was energetic and gregarious, turned to Larry and said there was something he needed to tell him.

"I'm not really enjoying this," Bertarelli said of the weeklong Newport America's Cup class sailing event, which followed the Moët Cup on San Francisco Bay. Bertarelli said that he didn't want to sail against Larry anymore, and that he needed to focus on the problems he was having with Russell Coutts. "Russell refuses to drive," Bertarelli said. In Coutts's absence, Bertarelli had deputized Holmberg, who had sailed for Larry in the previous Cup, to drive in the professional helmsman part of the Newport regatta. Larry had the same lineup as in the Moët Cup: Kiwi Gavin Brady as helmsman and Dickson as tactician.

Larry said that although he understood that Bertarelli needed to focus on the issues facing the Alinghi team, he hoped they could continue their owner-driver racing sometime in the future. Bertarelli then said, "Okay, you won in San Francisco, and now that our racing is over here, I win the regatta in Newport. That seems fair to me." Larry stared at Bertarelli and said, "Ernesto, what are you talking about? We've had three races in Newport and I won two of them." Bertarelli told Larry to read the rules for the scoring of the owner-driver series. "The first two races count one point, the third and fourth races count two points. I won the third race." Larry said, "Then we're tied at two each." Bertarelli countered, "No, according to the rules, if there's a tie in points, the boat that wins the last race wins the regatta."

After a long pause, Larry looked at Bertarelli, shook his head, and laughed. "You're joking, right?" Except for the sound of dishes being cleared there was silence. Seeing he was getting nowhere, Larry finally said, "Ernesto, the score is tied two-to-two. We don't *have* to race again. We can call the whole thing off and no one gets a trophy. Or I'll see you at the starting line tomorrow."

Another awkward silence fell over the room. Larry stood to leave and Bertarelli said nothing.

When Larry returned to his yacht *Katana,* shrouded like a giant iceberg in the Newport fog, he relayed the story to Melanie. "Ernesto is acting like a spoiled child: 'I won the trophy!' 'It's my trophy!' 'It's mine 'cause it's mine!'" He wondered if the attitude came in part from Bertarelli's silver-spoon background. Born in Milan, Italy, where his family had a controlling interest in Serono SA, Europe's largest biotechnology company and a leader in fertility drugs, Bertarelli spent his summers sailing on Lake Geneva, attended Harvard Business School, and joined his father's company as chief executive. Larry had been hearing rumors about Bertarelli and Coutts, about Bertarelli ignoring his contractual obligations and his deriding Coutts over silly things like wearing the wrong color shorts to team practice sessions. Of Coutts's absence in Newport, Bertarelli had told Larry that he had Coutts on the crew list and had hoped he would helm. "Unfortunately, he didn't want to helm," Bertarelli had said.

The next day, the battle of the billionaires resumed on the waters off Newport. Larry was not about to hand anyone an unearned victory. The start of the race was going to be critical. The boat that won the right-hand side of the Newport racecourse would have a big advantage. The men jockeyed for position behind the starting line for several minutes. With about twenty seconds to go before the start, Alinghi tacked onto port and aimed directly at the committee boat at the right end of the starting line. Larry, in the leeward position, immediately jibed *USA-76* onto starboard, calculating that he could get up to Alinghi in time to stop *SUI-64* from crossing his bow and thereby winning the right. It was going to be close and come down to how well *USA-76* accelerated after the jibe.

"Beautiful jibe, guys," Larry yelled as Ross Halcrow trimmed *USA-76*'s headsail on the wind. Larry made slight, almost imperceptible adjustments on the helm as his boat steadily surged forward approaching full speed. *USA-76* was now on a direct collision course with Alinghi. Larry's bowman Brad Webb started screaming "Starboard! Starboard!" demanding that Alinghi turn away and avoid a collision. *USA-76,* on starboard tack, had the right-of-way over Alinghi on port tack. Unable to cross *USA-76*'s bow, Bertarelli had no choice but to turn the wheel and tack *SUI-64,* heading out toward the dreaded left-hand side of the course. *USA-76* was now fully in control of the race.

Larry extended his lead by tacking on Alinghi again and again, blocking its wind and keeping the America's Cup champion pinned on the left hand side of the course for most of the first upwind leg. But as *USA-76* approached the first windward mark the winds became lighter and shifty, gradually changing direction by as much as forty degrees. Larry used this to his advantage, and *USA-76* just kept stretching away from *SUI-64* on upwind and downwind legs. With the finish line in sight, *USA-76* was more than a half a mile in front of *SUI-64.*

Larry had pushed *USA-76* as hard as he could for the entire race, content only with a win that would send a message.

At the ceremony, BMW Oracle Racing was awarded the trophy for beating Alinghi seven victories to four in the professional driver series. Larry received a plate, having defeated Bertarelli by three races to one in the owner-driver competition. At the news conference, Bertarelli gave away none of his discontent, saying graciously, "This is exactly what we both wanted after the last America's Cup, not to wait, Larry in California and me in Switzerland, waiting for the next America's Cup. We wanted to enjoy the investment of having two fantastic teams with beautiful boats and go at each other again. So I think it was a very successful week."

Larry, only hinting at the tension from the night before, said, "I'd say the owner-driver series maybe had a little more adrenaline than it should have had. Both Ernesto and I wanted to win."

After the races were wrapped up, Larry and Melanie spent time in Newport, where history and literature, not to mention decades of drama around the America's Cup, came together, where the rich and famous—the Vanderbilts, Belmonts, Manvilles, Astors, and J. P. Morgan—had passed their summers in "cottages" that included spacious servants' quarters and verdant, carpetlike lawns. Melanie knew Newport as the setting of Edith Wharton's *Age of Innocence,* which captured how the nineteenth-century upper crust lived. Newport was also where Presidents Eisenhower and Kennedy had both established their "summer White House," and Jackie and John F. Kennedy had their wedding reception there, at Hammersmith Farm, Jacqueline Bouvier's childhood home. The town once had a strong navy presence, and sailing for fun and commerce had defined the region; a downtown street was named America's Cup Avenue. Many still called Newport the spiritual home of the Cup, as it had been the location for the high-stakes showdowns for more than half a century, from 1930 to 1983. It was at Marble House, a palatial spread once owned by Mike Vanderbilt, great-grandson of the railroad tycoon Cornelius Vanderbilt, that the trophy had been in Americans' hands for so long before it was handed over to the Australians. And it was here that, decades earlier, in September 1962, John Kennedy spoke before the start of the America's Cup about the allure of water and of the Cup, saying, "All of us have in our veins the exact same percentage of salt in our blood that exists in the ocean, and, therefore, we have salt in our blood, in our sweat, in our tears. We are tied to the ocean. And when we go back to the sea—whether it is to sail or to watch it—we are going back from whence we came." Of the race, which that year was between America and Australia, Kennedy said, "I want to toast tonight the crew, the sailors, those who made it possible to come here, those who have, for a hundred years, defended this Cup from the New York Yacht Club, to all of them. They race against each other, but they also race with each other against the wind and the sea."

Not long after arriving back home in Woodside, Larry received an e-mail from Chris Dickson. He read it several times, as Dickson was not one to hand out compliments.

> Larry,
>
>   Nice job driving in the last race in Newport. In my biased opinion that first beat and first run you achieved the highest level of helming that could have been achieved (by anyone) and in those Newport conditions it wasn't straight forward. Fantastic job, that was some of the best I've seen. (and at a time we needed it!) No shit!
>
>   Well done,
>   cd

Larry had also been sent an early press release that announced Bertarelli's firing of Russell Coutts, effective immediately. Bertarelli contended that Coutts had violated his contractual duties, refusing to helm Alinghi in Newport and deciding not to sail with the team in regattas in Sweden, Italy, and Portugal. Bertarelli said that Coutts also had planned and developed a new race series, something "incompatible with his responsibilities and duties."

Larry rolled his eyes as he read, in the last paragraph, that Bertarelli, "Leader of Team Alinghi, has expressed his regret and disappointment that it is no longer possible to cooperate with Russell Coutts. He further points out that he will continue to do whatever is necessary to protect Team Alinghi and to secure the attraction and uniqueness of the America's Cup."

Larry had indeed seen how Bertarelli would do whatever was necessary to protect his interests.

16

Valencia, Spain

Early 2006

TUGSY TURNER AND his crew had been arriving at work before dawn and leaving after dark, putting in eighty-hour weeks in their temperature- and humidity-controlled warehouse in Anacortes, Washington. BMW Oracle Racing had set up its building shop there to be next to Janicki Industries, with its proprietary five-axis high-precision tools to make complex molds for composite fabrication for the marine and aerospace industries. Janicki had started out working for the marine industry but its primary business of late had been for Lockheed-Martin and Boeing. BMW Oracle Racing had employed Janicki to use its one-of-a-kind machines and tools to make the molds for Oracle boats. Oracle engineers worked with their partners at BMW, including two PhDs who brought a different approach to analyzing structures and stress loads. Employing finite element analysis software to look at the strength of different parts of the boat, they had also done three-dimensional complex analyses, modeling the hull, rig, and sails. And the BMW engineers had brought their own data logging systems developed for car racing to apply to the boat design and testing process.

Tugsy and his partner at Core Builders, Tim Smyth, were finishing the building of *USA-87*, the first of Oracle Racing's two new-generation yachts (the other would be *USA-98*). The yacht's two-ton hull, made of carbon fiber, was two feet shorter than *USA-76* and used a conventional single-strut keel and had a distinctive bowsprit, a bar that extends beyond the bow.

Tugsy had tracked down what he considered to be the very best carbon fiber for the boats, locking up huge quantities of a custom blend from the best supplier, and he had studied the level of resins impregnated in the fiber, searching for that point where the best bond could be achieved with the least resin, given that resins can be heavy. The laying of the carbon fiber was done in a matrix, with more materials placed in the areas of greatest stress, such as where the mast attaches. The outside skin was extremely thin but grew thick in high-load areas. Each laminate was laid, vacuumed, cooked, and cured, layer after layer. Tugsy made sure that everyone wore gloves, not just to protect the workers but to avoid contaminating the materials. Throughout the process, Tugsy watched, paced, and stepped in. He tried to train employees to take over various jobs but ended up doing much of the work himself. He was on-site all day every day to ensure that no mistakes were made, whether it was someone leaving a piece of plastic in the laminate—something that was easy to do—or having one of the workers mix the wrong paint formula for the hull or seeing the power go out in the middle of a cook. Every step along the way was risky, and every part had to be exactly right. In the summertime, they had to keep the temperature in the warehouse down, and in the wintertime they had to keep it up. They liked it at a steady twenty degrees Celsius, or about sixty-eight degrees Fahrenheit.

Tugsy was aware that few people understood what went into the making of a sailing machine like this. It was his life, and anyone who signed on to an America's Cup building team had better be prepared to put everything else on hold. There was little time for friends and family, and days off were rare. Tugsy had a home in

New Zealand that he rarely saw. He had built a simple, split-level bungalow on twelve acres of coastal property running to the beach, not far from where his parents and sister lived. But most of his time was spent in this sterile building in this seaside town about two hours north of Seattle near the Canadian border. It was a quiet and beautiful place, though the gray, wet winter months dragged on.

Throughout the science and engineering–driven process intuition played a role. It was something that came with experience, with seeing what works and what doesn't, and having a feel for the materials and the geometry of the designs.

By early February, work on *USA-87* wound down. After thirty thousand man-hours of work—or the equivalent of nearly three and a half years—the first of the boats was readied. Bound in thousands of feet of shrink-wrap for protection, the yacht was transported in an eleven-hour flight from Seattle's Sea–Tac airport to Valencia, Spain. She went on a massive Russian Antonov jet, a cargo plane capable of carrying more than a hundred tons. BMW Oracle Racing's load included the hull, the masts, and the appendages in containers. They would start building *USA-98* within a month.

Before *USA-87* hit the waters off Valencia, about one hundred members of the team gathered at dockside before the keel was lowered. The team splashed a red wine called "Sangre de Toro" (blood of the bull) over the bulb keel and Dickson, with design coordinator Ian "Fresh" Burns and Tugsy, poured the wine one measure at a time to appease Neptune, Poseidon, and Aeolus, the gods of the sea and wind. For a few moments, the dock had the silence of a cathedral. And in a moment the team considered fortuitous, rain began to fall and the clock tower on the Valencia *dársena* (harbor) rang out, the deep baritone drifting from land to sea.

Not long afterward, on a cold February day, Tugsy stepped onto *USA-87*. Dickson and the racing team checked the rigging and got the boat ready for her test drive. Tugsy was there to watch and listen. He could look at the reams of data that came in off the boat's sensors and he could get feedback from the sailors. He understood the predictions that were made and the data-driven analysis. But his years of experience had taught him there was nothing like listening to the boat herself. The sounds would tell him all he needed to know and whether or not some of the world's best engineers, designers, and builders had come together in the right ways.

Tugsy stood on *USA-87* as she was put through her paces, the sails unfurled, the winches flying, the bow cutting through the waves. It was Tugsy's favorite moment in any campaign. There would be tweaks to the boat, even major changes. But this was the moment when he knew if he had done his job: whether he had taken the designs and intricate engineering plans, applied the best raw materials available anywhere on the planet, and built one of the lightest yet strongest boats ever made.

He listened to the groaning, grinding, creaking—the good sounds—and watched the use of the winches, mast, wheel, and rudder. What he didn't hear were any of the untoward sounds: of composite coming unstuck; of the wrong cracks, creaks, or bangs. The sound of carbon fiber breaking was one sailors don't soon forget. As Dickson put the boat through a series of jibes and tacks, the loads were transmitted and more sounds came through: bangs and creaks and drawn-out moans as the spinnaker sheet went through its turning block. So far, the sound track was sonorous. Occasionally, the sounds would stop and there was only the splashing of the sea.

Tugsy had come a long way from his early boatbuilding days in New Zealand, when he began to think about such things as the standard definition of floating—first recorded by Archimedes—that "an object in a fluid experiences an upward force equal to the weight of the fluid displaced by that object." Now when Tugsy talked about a boat, he talked about displacement. If a boat weighed ten thousand pounds, it would sink into the water until it had displaced ten thousand pounds of water. If the boat displaced the same amount of water before becoming submerged it floated. When Tugsy learned the craft of boatbuilding, he worked on wooden boats whose hulls were shaped like fish, and whose planking was fastened to frames and a keel. The keel and the frames were typically made out of a hardwood such as oak and the planking used softer woods like pine or cedar. Tugsy's first boat when he was a child was a Sabot, a seven-foot, single-person dinghy. His father gave it to him when he was seven years old, and he considered the boat's number, 17, to be good luck.

Looking across the deck of *USA-87*, Tugsy felt he had delivered a great boat. The engineers had done their part. The builders had done theirs. The maiden structural sail was a success.

A month later more than 500 people and some 150 members of the international press gathered at BMW Oracle Racing's base in Valencia to watch as Sue Dickson, Chris's wife, christened *USA-87* with a bottle of Moët & Chandon champagne against the bow. The tradition of cracking a bottle of spirits against the bow was said to date to the Phoenicians, with the idea being that flowing liquid was a symbol of good luck. And because lady luck was considered important, most bows were christened by women. Hundreds of champagne flutes were handed out and a local priest, Padre Antonio of the Santa María del Mar church in Valencia, clad in a black clerical robe and a long white sash, blessed the yacht.

The new base, sleek and modern and open to the public, included about sixty thousand square feet over three floors and featured a public interactive center, a food court, a gym, an engineering facility, and facilities for the team and builders.

"This is a great moment and milestone for our team," Dickson said. "A boat christening is always a moving event, for every designer and boatbuilder, for every sailor." The boat was the result of a thousand hours of full-scale two-boat testing (using the previous campaign's two boats for modifications and testing). "Over the coming weeks," Dickson said, "the challenge will be to tap the yacht's full potential."

The 32nd America's Cup would begin in mid-April with the first round-robin of the Louis Vuitton Cup and eleven challenging syndicates. A second round-robin would start on April 25, and the Louis Vuitton Cup finals would begin on June 1. The teams represented a dazzling array of talent and countries, from Italy, South Africa, New Zealand, France, Sweden, and Spain to Germany and China.

17

South of Market,
San Francisco

Spring 2006

IN THE SPRING of 2006 Norbert received a call out of the blue from Terry Anderlini, a friend and former commodore of the St. Francis.

"Hey, Norbert, can we talk?" Anderlini asked.

"What's it about?" Norbert said, on his way home from work.

"Let's talk when we meet," Anderlini said cryptically. "And let's go somewhere besides our yacht clubs."

The next day, Norbert headed to the South of Market area to meet Anderlini and Terry Klaus, another former St. Francis commodore. Norbert was on good terms with both men but considered himself friends with Anderlini, who was head of the St. Francis when Paul Cayard had launched his *AmericaOne* syndicate and was also the father of Gina von Esmarch, who in earlier years had been a member of Oracle BMW Racing's administrative team.

The three men found an out-of-the-way table at MoMo's, a restaurant and bar situated across the street from the San Francisco

Giants' ballpark. On game day, the place was standing room only, but the Giants were not playing today so it was quiet.

Anderlini began by saying that the St. Francis's lease was coming up for renewal and that the club was looking at "all of our operations." He and a few others had been mulling over a certain idea.

Norbert sipped his drink.

"We have the idea of merging our operations," Anderlini said.

Norbert smiled. For years he had secretly flirted with the idea of having one great yacht club along the San Francisco marina that served people from all walks of life. Shortly after landing the deal with Larry to be the sponsoring yacht club for Oracle Racing, Norbert had talked casually with Commodore Charlie Hart about the idea of a merger of sorts. The idea was appealing but didn't go anywhere. Since then, anytime Norbert brought it up with close friends or yacht club members he got looks of disbelief. But Norbert felt the rivalry between the clubs should be a thing of the past. He knew the St. Francis had major Cup envy, but he also knew that members of the Golden Gate would get a great deal in a merger. They would have the world-class facilities of the St. Francis, and they'd have access to Tinsley Island. Norbert had been invited to Tinsley—the first such invitation extended to the commodore of the Golden Gate—to attend one of the St. Francis's all-male weekend bacchanals, which involved copious amounts of alcohol and little sleep. Norbert spent much of the weekend being ribbed by members who said things like, "I heard Larry Ellison bought the Golden Gate." Norbert replied drily, "Yeah, sure, and you see me driving a Rolls-Royce?" Then some of the members would come to Norbert's defense and say it was the St. Francis that screwed up the Ellison deal.

Norbert was more than aware that although the Golden Gate was no longer in debt it was hardly cash rich. Without Oracle, it would have to live lean and start looking for new streams of revenue.

"I like the idea of going one step further," Norbert said. "I've always been a fan of this idea. I see some really good things coming out of it." He said he would love to see the Golden Gate be the kids' annex, the dedicated spot for youth sailing. They'd have the downstairs as a classroom, the upstairs for the program, and the docks for the kids' boats and events.

The St. Francis reps seemed to like the idea, too, and even talked about a tentative name for the merged club: the St. Francis Golden Gate. Their burgees wouldn't have to move, as the Golden Gate's could stay at the youth annex. The one thing that Norbert saw as a sticking point was approval by the St. Francis membership. The Golden Gate's members paid $125 a month but would not have to pay the $25,000 initiation fee to join, as members of the St. Francis did. How would Norbert make sure the Golden Gate's members weren't treated like second-class citizens? Norbert was no longer commodore—he had served for two years—yet he had remained the public face of the club and was the liaison between the Golden Gate and Larry Ellison. Anything having to do with the America's Cup went through him.

The men agreed to think about it and draft plans from each side. Norbert made it clear that he would have to talk with Larry before anything happened, and that BMW Oracle Racing's America's Cup operations would remain with the Golden Gate. He also was in agreement that the St. Francis would not "buy" the Golden Gate, but that the Golden Gate would become a subcorporation of the St. Francis.

"These institutions have served different roles," Norbert said. "The Golden Gate has been more blue collar. But hey, this is mergers and acquisitions." Norbert took inspiration from being in Larry's life. He wasn't going to be sentimental about progress. Larry made decisions and moved forward. Oracle had become one of the world's great success stories not by worrying about the role that it played in the past but by thinking about the future, by merging with or buying up competitors. Norbert envisioned an even greater Golden Gate Yacht Club.

The yacht *America,* seen here years after winning the race that would come to bear her name.

In 1885, *Puritan,* sponsored by the New York Yacht Club, defeated *Genesta,* from the Royal Yacht Squadron, as depicted by Currier & Ives. It was the sixth straight victory for the United States.

The coveted "Auld Mug," c. 1958

The satirical magazine *Puck* weighed in on the winning streak in November 1900.

Sir Thomas Lipton, the Irish tea magnate, became beloved in America for his pursuit of the America's Cup.

Lipton's second try for the Cup saw his boat, *Shamrock II*, defeated by the New York Yacht Club's *Columbia*.

A 1903 cartoon from *Puck* shows the "American Sportsman" declaring, "If we can not keep both, we would rather lose the Cup than lose you, Sir Thomas."

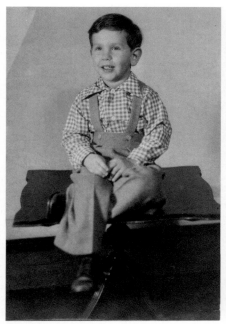

Larry Ellison at age two.

Larry's adoptive parents, Lillian and Louis Ellison.

Larry at twenty-four years old, rock climbing in Yosemite.

Larry with his children, David and Megan, in 1989.

Sayonara during a relatively calm moment in the 1998 Sydney-to-Hobart race.

Larry Ellison and Melanie Craft at their wedding in December 2003. From left: Rep. Tom Lantos with his wife, Annette Tillemann, Steve Jobs, Melanie, Larry, Megan Ellison, David Ellison, Laurene Powell Jobs.

Larry with his Marchetti S211 jet fighter.

Larry and his friend, Rafael Nadal, on the courts of his Palm Springs estate.

The Golden Gate Yacht Club was founded on a barge in San Francisco in 1939.

Norbert Bajurin with his parents, Jozo and Gertrude.

Norbert and Jozo Bajurin's shop, Alouis Auto Radiator and Air, in San Francisco's Western Addition.

Norbert and his wife, Madeleine, aboard Larry's yacht, *Katana*.

Kiwi sailor Chris Dickson, who ran Larry's America's Cup teams from 2003 to 2007.

Norbert and Larry on the deck of the Golden Gate Yacht Club.

Kiwi Russell Coutts with Swiss pharmaceutical heir and Alinghi head Ernesto Bertarelli after winning the America's Cup in 2003.

Gilles Martin-Raget

Fleet racing before the start of the Louis Vuitton Cup in 2007.

Gilles Martin-Raget

Gilles Martin-Raget

BMW Oracle Racing in the 2007 Louis Vuitton Cup semi-final against the Italian team, Luna Rossa, skippered by Jimmy Spithill.

Racing in the early stages of the 32nd America's Cup in Valencia, Spain. Here, *USA-76* takes on a Spanish team. Both teams are using boats from previous campaigns, as new boats were being built.

The last race of the 2007 Louis Vuitton Cup semifinals, when Larry replaced Chris Dickson with Sten Mohr.

Larry thanking the Oracle team members for their hard work and efforts, after the painful loss to Luna Rossa in 2007.

The young Australian Jimmy Spithill was Coutts's first hire.

Kiwi skipper Russell Coutts was hired by Larry to run his third Cup challenge, in 2007.

Mark "Tugsy" Turner heads up Larry's boat-building operations and has been with Larry since 1998.

Getting the twenty-three-story-high rigid wingsail onto the trimaran, *USA-17*, took up to eight hours, 2009.

The wingsail is finally on the boat, and *USA-17* is ready for her maiden sail, 2009.

USA-17 arrives in Spain just weeks before the start of the 2010 America's Cup and is unloaded in the middle of the night when there is little wind.

Jimmy Spithill at the helm of the massive *USA-17* during the 2010 America's Cup against Alinghi.

The trimaran that Larry called a "pterodactyl" wins the 33rd America's Cup in Valencia, Spain.

Finally, after two painful and costly losses, Oracle Racing wins the America's Cup. Top row, from left: Russell Coutts, Jimmy Spithill, Larry Ellison, Thierry Fouchier, John Kostecki (obscured), Ross Halcrow, Joey Newton, Dirk de Ridder; Bottom row, from left: Matteo Plazzi, Matthew Mason, Brad Webb, Simone de Mari.

Norbert and Larry embrace right after the February 14, 2010, victory.

Victory for Oracle Racing. From left: Jimmy Spithill, Russell Coutts, Larry, John Kostecki.

Spithill, the youngest skipper ever to win the America's Cup, celebrates.

Spithill and Norbert bring the America's Cup back to America for the first time in fifteen years.

The America's Cup is engraved with the results of the 2010 victory at Biro & Sons in San Francisco.

AC45s compete on San Francisco Bay in a World Series regatta in 2012.

Oracle Team USA capsized its AC72 on October 17, 2012, setting back the team by months.

Italy's Luna Rossa faces Artemis Racing of Sweden in the Louis Vuitton Cup semifinals.

Following the crash, and Artemis Racing's fatal accident, Team USA added more training, here at Stanford's pool.

ACEA/Guilain Grenier

Oracle Team USA, Jimmy Spithill in the center, with *USA-17*.

ACEA/Balazs Gardi

ACEA/Abner Kingman

ACEA/Abner Kingman

ACEA/Gilles Martin-Raget

Oracle Team USA vs. Emirates Team New Zealand in the 34th America's Cup.

Oracle Team USA sails home to victory, pulling off one of the greatest comebacks in sports history.

Celebration after winning the 34th America's Cup. From left: David Ellison, Judge Jimmy Linn, Sandy Ellison, Meir Teper, Nikita Kahn, Larry Ellison, Kim Dubin, Pam Tilton, FBI Agent Jonathan Dubin, Jon Weis.

Jimmy Spithill, Larry Ellison, and Norbert Bajurin celebrate the remarkable victory in 2013.

Norbert laughed and said, "Sure, at the St. Francis, you gotta turn your cell phones off. At the Golden Gate we don't care. The St. Francis has its history and the Golden Gate has its past." Norbert pointed out that he wasn't a part of the Golden Gate in its heyday. When he'd arrived it had a gold-toothed bartender and a sinking debt.

"We got another step in life," Norbert said. He felt as if the club could always maintain its history. They could have the story of the Golden Gate on the walls of the St. Francis and put up pictures of past commodores. "It could be really good," he said.

Walking out of the meeting, the men shook hands and agreed to keep the talks to themselves.

On the way home, Norbert thought of someone he had to call.

"Dad, I've got a question for you," Norbert said, feeling playful. "What would you do if I joined the St. Francis?"

"Join another yacht club," Jozo replied.

Norbert laughed. That was all he could do.

A few days later Norbert was at home when he received a call from a member of the Golden Gate who had stepped out of the bar at the San Francisco Yacht Club in Belvedere in Marin County. He had overheard a St. Francis Yacht Club member talking about how the St. Francis was going to "buy" the Golden Gate.

That was all Norbert needed to hear. He called Anderlini.

"People are gossiping about this, and I can't have word of it get out before I've even had a chance to talk with Larry," Norbert said, feeling his blood pressure rise. "The deal is off."

At least for now, Norbert thought to himself.

A week later, Norbert drove to Redwood Shores to meet with Larry, who was flying to Valencia later that day. Judy Sim, who had become a friend of Norbert's and served as liaison between Oracle Corporation and Oracle Racing, found time for the two men to meet. Norbert had something pressing to discuss.

The two met in the television production studio where Larry had just finished a taped interview. They talked briefly about Valencia and Larry said he looked forward to going back and hitting some of the local restaurants.

"I think I've eaten at every great paella restaurant in Valencia and there are a lot of them," Larry said. "The best ones are pretty small, so you have to have just enough Spanish to understand the menu and order. The food in Valencia is pretty fabulous. The pigs are fed hazelnuts. I don't like hazelnuts, but I guess they do. The ham is amazing."

Larry continued, "I really like Valencia. But right now it's Ernesto's town. The mayor is Ernesto's buddy and it feels like Alinghi owns the place."

Norbert mentioned one of his favorite places, called the Docks, in the old town of Valencia. "You didn't really have to order, as they had a routine of serving you."

Knowing Larry was on a tight schedule, Norbert got to his point.

"I was in Valencia a month ago," Norbert said, "and I heard from Chris Dickson that he is planning on changing a part of the agreement with the Golden Gate."

"Changing the agreement?" Larry asked.

Norbert explained that Dickson wanted to change the team's relationship with the yacht club. "He acknowledges he needs a yacht club," Norbert said. "But he doesn't think he needs to pay dues at our club."

Norbert added that when he told Dickson he still needed to have BMW Oracle Racing team members on the Golden Gate Yacht Club's board of directors, Dickson said he understood but that they weren't required to continue paying dues.

Norbert noted that this was not the original commitment that Larry and Erkelens had laid out, but if Larry wanted to change it he certainly understood. Norbert also quickly mentioned that American flags were not flying at the base, which was unusual, as every syndicate had its country's flag flying. Norbert said that when he'd asked about it, Sue Dickson replied the decision was made so the team wouldn't become a target for terrorists.

"Okay, I'll take care of it," Larry said, as Sim appeared to collect him.

Norbert never heard about it again, and the dues kept coming. When he returned to Valencia, a huge American flag was flying over the Oracle base.

18

Valencia, Spain

Spring 2007

IN APRIL 2007, eleven teams began racing for the Louis Vuitton Cup in the waters off Valencia. Each team raced every other team twice in two round-robins, which ended in May. After the round-robins, which consisted of over a hundred races, the top four teams advanced to the Louis Vuitton semifinals and the other seven teams were eliminated.

The round-robins were now complete. Chris Dickson had skippered and driven *USA-98* to seventeen wins with only three losses. Dean Barker's Team New Zealand had the identical record: seventeen and three. The Italian team sponsored by Prada and helmed by Australian Jimmy Spithill was in third place with a record of sixteen and four. The host Spanish team rounded out the top four qualifying for the semifinals with a record of thirteen wins and seven losses. The teams from Sweden, South Africa, France, Germany, and China plus two other Italian teams had been eliminated.

BMW Oracle Racing was heavily favored to beat Prada's Luna Rossa in their semifinal series. Dickson and *USA-98* had dominated *ITA-94,* beating the Italian boat in the first round-robin, and again in the second round-robin. New Zealand was even more heavily favored over the Spanish. Just about everybody expected BMW

Oracle Racing and Team New Zealand to easily win in the semis and then battle each other in the Louis Vuitton final for the right to face Alinghi in the 32nd America's Cup.

For months, Prada helmsman Spithill had been watching and recording Chris Dickson's every move. Spithill's coach, Philippe Presti, tall and silver-haired and an accomplished sailor himself, scouted Dickson on the water to understand his strengths and weaknesses. Presti filmed Dickson and returned to base to analyze the footage. Presti knew Dickson well, not just as the legendary skipper but as someone he had sailed against in the 2003 America's Cup, when Presti was skipper of the French team Le Défi Areva.

Spithill was out for blood, as he and Dickson had had earlier dustups. "I want to kill him," Spithill told Presti.

Spithill grew up in Pittwater, Australia, and had dreamed of the America's Cup ever since he was a young child. His family's neighbors were the Beashels—Colin Beashel was a national hero for his role as mainsheet trimmer on the winning *Australia II* team, in 1983. In the days and weeks following the victory, every family in Pittwater held raucous celebrations. Jimmy was all of four years old but aware enough to declare that he would one day win the Cup. Now twenty-seven and tall, wiry, and agile, he had the quick reflexes of the boxer he'd been as a teenager. He had shown uncommon talent in boxing and reached a point in his competing when he had to decide whether he'd go in that direction or pursue sailing. One virtue of sailing was that it could be done with a team, whereas boxing was solitary. To his mother's relief he went for sailing. He was the kid who sailed to school, arriving with his clothes all wet. And he was the kid who failed to do well behind a desk or in exams. His teachers reassured his parents—his father was an electrical engineer—that Jimmy would find his way but that it wouldn't be an academic path.

At the age of eighteen, Spithill was given the opportunity to sail in the 1998 Sydney-to-Hobart race, where Larry and crew took line honors and finished first overall. He debuted in the America's Cup at age nineteen, in 1999, showing precocious talent as helmsman of *Young Australia;* he was the youngest skipper in the oldest boat with the smallest budget. He reached the semifinals of the 2003 America's Cup as skipper of *OneWorld,* funded by the Craig McCaw and Paul Allen syndicate. He then did what many considered impossible: he beat Russell Coutts in the World Match Racing Championship on Lake Garda in 2003. Now, he was skipper of the Italian America's Cup team, Luna Rossa, backed by Patrizio Bertelli. Bertelli believed Spithill had great talent as a helmsman and sailor but also saw his determination and what Bertelli dubbed his "killer instinct."

Spithill and Presti, who is French, had been preparing for the 2007 LouisVuitton Cup by spending a part of each day working on their playbook. Presti believed in building plays for the water in the same way football teams hit the turf with a plan. Plays had names like "Eddie Baby" and Presti worked with Spithill to read what the other team would do, all the while hiding his own intentions. He believed that match racing—the one-on-one races of the America's Cup and LouisVuitton series—was like boxing, in that the boats went into the ring and faced one another, knowing opponents' strengths and weaknesses. Presti told Spithill that he knew Dickson's abilities, knowledge, and tricks. He knew what his opponent would do under pressure and he could predict the opponent's moves. Presti had spent hours studying videos of Dickson driving. He figured out Dickson's patterns: how he liked to enter the starting box, when he liked to turn and pursue and maneuver against his opponent, and how he liked to sail once the race had begun. Presti also planned to use psychological warfare, as John Bertrand, helmsman of *Australia II,* had done with Dennis Conner. Bertrand built up a formidable mystique around his boat's winged keel design, which made its debut on the 12-Meter-class yacht that year. The keel was designed with horizontal winglets angled slightly downward, providing more lift than drag, thus allowing *Australia II* to sail closer to the wind. It came to preoccupy Conner and the American team.

Spithill would look for weakness wherever it could be found. It was well known in sailing circles that Dickson's temper caused trouble with his team. Presti and Spithill would use any lack of cohesion against him.

During a regatta preceding the start of the Louis Vuitton Cup months earlier Dickson had intentionally slammed the bow of *USA-87* into the most vulnerable part of Luna Rossa's hull, the heavily loaded spot where the running backstays attach. Dickson had been slightly behind at the time but the impact caused such severe structural damage that the Italian boat had to withdraw from the race. What further enraged Spithill was that Luna Rossa was penalized and forced to pay for the considerable repairs to both boats.

So as Spithill readied for the first of the Louis Vuitton semifinal races, he and Presti went over the game plan. They focused on the prestart, that all-critical five-minute period right before the start of the race when the two boats maneuver against each other attempting to gain an advantageous position when the starting gun goes off. The prestart begins when both boats enter the starting box, the area directly downwind of the starting line. The boats enter from opposite ends of the starting line, and as they come together, the boat entering from the right, the one on starboard tack, has the right-of-way. Typically, the boat entering from the right will aim directly at the boat entering from the left, and the boat on the left *must* avoid the boat on the right or incur a penalty. The standard way for the boat on the left to avoid a penalty is to complete a tack onto starboard and then point its bow directly into the wind, thus forcing a "dial-up," a position where both boats are close together, side by side, pointed directly into the wind. Once in the dial-up position, both boats begin to slow down; then they stop going forward and start to go backward. Driving a sailboat backward takes constant coordination between the helmsman and the sail trimmers. If it is done well, the driver can come out of the dial-up with enough speed to put his boat in a position to control the other boat, and to gain an advantage in winning the start.

"Chris always prefers to keep moving, not stopping, so dialing up head to wind is a position he's not comfortable with," Presti said. Spithill, however, had been practicing the dial-up to the point of tedium and the subsequent offensive and defensive moves that could be used against his opponent during and after it. To prepare for the races, Presti, skippering Luna Rossa's other boat, had pretended to be Dickson, driving the way he drove, glaring the way he glared, and making the moves the Kiwi was known to make.

Spithill began the prestart by getting Dickson into a dial-up. The boats stayed side by side for about a minute before both boats bailed out of the dial-up at the same time. Spithill and crew did a better job of accelerating their boat, and used the momentary speed advantage to gain control of Dickson by positioning *ITA-94*'s bow close behind and slightly to leeward of *USA-98*'s stern. The position of the Italian boat prevented Dickson from jibing and turning *USA-98* back toward the starting line. Spithill maintained control throughout the last two minutes of the prestart and led Dickson off the starting line. On the first upwind leg Spithill used the lead he gained at the start of the race to force Dickson to sail to the less favorable left side of the racecourse, while Prada found better wind on the right. Spithill led comfortably around the first weather mark and held on to win race one.

Race two showed Spithill again strong in the prestart, winning the start, and leading around every mark until the last downwind leg when Dickson found better wind on the left-hand side of the course and drew even. As both boats approached the finish line, *USA-98* and *ITA-94* were on a collision course, coming together bow to bow. Spithill jibed on top of Dickson in an attempt to roll over him and Dickson responded by turning *USA-98* directly downwind to keep the Aussie from blocking his wind. Spithill then pointed *ITA-94* in exactly the same direction, paralleling *USA-98*'s course. Now both boats were going at the same speed, sailing side by side, an arm's length away from each other, headed due downwind (180-degree true wind angle) directly toward the finish line. There was silence on both boats until suddenly *USA-98* tactician John Kostecki started screaming, "We are winning this game! We are winning this game!" *USA-98* was slowly inching ahead of the Italian boat. As BMW Oracle

Racing crossed the finish line first, Larry, sailing as a member of the afterguard, grabbed a surprised Dickson, slapped him on the back and said, "Great job Chris, great comeback guys. We really needed that one." The score after the first two races was even: Prada one, Oracle one.

In race three, Spithill won the start again, was twenty-nine seconds ahead at the first mark, and never looked back. And in race four, Spithill—dubbed "Pitbull" and "Spitfire" by a press that adored his aggressive starts—entered the box smiling at Dickson. As the commentators noted, these starts were not for the weak of heart. The boats entered the starting box from opposite directions and headed straight toward each other, like two trucks playing chicken. All the while, commentators noticed Spithill appeared to be looking straight at Dickson and grinning. Presti knew that Spithill was actually watching Dickson's hands, as the skipper's hands told him where his boat would go.

Now, Oracle was down three races to one in the first-to-five series. It was a situation no one would have predicted. BMW Oracle Racing had handily defeated Luna Rossa in both of the round-robins. The American team was favored to win, and Larry expected to win.

Throughout the Louis Vuitton Cup, Larry was a part of the crew onboard *USA-98*: trimming the tab during the prestart, easing the weather runner as they tacked around the upwind mark, sheeting in the leeward runner as they rounded a downwind mark, and alerting the helmsman whenever *ITA-94* began a maneuver. But he also watched Dickson drive. Larry had seen him sail brilliantly during the first round-robin when he ducked underneath Dean Barker and Team New Zealand during a dial-down, giving *USA-98* the favored right side of the course and the lead in the race. But now Dickson was not sailing brilliantly; he was being outmaneuvered by Spithill in every prestart. Larry had seen that happen once before, when they were practicing match racing forty-footers in San Francisco Bay. Larry was driving one boat with Gavin Brady as his tactician and Dickson was driving the other boat. Larry and

Brady won the first prestart, then the second, and then the third. Dickson got more and more upset as Larry and Brady kept winning most of the practice prestarts. Larry thought Dickson must have been rusty or jet-lagged, or something. But Brady, who had been practicing against Dickson on a regular basis, looked at Larry and said, "I told you we'd beat him."

Now Larry was seeing exactly the same Dickson—losing the prestarts to Spithill, then losing his confidence. He knew that unmanaged stress eroded confidence first, skills second. A few crew members pulled Larry aside and suggested that his presence on the boat was adding to Dickson's stress. So for race five, Larry watched from his chase boat.

The prestart is the most difficult and most important part of a match race. It requires extraordinary teamwork among all seventeen crew members as the boat is steered, not only by the rudder controlled by the helmsman's wheel, but also by the sails manned by the trimmers and the bowman. Both sails must be trimmed in precisely the right time and in sequence to accelerate and decelerate the yacht as it tacks and jibes in response to its opponent's maneuvers.

The prestart of race five was an encounter that commentators and announcers could not believe, and they called it one of the most dramatic in America's Cup history. In less than five minutes, the legendary skipper of *USA-98*—to whom Larry had entrusted his dreams for not one campaign but two—came unglued at the hands of this young freckle-faced Aussie, who was taking him apart. Dickson already picked up one penalty early in the prestart, and now Spithill had Dickson pinned up against the port end of the starting line, the area of the starting box sailors call "the zone of death." Trying to extricate himself from Spithill's tight control, Dickson swung his transom hard into Luna Rossa and was penalized a second time for causing a collision.

Presti, watching Spithill, nodded. Sailing was a mental game—tough, like chess—and Presti loved it.

The sailing commentators were breathless: "The prestart between Chris Dickson and Luna Rossa's James Spithill is just electric. Dickson copped not one but two penalties. This is just hard to believe what we are seeing." Immediately after the start Dickson was required to perform the first of his two penalty turns, and Spithill sailed away.

This cannot be happening, Larry said. *Two penalties in the prestart.* He sat down in the chase boat. The race was over before it began. And their campaign appeared to be over too. This time they weren't even going to make it to the Louis Vuitton final. Seven years and a couple of hundred million dollars had gone into his quest for the America's Cup. He would go to work and earn that money back, but he knew he could never get the time back.

The commentators posed the question: "Should the America's Cup still be called the America's Cup?" They noted that BMW Oracle Racing was the only American team in contention, and that the Cup had been out of the country's hands since 1995, when Dennis Conner lost to Russell Coutts and Team New Zealand.

Not far away in the gulf, Norbert watched the action from a spectator boat he'd rented to host the eighty-four members of the Golden Gate Yacht Club (twenty-two members of the club had gone to Auckland in 2003). At the start of the race, Ned Barrett asked Norbert, "Did you see that smile on Jimmy Spithill's face as he looked over at Dickson? He's out to kill him, but smiling as he does it." Norbert and Madeleine had been busy playing host to the huge group, handing out passes and organizing tours at the start of each day and running the parties at day's end. They were exhausted, and Madeleine found herself glued to the news of another Madeleine, the little Madeleine McCann, who was on holiday with her family in Portugal when she was kidnapped. The news competed with the America's Cup for front-page headlines.

Tugsy was also out near the racecourse. He knew this was not going to end well for the Oracle racing team. In his mind, Dickson had been given the keys to the kingdom, not wanting for a single thing, whether with his own multimillion-dollar salary or funding for the latest innovations in technology and training. Tugsy had stayed with the team out of loyalty to Larry. As the race played out, Tugsy turned to one of his crew and said, "Chris had all of the resources in the world and he's just fucked it up. Larry never saw Chris like other people saw. Now he gets to see him come undone."

On board, fighting to catch Spithill, navigator Peter Isler, an American who had sailed in four Cup campaigns, including one with Dennis Conner when Conner won the trophy back for America in Australia in 1987, tried to talk to Dickson, who had gone silent. Isler knew that in this race, with the boats about even in speed because of their similar designs, the first ten minutes of the race were crucial. Hired by Dickson in 2005, Isler had seen his brilliance at the helm and also his weakness at delegating. Dickson was the team's great strength as well as its Achilles' heel. Everyone aboard was working to try to keep him in his mode of strength. Oracle had beaten Team Luna Rossa in the earlier races, and Dickson had said, "We have their number." But they had raced against each other a few times more recently and the outcome had been closer to fifty-fifty. Isler worried that it had created a potential psychological wedge.

Watching Dickson, a man he respected, Isler knew that he was alone in that moment, with a multimillion-dollar campaign resting on his shoulders. It was up to Dickson to decide, like a gambler, what risks to take. And when Dickson felt he wasn't getting the correct information, he would fall back on what had served him well through his years of sailing, his own intuition and strength. But Isler understood that this didn't work in the America's Cup, where the team has to operate flawlessly, where there is no room for second-guessing.

As they sailed to the first mark, with the Luna Rossa boat ahead, Dickson collected himself. The race wasn't over but the mood on board was bleak. They had a great team and a strong boat, and they could've won the whole thing.

"I should have seen this coming but I didn't—*why*?" Larry said in a near whisper on the chase boat, as Luna Rossa increased its lead. He had seen professional athletes melt down before, and he knew their moments of heartbreak would never be erased. He had watched as the French midfielder Zinedine Zidane head-butted his Italian opponent in the 2006 World Cup final, ending his team's chances and marking his last professional match. There had been the heavyweight championship fight of 1997, when Oliver McCall broke down in the middle of the third round, dropping his gloves to his sides and refusing to fight. He wandered around the ring and wept and seemed oblivious of the gargantuan Lennox Lewis pounding his face. And during the French Open in 1999 Martina Hingis had been just three points away from victory over Steffi Graf when a line judge made a bad call in Graf's favor—and Hingis unraveled from there, losing the match. A lifetime of training, sacrifice, and dreams ended, replaced with a new reel that would mercilessly play over and over. When Dennis Conner had lost to Bertrand on the Rhode Island Sound in September 1983, it was after sailing in seven races covering two hundred miles. *Australia II* defeated *Liberty* by forty-one seconds—all of eight boat-lengths.

Race five was lost. Luna Rossa trounced BMW Oracle Racing by nearly two minutes. Now Dickson and company were down 4–1, and the Italian team had them by the throat.

A teary-eyed Dickson, reaching the docks, said to Larry, "I just didn't sail as well as I did when I was younger." Larry shook his head. He didn't believe it had anything to do with age. He had seen Dickson sail brilliantly over the past few months. He just couldn't do it when it mattered most. What bothered Larry even more than the loss of race five was the collision during the prestart. Larry was on board *USA-87* when Dickson slammed into Luna Rossa. When Larry quietly said to Dickson, "*You did that intentionally*," Dickson responded, "*Did I?*" Larry could not risk a third collision.

That night Dickson got a call from Larry.

In the months leading up to the Louis Vuitton series, Dickson had told Larry that at forty-three years old he wasn't as good in his reaction time as he used to be. He had noticed he wasn't as quick at processing the numbers and data needed to make the split-second decisions. He had told Larry, "I'm getting older. I'm not as good." Larry had replied, "Chris, you at eighty percent are way better than those other guys at one hundred percent." Larry didn't believe Dickson's problems had anything to do with age. It was all about the mental game, about who performs in the clutch and who caves.

In their conversation that night, the two talked about changing rudders, keels, and people. But Dickson insisted, "We are doing everything we can. We are racing this package because this is the best we've got," Dickson concluded. "They've beaten us four out of five and the odds are they will beat us again. They have a stronger package. I know that I sailed better when I was younger."

Without being specific, Larry reiterated that it was time to change some things.

"You can change whatever you want, but it will be a weaker team and a weaker package," Dickson said. "You change things, and it will make the odds even worse. But if you want to be seen as doing something, that's your call."

Larry was silent. "We all make mistakes," he said. "I just didn't see this coming." What he did see all too clearly now was that his skipper wasn't a Michael Jordan who at the end of the game, when the pressure was on, said, *Give me the ball.*

Dickson added, "Larry, my advice—and you can obviously do what you want—is that we go out there tomorrow to try to win the race. We will probably get beaten and you should be prepared to lose gracefully."

Larry was stunned by the suggestion. After a long pause, he said that he could be gracious after losing, but he wasn't capable of being gracious while losing. He had come here to win.

The next morning, as Dickson got ready for the race of the day, a call came in. It was from Laurent Esquier, a team manager. Dickson was told he didn't need to show up for work. He was off the boat.

Dickson sat quietly for a few moments. He had come at Larry's invitation, and he would leave at Larry's invitation. He felt Larry's decision was the wrong one for the team, and he was disappointed that Larry hadn't made the call himself. After all their years together, Larry had ordered someone else to make that call.

But Dickson knew Larry. He knew that, when the chips were down, Larry would always come out swinging. He would never do nothing. He would take a risk and make a change and, nine times out of ten, it worked for him.

Dickson was replaced at the helm by the Danish match racer Sten Mohr, with Gavin Brady returning to the team as skipper. Brady had been on and off the boat because of disagreements with Dickson; Brady also was famously headstrong. Now he was back again. It was Mohr's second America's Cup race. He had been at the helm when BMW Oracle Racing suffered its most ignominious defeat of the round-robin series, losing to the last-place Chinese team because its jib kept coming off the headstay, forcing Oracle to sail the upwind legs with only its mainsail.

As they headed out in *USA-98*, Larry rejoined the afterguard. He was an optimist but reality had set in. He had no delusions about the outcome of the day's race. It was over long before today. He was back to the thoughts that had consumed him in the first campaign: *How did I make so many mistakes? I can't believe I fucked it up again!*

In strong breeze, Luna Rossa led by thirty-two seconds at the first mark and by the same margin at the leeward gate. Spithill led around the final mark by thirty-five seconds and seemed to lope across the finish line well ahead.

Back at the docks the team gathered in the sail loft. Larry thanked them all for their efforts and dedication. Dickson was there, as he had been all day, helping where he could and putting an upbeat spin on the helmsman change when grilled by the press.

Larry knew how hard everyone had worked. There had been a daily commitment from hundreds of people on this shared dream. Lives had been put on hold to win the Cup.

"Thank you for the hard work," Larry said. "Thank you for your years of dedication and effort you have all put into this team. I appreciate that enormously. I know that people made personal and professional sacrifices to be here. I was pretty confident, but we lost. There will be more sailboat racing."

On his way out of the team base, Larry was asked by a reporter whether it was worth a hundred million dollars—he had spent far more than this—to win the America's Cup. He paused and said, "I don't know. I've never won the America's Cup. But I can tell you this, it certainly isn't worth a hundred million dollars to lose the America's Cup."

Many in the press, particularly sailing bloggers, jumped on Larry's loss. He was criticized, second-guessed, and called a "chump." One writer said, "BMW Oracle Racing was destined to fall apart," and "Boat designer Bruce Farr was capable of designing boats only for a certain type of wind and can't design boats in all around winds." A blogger wrote, "This marks the end for Chris Dickson," and, "Larry should be sent packing. However, at the end of the day, it's his money and he is entitled to waste it how he sees fit." Another blogger wrote to Larry, "You probably need to bring in someone fresh who doesn't get weak kneed at the site [sic] of James Spithill." The most popular refrain, though, was to refer to

Larry as the "modern-day Sir Thomas Lipton," a comment Larry brushed off with humor by saying, "I drink tea, but I don't make it." Of course he knew Lipton's story well.

After three decades of effort and *five* unsuccessful challenges, Lipton had failed to win the Cup, but along the way he had won the hearts of the sporting world. He was beloved as the "winningest loser" and helped to pull America out of the pains of the Great Depression, when Americans had turned to sport, notably baseball and the America's Cup. When Lipton arrived in New York in 1930, he was greeted by police boats and fire department bands. Reporters covered his every move. He was the underdog, and New York's mayor Jimmy Walker suggested a trophy for Lipton with the inscription: "To possibly the world's worst yacht builder, but absolutely the world's most cheerful loser. You have been a benefit to mankind Sir Thomas. You have made losing worthwhile." His good sportsmanship inspired America, and the "Loser's Cup" was fashioned by Tiffany, made out of eighteen-carat gold and with a lid decorated in carved shamrocks. When Lipton received the trophy before a crowd of thousands, he said with great emotion, "Although I have lost, you make me feel as if I had won."

Larry appreciated Lipton's perseverance but found nothing inspiring in losing. He preferred to think about the story of Australian businessman Alan Bond, who, having been beaten three times in a row, persisted with a fourth challenge. He came to America with *Australia II* and a golden wrench, which he said he would use to unbolt the trophy from the New York Yacht Club. President Ronald Reagan congratulated Bond and his winning team during their visit to the White House. Referring to the Australians and to Conner's American team, Reagan said, "You captured the imagination of the people, and the world over." And to Bond, known as "Bondy," he said, "Alan, you represent the kind of tenacity with which Americans and the Australians identify. For eleven years and four challenges, and at heavy financial sacrifice, you have been trying to accomplish this feat. You just kept on coming." Then Reagan said with a smile, "But don't relax. Americans, from deckhands to their head of state, don't take kindly to defeat. And they never give up."

Larry had endured two painful losses. Two losses for a guy who hates to lose. *Why go again?*

The one thing that tempted him was the knowledge that a certain sailor, one with the most impressive record in the modern history of the America's Cup, was now a free agent. Only three skippers in the history of the race had as many victories: Charlie Barr, who skippered winning America's Cup boats in 1899, 1901, and 1903; Mike Vanderbilt, with Cup wins in 1930, 1934, and 1937; and Dennis Conner, "Mr. America's Cup," who skippered winning boats in 1980, 1987, and 1988.

But for now, Larry wanted to think about anything but the America's Cup. If so much as a commercial with a sailboat in it came on TV, Larry changed the channel. It reminded him of when he was a teenager in Chicago and his first job was as a lifeguard. On his days off, when his girlfriend wanted to go to the beach, he would say, "Not unless you pay me." Now he felt the same way about sailing.

PART III

"It's not whether you get knocked down, it's whether you get up."

—Vince Lombardi

19

Woodside, California

Early Summer 2007

A GREAT BLUE HERON moved with a ballerina's high-stepping precision twenty feet from where Larry sat having breakfast outside. The heron, with a pale white face, yellow bill, and black plumes running from its eyes to the back of its head, seemed to tiptoe from the edge of the koi pond, filled with the big, colorful ornamental fish, to the nonreflecting glass wall of the great room, where Larry held meetings, and over to the lake, where a mallard chased its mate, wings flapping madly, cutting a thin wake behind.

Shigeru Namba, Larry's Japanese rock artist, was on the property, moving rocks and adding paths. The hardest part of garden design was rock placement, and Shigeru was a star in his native land. Larry also had employed a well-known landscape architect, Ron Herman, to work with Shigeru. Herman would do something and Shigeru would undo it. The pattern was repeated until Shigeru prevailed. Larry found that whenever he tried to make a suggestion to Shigeru about the garden, the artist's English fluency would vanish and the suggestion would be met with a blank stare. Larry went along with the feigned nonfluency only because Shigeru was the best at what he did. Also on the property were a green clay tennis court and a stable, where Larry kept three Icelandic ponies, which were as friendly as puppies and had the smoothest gaits imaginable.

Looking out at the placid lake, Larry knew he could suppress thoughts of sailing for only so long. In the same way Scarlett O'Hara declared in *Gone with the Wind*, "I can't think about that right now. If I do, I'll go crazy. I'll think about that tomorrow," he had pushed aside decisions on the next America's Cup. Oracle's campaign for the 31st Cup in 2003 in New Zealand had been respectable; the team had made it to the Louis Vuitton Cup finals on its first try, and had done so when Larry was focused on national security and a bad economy. But the second campaign was a disaster and it was depressing. He had put his faith in the wrong man. Larry had driven *Sayonara* to five consecutive world championships with Chris Dickson as his tactician. Larry and Gavin Brady had driven *USA-76* to consecutive victories over Alinghi in regattas in San Francisco, Newport, and Marseilles with Dickson as tactician and skipper. But when Brady left the team and Dickson switched from tactician to helmsman, things began to unravel. The pressure on Dickson was intensified, and he had more interaction with the team. Larry knew now that he should have taken Dickson off the helm the day he saw him intentionally ram another boat.

Larry closed his eyes and listened to the sounds. He was a Shintoist by choice, finding God in nature. He worshipped the sunrise in Kyoto, cherry blossoms in spring, maple trees in the fall, and the strength of the redwoods at home. His connection to nature crystallized when he'd worked as a programmer in Japan in the mid-1970s for Amdahl, partially owned by Fujitsu. Every weekend, he commuted by bullet train from Tokyo to Kyoto. It was there he discovered the artful serenity of the Japanese garden. After a long walk from the Kyoto train station, Larry arrived at the Heian shrine at noon, and stayed until sunset. This Jew from the Lower East Side of Manhattan who grew up in the South

Side of Chicago felt truly at home—for the very first time in his life—in the garden of a Shinto shrine. He connected with the sound of water, and inhaled the scent of moist soil. He was taken by the minimalist style and the structures made of wood and paper. He listened to the wind rustling the bamboo. And for a welcome moment, he felt safe.

His favorite Japanese saying was, "Your garden is not complete until there is nothing else you can take out of it." To Larry, it meant that if he had forty friends it was probably too many. It was a reminder to spend time with the people who mattered, and on the things that were important.

While he was playing tennis with his friend Rafael Nadal, the Spanish tennis champion, Nadal asked how Larry had made his life such a success. Larry launched into a long philosophical musing about how innovation in technology is quite often based on finding errors in conventional wisdom, and when you find an error you have to have the courage take a different approach even when everyone else says you're wrong. Then Larry abruptly stopped himself. "Forget everything I just said. The answer is simple. I never give up." Earlier, Nadal had said something that made a deep impression on Larry. When asked if he loved winning, Nadal shook his head and replied, "No, I love the fight. If you fight hard the winning will come." Larry loved the fight. But in between the fights, his mind needed to rest in the sanctuary of his garden.

Larry headed inside, pausing to pick up his Kindle so he could finish reading *Lone Survivor: The Eyewitness Account of Operation Redwing and the Lost Heroes of Seal Team 10*, by Marcus Luttrell. It was the harrowing true story of a 2005 mission by four U.S. Navy SEALs in the mountainous Pakistani borderland. Less than a day after they started their mission, only one SEAL—Luttrell—was still alive. He'd been blasted unconscious by a rocket grenade, was blown over a cliff, and watched helplessly as his buddies died, but he refused to die. Larry had noted a page: *The real battle is won in the mind. It's won by the guys who understand their areas of weakness,*

who sit and think about it, plotting and planning to improve. Attending
to the detail. Work on their weaknesses and overcome them. Seals never
put up their hands, never wave the white flag.

Larry had just spent seven years trying to win the America's Cup.
He had taken his childhood romance with sailing, inspired by a
teenager's voyage of discovery in a small sloop, to an obsession. He
was incapable of waving the white flag.

It was early evening in New Zealand when Jenny Coutts got a
call from Larry Ellison's office, asking to speak with her husband.

Jenny explained that Russell had arrived home exhausted from
a trip overseas and had gone to bed early. She asked if he could
return the call in the morning.

Over breakfast the next morning, Russell sat with their three
young children: Michael, six; Natasha, four; and Mathais, two.
Jenny, clearing dishes, said, "Oh, by the way, Larry Ellison called
last night."

"What?" Russell said, sitting back in his chair. "Why didn't you
have me take the call?"

"You were sleeping," Jenny said. "Besides, you're not going
to do the America's Cup again, are you? After what we've been
through?"

Russell's former boss the Swiss pharmaceutical heir Ernesto
Bertarelli, and his Team Alinghi, had won the Cup for the second
time on July 3, beating Emirates Team New Zealand five races to
two. Russell, locked in a legal battle, had sat out the 2007 races,
and under his contract he was not allowed to sail for another team.
Rumors had swirled in sailing circles that Bertarelli refused to pay
Coutts, though Bertarelli insisted Coutts was doing too many things
outside of Alinghi. Now, Coutts was free to work with whomever
he wanted, and he had been in talks for several weeks with Patrizio
Bertelli, head of Prada, about running Bertelli's next Cup effort.

"I know the America's Cup isn't exactly the flavor of the month
in our household," Russell said, looking out at the beach of Tindalls

Bay, north of Auckland. "But we should at least hear what Larry has to say."

Russell had first met Larry in Hawaii after the Oracle chief won a race with *Sayonara*. Russell had been impressed with him in 2003, seeing how gracious he was in defeat in the Louis Vuitton finals—against Coutts's team. He also knew Larry could really sail. When Bertarelli informed him he was going to race against Larry in the owner-driver part of the Moët Cup in San Francisco, Russell had said, "I don't think that's such a good idea." But Russell needed to be cautious; he wanted to get involved in the right campaign this time. Larry had a reputation for wanting to win at all costs. And Russell was sure that the tech titan didn't get to be among the world's most successful people by pandering to others. Larry could set his own rules, and Russell wasn't eager to get into another relationship with an autocratic billionaire. He had won the Cup three times, always as a hired gun. This time, he wanted control.

Russell, who spent a part of his youth in the city of Wellington at the southwestern tip of New Zealand's North Island, started sailing at around age seven. His first boat, a P-class dinghy—a seven-foot-long single-hander—was made by his father, Allan, who was a tradesman, and given to him when he was eight years old. He and his two brothers, Grant and Rob, landed in hot water with their mother, Beverly, when they sneaked the hull of the new boat into the "lounge"—the Kiwi term for living room—in the middle of the night to paint it. When Russell was a teenager and the family moved to the town of Dunedin on New Zealand's South Island, he and his older brother sailed competitively in a youth league and were winning enough races to generate some fame. One year, when Russell's brother Rob was set to compete in the World Laser Championships in Dunedin, the local television station called Allan Coutts to say it wanted to run a segment on the promising Coutts brothers. Russell and Rob were to be filmed having a friendly rivalry on the water, with one boy in each boat. On the day of filming, cameras rolled as Russell and

Rob set sail. Things went smoothly for about one minute. Then an argument broke out and Rob slammed his boat into Russell's and jumped on board. The brothers were nose to nose, yelling. Then the fighting began, and the sailboat rocked and capsized, sending the boys overboard. They fought even as they hit the water.

That night, Allan Coutts, after a long day at work, sat down in front of the television to watch the story of his talented sons and the genteel sport of sailing. The clip started auspiciously, with the sun shining and the water glistening. Allan's boys looked adept in their boats—until, that is, the prizefighting began and the boys pulled each other into the drink.

Although the family never had a lot of money they always sailed, and soon it became clear that Russell was the Coutts to watch. He won a gold medal in the Finn class in the 1984 Olympic Games and earned his bachelor's degree in engineering from Auckland University in 1986. In 1987 stock markets crashed around the world and New Zealand's economy collapsed overnight. At the same time, incongruously, a merchant banker named Michael Fay, one of New Zealand's wealthiest men, announced he was forming a local team to challenge for the America's Cup. The country had no money, boatbuilding operations were done mostly out of small shops and garages, but Fay was a believer in New Zealand's homegrown talent. Fay chose as his skipper none other than a young, curly-haired Chris Dickson, and they built three fiberglass—rather than wood or aluminum—12 Meters, which came to be dubbed "Plastic Fantastics." This was the first time the hull of an America's Cup boat was made of fiberglass. Russell, who was twenty-five, sailed briefly with the team—with Dickson as his boss. The team stunned the sailing world with its performance, romping through the challenger series, winning thirty-seven of thirty-eight matches, halted only by Dennis Conner in the Louis Vuitton Cup finals.

With the economy still depressed and no work to be found, Allan Coutts told his son to give sailing a try for a few years, "as there's no work around anyway." Once he was done with that, the economy would come back and Russell could get a "real job." Russell was hired by Fay, now anointed "Sir Michael" by Queen Elizabeth for his contribution to sports, as backup helmsman for the next campaign, in 1992. Team New Zealand again made it to the finals of the Louis Vuitton Cup, where it faced American sailor and St. Francis favorite Paul Cayard as helmsman of the Italian syndicate, Il Moro di Venezia. After a controversy over Team New Zealand's bowsprit—the boat was being called a "skiff on steroids"—judges ruled that the Kiwis had to change the way they used the bowsprit when jibing, and the team lost, five races to three. Russell walked away from the loss with lessons learned. The crew had the talent to win but the men had not figured out how to make the right decisions at the right time. They hadn't become a team. In 1995 Coutts was named helmsman. He selected the crew and Team New Zealand became a formidable force. This time, the New Zealand boat *Black Magic* won the Louis Vuitton series with relative ease and went on to trounce the competition in the America's Cup, with a 5–0 win over Conner's *Stars & Stripes*. The syndicate, which had been organized by Peter Blake, a noted Kiwi yachtsman, had a group of managers that few on the team had ever heard of, let alone met. Heading into the 2000 defense of the Cup, Coutts and his teammates were told that if they won, they would be rewarded with management roles. Eleven syndicates from seven countries competed in Auckland in 2000, and it was Bertelli's Prada that went up against Team New Zealand for the America's Cup. Russell and his crew eliminated Prada 5–0 and he and the sailors were minted as national heroes. The America's Cup, held by the Royal New Zealand Yacht Squadron, infused the New Zealand economy with hundreds of millions of dollars, prompted the redevelopment of a run-down waterfront in Auckland, and gave rise to a thriving boatbuilding industry; and because of the newfound prestige and the country's natural beauty—the *Lord of the Rings* trilogy was filmed there—the islands became a popular holiday destination.

But the promises made to the team never materialized, and the sailors learned the details of their next challenge only by watching the press conference on TV. Russell, dispirited, ended up in line at the airport one morning with one of the team managers, who tried to go unnoticed. Finally, the man was forced to acknowledge that Russell was standing there and said, "How's it going?" Russell replied, "Not great. It's not working out." The manager said, "Well, you can always go away and do something else."

The comment hit like a punch. Russell had been mulling over the idea of chartering one of the old Team New Zealand Cup boats and raising his own money to form a syndicate. He began to put out feelers, and one of the first trips he made was to Geneva to meet with a Swiss group that had expressed interest. One of the first meetings was with Ernesto Bertarelli at his home on Lake Geneva.

When Russell told him about his plan to charter an old boat, Bertarelli looked at him and said, "Why would I be interested in buying old technology? And why would I be interested in buying the hardware if I couldn't buy the software?" Talks pivoted to how the Swiss billionaire could have both new technology and winning software—new boats *and* a new team.

Bertarelli, a hobbyist sailor, was stunned when he realized that Russell Coutts—considered one of the world's greatest sailors, having won back-to-back America's Cups—was considering leaving the Kiwis. In a matter of weeks, Bertarelli hired Russell and a handful of the Team New Zealanders. For Russell, it was the biggest decision of his life: have the freedom to build a team and get paid well but do it for Switzerland, or have no money and no say but work for his native land, New Zealand, where the management would benefit and, once the sailors reached the end of their sailing careers, there'd be nothing for them. They'd be expected to *go away and do something else.*

In a move fraught with risk, and met with public outcry and derision, Russell and his family packed up and moved to Geneva, knowing only their teammates. Although there had been other high-profile defections—Dickson sailed for Japan in 1992, Cayard for Italy—Coutts and company were New Zealand treasures. Unlike the others, they had *won* the Cup. They had started sailing as

Team Alinghi one year after other top teams started sailing. The decision paid off but exacted a price.

Russell, in his home on Tindalls Bay, a former village where the Maori used to fish for sharks, picked up the phone. It was time to call Larry Ellison.

The two had a few minutes of banter before getting to the point. Russell told Larry he was in talks with Patrizio Bertelli about Bertelli's next campaign, but that he hadn't made a formal commitment. Larry said he wanted to challenge for the Cup and wanted Russell to head his team.

"Well, I'm interested in doing the next one," Russell said. "I don't want to sit another one out."

"What are your terms?" Larry asked.

Russell outlined his financial terms and management terms, saying, "I need to be the CEO. I need to be in control."

Larry listened to the amount Russell requested and paused. "That's a lot of money," he said. But Russell was the guy who had never lost a single race in the America's Cup. He was the modern-day Charlie Barr—separated by a century. Barr, a commercial fisherman and yachtsman born in Scotland, was hired by the American banker J. P. Morgan to sail for America against a Scottish syndicate. Barr repeatedly defeated none other than Sir Thomas Lipton.

"Okay, we have a deal," Larry said.

"We have a deal?" Russell said.

"Yes."

Russell was stunned. Larry was certainly direct. There was no gamesmanship, no back-and-forth. But, Larry did make one thing very clear. While Russell had proved himself over the years and deserved to be rewarded for his successes, he would have control of the team only if he continued his winning ways and won the America's Cup again, this time for Oracle Team USA.

In the first two campaigns, Larry had operated under the Japanese business principle *kaizen*, a term used to describe continuous improvement or incremental change through constant work. Larry was starting over with someone who had never lost an America's Cup race. "I tried *kaizen,*" Larry said, "It didn't work. So we're making radical changes, starting with a new leader for our team."

The two losses had taught many lessons. Larry found out the hard way that personal loyalties sometimes got in the way. He had relied on the people he knew and had sailed with for years.

"Sometimes your relationships, your friendships, get in the way of making the right decisions and prevent you from picking the people who allow you to compete and win at the highest level," he said. "After losing twice, I'm putting personal loyalties aside and picking you—the guy who beat us. I also have decided I need to put the time in and be a part of the team." With the first campaign, Larry was never a part of the team. With the second campaign, he was involved at the beginning during the regattas in San Francisco and Newport, but then lost control after the team moved to Europe.

Larry had come to realize that it was important for him to get to know the team, and for the team to know him.

"I detached from the first campaign because of 9/11 and the Internet stock market bubble bursting," he said to Russell. "But there's no excuse for the second campaign. I thought we had the right formula when we won in San Francisco and Newport with Chris Dickson as tactician and Gavin Brady driving. But then Chris decided to drive, Gavin left the team, and the die was cast. Everything depended on Chris, who was at the helm of the team and the boat. I made a mistake. I had no Plan B. I should never have let Gavin leave."

He explained to Russell that when he sailed with Dickson on *Sayonara,* he drove and Dickson was tactician. "Whenever we were under pressure during the start or the first upwind leg he made good calls. We always won. He did a great job as tactician."

Larry paused. "Obviously there is a lot more pressure when you're driving during the America's Cup than there is as tactician during a maxi world championship. I made a mistake. I take responsibility for screwing that up." Larry noted that when he made mistakes at Oracle, he learned from his mistakes and fixed the problem.

"I don't have to run the team," he said, "but this time I have to be a part of it starting at the beginning and going to the end."

Russell was impressed. Larry was not the swashbuckling, win-at-all-costs warrior he was usually portrayed as being. He agreed that it was important for Larry to be a part of the team, to see the issues firsthand, to understand what they were doing well and not doing well. "That way, you won't get secondhand or thirdhand information and then try to make a decision based on that," Russell said.

Larry laughed and said, "By being a part of the team, being close to the team, I'm less likely to ask you to do something stupid."

Russell said that he planned to get the Oracle racing crew out competing in RC44s, ultrahigh-performance monohulls that he had designed (RC stood for Russell Coutts). The boats were used in one of the most competitive series of weeklong regattas on the international yacht racing circuit, held in a range of challenging venues. Russell proposed that he drive during the professional match races held during the week and Larry could drive the amateur owner fleet races on the weekend.

Larry was silent. Finally he said, "Russell, I don't know if I want to fly to Sweden for a weekend of fleet racing against a bunch of amateur drivers. I've already done that."

Larry felt that, in sport as in life, you work your way through your weight class and then you move up. "I've raced against Hasso Plattner a dozen times and won them all. What does that prove?" he said. "I'd rather lose to Dean Barker or Ben Ainslie or Jimmy Spithill than beat a Hasso a hundred more times. That's the only way I'm going to get any better." That was the weight class Larry wanted to fight in.

"Okay, okay," Russell chuckled. "You can drive in the professional match races too." But, he warned, it meant that Larry would have to practice, and practice a lot.

"I'm there. I'll put in the time," Larry said. "Just tell me when and where—send me the dates."

Hanging up, Russell knew that his contract still had to be drawn up, and that there could always be surprises. But he had a good feeling he was teaming up with the right guy this time. He already knew the sailor he wanted to hire first, an Aussie with an easygoing disposition off the water but a killer instinct on. A guy who reminded him a lot of himself as a young man.

For now, though, he had to deliver the news to his wife, Jenny, who had visions of a quiet life away from the stress of an America's Cup campaign. The two were married in 1999 and Jenny had weathered the fallout from his leaving Team New Zealand to join Alinghi and lived through the legal problems with the Swiss billionaire.

"I am a professional sailor," Russell said to Jenny, sitting down. "This is what I do."

She said, "Well, at least we know nothing can be as bad as what you've already been through."

"Yes," Russell said. "How bad can this next one be?"

20

Woodside, California

Summer 2007

L ARRY SAT AT HIS DESK, made from the reclaimed stump of a massive sequoia tree cut down a century ago, and read over the Protocol that had just been released by Ernesto Bertarelli to govern the next America's Cup. The Protocol was sent out to interested parties and past syndicates, and defined in detail all the rules before the next race.

Is this a joke? Larry wondered to himself.

Glasses on, he read the document again. Among the more eye-opening points were:

Umpires and race officials would be employees of Alinghi's management company, and could reject or eject competitors at any time.

Alinghi would set the rules for racing and could restrict or sanction competitors as it saw fit.

Alinghi would select the umpires on the water and the jury who would judge the races.

Larry looked at the named Challenger of Record, Club Nautico Español de Vela. He had never heard of it. Under the Deed of Gift that governs the America's Cup, the Defender must accept the first valid challenge from a legitimate yacht club. The club to issue the first valid challenge then becomes the Challenger of Record. The Defender and the Challenger of Record then jointly negotiate and agree upon the Protocol that governs the next America's Cup race. The Defender usually picks the Challenger of Record it wants for the next America's Cup by prearranging for the challenge to be made a few moments after the final race of the current America's Cup.

Larry hit the button on the phone on his desk for his longtime assistant Joyce Higashi and asked her to get Bertarelli on the line. Their friendship, cemented over a shared interest in sailing and a desire to modernize the America's Cup, had ended years before. Larry had not forgotten how Bertarelli insisted he'd won the UBS Cup in Newport when Larry had won two of first three races with one more race to go. The men were civil when they saw each other, but any pretense of a friendship was gone. Larry was amused by how Bertarelli had convinced himself that he was a great sailor, despite evidence to the contrary, and now he wanted to use a rigged 33rd America's Cup to convince everyone else. One of Larry's favorite sociobiology maxims was, "The brain's primary purpose is deception, and the primary person to be deceived is the owner."

With Bertarelli on the line, Larry began by congratulating him on his second America's Cup win. Larry then said, as casually as he could, that he had read the Protocol and he thought that none of the other teams would want to enter a race they had no chance of winning.

"Ernesto, why are you doing this?" Larry asked.

After a moment, Bertarelli replied, "Larry, wouldn't you want a set of rules like this if you could get them?"

"No—I don't think so," Larry said, speaking slowly, still in disbelief. "Why would I enter a race that I couldn't lose? Winning is meaningless if you can't lose." He went on, "Your rules say you can disqualify a competitor at any time, and you can change the rules at any time. That means there are no rules at all."

"I think you *would* want these rules," Bertarelli insisted. "Everyone would."

After a long pause Larry continued, "Ernesto, even the umpires on the water work for you. If the referees in the NBA worked for me I could easily break Wilt Chamberlain's single-game scoring record of one hundred points, all from the free-throw line. But nobody would be fooled into thinking I'm a great basketball player."

"You're just upset because it's not you doing this," Bertarelli said.

Larry then suggested they go back to the rules of the 32nd Cup. "They're fine. Why change them?"

Ernesto said, "I prefer the new rules."

Realizing the conversation was going nowhere, Larry ended the call quickly but coolly. He wasn't about to hint at his next step.

Larry liked having opponents, even enemies. "I learn a lot about myself when I compete against somebody," he later said to Melanie. "I measure myself by winning and losing. Every shot in basketball is clearly judged by an orange hoop—make or miss. The hoop makes it difficult to deceive yourself." He thought about his love of driving fast and flying his own planes. Flying was all about being in control. But without a cloud, there was no sense of speed. Driving a car one hundred miles an hour was great, but it didn't require a lot of skill. What he liked best was being on a racetrack and breaking late into a turn, passing another car, and accelerating ahead of the competition. Right now Bertarelli was out front and in control, but Larry had every intention of changing that.

Larry was certain that Bertarelli had orchestrated the one-sided rules out of fear. In the next Cup, Bertarelli would be competing against Russell Coutts. Before going to sleep, Larry reviewed the latest information he was getting on Alinghi's chosen yacht club, Club Nautico Español de Vela. He had never heard of the club because apparently it had been created just a few days before the end of the last America's Cup for the sole purpose of becoming the Challenger of Record. The "club" had no clubhouse and no boats. It seemed to Larry that Bertarelli had created this fake club so he could be both the Challenger and the Defender and negotiate with himself over the rules for the 33rd America's Cup. But if the Challenger of Record were found to be invalid, Bertarelli would have to accept the next legitimate challenge he received.

Larry loved the idea of watching Bertarelli receive a challenge from the Golden Gate Yacht Club and insist he already had a challenger. Larry would then respond, *We don't think you do.* And if Oracle did become the challenger and the two parties failed to agree on the terms of the race—at this point he couldn't imagine agreeing with Bertarelli on the color of an orange—the rules would revert to what was called a Deed of Gift or "DoG" match. In a DoG match just two teams—challenger and defender—fought it out for best two out of three races, winner take all. In such a match, the teams were freed from most of the rules that limited what type of boat could be designed and raced.

Believing that the Golden Gate Yacht Club would ultimately replace Alinghi's bogus challenger, Larry began to think about what kind of boat they would need to build for what would surely be a DoG match. Larry then made a decision: they needed to immediately get under contract the world's best multihull designers. The battle, as he imagined it, would be fought in multihulls—which are much faster than monohulls—and he wanted all of the top designers locked up and working for him. Larry envisioned a boat the likes of which had never been seen before in America's Cup history: a predator on the water.

It was around 11 p.m. on Sunday, July 8, 2007, when Oracle Racing's rules adviser Tom Ehman, who had served as director of external affairs in the 2003 and 2007 campaigns, got a call from Ian "Fresh" Burns, a good friend, a world-class sailor and navigator, and the mechanical engineer who had managed Oracle Racing's boat design operations. Ehman, Burns, and Burns's girlfriend Judy Sim, the chief marketing officer at Oracle Corporation, were scheduled to have dinner at their favorite restaurant, Lambrusquería, the America's Cup hangout in central Valencia, also known as the Docks. Burns had been doing an Oracle Racing presentation in Palma de Mallorca and was coming directly from the airport, and Sim was taking a taxi to the restaurant from their flat minutes away. They were in Valencia to wrap up racing operations after the Cup.

"Coffee up," Burns said to Ehman by way of hello.

"What's going on?" Ehman said, having gotten to the restaurant early, when diners were just arriving.

"You're going to get a call from Melinda Erkelens," Burns said. "We're going to file a challenge and Larry has given strict instructions not to say a word to anyone else about this."

"Okay," Ehman said, moving into his war plan mode. "We obviously can't do this at a restaurant. We need phones, computers, fax machines." They quickly decided they'd head back to Burns and Sim's apartment, and Erkelens, still general counsel for the team, would meet them there. Ehman ordered a double espresso at the bar before hailing a cab.

Ehman was already thinking strategy. The Protocol produced by Alinghi was the talk of the town, having ignited a firestorm in the America's Cup community. Bertelli of Prada, among others, said the new rules set the stage for the "Alinghi Cup," not the America's Cup. A meeting had been called at Luna Rossa's base for the next night to discuss the rules and a nascent belief among syndicate heads and sailors that the challenging club was a sham created by Alinghi. If they could prove that Club Naútico Español de Vela was invalid, Bertarelli would have to look elsewhere. Ehman had no doubt that Larry intended to be the first to challenge, but this meant moving fast.

Ehman, who grew up on a small lake outside Ann Arbor, Michigan, where he'd spent his every free minute sailing or playing hockey, was boyish at fifty-three. He had been involved in ten America's Cup campaigns, starting in 1980 when he served as rules adviser to the New York Yacht Club and its defending teams. He had worked for teams from San Diego to New York and back to San Francisco, and he had been traded by Conner when he ran out of money, to Paul Cayard for the *AmericaOne* syndicate. Ehman knew the America's Cup game, players, rules, and history better than anyone else and was adrenalized with four hours of sleep and constantly changing time zones. His involvement with Oracle Racing had begun in 2000, when he was doing marketing for Formula One racing in Germany. He got a call at 4 a.m. from a group of *Sayonara* sailors in Antigua, where the team had just won the Caribbean's biggest regatta.

"Larry is going to file a challenge for the America's Cup," said Jim Nicholas, a *Sayonara* team member.

"You guys must be fully on the piss," Ehman had said, trying not to wake his wife, Leslie.

"No, no, no," Nicholas laughed. "We haven't been drinking—well, not much. You gotta get to Newport. They want to hire you."

A week later, Ehman met with Bill and Melinda Erkelens in their rented cottage in Newport. Ehman, with the Erkelenses and Chris Dickson, sat at the edge of a bed with a small card table before them and began to map out what needed to be done to compete for the America's Cup. It was Oracle Racing 1.0, and the Silicon Valley garage was a seaside shack.

In Valencia, Ehman jumped out of the taxi and buzzed Sim's apartment. Burns was on his way, and Melinda Erkelens arrived just as he was closing the gate.

The first call Ehman made was to his wife, to tell her he wasn't coming home that night. "It's on the up-and-up," he said, "but I can't tell you why."

In the one-bedroom apartment, Ehman took over the small dining table. Erkelens sat on the couch, blanketed in documents, and Sim, after ordering food from a restaurant downstairs, was on a sofa nearby. Ehman, who had been through a lawsuit when Conner was challenged by Michael Fay, knew the Deed of Gift the way Tugsy knew carbon fiber, Larry knew database systems, Norbert knew radiators, and Burns knew velocity prediction programs.

The America's Cup had had its share of legal wrangling and accusations of unfair play, starting with the very first race in 1851, when members of the British fleet who had been beaten by *America* argued the U.S. schooner had an unfair advantage and may have had a secret motor. Fay's challenge in 1988 involved his suing the San Diego Yacht Club syndicate Sail America, run by Conner when Ehman was Conner's rules adviser. Fay's New Zealand team was successful in getting the court to order an unwanted Deed of Gift challenge against Conner's team. Fay had prepared for his challenge by building a huge Bruce Farr-designed 130-foot mono-hull, *KZ 1*, nicknamed the "Big Boat." When Conner announced he would defend the Cup in a sixty-foot catamaran called *Stars & Stripes,* Fay sued again, arguing that the Deed of Gift prohibited the use of multihulls and required both parties to use "like or similar" boats. Fay also asserted that the deed allowed the challenger to dictate the size and type of yacht to be used by the defender. The New York Supreme Court eventually ordered the parties to sail with their respective boats, stating in its decision, "Neither this court's order, nor the terms of the Deed of Gift incorporated therein, so unequivocally state that multihulled boats are prohibited or that a defender must face the challenger in a like or similar yacht." Conner's catamaran easily beat the Big Boat.

Having been through the court process before, Ehman was versed in what to do. Had he not been through it, the group would have spent weeks just trying to understand the process and possibilities. The first thing Ehman needed to do was come up with the language for the challenge. He had a trove of computer files and unearthed the 1988 Fay challenge. Talking with Melinda Erkelens, Ehman started by reiterating what they already knew: the Spanish yacht club, formed right before Alinghi won the America's Cup, had no clubhouse, no members, no boats—"but, importantly," he said in a eureka moment, "they have never had a regatta on the 'arm of the sea'—as the Deed of Gift specifies." Ehman agreed with Larry that Berteralli had set up the yacht club "basically to challenge himself," so he could negotiate with himself and effectively dictate the Rules of Protocol. Erkelens and Ehman talked about the likelihood of Bertarelli rejecting their challenge and agreed that they needed to be ready to sue in the New

York Supreme Court. From what Ehman knew, the Swiss billionaire was not the type to compromise or capitulate.

It was now 1:30 a.m. and Ehman sipped coffee and marveled, saying, "Ernesto is going for the most audacious power grab in the history of the Cup. We need to stop this lucky sperm club guy from hijacking the Cup." In Ehman's mind, Bertarelli was trying to become the "Bernie Ecclestone of the Cup." Having worked for Formula One, Ehman knew Ecclestone, a fisherman's son who became England's fourth-richest man. Ecclestone had done a deal with Formula One where he went around to different teams, when Formula One was still like a country fair, and said he would set up a circuit with sponsors. He got everyone to agree to a program, asked for the commercial rights—which at the time were worth next to nothing—and said he would pay the teams and build it into something worthwhile. Ecclestone built it into one of the greatest properties in sports and he became known as "F1 Supremo."

"Ernesto," Ehman said, "is trying to become the 'AC Supremo.'" He wanted to set all of the rules and reap all of the profits. As he studied the papers and jotted down notes, he heard Sim and Erkelens working on another critical part of the challenge. Sim was talking to Norbert in San Francisco.

Norbert was in the middle of a meeting at the Golden Gate Yacht Club when he saw Sim was calling. He answered quietly so as not to disrupt the meeting and headed in the direction of the small upstairs deck.

"Norbert, I need to talk to you about something," Sim said.

"Just one minute," Norbert said, stepping outside and closing the door behind him. "What's up?"

"We are going to race again," Sim said, catching Norbert by surprise. Considering how badly the 2007 Cup had ended, Norbert had been certain Larry wouldn't be back in.

"Wow, that is news," Norbert said, watching a fishing boat pick up speed as it left the San Francisco Marina yacht harbor. The hiring of Russell Coutts had not yet been announced and Norbert hadn't heard a word from Larry on his feelings about doing a third Cup campaign.

"There's something else," Sim said. "Larry is going to file papers to be Bertarelli's Challenger of Record for the thirty-third America's Cup."

"I thought he already had a challenger," Norbert said, having read Alinghi's Protocol, published two days after the Swiss team's second Cup victory on July 3. He knew that a Spanish yacht club was named as challenger and Valencia was assumed to be the venue.

Sim said Larry didn't believe the challenger was legitimate and would fight to have the Golden Gate Yacht Club named as Challenger of Record.

Norbert whistled. The America's Cup, the jewel in sailing's crown, conjuring images of lords and counts, of Morgans and Vanderbilts, seemed to invite more name-calling, mudslinging, undermining, spying, and lawsuits than anything else he'd ever encountered.

"What do we need to do?" Norbert asked, looking in at the membership meeting.

Sim explained that the Golden Gate Yacht Club had to file the challenge. "Melinda is here with me in Valencia and she's putting together the papers as we speak."

"I'm your man," Norbert said. A few minutes later, the two hung up and Norbert headed back inside. Walking past the bar and toward the bathroom, he stopped to look at a photomontage of Ruth Gordon Schnapp, one of the founders of the club, holding a trophy and standing next to a modest boat she had loved. She had always worried that the club was not going to make it.

Norbert walked out to the main room and looked straight ahead at Alcatraz, then over to the stunning Golden Gate Bridge, which had opened just two years before the Puerta de Oro. The now iconic 2.7-mile span from San Francisco to Marin opened in May 1937, and saw more than two hundred thousand people cross by foot or roller skates the day before traffic was opened to cars. Norbert had a feeling this little club, in the shadows of that famous bridge, would one day have its own place in history.

Burns finally made it to the Valencia apartment at around 2 a.m. His flight had been delayed for hours.

"Fresh, not to put any pressure on you, but the boat we arrive at the starting line with has to match the dimensions you conjure up tonight," Ehman said to his friend, who had started with the Oracle Racing team in October 2000, was a navigator in the 2003 America's Cup, and served as design coordinator for the 2007 campaign. The boat specifications had to be laid out in the original challenge and couldn't be amended, according to America's Cup rules.

Burns, who grew up in Sydney, Australia—and had earned his nickname "Fresh" as a kid delivering milk—spent his time at the airport considering the type of boat they would want to challenge Alinghi in. The only constant with the America's Cup yachts was change. Different "class rules" were used to regulate the size and, to varying degrees, the design of the boats—hence their performance.

In the 1930s, the J-class yachts were large, powerful sloops (single masted) that came in at about 125 feet in overall length (LOA) and around 84 feet on the waterline (LWL), with exceedingly tall (for the size of the yacht) 165-foot masts. The J boats were sponsored by some of the world's wealthiest men, including Lipton and Vanderbilt.

When racing resumed in 1958, after the wartime hiatus, it was contested in significantly smaller and less expensive 12 Meter–class yachts. Also sloop-rigged, the mast was a much more modest 85 feet, and the 12s ranged in size from 65 feet to 75 feet LOA and about 45 feet LWL.

After the controversial 1988 DoG match between Fay's Royal New Zealand Yacht Squadron and the defending San Diego Yacht Club's Team Dennis Conner, a new class rule was worked out by an international committee of America's Cup designers and sailors. Dubbed the International America's Cup Class (IACC), it was based on the 12-Meter class but had an updated formula. The IACC rule produced slightly larger but relatively lighter and much more powerful monohull sloops, significantly faster than the 12-Meters. Considered cutting edge at the time, the IACC yachts first raced for the 1992 Cup in San Diego, won by Bill Koch's *America Cubed* representing the San Diego Yacht Club, which defeated Italy's team Il Moro di Venezia (with Cayard). The IACC rule had a twenty-year run. With minor amendments, the original 1992 IACC rule was used for the 1995, 2000, 2003, and 2007 Cups, producing one hundred yachts.

Burns knew that with the option of a monohull or a multihull, a multihull would be favored, as multihulls were to monohulls what thoroughbreds were to camels: sleeker and faster. During races held by the New York Yacht Club off Long Island Sound in the late 1870s, boatbuilder Nathanael Herreshoff showed up with a catamaran called *Amarayllis,* which handily defeated all of the monohulls and prompted yacht club members to ban the boat. A story that appeared at the time related: "The *Amaryllis* was sailed by Capt. Nat two hundred miles from Bristol to New York in the remarkable time of fourteen hours. Then he entered her in the Centennial Regatta and beat all comers with this radical sailing machine. The utter shock to the other contestants sailing much larger boats led to disqualifications of the *Amaryllis* and the barring of catamarans." Only once in the history of the America's Cup had a multihull sailed, and that was Conner's in 1988.

Burns, who set up his papers in the small bedroom of their rented flat, made his first call to Michel Kermarac, a member of the Oracle Racing design team and a Frenchman considered the best in the game at predicting the performance of a boat and designing a boat's appendages, including rudder, keel, and bulb. Kermarac, referred to as a "genius" by team members, had been working in Europe designing sixty-foot multihulls, a light and powerful class of catamaran, for a new series of regattas.

Burns and Kermarac talked on the phone and quickly agreed that if Alinghi would come in with a catamaran, then they needed an even stronger hand.

By early afternoon the next day, Monday, Kermarac produced the dimensions for the Challenger of Record submission: ninety feet long on the waterline, ninety feet at the boat's widest point. In the America's Cup, part of the trick was to make the boat sail longer than it measured. Kermerac's idea for a stronger hand was a trimaran, which has three hulls and which when measured on the waterline would meet the regulation of under ninety feet. But its outer hulls would measure closer to 113 feet. The farther a designer could get the bow away from the stern, the less suction—or drag—there would be in the water. By anyone's standards, what Kermarac had drafted was an imposing boat. More important, it was seen as a boat that could do well in any type of breeze.

Before a challenge could be filed, however, Burns was given another set of strict orders by the boss. "We need to corner the market, lock up every talented multihull designer," Larry said. "By the time Ernesto realizes he is vulnerable, all the top designers will be working for us."

At around the same time the design specifications were done Larry called Ehman.

"Have you got the challenge ready yet?" he asked.

"No," Ehman said, looking at the bedraggled group. "Not yet." They were all in Fresh's apartment, having pulled an all-nighter, and Norbert was putting the documents together in San Francisco. They were looking at flights to get to Geneva the next day and found there were no direct flights.

Larry told Ehman to talk to his secretary. He would send a plane and it could be in Valencia the next morning. Before hanging up, Larry said, "When you serve papers at Société Nautique de Genève, take pictures. Get it notarized. Document everything."

After working for two days and two nights straight Ehman had a press release drafted. The major point to make was that the Deed of Gift required the challenging yacht club to hold an annual regatta on an arm of the sea. This was intended to allow entries only from big, open ocean clubs, rather than clubs on lakes. Ehman wrote that Alinghi and the Spanish club had failed to come up with a specific date for the Cup, a location, or a class of boat. "Virtually all Challenger rights are eliminated and total control of the event and its rules are granted to Alinghi," Ehman wrote, "altering the very nature of the competition by giving unprecedented and unfair advantages to the Defender."

In all of the years Ehman had been involved in the America's Cup, he had never seen a power grab like this. It was as if Bertarelli had looked at the rules at the end of the 32nd Cup and had torn them up. Ehman had talked with all of the major players from other syndicates and the fear was that the event would go on, and it would be called the America's Cup, but the sailors would know it wasn't the real thing and sponsors and fans would come to feel the same way. It would be a rigged match.

Ehman had attended the Monday night meeting at Luna Rossa's base and was in the awkward position of not saying a word about their challenge to the other teams. But he walked away with strong letters of support, including one written by Vincenzo Onorato, head of the Italian team Mascalzone Latino:

Alinghi claims the right to choose, at its sole discretion, the regatta judges, the committee, the umpires, and the measurers, even going so far as to state that they must be its employees. Alinghi, again at its sole discretion, claims the right to accept a challenge or to penalize a rival and to change the rules at any time. Little wonder this protocol was immediately opposed by seven syndicates.

Faced with a stacked deck, top-level syndicates will stay away. You can argue it is still better to join and hope for change, but that's how a lamb thinks before it gets into bed with a wolf. We might as well rename it the Alinghi Cup now. What looks like a race will in fact be a procession. Ernesto Bertarelli's vision turns out to be a cynical marketing ploy that gives his commercial subsidiary total control.

The organizers of the Louis Vuitton Cup also voiced their displeasure, announcing they were not going to be a part of the regatta, which they had run since 1983. There were simmering problems with Bertarelli and they felt as though Alinghi had treated them as a source of money, not as a collaborator. In the past, Louis Vuitton had run the media center parties and helped promote and guide the look and theme. When they heard of Bertarelli's new rules and the outcry from other yacht clubs they said they'd had enough.

The plan now was for Ehman and the others to take Larry's plane to Geneva on Wednesday. Jane Eagleson, Oracle Racing's communications director, would fly in on Larry's plane and she and Burns would work on a press list.

"We have to be ready, because the shit is going to hit the fan," Ehman said, pleased at the prospect.

On Wednesday, the group boarded Larry's jet in Valencia for Geneva. Arriving in Geneva, they piled into the back of a black SUV and headed to a law office in downtown Geneva to get papers notarized. It was a hot summer afternoon, and they were greeted in the otherwise empty office by a tall, thin man wearing a black suit, white shirt, black tie, and somber expression. Ehman's first thought was *undertaker*. Ehman knew that Ernesto's yacht club, Société Nautique de Genève, had a regatta on Wednesday nights, so the club would be open late. But the notary was painfully slow. Finally, with everything stamped and copied and assembled into a booklet, he told Ehman it would be 800 Swiss francs.

"Just bill our law firm," Ehman said, having enlisted the New York firm of Latham & Watkins, which he had used in the 1988 Conner versus Fay lawsuit.

"We only take cash," the notary said.

"I don't have that kind of cash on me," Ehman said.

The man stared impassively, and the forever cool Ehman had to think fast.

"Okay, we'll have to go to two ATMs to get the cash, and you are coming with us," Ehman said to the notary as the group rushed out of the office. After the second withdrawal of the daily maximum amount, Ehman sat in the back of the sedan and counted the money for the undertaker. The driver studied the situation in the rearview mirror and asked Ehman, "Would you like me to step out of the car, sir?"

Ehman laughed.

They arrived at the steps of Alinghi's yacht club, Société Nautique de Genève, founded in 1872 on the shores of Lake Geneva. Ehman, a founding member of the Gstaad Yacht Club, not far away, was known by the club's general manager and was greeted warmly. Ehman and the others, including the notary, were asked if they'd like to head upstairs, as a board meeting was taking place and they might want to say hello.

"I know you know Fred Meyer, our vice commodore," the general manager said to Ehman.

Ehman, noticing the America's Cup trophy on display, thanked the general manager and handed him the notarized letter. The man smiled as if he were receiving a commendation. Ehman quickly snapped the first picture with his small Canon camera. As the general manager continued to read, his expression changed. Ehman snapped the second picture.

The general manager was reading from the challenge cover letter. It read:

We respectfully submit that the challenge from [the Spanish club] CNEV is invalid. Among other deficiencies, it is not from a bona fide yacht club, but from an entity organized in the form of a yacht club only a few days before the challenge was accepted by SNG, and which has never had an annual regatta on an open water course on the sea or an arm of the sea as required by the Deed of Gift. It is also apparent that this "Challenger of Record" has not performed the duties of the Challenger as contemplated by the Deed of Gift, but has simply delegated to the Defender the authority to determine all of the "conditions" governing the match. This undermines the fundamental purpose of the Deed of Gift to preserve this competition as a Challenge Cup. Attached is a bona fide challenge from the Golden Gate Yacht Club (GGYC). GGYC hereby demands recognition as the legitimate Challenger of Record for the 33rd America's Cup.

Ehman and the others bade their farewells, turned on their heels, and bolted to the waiting car. Ehman called Eagleson and Burns and said the papers had been served. It was time to alert the global press. The notary was dropped back near his office, giving a hint of a smile suggesting the adventure was appreciated.

Ehman and the others headed to a Chinese restaurant down the street from their hotel. By the time they had ordered their food, cell phones had begun to ring—and didn't stop.

Less than three weeks later, after Bertarelli rejected the bid by BMW Oracle Racing to be named as the Challenger of Record, Larry sued in New York's Supreme Court, the trial court where the Deed of Gift is registered, calling Bertarelli's challenging yacht club a "sham." In the suit, the Golden Gate Yacht Club asked that Société Nautique de Genève void the challenge of the Spanish club, declare the Golden Gate Yacht Club as the legitimate Challenger of Record, and work with the Golden Gate Yacht Club to create a new protocol.

Bertarelli responded with a press conference, lashing out at the challenge. "It is a shame that having failed to win the America's Cup on the water, [Larry] now wants to win in a court of law," he said. He insisted that there were precedents in the 156-year history of the Cup of a new club challenging and a protocol being signed with neither a time nor a place set for the next event and said that the new club was organizing two open-sea regattas in northern Spain to be held in coming months. Bertarelli declared, "It is not possible that we will lose. We have the best lawyers." Bertarelli also let Russell Coutts have it, saying, "I paid him millions, but he had other projects that he thought were more important."

In a Swiss newspaper article Bertarelli, the fourth-richest man in Europe, called Larry, his former friend, a "loser" who had failed on the water and would fail in the courts as well. Before long, there was talk of getting Juan Carlos, the king of Spain, to negotiate a truce between the warring parties.

Larry held his own press conference, saying, "All we want is a fair set of rules for the next America's Cup. If Alinghi will agree to use the same rules we sailed under during the last Cup, we will immediately drop our suit, enter the next Cup, and compete as one of the challengers." When Larry was asked about Bertarelli calling him a "loser," he responded, "Well, we raced against each other a couple of times. The first time was in San Francisco and *he* lost. Then we raced again in Newport and *he* lost again. And then *he* quit. He refused to do any of the additional owner-driver races we had planned. I think calling me a loser says a lot more about him than it does about me."

21

Bangkok, Thailand, to Cagliari, Italy

November 2007 to Spring 2008

I**T WAS LATE** fall and Norbert was in Bangkok on business when he got the news he had been anxiously waiting for, knowing a court decision was imminent on Golden Gate's claim to be Alinghi's Challenger of Record.

"We won!" Judy Sim said. "We are the Challenger of Record. The court concluded that the Golden Gate is the legitimate challenger."

Norbert was thrilled. The Golden Gate Yacht Club had been to Auckland. It had been to Valencia. Now it was being heard in New York's Supreme Court and it looked as if it would be getting another chance at that elusive Cup. "Third time's going to be a charm," Norbert said, as his radiator buddies lingered nearby.

It was a huge win for Oracle Racing, after motions and cross motions and letters from seven challengers strongly opposed to Alinghi's new protocol. Russell Coutts had been trying hard to negotiate a settlement based on reinstating the old protocol, something all of the challenging teams would willingly accept. He had even written to his former boss, Bertarelli, and his best friend and sailing buddy, Brad Butterworth, who remained with Alinghi: *"Time is running out, and a key requirement for all competitors is certainty,"* Coutts wrote. *"If there are any points in this proposal that are unacceptable to you we would ask that you negotiate these with us as soon as possible. We are approaching a point where we have to know what sort of race we will be competing in. It is simply not feasible to carry on trying to be prepared for both a conventional regatta and a Deed of Gift race. Accordingly, we request that you indicate if you accept [our challenge] as soon as possible."*

Alinghi didn't reply. But Bertarelli continued to criticize Coutts in the press and blame him for Larry's decision to sue, saying, "Russell Coutts wins by destroying," pointing to his defection from Team New Zealand to Alinghi. "He destroyed Team New Zealand and he tried to destroy Alinghi," Bertarelli went on. "And now he is destroying the America's Cup. He is destroying the game that gave him everything."

In the eighteen-page judgment in favor of the Golden Gate, Justice Herman Cahn found that the Spanish yacht club had no clubhouse, no telephone number, no members, no Web site, and no races on the all-important arm of the sea. He wrote: "The deed expressly requires one specific attribute, namely, that the club have an annual regatta."

Norbert returned to the meeting, where he had been listening to colleagues talk about problems customers were having with aluminum radiators. A handful of the top radiator distributors from across the United States and Canada were in Thailand to attend the meetings and Norbert was there in part to talk with the company that made the radiators sold by Alouis in San Francisco.

Norbert figured that while Fresh Burns and Tugsy and the Oracle Racing designers and engineers focused on the latest in boat design, he needed to concentrate on the inner workings of cars. As the industry had moved away from copper and brass radiators to an aluminum core with a plastic tank, complaints had come in about leaks caused by decomposition from electrolysis. Aluminum was cheaper and lighter, and had been used in radiators starting in the 1980s, incrementally at first, with about ten percent of the radiator composed of aluminum, and the rest made up of brass or copper.

More aluminum was added each year, until radiators were made entirely from the metal.

The goal of the annual meeting in Bangkok, with distributors from New York, Seattle, Los Angeles, Miami, and Canada, was to find ways to improve the overall quality of radiators being made in Thailand and to stop the leaks.

"One thing we do in the boating industry to protect against corrosion is to put zinc anodes in boat cooling systems," Norbert said at the meeting. "These 'sacrificial zincs' deter corrosion. We should take zinc anodes and put them inside the radiators, as a cheap kind of insurance policy." The electrolysis current would be drawn to the anodes instead of the radiator. "And it's cheap, a dollar a radiator," Norbert said. The idea was well received and the manufacturer agreed to start putting zinc anodes in the radiators to absorb the electrical currents.

At the end of the meeting, Norbert and his radiator pals agreed to meet back at the hotel bar. Even some of the mechanics he met in Thailand knew of the America's Cup and congratulated him when they learned he was a commodore.

That night, Norbert and his colleagues hit the bars in Bangkok. Norbert's back was killing him and there was no aspirin to be found. Sitting at the bar, self-medicating on beer, he caught his reflection in the colored glass. His hair was thinning and he looked enviously at tough-guy baldpate types such as Bruce Willis and Ben Kingsley. As he downed his final Stella Artois he made a decision. With buddies in tow, he located a barbershop, sat down in a chair, and signaled that he wanted it all shaved off. He looked at his bald head in the mirror and smiled. It was a defiant act, like joining the military while still a senior in high school. Something about being a rebel suited him.

The spring of 2008 saw Larry fulfilling one of his dreams: he was in Cagliari, Italy, sailing in the most competitive series of races of his life.

He was at the helm of an RC44, with Russell Coutts as his tactician. The Cagliari Cup was considered the number one professional match racing event of the spring, and it drew the best sailors from across the world, with everyone competing in identical one-design boats. Many of the sailors were America's Cup veterans, Olympic medalists, or both.

The winds were strong in the waters off the coast of Sardinia, and Larry was the only nonprofessional helmsman in the regatta. He was competing against sailing's superstars including the British three-time Olympic gold medalist, Ben Ainslie, and his new Oracle Racing teammate, Jimmy Spithill, who hadn't lost a single match race that year.

This week Spithill was competing in Cagliari against both of his bosses—he had been Russell's very first hire—honing his skills in a range of regattas and types of boats, as was standard practice for the world's top sailors. In an interview prior to the start of the Cagliari Cup, Spithill said, "This is simply the best level you can get in match racing, worldwide. You have match race world champions, America's Cup skippers, world champions of several classes. It's just very tough. The boats are great, and very fast. Thanks to their speed, there are always great passing opportunities. It's very exciting."

There were ten RC44 teams in the competition, and Larry would be facing a world-class professional helmsman in every race. News that Larry would drive against the pros was met with more than a little skepticism. A few years earlier, when Larry entered his first professional match race regatta, he managed to win only two of seven races, prompting a San Francisco television journalist, reveling in his losses, to say, "Larry Ellison is very good at helping his sailing team by writing checks, but he's not very good at driving the boat." Larry, who happened to see the clip on TV, shot back, "What are you good at—asshole?" He clicked off the TV, stared at the blank screen for a few seconds, and turned to Melanie and said, "Maybe he's right—maybe he's not. One way or the other,

I'm going to find out." Larry was even more sensitive about put-downs in sports than in business.

An hour before the first race in Cagliari was scheduled to start, as the crew and boat were put through their paces, Russell appeared calm, smiling and joking. He loved the rugged beauty of Sardinia, and was happy to be sailing with Larry. Then, with a minute to go before the prestart, Russell's expression changed. The smile was replaced with a clenched jaw. Larry felt just the right amount of stress. He was nervous but focused, and the weather was to his liking, blowing hard at around twenty-five knots. The conditions were similar to windy summer afternoons on San Francisco Bay.

Russell and Larry were now moments away from their first race together, and their opponent was America's Cup helmsman Cameron Appleton from New Zealand. The countdown continued—five, four, three, two, one—Larry entered the starting box from the port side, crossed Appleton's bow; Appleton jibed and followed. Both boats sailed away from the line, made a couple of circles, and headed back toward the starting line. Then with more than a minute left, Appleton set up on the starboard lay-line with Larry sixty feet to his left. It was clear that Appleton wanted the right but he gave Larry enough time and enough room to do two tacks and close down the distance between the boats to fifteen feet. Appleton won the right, but Larry was positioned just to leeward. As the gun went off, both boats crossed the starting line at the same time, sailing right next to each other. Larry's goal was to shrink the distance between the boats from fifteen feet to around three feet, and force Appleton to tack away or get a penalty. In match racing involving identical boats, the first boat to tack usually loses.

Sailing side by side, Russell started yelling, "Come on guys. Get over the side. Hike it out hard. Cheese [Dirk De Ridder], try a little more traveler down. Roscoe, more runner—max runner. Larry, sit down and smooth it out. You're going to get to him, but only if you smooth it out." Larry and the crew were all on the same side of the boat, leaning overboard as far as they could. They were using their weight to prevent the boat from heeling over too much, making them go faster. With every gust of wind Larry eased his hold on the wheel, letting the bow of his boat come up a degree or so; then he brought the bow back down a degree, repeating this again and again as he tried to close the gap between his boat and Appleton's.

"Come on Larry," Russell yelled. "We've got to make him tack before he gets to the lay-line." Larry, focused on driving, didn't say a word. When the two boats closed to within eighteen inches of each other—Larry was in the leeward right-of-way position—Appleton was out of room, and forced to turn his wheel and tack away onto port to avoid a penalty. Larry exhaled and momentarily glanced back at Russell, who was right behind him and sitting on the rail of the racing boat that bore his name. Russell nodded and said, "Nice job. Let's keep it going here guys. We're going straight—all the way to lay-line."

When the two boats got to the first weather mark Larry was ahead. He had done only one tack, while Appleton did two. Larry maintained his hard-earned lead throughout the two-lap race and crossed the finish line eight seconds in front. "Okay, guys, good job," Russell said of their race one victory.

Race number two was against the Danish champion Morten Henriksen. With minutes to go before the start, Russell began barking out information and orders, "We're starboard entry this time guys. Everyone stay focused. Larry slow it down, you're three seconds early here. Kill it high. Okay, go—go now!" Larry entered the starting box and used his starboard advantage to control Henriksen throughout the prestart, earning Oracle Racing the right side of the racecourse and a solid lead of half a boat-length at the gun. He extended this lead by making Henriksen do two extra tacks before the weather mark. Larry started the first downwind leg with a lead of over three boat-lengths as his RC44 planed downwind at a speed of seventeen knots. He was continuing to increase his lead over Henriksen, when disaster struck. A thirty-knot gust of wind hit their spinnaker and exploded it into tatters. Their speed dropped to twelve knots as they continued with just the mainsail.

Russell screamed, "Get that other chute on deck, fast guys. Larry, keep it going here." By the time they hoisted their spare spinnaker and got back up to speed Henriksen had flown past them, and as he approached the leeward mark Henriksen had built up what seemed to be a safe five-boat-length lead.

Larry turned his boat close around the leeward marker buoy, almost touching it, and held his speed as he nailed his upwind angle. "Great rounding, guys," Russell yelled. "We just got some of it back. It's not over. Keep it up. Hike it out, get over the rail. Larry, that's too much heel angle. Cheese, main on. Help him bring it up." After the leeward rounding, Henriksen's lead was down to four lengths. By the time they rounded the second weather mark and hoisted and set their spinnaker, the lead was down to three boat-lengths. Both boats raced downwind toward the finish line, and Larry was sailing as high and as fast as he could, pushing his boat to over eighteen knots and closing the gap with Henriksen. "Larry, careful, not too high, you're going to broach," Russell yelled. "Keep your speed up during the jibe. Ready jibe, jibing, Larry, turn the boat." Larry turned the wheel and pointed his bow due downwind, pausing as the crew brought the spinnaker and the main across. Then he brought the bow up to accelerate. As both boats completed their jibes, Henriksen's lead was almost gone. Larry was consistently sailing higher and faster, on the edge of losing control and broaching, but it was paying off. As they neared the end of the race, both boats were dead even, bow to bow, aiming right at the middle of the finish line, converging rapidly—on a collision course.

Just before crossing the finish line, Larry altered course ever so slightly, by one or two degrees, to avoid hitting Henriksen. Russell screamed, "No, no, hit 'em, hit 'em. Fuck! I said hit 'em. What are you doing? Why didn't you hit 'em?" Larry was startled; he stared at Russell for several seconds. The race was over, except for the shouting, as they say, and Russell was doing a lot of it. Everyone on the crew stayed absolutely silent until Larry said slowly and clearly, "Okay, Russell, it's your boat. Next time I'll hit them."

Larry and his teammates shared a knowing look about the Kiwi nicknamed "Crash Coutts," that mild-mannered engineer and team leader by day who turned rabid on the water. Russell, for his part, wasn't one to stop and think about who he was yelling at. The race hadn't been called yet, but Larry knew one thing for certain. Russell drove the crew hard and himself harder. And the guys *loved* him.

While Larry was busy feeling good about his choice of Russell Coutts to run his America's Cup campaign, the crew learned that they had lost the race by less than three feet. They had fought all the way back from a five-boat-length deficit, only to lose by the narrowest of margins at the end. Larry wondered whether, if he had held his course longer, Henriksen might have turned first to avoid a collision. He was certain that Russell didn't really want him to hit the other boat; Russell just wanted him to force Henriksen to turn away first. It was a game of chicken, and Larry lost.

Larry was filled with adrenaline, and determined to win the next round. And he did, winning the start of race three against former match racing world champion Sebastien Col of France. He extended the lead on every leg and crossed the finish line comfortably ahead. Then he won race four in pretty much the same fashion.

As Larry had been focusing on the races, Russell had been watching Larry and assessing his skills. Larry, who was tall and fit and quick to laugh, was also hard on himself. Russell was gleaning insights into the man, and liked what he was learning. Larry had an engineer's mind on and off the water, assimilating loads of information quickly. In the races, Larry was quick to recognize and react to all the changing variables of sailing, including apparent wind angle, heading, boat speed and other readouts from the instruments, telltales flying or stalling along the luff of the jib, and heel angle. Larry's ability to get the maximum speed out of the boat while driving in high winds had impressed the crew. Russell was also pleased that Larry was out sailing with the team, and that he wouldn't spend his third America's Cup campaign hearing about the ups and downs, strengths and weaknesses secondhand.

Larry now had a record of three wins and one loss going into his last race of the day. But race five was going to be more challenging than the first four. Race five was against Jimmy Spithill, who had beaten all four of his opponents in Cagliari, including Ainslie. He also was the guy who hadn't lost a race all year. Larry exhibited a bit of gallows humor by saying, "What's the big deal about being undefeated for the year? It's only April!"

The team was not in a joking mood. "Come on, Larry, we work with these guys every day," said mainsail trimmer Cheese De Ridder. "We want to beat Jimmy." For emphasis, and just in case Larry was still uncertain about the seriousness of the intramural competition on the team, Russell added, "This is an important one guys. We've got to win this race. Everyone stay focused and do your job."

Larry remembered the first time he practiced match racing against Jimmy. It was on San Francisco Bay, and he and Russell took turns driving their boat against Jimmy. On the first day, Jimmy won every race. Switching boats didn't make any difference. Jimmy just kept winning. Larry had never been crushed like this, race after race. At the end of the day, Larry turned to Russell and said, "This is embarrassing. I'm not looking forward to coming out here tomorrow." Russell smiled, pointed at Jimmy, and said, "Aren't you glad he's on our team." Their practice sessions on San Francisco Bay made it painfully clear that he needed to improve, and fast, or face humiliation on the water.

After several more practice sessions, Russell was winning almost as many races as Jimmy. Even Larry was winning a few races every day. Through the wins and losses, Larry had been wowed by Russell's skills. The Kiwi champion had a level of precision and aggression in sailing that Larry had never seen before. In Larry's mind, Russell sailed the way Roger Federer played tennis. He wasn't just better than everybody else; he was different, a kind of artistic genius of the sport. And if Russell was Federer, then Jimmy was Rafael Nadal. Larry wondered, *What the hell am I doing here with Roger and Rafa?*

Larry was about to sail against the best match racer in the world. Russell pulled a piece of paper from his pocket, looked at it, and said, "We're first up, port entry, time to get into it guys." As the horn went off marking the beginning of the prestart, Larry entered the box, crossed Jimmy's bow, and sailed away from the starting line. Jimmy jibed and followed, but not quite close enough to keep Larry from jibing.

The beginning of a match race is as choreographed and well-studied as the beginning of a chess game. Larry was doing what Jimmy expected, and Jimmy was doing what Larry expected. As in chess, the improvisation would come later. The beginning of the prestart was planned. They did their circles, they turned and ducked, they tacked and jibed, and Jimmy did it all better than Larry. The young, undefeated Australian won the right and hit the line with more speed, giving him starboard advantage with his bow slightly in front.

But Larry was satisfied with his start. He was in the race. It was close, and if he could keep it close, he'd have his chances. Separated by less than a boat-length all the way up the first leg of the race, Larry rounded the windward mark right on Jimmy's transom. Russell yelled, "We need a good set here guys—ready—hoist." Jimmy's spinnaker set just before Larry's, and the two boats started racing toward the leeward mark. Jimmy gradually extended his lead to almost two boat-lengths as they sailed downwind and then back upwind. But while Jimmy's boat was rounding the second windward mark, a crew member was too slow easing the runner, and that forced Jimmy to delay his turn and spinnaker hoist for a few precious seconds. Larry had his chance; he was able to complete his turn downwind before Jimmy. His team hoisted the spinnaker, as it filled in the breeze, and they took the lead.

At this point, Larry knew that he had only one more maneuver to make before they got to the finish line. If he didn't screw up the tricky, high-speed jibe, they just might win the race. Halfway down the final leg Russell yelled, "One jibe and in guys. Ready— ready—jibing." Larry turned the boat, waited for the spinnaker set on the other side, and brought the bow up. The RC44 accelerated to over eighteen knots—they were headed straight toward the finish line—and they were still in front.

When they crossed the finish line the entire crew raised their arms up in the air and started jumping and screaming. Russell yelled, "Way to go, guys. Awesome race, guys. Jimmy's buying dinner tonight." Then Russell put his hand on Larry's shoulder and quietly said, "Good job. But it's too early to celebrate. We have a lot more sailing to do." Larry didn't say a word. He gave the wheel to Russell, shook hands with the crew, and walked to the back of the boat and sat down by himself. Larry was glad that the first day of racing was over and—so far—he hadn't screwed it up.

After the first day of racing, three drivers had identical four-and-one records: Spithill, Ainslie, and Larry. However, the press noted, "Larry Ellison's team is the provisional leader thanks to victories against its direct opponents. A great achievement for the only nonprofessional helmsman involved today."

That night at the crew dinner Larry told a story about the time he was out racing *Sayonara* with his friend Rupert Murdoch, the Australian media mogul, as a part of his crew. It was back in 1995 and Larry had invited Rupert to join him on the Sydney-to-Hobart race. Two days prior to the start of the Hobart, *Sayonara* sailed and won a short around–the-buoys race in Sydney Harbor. After crossing the finish line, the crew dropped the spinnaker and then Larry spun the boat around head-to-wind so they could lower the mainsail. As Rupert walked over to congratulate Larry, he casually grabbed the mainsheet, the rope that attaches to the boom and is used to trim the mainsail. Larry had started to yell, "Rupert don't!" but it all happened too fast—the mainsheet suddenly went taut—and the tip of one of Rupert's fingers was shaved right off. The sailors recovered the severed fingertip, put it on ice, and put Murdoch into a tender; and off they went to the hospital, where surgeons operated on his finger. That evening, fingertip reattached and in a cast, Rupert showed up for the crew dinner. He sat down next to Larry and said, "If I'm going to be a member of the crew, I'm not going to miss any crew functions."

Thirty-six hours later, Murdoch climbed on board *Sayonara* for the start of the Sydney-to-Hobart race. The 1995 Hobart was rough, but nothing like the hurricane of 1998. During the race, Murdoch performed all assigned duties and was a member of the crew. Each day he was on deck for two eight-hour watches and then went below to rest for eight hours, just like everybody else. After one group finished resting down below, the custom was to bring hot drinks—coffee, tea, chocolate—up to the guys working on deck. Rupert refused to be treated any differently from any other member of the crew, so when it was his time to come back on deck, he popped his head out of the hatch and asked, "What do you guys want—coffee, tea—what?" The Kiwis asked for "coffee white," coffee with cream, or "coffee black." Larry went on with the story, "So, Joey Allen says, 'Coffee white,' and Robbie Naismith says, 'Coffee black with sugar.' Rupert goes back down below and comes back a couple of minutes later with the coffees. He gives Joey his coffee and he gives Robbie his coffee. Joey says thanks. Robbie starts drinking his coffee, then he makes a face, looks at Rupert, and says, 'Goddammit Rupert, I said *two* sugars!' Everybody is shocked and nobody moves. Then Robbie gets this big grin, Rupert cracks up, and we all crack up." Rupert loved and appreciated the moment. For a few days he was one of the guys. He was part of a small tight-knit team rather than the head of a giant corporation. He had a chance to take a break from being Rupert Murdoch.

Larry's second day of racing in Cagliari began with a match against Mateusz Kusznierewicz from Poland, the recent Star-class world champion and two-time Olympic sailing medalist who was still trying for his first win in the regatta. Despite entering the starting box on port, Larry controlled the action throughout the prestart and led the race from start to finish, handing Kusznierewicz his fifth consecutive loss. In his next race, Larry sailed well again and won again. He was leading the regatta with a record of 6-1, and there were only two more races scheduled.

The weather in Cagliari was getting worse, and there was talk of calling off racing for the rest of the day. The wind was a solid thirty knots, and the race committee decided to suspend racing for a while. Racing RC44s—forty-four-foot, ultralight, carbon fiber "windsurfers"—in thirty knots of breeze was dangerous. After an hour or so, when it became clear that the weather wasn't improving, Russell looked at Larry and told him to sail over to the committee boat to talk with the principal race officer, Peter Reggio, popularly known as "Luigi." Larry shrugged, nodded, and slowly sailed over to the race committee boat located at the right end of the starting line. When Larry got close to the committee boat, Russell started shouting at the top of his lungs, trying to be heard over the howling wind, "Luigi! Luigi! Can you hear me?" Reggio answered, "Yes, Russell, everyone in Cagliari can hear you." Russell continued shouting, "Luigi, don't stop the racing. We don't want to win this way. We want Ainslie! We want Ainslie! Do you hear me? We want Ainslie!"

Larry's next scheduled race was against the British Olympic superstar. If racing was called off for the rest of the day because of the bad weather, then the professional match racing part of the regatta would be over, and Larry would be the winner. Larry, maneuvering to stay close to the committee boat, wondered, *Who is this "we" in "we want Ainslie"? I don't want Ainslie. He's got a drawerful of Olympic gold medals. I watched the Olympics on TV. The only one who wants Ben Ainslie is Russell Coutts.*

But Russell got his wish and the race was on. Ainslie entered from the port side and crossed Larry's bow, and Larry jibed and followed. Both boats sailed deep into the right-hand side of the starting box. There were no circles with the wind blowing around thirty knots. After a little over a minute, Ainslie decided to jibe and lead Larry back toward the starting line. Larry timed his jibe perfectly and tucked in right behind Ainslie. As both boats sailed on starboard toward the starting line, Larry was in a strong controlling position to leeward, and slightly behind Ainslie. Both RC44s were on the starboard lay-line, pointed directly at the committee boat. Russell started screaming, "He's way early here. He can't jibe, he's going to have to tack." Ainslie was forced to tack onto port and go behind the committee boat. Larry tacked right underneath him, maintaining control, pushing him farther and farther to the right of the committee boat and above the starting line. Then Ainslie tacked back onto starboard, and Larry immediately did the same. Larry now had Ainslie trapped above the starting line and to the right of the committee boat. Ainslie tacked back onto port and Larry did the same. Both boats were to the right of the committee boat and above the starting line, with time running out. Larry was in position to get a "kill start" against the great Ben Ainslie, to win the race before it begins. Ten seconds after the starting gun went off, Larry had control. Ainslie tacked back onto starboard; then Larry tacked back—too slowly, too late—letting Ainslie escape, dive down below the committee boat, and come up hard on the wind and start in the middle of the line. Larry did a similar maneuver and started at the committee boat a second behind Ainslie. Larry screamed, "Fuck, fuck, fuck—I had him."

Russell told Larry, "Calm down, sit down and drive the boat. We've got the right. We're in the race." If Larry didn't lose any ground during the first leg of the race he could use his starboard right-of-way advantage to pass Ainslie at the weather mark. The two boats sailed side by side all the way up the first leg, but Ainslie gained just enough to break the overlap and round the first mark in front. Larry rounded so close behind that he almost hit Ainslie. The two boats bore away, set their spinnakers, and started racing downwind, still right next to each other with Ainslie about half a boat-length in front. In thirty knots of breeze, the boats were hitting speeds of twenty-two knots, creating huge wakes and leaving rooster tails of water spray behind them. The boats executed simultaneous high-speed jibes onto starboard and continued to race side by side toward the leeward mark. Ainslie was still half a boat-length in front, but Larry was positioned to Ainslie's right and both boats had to make a right turn around the leeward mark. As they approached the leeward mark, Larry was actually closer to it than Ainslie and certain he had the room to turn inside the Brit and make the pass. As they dropped their spinnaker and started to sheet on the jib, Russell started screaming, "Turn inside of him.

Turn inside of him." Larry had already started to turn before Russell started screaming. He turned inside Ainslie and went from being half a boat-length behind to being half a boat-length ahead.

The two boats raced upwind tacking simultaneously and still overlapped all the way to the windward mark. Larry had starboard advantage and a half-boat-length lead as he rounded the final mark just ahead of Ainslie. Both teams got their spinnakers up and set at about the same time and continued their side-by-side battle as they raced toward the finish line. Both boats were sailing on the edge, hitting twenty-three knots in more than thirty knots of breeze. Larry had a lead of less than half a boat-length, which was around one second at this speed. Both boats completed their jibes and accelerated back up to speed. They were pointed directly toward the middle of the finish line, with Larry in front—but just barely. The RC44s, looking more like speedboats than sailboats, flew across the finish line still side by side. Larry was first, Ainslie second.

There were screams and high fives all around. Russell grabbed Larry's shoulders and yelled, "Awesome fucking race. That's one of the best races I've ever been on in my life." Larry screamed back, "It's the best fucking race I've ever been on." Larry congratulated the crew, and said, "I don't believe it! We just beat fucking Ben Ainslie." Russell added, "That's right. We just beat fucking Ben Ainslie. Boys, it's just about time to clear a place on the mantel for the trophy. You can see it right up there. All we have to do is sail our last race sensibly—not break anything—and we're going to win this regatta."

The last race was against yet another world champion, Jesper Radich from Denmark. As Larry entered the starting box on starboard, Russell whispered to him, "Larry, we want to sail conservatively here, we don't want to break anything. We don't want to do anything stupid." Larry followed Russell's instructions, keeping his maneuvers in the prestart to a minimum, setting up to the right of Radich and starting in front. Larry rounded the first mark three boat-lengths ahead and turned downwind to a safe angle—not too high—and the boat accelerated to about sixteen knots, enough to hold his lead.

Suddenly Russell laid into him, "What the fuck is wrong with you? Did you forget how to sail? Bring her up and let's get going." Larry shot the agitated Coutts a look, pointed the bow higher, and felt the black boat power up and accelerate: seventeen, eighteen, nineteen, twenty knots. When their lead over Radich grew to a commanding eight boat-lengths, Russell exhaled, patted Larry on the back like a puppy, and in a totally relaxed tone said, "That's better. That's how to do it." Larry thought, *So that's what Russell Coutts means when he tells me to sail conservatively.*

When the Oracle Racing RC44 crossed the finish line, Larry had won his first professional match racing regatta. At the awards ceremony that evening, when it was announced, "The winner of the Cagliari Cup match racing event is: Oracle Racing—professional driver, Larry Ellison—boat owner, Russell Coutts," the place went wild with cheers and laughter. When Larry went up to the podium to accept the trophy, he addressed the raucous crowd, "I know, I know—it sounds like they must have gotten that backward. Normally, I have to buy the boat to get a chance to drive. So thank you, Russell, for letting me drive your boat. And thanks to all the guys on the crew. You did an amazing job. It's a team sport and I'm very proud to be a part of this team."

Coming off the stage Larry was cornered by a reporter who incredulously asked, "Ben Ainslie third, James Spithill second, Larry Ellison first. How do you explain *that*?" Larry paused, thought for a moment, got a huge grin on his face, and said, "Well—maybe there *is* a God."

The reporter then walked over to Jimmy Spithill and asked him to comment on the results. "We didn't sail too well today, and made some mistakes. But we are very happy to finish the event in second. It was absolutely superb. I am very impressed by Larry Ellison's performance. He sailed extremely well. What he's done is amazing." Early on—during their practice races in San Francisco when Jimmy was beating Larry in every race—one of Jimmy's teammates said, "Why don't you just let him win one?" Jimmy replied: "You think he'd let me win one if he was in this position? No way. The guy's a competitor. I view him as a peer."

Larry followed up his win at the Cagliari Cup with a respectable third-place finish at the next RC44 match racing event. Then lightning struck a second time. Larry won the Malcisine Cup professional match racing regatta on Lake Garda, Italy, beating both Jimmy Spithill and Team New Zealand's Dean Barker along the way. With two victories in his last three professional match race events, Larry impressed his teammates, silenced the critics, and quelled a few of his inner demons.

As Larry and Russell continued winning RC44 races throughout that spring and summer, Jimmy and Larry also teamed up, shared the driving, and won the TP52 professional fleet racing event, the City of Marseille Cup in June, and Jimmy and his crew won in catamarans in July. Then they were handed an unexpected defeat.

The Appellate Division of the New York Supreme Court, in a three-to-two split decision that surprised everyone, reversed the earlier ruling establishing the Golden Gate as Challenger of Record. The Spanish yacht club was back in, and Bertarelli declared victory. The ruling said that one disputed phrase—"having" a regatta on the arm of the sea—was "ambiguous." Oracle had argued that having a regatta on the arm of the sea meant a club has *had* a regatta. Alinghi argued that "having" could mean a regatta was in the works. Bertarelli could now come up with new boat specifications, create a new protocol, and bar Larry from being a part of the race at all.

"We are out," Russell said to Larry, as the two discussed the ruling. Larry contemplated the situation, and listened to Russell. It had been a year since they filed to be the legitimate Challenger of Record, and they had won the first decision. Predictably, Alinghi appealed, and now had its victory. But Oracle Racing still had one last legal move, in New York's highest court, the Court of Appeals.

Larry didn't normally overrule Russell. There were a few people Russell had hired who Larry wasn't entirely thrilled about. Larry told Russell what he thought about them and then let Russell make the call. There was a decision made early on in the campaign for the 33rd Cup to let BMW go as a sponsor; they couldn't come to financial terms, and Russell had been confident others would step in. Larry approved the decision to walk away from the BMW deal, but with the economy faltering, those other major sponsors had failed to materialize. Now, the team's lawyers were losing in court. As Larry saw it, the attorneys were making a hash of things.

Larry told Russell that he was taking over the lawsuit and planned to bring in someone who doesn't lose.

"His name is David Boies," Larry said. "Like you, he's the best at what he does. He's going to be our lawyer moving forward."

Boies, considered by many to be the greatest trial lawyer alive, had successfully defended CBS and IBM, led the government's antitrust suit against Microsoft, and defended Napster when the recording industry charged it with copyright infringement. He had helped win judgments establishing the constitutional right to marry for gay and lesbians in California in federal district court and had represented Al Gore before the United States Supreme Court in the case that decided the 2000 presidential election. He also litigated a range of cases in the world of sports, defending NASCAR against antitrust charges from Kentucky Speedway, and he had a long working relationship with George Steinbrenner and the New York Yankees. Boies's knowledge of the America's Cup was limited, though he had represented Bill Koch (*America Cubed*) in various cases, and was on both sides of litigation with Ted Turner. He quickly began to read everything he could on the Cup, poring over nineteenth-century sailing screeds and the Deed of Gift, which had been written in 1852, adopted by the New York Yacht Club in 1857, and amended four times—in 1882, 1887, 1956, and 1985.

In many ways, Boies and Larry were a natural fit. Boies was hypercompetitive and once remarked that he "could sleep or win." He had been called the "Michael Jordan of the courtroom" and spent the eve of his deposition of Bill Gates watching *Tombstone* (one of Larry's favorite movies), with its showdown at the O.K.

Corral. He wore inexpensive suits, collected expensive wine, and had a memory like one of Larry's database systems. He even liked to sail and had an interest in an eighty-foot Dynamique sloop named *Coconut* that he sailed in the Caribbean, in the Aegean, in San Francisco Bay, and at Martha's Vineyard.

Larry had instructed Russell to tell everyone on the team that they were moving forward with the campaign. "We'll win in court," Larry said, "Then we'll win on the water." Russell admired his boss's conviction. Larry had them racing ahead with the goal of winning the America's Cup, and they didn't even know if they'd be allowed to show up at the starting line.

Russell may have been teaching Larry about sailing, but Larry was teaching the sailing master about other kinds of high-stakes decision making. Larry had told Russell a story of when he was working with the Israeli Defense Forces, reviewing the progress on one of their new Oracle systems. The Israeli general began the meeting by studying Larry and asking him, "What did you bring me today: results or excuses?"

The Golden Gate filed an appeal to be reinstated as the Challenger of Record. With the appeal came the support of the New York Yacht Club, which until now had remained neutral in the lawsuit. The New York club submitted an amicus curiae brief, saying it had no stake in the upcoming race, but that its interest "stems from its long, unique involvement with the America's Cup and its desire to have the competition remain faithful to the Deed of Gift drafted by the [New York Yacht Club founders] and to see that the races for the Challenger Selection Series and the America's Cup are fair and even-handed competitions for all participants." It went on to say that when "[the Spanish club] CNEV issued its challenge on July 3, 2007, it had never held an annual regatta and was not an 'organized Yacht Club' because it had only five members, no yachts, was formed just days before submitting its challenge for the America's Cup, and was formed solely for the purpose of submitting that challenge."

Bertarelli wasted no time in responding, saying Larry's actions showed a "tremendous arrogance and lack of respect for the teams involved" in trying to organize the 33rd America's Cup.

What fascinated David Boies, though, as he began to research the history of the America's Cup was that there was no governing body, and the race continued in perpetuity based on the nineteenth-century Deed of Gift. This meant that the sport, which epitomized the cutting edge in modern technology, was rooted in the nineteenth century. It also meant that with no governing body, the defending club served as both competitor and trustee, with substantial power to control and enforce the rules—something Boies likened to giving one of the teams in the baseball World Series the right to supply the umpires. As Boies saw it, Alinghi was trying to use that power to "disqualify, or alternatively disadvantage, Larry's boat." His task would be to convince the court that it had the power and obligation under the deed to ensure the defender did not abuse its power. To do this, he needed to explain to the judge—unfamiliar with the America's Cup—the intricacies of the race today and of the race in the early 1880s. Every case was different, and this one had him delving into such things as what it meant to measure a boat on the "load waterline" and why centerboards and sliding keels were used by American yachtsmen but not British yachtsmen. Boies, who loved to litigate and believed the smallest details could make a difference, was not about to let his new client lose.

22

Anacortes, Washington

August 2008

Tugsy and his building partner Tim Smyth had studied the plans for the team's next America's Cup boat—a design hastily but brilliantly drawn up by Michel Kermarac—and wondered if putting together such a monster in less than a year was humanly possible. The boat would be 135 feet long and 90 feet at the waterline. The beam would be just under 90 feet, the mast 185 feet and three and a half tons. The yacht would have a displacement of sixteen tons. Tugsy had never built a trimaran, but this inexperience was not unusual, in that all but one boat in the history of the America's Cup had been monohulls.

Not knowing the date or location of the next Cup, or whether they would even get to compete, Tugsy was struggling to keep the crew motivated to get the boat ready for whenever the next decision was handed down. With each new rumored venue, the builders and engineers had to consider new designs suited for those conditions.

From their headquarters in Anacortes, Tugsy directed eighty builders working sixty-five-hour weeks. The outlying hulls were made first, and then the mast and appendages followed. The three-dimensional shape of the hull was programmed into Janicki

Industries' five-axis cutters, which created full-size molds that would become the hull. Layers of high-grade carbon fiber were applied to the mold and the heating process was begun. Temperatures were set at around 180 degrees Fahrenheit. Once the temperature was reached, it "cooked" overnight and then temperatures were slowly lowered. An aluminum honeycomb core was then applied to the cured carbon skins, like meat in a sandwich, before another thin layer of carbon fiber was laid on top of the core to complete the structural sandwich. The appendages, deck, and bulkhead items were put together in similar ways, all with their own molds. The only subcontracting that was done was with a company in Rhode Island that was making masts for the soft sails. And this time around, design guru Bruce Farr had been replaced by the French naval architects Van Peteghem Lauriot Prévost, who started the process before it was taken over by Oracle's in-house design team headed by Mike Drummond. Franck Cammas, an accomplished French sailor and specialist in trimarans, was a design consultant and also trained the crew in sailing multihulls.

After nine months of nonstop work, *USA-17*—originally named *BOR 90*—was christened with a bottle of champagne on the bowsprit by Melinda Erkelens, then lowered into Fidalgo Bay, off Puget Sound near Core Builders. The boat was loaded with more than 250 sensors, from rudders to sails, bow to stern. Russell's first take on the boat was that it was "incredibly challenging," a comment that made Tugsy smile. That was an understatement when it came to this boat. There was also talk of building a new boat from scratch, and using *USA-17* for practice. The most titillating talk, though, centered on the building of a certain type of sail, the size of which had never been seen before. The secretive project, code-named "Kopis" after a Greek sword with a forward-facing blade, was started as a side project in December 2008 and was now nearing completion.

• • •

In November, Jimmy Spithill drove *USA-17* in a practice session off the San Diego coast. He and the crew, flying through the choppy waters at twenty-five knots, were trying different configurations of the mast and had moved it slightly forward. Mike Drummond had been asked to come aboard and take a look. The entire crew was on edge, as not a day of sailing went by without something breaking.

Jimmy stood on the steering platform, forty feet above the water, looking as the mast moved windward. "It has too much inversion," he said of the 193-foot-high mast, weighing one and a quarter tons. The crew all wore hard hats and life jackets. Cranes and special booms were needed to pick up sails and get them onto the boat. They'd had winches break and the bowsprit had violently cracked on six different occasions when they were testing loads. Bowman Brad Webb had admitted the boat terrified him on a daily basis, saying, "Stuff is falling out of the sky and just missing us."

Tactician John Kostecki told Webb, "I am more scared on this boat than I've been on any boat in any open ocean race."

As Jimmy pushed the boat in the San Diego Bay that fall day, the fiber-optic alarm system sounded the siren. Jimmy studied the computer screen next to him. The siren was a part of his daily routine, a constant, like chatter to a teacher. His challenge was to push the boat as hard as he could while monitoring the loads—the pressure and strain gauge readouts on parts of the boat—without pushing too far. He likened it to redlining a race car, a process in which drivers take the car up to the redline, the maximum rpms, without going over. It was a mental strain every day, but when it all worked—when they were sheeted on and launched across the ocean—it was pure ecstasy. *USA-17* was bigger and more technologically daring than any other trimaran ever built.

"This really doesn't look right," Drummond concurred, as the mast started to bend sideways. Jimmy could see that the mast was close to tolerance. Suddenly, there was a terrifying boom—a boom like a cannon firing—and the rig came down in an avalanche. Jimmy hammered his ribs on the wheel and yelled, "Move out of the way!" to navigator Matteo Plazzi, in the boom's line, and to sail trimmer Ross Halcrow, working directly under it. Halcrow did the only thing he could do: he lay flat on the trampoline, close to the hull, and tucked himself into the netting. The mast landed just above him, with six inches separating the two. Meanwhile, Joey Newton, who was terrified on the boat most of the time, took a step and jumped into the water at twenty-five knots, flailing his hands so the chase boats wouldn't run him over. Another sailor also jumped off the boat and the guys heckled them about it later, prompting Newton to joke, "Roscoe, poor bloke, was under it. He needs to do more speed work so he can get out of the road quicker."

Jimmy—who suffered several cracked ribs—took a head count. Members of the team had gone overboard and the chase boats were heading to retrieve them. The biggest concern now was the boat. A dropped mast could start rubbing on the boat, creating "sores" that could cut all the way through. If that happened, it would be catastrophic to the campaign, as there was no backup. The mast was sheared off, jagged and broken like a thick trunk, with splinter-like fibers sticking out. The sail was partly on the boat, partly in the water. Before long, the shore crew arrived with a giant cutter, which was used to saw through the dropped mast to prevent damage to the boat.

After the mast was separated from the boat, chase boats dragged the mast and sails in the water back to the San Diego harbor, a fair distance away, and another boat towed USA-17 to shore. All Jimmy could think of was, *What are we going to do now?* The mast alone had taken more than ten thousand hours of work. They didn't have another one of sufficient size lying around.

A team meeting was called. Tugsy, who was in Anacortes, was conferenced in.

"Breaking our mast today eliminates a whole lot of options," Russell said to the sullen team.

"We can try to build another mast for the soft sails," Tugsy said. "And we could probably do it in eight thousand hours of work."

For nearly a year, a different type of sail—a rigid wing modeled after the wing of a plane—had been in the works. A discussion ensued about the wing. Wing sails, uncommon on private sailboats, had been used for decades by speed sailors and popularized by a 1963 book, *The 40-Knot Sailboat*. The difference, though, was in scale. The boats that had used hard sails in the past were small, and the only rigid wing used in the history of the America's Cup was Dennis Conner's wing sail on his sixty-foot catamaran *Stars & Stripes*, the winner of the 1988 Cup. That wing was 108 feet tall. The rigid sail that Oracle had under development was more than twice as tall and over six times larger in surface area. If they could pull it off, the Oracle wing would be by far the largest wing ever built—longer than the tip-to-tip wingspan of a Boeing 747 jet.

Larry, who was a part of the meeting, said encouragingly, "The wing is going to generate a lot more power than any soft mainsail. Everyone knows that. What's at least as important is the fact that the wing will dramatically reduce the loads on the boat. Using our soft mainsail, we saw the massively loaded mainsheet crush the largest winch Harkin makes as if it was an egg. The wing has no mainsheet to overload, just a traveler. We've seen extreme loads compress and snap our mast like a twig; there is no compression on the wing. The wing will generate more lift with less load. We'll go faster, much faster, and reduce the likelihood of something breaking."

Larry went on, "I know that most people think trying to build a hard wing of this size is crazy. But that's the beauty of the idea. The other side *isn't trying* to build one." And, savoring his words, he added, "So we'll have a wing, and they won't."

While most of the sailors and builders had dismissed the wing as an experimental side project, Jimmy was an early champion of the rigid sail. He had told Larry that he believed the wing would give them an advantage in a range of conditions. Jimmy had been out sailing in a new C-class wing-sailed catamaran, owned by the Canadian sailor Fred Eaton, who had been teaching him the ropes of the two-person cat. Jimmy had told Larry over the phone, "It's a no-brainer to do the wing," thinking only later, after the two had hung up, *Shit, I hope it works.*

Russell ended the meeting by saying, "We can't play both sides anymore. We can't advance with soft sails and the rigid wing. Now, we are all going to focus on the rigid wing. We won't have a backup. So all I can say is focus."

The wing-sail project began in the late fall of 2008, when Mike Drummond asked Joseph Ozanne, a twenty-nine-year-old aeronautical specialist who had joined Oracle Racing's engineering team in 2004, to "go off and investigate the rigid wing and see if this can be done." The men agreed the idea was far out and "utopian," but both wanted to pursue it.

Ozanne had graduated from the École Nationale Supérieure de l'Aéronautique et de l'Espace, or "Supaero," which was founded in 1909 as the world's first dedicated aerospace engineering school and had become one of the most prestigious and selective schools in France. Ozanne, whose family had moved around a great deal when he was a child, had a constant in his love of sailing. As a boy, he dreamed of one day winning the America's Cup. But his dream wasn't about *sailing* a winning boat; it was about *designing* a winning boat. To him, the America's Cup represented the best in human engineering. At Supaero, which did not have a sailboat program, Ozanne was routinely ribbed by professors who laughed and asked, "Why come here to design sailboats?" If they had sought an answer, he would have said that he found the physics of a yacht more intriguing than the physics of an airplane, as planes were designed to function in the air, while boats were engineered to work in water *and* wind. A plane had to take off, fly at altitude and conserve fuel, and then land. A boat had to go upwind, go downwind, and turn. The boat was in the water but the sail—the boat's engine—was in the air, and it was always changing shape.

Ozanne believed that his training in aerodynamics and flight dynamics, in aircraft and space shuttles, would translate to boats.

Before coming to BMW Oracle Racing—he was hired by Chris Dickson—he had worked with Kermarac and Cammas at Van Peteghem Lauriot Prévost. Ozanne was seen as especially skilled at velocity prediction programs, which used algorithms to predict the performance and behavior of a yacht, factoring in boat speed, heel angle, and propulsive and resistive forces.

After getting his marching orders to explore the possibility of a hard sail, Ozanne had come to see the wing as the best way to give their multihull more power. A hard sail could be shaped, or trimmed, more accurately than a soft sail; was easier for the sailors to shape; and lightened the pressure loads on the boat. The articulated flaps running up the wing would give it aerodynamic properties that couldn't be had with a soft sail, and because *USA-17* was massive the wing also needed to be massive. Ozanne, working from the team's design offices in San Diego and Valencia, started with a rigid sail of about 150 feet and grew it from there. He designed the wing to have nine articulated panels like the trailing edge flaps of an airplane. Cables running up the wing would control the panels, or "arms," and the panels could move in relation to one another and to the spar, the pole running up the main element. The adjustable flaps controlled the airflow, increasing lift in one part of the wing while reducing lift in another, maximizing overall power without overdoing the heeling force.

Through his velocity prediction analysis, Ozanne would be able to tell the trimmer the best angle for each flap under changing wind conditions and sea states. At the same time as he was working on the wing, he was creating his own playbooks to give to the sailors, showing, for example, that if they were sailing in ten knots of breeze certain sail flaps should be set at twenty-five degrees. And he was doing the same prediction performance analysis for Alinghi's boats. The more time Ozanne put into the wing, the more convinced he was that it would soon move from an engineering fantasy—something that few on the team took seriously—to their ultimate secret weapon.

23

San Diego, California

Spring 2009

IN A UNANIMOUS SIX-TO-ZERO VERDICT delivered in early spring, the New York Court of Appeals handed down its decision: the Golden Gate Yacht Club was back in and the Spanish yacht club chosen by Alinghi was out. This time, the word "having" was declared by the justices "unambiguous." Before David Boies had taken over, an appellate specialist named Maureen Mahoney, a superstar in the offices of Latham & Watkins in Washington, D.C., had argued the Golden Gate's case brilliantly. The justices found that a yacht club did not qualify as Challenger of Record unless it had held at least one annual regatta prior to its challenge. There was no higher court to appeal to, and Bertarelli was ordered to choose a date and location for the 33rd America's Cup within a ten-month window.

Immediately, Alinghi named the emirate Ras al-Khaimah of the United Arab Emirates as the venue, and just as fast the Golden Gate—now represented by Boies—objected to Ras al-Khaimah and asked that Valencia be reinstated as the venue.

Ras al-Khaimah had a "hotel and a marina, and that's about it, so we would have to build everything," Tom Ehman told Larry. But the real bad news was that Ras al-Khaimah was a trading partner with Iran, and two Iranian islands were within a couple of miles of the racecourse. Women were not allowed to take cabs by themselves, and Americans were advised they should not try to drive anywhere at night. "We have no idea what would happen if the police were to stop our containers," Ehman said, adding, "and Jews with an Israeli passport won't be let into the country."

Boies argued that Alinghi's choice of the emirate was prohibited by the Deed of Gift, which required a southern hemisphere site for a race to be sailed in February. He also voiced security concerns, explaining that the proposed course was next to Iranian waters. "There couldn't be a more provocative target," Boies said, "than a huge yacht flying an American flag."

Barry Ostrager, who represented Bertarelli, called Boies's objections to the emirate "a completely confected proposition" intended to delay the race. He also argued that earlier rulings in the Manhattan court had given Bertarelli the "sole right to pick the venue" and trumped the Deed of Gift. Ostrager dismissed Boies's assertion that the location was unsafe, citing an affidavit from Noah Feldman, a comparative constitutional law expert at Harvard Law School, who said that a terrorist attack was more likely in Spain, where the Cup was originally to be held, than in the United Arab Emirates. And Ostrager called Boies's opposition to the venue "an affront to the UAE . . . and an affront to the sport."

Within a month, the New York Supreme Court justice Shirley Kornreich ruled that Ras al-Khaimah could not host the next America's Cup. She based her decision on the Deed of Gift's southern hemisphere stipulation. But she also said that she was not going to force an American team to go to a place that practiced discrimination based on both sex and religion.

Bertarelli, who had already moved his boats and base to Ras al-Khaimah, which was run by Swiss technocrats—the emirate's right-hand person was a Swiss national—and famously had no wind, responded to the ruling by saying, "Ras al-Khaimah has put enormous time and effort into this thirty-third America's Cup project. We thank them and feel sorry for this unexpected result out of the New York court." Bertarelli's skipper Brad Butterworth said, "BMW Oracle should clean up their unsportsmanlike behavior with a dose of salt water and sunshine."

After claims and counterclaims, after years of uncertainty, the case was finally settled and they would sail in Valencia in February 2010. It would be a DoG match, decided on the water by two of the fastest multihulls ever built.

One month after the issue of the venue was decided, fifty men and two enormous cranes came together on the San Diego docks to hoist a brand-new rigid wing, made of carbon fiber and Kevlar and wrapped in a white aeronautical film skin, onto *USA-17*. The wing had grown from 150 feet to 196 feet to 206 feet and finally to an astounding 230 feet. At twenty-three stories, it was too tall to fit under the Golden Gate Bridge. The wing was approximately the same area as a football field, but as fragile as an egg.

They planned to raise the wing in the middle of the night, when there is less breeze. Tugsy watched as the crane operators worked in tandem to lift this kite, which had never been flown. "This wing is so light, in five knots of breeze, it will literally fly away," he said. The system involved a crane carefully lifting the wing from the dock and moving it so its base could be attached to the mast step on the boat. A hoisting line ran from high up on the wing to the end of a thirty-six-foot-long pole known as a "gin pole," which acted as a lever to raise the wing, and back to the winch on the boat. Other lines were rigged to secure the wing. The men's workday had started at 2 a.m. with maneuvering the wing from the tent out onto the dock, and eight hours later, they had the wing on the boat.

Fresh Burns watched the wing go up. "This is not born of the ocean, to live on the ocean," he said. "It's like some piece of land-based architecture."

To better understand the power of the rigid wing, Jimmy had spent two weeks taking an intensive course in flying. He figured the best way to learn to sail this aerodynamic wonder was to get his pilot's license. So on a rare break he returned home to Australia, visited a small country airfield, and explained to the guys what he wanted to do. His flight instructor, also a sailor, took him out every day for hours at a time and in weather that grounded other planes. Jimmy was immediately struck by the similarities between flying and sailing. A well-set-up plane, one driven smoothly, was easy to fly and had less drag. In the same way, a properly balanced boat, trimmed well, was easy to sail. The experience hooked him on flying.

When Jimmy stepped aboard *USA-17*, which was called "the Beast," he briefly looked up. It was as if someone had ripped the wing off a jetliner and placed it on his boat. Jimmy held the wheel lightly, as was his way. The day before, in a meeting that raised eyebrows with the sailors, Mike Drummond and Joseph Ozanne had advised the sailors to forget everything they knew about reading soft sails. "An airplane pilot doesn't look at the wing to see how he's flying," Ozanne had told them. "He looks at the instruments." (Though Jimmy knew that, with time, the sailors would start to feel changes on the boat without studying the instruments.) The sailors needed to understand the physics of the wing, and study their new playbooks, which were filled with numbers showing the best way to trim the sail according to the data coming from the onboard sensors. Out on the boat, wing in, *USA-17*'s trimmer, Dutchman Dirk "Cheese" De Ridder, wore a waterproof electronic display on his arm, showing boat speed and wind speed and optimal positioning of the nine articulated panels. Ozanne and Drummond followed in a performance boat. At first, the sailors floundered and the guys on the boat griped that the wing wasn't working right. Ozanne knew it was asking a lot for some of the world's best sailors to listen to a "computer guy" tell them how to sail. He had to sell them on the wing by proving it would work. And he would listen to their feedback on the water. It was an exchange between the two worlds that he welcomed.

From the performance boat, Ozanne talked with the sailors again about the specifications for the wing. He asked them to follow the numbers, not the telltales. Soon, with the wing position reset, the boat took off and Jimmy was tacking and jibing. In a moment that no one would forget, he had *USA-17* doing figure eights at twenty knots in the San Diego harbor. De Ridder exclaimed to Ozanne, "You proved physics is right! It works!"

Jimmy, whose first boat had been his family's neighbor's old, discarded Manly Junior, beamed. This was one of the best days of his life. What struck him, besides the speed, was the quiet. In that rare moment when the sensor alarms stopped, there was one sound missing: the flapping of the sails.

Russell, at a meeting in New York, got a call from Stephen Barclay, the team's chief operating officer, who was out in the harbor on a chase boat. Barclay told Russell he could watch a live video stream of *USA-17*. When Russell saw Jimmy showing off a series of hotshot sailing moves, with a wing that looked like a gigantic knife that could slice through the clouds, he sprang up from his office chair, pumped his fist in the air, and screamed "Yes—yes—yes!"

The plan for the day had been to go out and take it slow and easy, so the crew could gradually begin to get a feel for the huge wing-sailed boat. But the boat wanted to fly and, once De Ridder started to trust the data, Jimmy felt like a jockey trying to hold back his horse. He asked Scott Ferguson, a designer on board, whether he could fly a hull—push the boat hard enough to raise a pontoon out of the water—and accelerate *USA-17* to a much higher speed.

"Now is as good a time as any," Ferguson said, holding his breath.

As the boat outperformed anyone's expectations, Ferguson had tears in his eyes. Ozanne and Drummond watched in awe as their experimental side project became the main event. Larry had been told to get to San Diego as soon as possible, so he could see the wing sail. As he approached Lindberg Field, near the San Diego harbor, he banked his CJ4 twin jet over the harbor and looked down. That's when he saw the winged trimaran—taller than most buildings in the San Diego skyline—for the first time. Seeing the boat from the air, he thought to himself, *Ohmygod. What have we done. This is . . . madness.*

When *USA-17* returned to the docks the entire team of engineers, builders, and sailors were there. They still had a regatta to win in Valencia but they had already pulled off one of the biggest engineering victories in maritime history.

The next herculean task they faced—now a little over eight weeks out from the start of the America's Cup—was to get *USA-17* from San Diego to Spain. Again, the loading of the boat began in the middle of the night on December 9. The hull and all of the parts were tightly shrink-wrapped and everything was restrained on the ship that would go through the Panama Canal. The loading and unloading of the wing had to be done in the middle of the night, when there was little to no wind. It couldn't be moved in more than eight knots of breeze, as it would begin to fly.

Because *USA-17* was ninety feet wide, there were challenges in finding the right transport vessel. Tugsy had spent weeks searching for one wide enough to carry the trimaran, but narrow enough to fit through the Panama Canal. The cargo ship *Oceanlady,* only a few feet wider than the trimaran, was chosen to carry two hundred tons of freight in twenty shipping containers, plus the trimaran, wing sail, and support boats.

For the next few weeks, as *Oceanlady* passed through the Panama Canal before heading across the Atlantic Ocean and into the Mediterranean, Tugsy and Larry received daily updates on the progress of their precious cargo.

Meanwhile, Alinghi had its 100-foot-long catamaran, *Alinghi 5,* with a flexible, 200-foot-tall mast, flown from Ras al-Khaimah to Valencia. In a dramatic spectacle in an earlier relocation, when it had moved from Switzerland to Genoa, Italy, *Alinghi 5* was wrapped in a cradle and dangled below as a Russian military helicopter carried it over the snowcapped Italian Alps.

On January 4, 2010, after twenty days at sea, *USA-17* arrived in Valencia. Larry's team now had a month before the racing finally began.

24

Valencia, Spain

February 2010

A T 4 P.M., now just days before the start of the America's Cup, an urgent call went out to the shore and sailing crews of Oracle Racing. A major storm was hitting, and *USA-17* was in trouble. Everyone was needed down at the docks as fast as possible. The trimaran was never left unattended, and the skeleton crew onboard had sounded the alarm. Gale force winds from a winter mistral were turning the waters of the Mediterranean dark and bearing down on Valencia.

Just two weeks before, a similar storm had pounded the city, sending Alinghi employees running for their lives as their sail tent was knocked down and massive equipment was hurled like toys by the menacing winds. When that storm abated the dock looked like a war zone, with thrown detritus, torn sheeting, and huge pieces of metal and wood scattered everywhere. Oracle, whose base was across the harbor, escaped with only minor damage, their wing sail safely stowed, flat on the ground, under tons of headsails, inside a heavy-duty tent reinforced with concrete blocks.

But this time, the storm came on too fast, and there was no time to get the wing off *USA-17*. The twenty-three-story wing was on the trimaran and directly in the storm's path. Russell and the team had done all they could to prepare for an event like this. There was a five-minute call list—the names of team members to be called in the first five minutes of an emergency—and another list to be on call within the first fifteen minutes.

As the men arrived at the dock, *USA-17* was threatening to pull away from its moorings. It was early evening, and the cold wind was now gusting at over sixty-five knots. Jimmy Spithill, who had rushed down to the docks, took one look at the trimaran and thought of a wild stallion trying to break free from its constraints. If the boat did break free, the crew onboard would *try* to sail her out to sea. But everyone knew that was a 50-50 proposition at best. More likely, the trimaran would crash hard against the dock or seawall, causing the wing sail to come loose and *simply fly away*, taking with it the hopes and dreams of everyone involved. The most technologically innovative wing ever built for air or sea would be lost to the fury of the storm. The game would be over before a single race was run.

Throughout that afternoon, Larry had been on *Rising Sun's* bridge, tracking the storm's approach on satellite radar and on the ship's array of Brookes and Gatehouse instruments. When he first went up to the bridge at around noon, the wind speed on the B&G instruments indicated a solid thirty knots; by the time the sun set, the wind was topping fifty knots and still building. After hours of pacing on the bridge, watching the storm's menacing approach, he decided it was time to head over to the harbor and see firsthand how *USA-17* was handling the mistral. Larry had been in more than his share of storms, and here in Valencia, Mother Nature was threatening to punish him again. Dressed in foul-weather gear, he hunkered down, as *Rising Sun's* tender plowed through the gale force winds toward the harbor where the trimaran would try to ride out the night.

The waves kicked up from all directions, reflecting off the docks and the seawall that surround the harbor. In the middle of that chaotic sea was *USA-17*, lunging back and forth, straining against her heavy mooring lines, while a gusting wind of sixty to seventy knots battered her giant wing sail. The wing was trying to weathervane into the wind, but when the wind gusted, the apparent wind angle changed, and the wing developed a huge lifting force—causing the 135-foot-long, 90-foot-wide, 230-foot-tall boat to suddenly leap forward, and then snap backward as her mooring lines went taut. This violent bucking motion happened over and over again every few seconds. *USA-17* could not survive this for much longer.

As sailors continued to arrive at the dock, many stood and stared in disbelief as the huge boat thrashed around. But they didn't stand there for long. Russell ordered them into the team's six large chase boats—42-foot-long rigid inflatable boats (RIBs) with powerful engines—and told them to form a circle around *USA-17*. Then, with great difficulty, the sailors rigged up towlines between each of the chase boats and the carbon fiber crossbeams of the trimaran. The chase boats acted like six tugboats—pushing and pulling the trimaran at full throttle—battling to keep her in the center of the harbor and away from the dock.

Larry and Tugsy watched as Russell directed Jimmy and the rest of the crew on board *USA-17*, and the guys in the chase boats as they fought to maintain control of the trimaran. During the long vigil, Larry's mind replayed other storms, particularly the nightmare of the 1998 Sydney-Hobart hurricane. He remembered the mistral that hit Marseille in 2004 and damaged *USA-76* beyond repair. Now another mistral was trying to destroy *USA-17*.

Tugsy thought about the one hundred thousand hours of work and *$40 million* that had gone into building this giant one-of-a-kind boat and wing. Every day of the last two years of his life had been dedicated to building her. What took him so long to build could shatter into countless worthless pieces of carbon and Kevlar in an instant.

Finally, as the morning sun began to lighten the charcoal sky, the wind calmed. Faster than it had surged, the tempest quieted, reminding Larry of the calm after the storm as he sailed along the southeast coast of Tasmania toward the Derwent River. The hurricane in the Sydney-to-Hobart did not kill him. The mistral did not kill *USA-17*. The wing had not taken flight, and the trimaran was at rest. They had tempted fate and survived, for reasons he believed were beyond understanding. It was a twist of fate, an unexplained gift, like that described in Ernest Gann's *Fate Is the Hunter: A Pilot's Memior*—"The peril was instantly there and then almost as instantly not there. We peeped behind the curtain, saw what some dead men have seen, and survived with it engraved forever on our memories. That one second's difference, its selection, the reason for it, must haunt the rest of my living days whatever their number."

Later that morning, when Larry stepped back onto *Rising Sun,* he knew the race was meant to be decided on the water. He had started this effort ten years earlier, endured two painful and costly losses, waged a legal war, and won twelve of fourteen court battles against Alinghi. He had been involved every step of the way in building a sailboat that Burns had taken to calling a "light air flying machine." Larry had a different name for the formidable boat. He called her "the pterodactyl." The black-winged trimaran was the flying predator of his dreams.

Now the time had come to find out how fast she could fly.

The first race of the America's Cup is what sailors and the sport's enthusiasts across the globe wait for, just as NFL fans are thrilled by the kickoff that starts the Super Bowl, hockey fans watch the drop of the puck in the Stanley Cup finals, and baseball diehards cheer the first pitch of the World Series. It is that moment when the history of the sport takes a big step forward, when human drama, grit, perseverance, and a bit of luck come together. The America's Cup creates a new ideal, a new vision of what is possible on the water.

It was unseasonably cold for the beginning of the best of three series between *USA-17* and *Alinghi 5,* between the Silicon Valley billionaire—who had lost two Cup challenges and was determined not to lose for a third consecutive time—and the Swiss billionaire, who had won the last two America's Cups and believed he would win again. The first race would be forty nautical miles (twenty miles to windward and return), and the second race would be a thirty-nine-mile equilateral triangle (with the first leg to windward and the other two broad reaches) with each of the three legs being thirteen miles. A third race, if necessary, would be another forty-miler, twenty miles up and back.

The first two days of scheduled racing in the western Mediterranean were called off because of bad weather. The question being asked was, *Bad for whom?* The wind had been all of twelve knots and the waves were between three and four feet high. The postponements were pushed by Alinghi team members on board the race committee boat who insisted it was unsafe to race in such conditions.

Larry and Russell believed the real reason the Swiss were pushing for postponement was the design of the *Alinghi 5* catamaran. The Swiss boat was built to be at its best in light air. Computer models predicted that *Alinghi 5* was faster than *USA-17* in eight knots of breeze or less.

Jimmy Spithill and his crew scoffed at the delays, saying they had sailed in more than twenty knots of wind and rougher seas during most of their practice days off the San Diego coast. The American trimaran was much stronger and heavier than the slender Swiss cat. That extra weight gave *USA-17* more stability—what engineers call righting moment—than *Alinghi 5*. The boat with more righting moment usually has an advantage once the wind speed increases past a certain threshold. Oracle's computer models predicted that their heavy trimaran would surely be faster than the light Alinghi cat in more than twelve knots of breeze, and probably faster in ten knots of breeze. In under eight knots of breeze, the Oracle computer could not pick a winner.

"They can run and hide for only so long," Jimmy told the crew. "At some point, they will have to come out and race us."

That day came on Friday, February 12. Breathless commentators called it an "epic duel," "extreme sailing," and "judgment day" for Bertarelli and Ellison. They noted that for the first time in history two multihulls were in competition. Alinghi had eleven boats and two ultralight seaplanes monitoring wind speed and direction; Larry had five weather boats and a helicopter. The wind was around eight knots, and the temperature was barely above freezing. The skies were a winter blue as team members strode to the boats as players to the field, passing fans waving Swiss or American flags.

Oracle crew members, dressed in as many layers as they could wear and still move, waited from ten in the morning until three-thirty in the afternoon for the race to start. Just when they thought it was going to be another postponement day—the breeze dropped to around five or six knots—*USA-17* got a VHF radio call from the race committee boat: "Twenty-five minutes to start." Skipper Jimmy Spithill adjusted his headset microphone and said, "Let's unfurl the jib, guys, it looks like they're going to let us race today." Crew members had small boom microphones and Bose noise-canceling earphones built into their helmets. Yelling didn't work on a boat as big as *USA-17*.

The countdown to race one continued: "Eleven minutes to start, guys—six minutes to entry, let's get into it," Jimmy said as he slowly sailed the black trimaran on port tack reaching along the starting line toward the committee boat. *USA-17* passed the committee boat and kept sailing for a couple of minutes. Jimmy said, "We're going to tack back in four boat-lengths, guys. Roscoe, furl the jib. Ready guys, tacking." Jimmy carefully turned the wheel, and the three bows of the trimaran gracefully arced through head-to-wind and then *USA-17* bore away onto starboard tack and headed back toward the committee boat and the starting line. "Six minutes to start guys, one minute to entry." Jimmy pointed the trimaran just above the bow of the committee boat. "Thirty seconds to entry, trim on guys." Ross "Roscoe" Halcrow sheeted on the jib, "Cheese" De Ridder trimmed on the powerful wing sail, and the big black boat accelerated to an astonishing eighteen knots of boat speed—in only seven knots of wind speed. "We're on time here guys, full speed," Jimmy said.

As the horn sounded, marking the historic start of the 33rd America's Cup, the trimaran flew past the committee boat and Jimmy began a fifteen-degree left-hand turn around the committee boat and down into the starting box. The trimaran crossed the line and entered at full speed—flying two hulls and going over twenty knots. At the opposite end of the starting line, Alinghi entered the starting box late and slow with both of her hulls flat in the water. *USA-17* had starboard advantage (right-of-way), and Jimmy intended to use it. Jimmy brought his bow up and aimed the flying trimaran right at the flat Swiss cat. The two boats were on a collision course. Alinghi had about thirty seconds to maneuver out of the way of the fast-approaching trimaran or get a penalty. The Swiss boat started to tack from port onto starboard, but the beginning of the turn looked as if it was happening in slow motion. *Alinghi 5* was still stuck on port tack when *USA-17* arrived going full speed on starboard tack. Jimmy maintained the collision course until the last possible moment, turning the wheel sharply to the right to avoid a crash.

Jimmy had made it easy for the umpires on the water. It was clear as can be that *USA-17,* on starboard tack, was forced to alter course to avoid a collision with the boat on port tack. The rules state that it is the responsibility of the boat on port tack to give way to avoid the boat on starboard tack. Alinghi failed to maneuver out of the way, and was penalized—only the second penalty in the long history of the America's Cup.

Larry and Russell watched the start from a chase boat. Larry could barely believe what he was seeing: Ernesto Bertarelli was at the helm of *Alinghi 5,* match racing against Jimmy Spithill. After the penalty, Larry said, "I've raced against both of those guys. Ernesto never beat me, but he thinks he can beat the best match racer in the word. How crazy is that?"

During a TV interview before the race, Bertarelli had issued a mocking invitation for Larry to take the helm of *USA-17* during the America's Cup. Larry loved to drive and was confident that he could have beaten Bertarelli, but he never seriously considered taking the helm. Jimmy was the best driver on the team, and Jimmy gave Team *USA* the best chance of winning.

After the penalty, both boats were dialed up, head-to-wind for a couple of minutes, with *USA-17* to the right in a strong, controlling position. Then, suddenly, a winch broke and the trimaran was unable to maneuver. The Swiss used the opportunity to slip out of jail, sail back behind the starting line, and start nearly on time. As *Alinghi 5* started race one of the 33rd America's Cup, *USA-17* was stopped dead in the water, stuck in irons, head-to-wind and still above the starting line. It took a minute and a half for the crew to get the winged trimaran moving again, sail back behind the starting line, and then start the race. By the time *USA-17* started, Alinghi had built up a huge half-mile lead.

As Jimmy and the crew struggled to get the trimaran sailing, Russell shouted, "Jimmy, you're fucking it up! Jimmy, you're fucking it up!" Larry was rather stoic as he watched Bertarelli, with Brad Butterworth as his tactician, drive *Alinghi 5* farther and farther away from the starting area, headed upwind toward the weather mark twenty miles away. This was not how either of them wanted the race to begin.

If this had been a race between two identical one-design boats, like RC44s, the race would have been over. There would have been no way to overcome such a disastrous start. But these boats were not identical; they were very, very different. And nobody knew how they would perform relative to each other while sailing upwind in seven knots of breeze. Now everyone was about to find out.

Larry's chase boat was following close behind *USA-17,* as the trimaran crossed the starting line and Jimmy and crew got her up to speed. He could clearly see both boats on port tack—*Alinghi 5*, half a mile in front and to windward—in the perfect position to block *USA-17*'s wind and slow her down. He watched quietly for a couple of minutes—almost said something but stopped himself—and kept watching for another minute. Then, when he was sure, Larry smiled and shouted, "We're sailing higher than they are—a lot higher—at least two, maybe three degrees. We're constantly gaining gauge, slowly sliding up to weather, out from underneath them." Larry's nephew, a judge from Chicago, asked, "Is that a good thing?" Larry laughed, put his arm around the judge, and said, "Yes, Jimbo, that's a good thing, a very good thing. And Alinghi is getting bigger. That means we're going faster than they are, we're catching up. We're sailing higher *and* faster than Alinghi. Unless they are sailing in less breeze up there, and I don't think they are, we have a *much faster boat*." The excited judge raised his hand in the air and the men high-fived and shouted in unison, "Fuck Alinghi!" Those two words had become Larry's regular benediction, akin to "Amen, brother," ever since the release of the controversial Protocol for the 33rd America's Cup.

Five minutes into the race, TV commentators, armed with continuously updated GPS coordinates for both boats, confirmed what Larry thought he saw from the chase boat. *USA-17* started 660 meters behind Alinghi, but five minutes later the American boat was less than 500 meters behind. The trimaran *was* sailing higher and faster than the catamaran. Jimmy was driving smoothly, consistently flying two hulls, while Bertarelli frequently dropped both of the cat's hulls in the water, markedly slowing his boat down. "Very different drivers and very different boats," Larry said as the lead continued to shrink. The black trimaran was closing in on the grey Swiss cat, a relentless predator chasing its prey.

Fifteen minutes later, the two boats were sailing side by side. The speed difference was stunning—*USA-17* was at least two knots faster—in wind conditions that were supposed to favor Alinghi. Even in light breeze, the perfectly trimmed rigid wing sail generated enormous lift and forward thrust. Fully powered up, *USA-17* flew past Alinghi and took the lead. The trimaran had sailed from underneath and behind the Swiss to on top and in front. *USA-17* had punched right through the catamaran's wind shadow, something that is supposed to be just about impossible in sailing.

The American boat's lead continued to stretch all the way up to the top mark. Round the windward buoy and turning downwind *USA-17* was a mile in front of Alinghi. It was clear to everyone that the wing-powered trimaran was much faster upwind than the lightweight catamaran. But one crucial question remained: which boat was faster downwind?

When *Alinghi 5* rounded the top mark and started pursuing *USA-17*, the question was answered. The American boat had an even bigger advantage downwind than upwind. When *USA-17* crossed the finish line *Alinghi 5* was literally miles behind. The Swiss boat didn't get to the finish until more than fifteen minutes later.

It was the biggest margin of victory in the 160-year history of the America's Cup.

Immediately after the race was over, Larry and Russell jumped on board the trimaran. There were handshakes all around, a couple of "Great job, guys," and a "Well done, Jimmy." The entire celebration, if you could call it that, lasted a few minutes. The mood on the winning boat remained serious. Race one was over, and it was time to focus on race two.

While they were shaking hands after the race, Jimmy asked if Larry wanted to drive the trimaran back to the harbor. Larry didn't hesitate. He had driven her several times before and he almost never passed up an opportunity to take the wheel. The racecourse was far away from the harbor, and the drive back would take around forty minutes. The sun was setting over the Mediterranean as Jimmy and Larry made their way along the back crossbeam of the trimaran to the starboard steering station. Jimmy spoke into his headset and told Cheese to trim on the wing sail. Larry turned the wheel and the trimaran smoothly accelerated to a comfortable sixteen knots. Then Larry brought the bow up a bit and pointed *USA-17* toward the Valencia harbor. The two of them stood next to each other in the steering station, high above the water, as they began the twilight ride home. After a couple of minutes, Jimmy turned to Larry and smiled, "You're having fun." Larry smiled back and nodded. Then Jimmy left the steering station, walked along the narrow black crossbeam, and joined Russell and the other guys in animated conversation.

Larry was all alone on the steering platform as the sky grew dark. He focused on the heel angle, and had two of the trimaran's three hulls flying above the water. As he brought the bow up a degree or so, Cheese trimmed the wing, the heel angle increased a bit, the hulls flew higher above the water, and the boat accelerated to over twenty knots. The power was incredible. Larry had continued to push the trimaran until she was going around twenty-six knots when Larry noticed Russell waving his arms. Russell shouted something but Larry shook his head and pointed to his ear. Russell carefully walked along the back crossbeam to the steering station and said, "Larry, your driving is not going to win us the America's Cup, but it could *lose* us the America's Cup. Back off! Stop pushing her so hard." Larry laughed and slowly brought the bow down a few degrees; Cheese eased the trim on the wing; and the boat settled back down to twenty-two knots. This wasn't the first time that Russell had asked Larry to sail conservatively. But Larry could see that this wasn't as it had been in Cagliari; this time Russell really meant it.

Joseph Ozanne and Mike Drummond watched race one from the team's instrument-laden performance measurement boat. Early in the race, as *USA-17* rapidly ate into *Alinghi 5*'s lead, the designers wondered aloud whether the Swiss catamaran had a rigging problem, or some other kind of technical difficulty. When they realized it wasn't that Alinghi was so slow but that *USA-17* was so fast, Ozanne beamed: "We finally get our answer. We *are* faster."

At a press conference that followed, Bertarelli acknowledged that the rigid wing "seems to be quite a weapon." Butterworth smiled and shook his head. "Today, they showed how fast they can get their boat going. They couldn't have come off the line in a worse position, and they ended up in a very strong position. We were sitting in front of them and they sail up and around you. That's speed."

Another reporter asked if the American team had won the engineering battle by building a faster boat than Alinghi. Butterworth paused, shrugged, and looked around, "What do you want me to say, mate? They sailed from behind us to in front of us. Did *you* see what happened? Did ya? Then you can work it out."

There was no champagne and not much beer for the Oracle team that night. In a short meeting Russell advised them all that they still had one race to go and that anything could happen. They had never sailed *USA-17* without something breaking or crashing down on them. Jimmy and the crew had done a great job overcoming the winch problem at the beginning of race one. Next time they might not be so lucky. Russell had seen expensive, space-age America's Cup yachts break their masts, capsize, and even sink, vanishing into the deep. They had one more race to go. Jimmy nodded and said, "It's never over till it's over," and Larry said, "We're focused on one thing—the race on Sunday."

Late that evening, back on his yacht *Rising Sun*, Larry watched a replay of the TV coverage of race one. As he watched *USA-17* chase down *Alinghi 5* during the early part of the race, he recalled the exact moment earlier in the day when he realized that the trimaran was far faster than anyone thought, or dared say out loud. It was at that exact moment that Larry believed they were going to win the America's Cup.

That moment of realization reminded Larry of another important moment in his life, this one during his early days at Oracle. Back then, nobody believed that a relational database could ever be as fast as the IMS database made by IBM. But Oracle had just finished a benchmark for the CIA that proved that conventional wisdom was wrong; the Oracle relational database was as fast as any database on the market. That exact moment was when Larry believed Oracle would be successful. Larry was leaving work, waiting for the elevator, when he tried to explain it all to one of the company's auditors, Tony Spoor. "Do you know what this means, Tony? Do you?" Larry asked after relaying the benchmark results. "It means that Oracle is worth at least a hundred million dollars." Larry never forgot Spoor's response: silence, and a facial expression that seemed to say, *Give this guy an injection of Thorazine—he's crazy*.

But Oracle's relational database was fast, and Oracle was going to be worth even more than the estimate he gave Spoor that night. The trimaran with the huge wing sail was fast too, and Oracle Racing was now the odds-on favorite to win the 33rd America's Cup.

Early Sunday morning, Norbert took a tender to *Rising Sun* for the second, and possibly final, history-making race. Norbert was to be sequestered for the race so that if they won they could accept, as Challenger of Record, Vincenzo Onorato, president of Mascalzone Latino, the Italian team he founded in 1993. Norbert had ordered the Golden Gate Yacht Club in San Francisco closed and told club manager Bob Mulhern not to open the door or accept any letters or packages. They didn't want what was called a "rogue" challenge served on them. Onorato and Larry were meeting on board, and Onorato had his attorney with him. When the race began Norbert, Onorato, and the attorneys would head out to the finish line in a chase boat, and—if *USA-17* won—legal papers establishing defender and challenger would be signed just seconds after the race finished.

On board *Rising Sun*, Norbert was greeted by Judy Sim, and the two went downstairs for breakfast. Just as Norbert was biting into a powdered-sugar doughnut, Larry's nephew Jimmy Linn, the judge from Chicago, appeared. When introduced, Linn stopped in his tracks and said, "*You're* the commodore!" Norbert did his best to wipe the sugar from his mouth. Linn went on, "I want to thank you for what you've done for my uncle. This is all because of you!"

Norbert demurred, trying to swallow the bite of doughnut.

"I'm going to give you the shirt off my back," Linn said, proceeding to remove his shirt and hand it to Norbert. After photos were taken of the two men, Norbert spotted Larry.

Larry had a friendly welcome for the commodore—he always addressed Norbert as "commodore"—and the two talked briefly about the race ahead. Larry was in game-day mode and, gesturing to his cold-weather gear, remarked that he was wearing so many layers he looked like the Michelin Man. He was heading out to *USA-17,* where he'd be sailing as part of the afterguard, monitoring and communicating Alinghi's maneuvers, speed, heading, and wind relative to their own.

Jimmy and his crew had hit the water before the sun came up, only to learn that the start was being pushed back as Alinghi again protested about the swells. *Alinghi 5* could be towed out, sails down, and the crew could rest while waiting. But Jimmy and team, with the wing sail in, had to work every minute. The boat always wanted to charge. "This is like a freakin' caged animal that wants to go," Jimmy said, as waves slammed the boat and sharp noises came off the wing. They sailed the trimaran slowly upwind, tacked, then back downwind, jibed, then back upwind, like an airplane in a holding pattern. Sailing at angles that minimized the loads on the boat, they were doing their best not to break something before the race even started. Meanwhile, the crew members were taking turns going down a small hatch into the engine room—a BMW diesel engine powered the winches—in the middle hull. The temperature was in the high thirties, and everyone fought for a chance to be in there, as it was the only warm place on the boat.

Finally, after a six-hour delay, the race was on.

This time, it was Alinghi's turn to enter the starting box from the right, on starboard tack, with the right-of-way. Jimmy would enter the box from the left, on port tack, as the give-way boat. It is harder to win the start of a match race when you enter from the left, but Jimmy always had a plan.

As the countdown to the start of race two began, the frozen sailors on *USA-17* got ready for action. "Twenty-five minutes to start guys, let's get into it," Jimmy said into his microphone. "Radio check, radio check, can everyone hear me?" Everyone on the crew gave him a thumbs-up. "Okay, let's go on the wind for a minute and then head down and take a last look at the starting line." Tactician John Kostecki, better known as JK and the only American on board other than Larry, said, "Eleven minutes to start, six minutes to entry. Jimmy, it looks like the pin end [left end of the starting line] is favored by quite a bit." Jimmy told the crew. "Thanks, JK. Guys, we might want to start on the left. Six minutes to start, one minute to entry, let's get her going—Roscoe, Cheese, trim on. Thirty seconds to entry, we're on time, full speed."

Larry was on board *USA-17*, about to experience the beginning of his first-ever America's Cup race, but rather than being pumped up and exhilarated, he was utterly bewildered. He'd been watching Alinghi during the countdown, and the Swiss boat was nowhere *near* where it was supposed to be. At thirty seconds to go before entry, Alinghi should have been outside the starting box, sailing toward the committee boat on starboard tack. Instead, they were deep *inside* the starting box, sailing on port tack. "What the fuck are they doing?" Larry wondered aloud. "Are they lost?"

The countdown onboard *USA-17* continued—"Three, two, one"—and then the horn sounded, marking the beginning of the five-minute prestart period. Jimmy turned the wheel to the right and the trimaran dug down into the starting box. "Entry," JK shouted, letting everyone know that *USA-17* had crossed the line and entered the box. It was a near-perfect entry for Jimmy. An entry is perfect when you enter a second or two *after* the horn goes off. If you enter the starting box *before* the horn goes off you get a penalty.

Right after the trimaran entered, Larry spoke into his microphone, "Guys, ignore Alinghi for the moment, she was deep inside the box when the horn went off and she's going to get a penalty." Jimmy responded, "Copy that. Okay, guys, let's stay focused here. It's going to take them a while to sail back over to the committee boat and make a proper entry."

A yellow flag was raised on the umpire boat. Penalty Alinghi. Commentators were breathless. It was an unexpected—and bizarre—penalty for the two-time Cup defenders.

It took almost a minute for Alinghi to sail over to and around the committee boat and reenter the starting box. Jimmy dominated Bertarelli during the remaining four minutes of the prestart period. When the gun went off, *USA-17* crossed the starting line well ahead and sailed on starboard tack toward the left side of the racecourse, while Alinghi sailed on port tack toward the right side of the course. As the two boats sailed on opposite tacks, they separated rapidly. Larry watched as Alinghi got farther and farther away. With every passing second, he was getting more and more uncomfortable.

After Alinghi was about a mile away, JK said, "Enough of this, ready tack." They furled their jib and Jimmy turned the wheel to the right and tacked the trimaran onto port. The two boats were now on the same tack, paralleling each other, with Alinghi about a mile to the right of *USA-17*.

"They're definitely in front of us now, and the wind is continuing to go right," Larry said. In other words, Alinghi had found better wind conditions by separating from *USA-17* and sailing out to the right-hand side of the course. The Swiss boat was going faster because she was sailing in more wind, and as the wind direction shifted more and more to the right, Alinghi had to sail less distance to get to the top mark. It was a double whammy. Halfway up the first leg, *USA-17* had gone from 300 meters in front to more than 600 meters behind.

Another big change was that Bertarelli had given up on driving the Swiss cat, turning the helm over to teammate Loick Peyron, the superstar multihull driver from France. Peyron was driving brilliantly, first pushing the catamaran into the lead, and then fighting hard to hold on to that precious advantage. Alinghi had more wind, a right-hand shift, and a new driver. Race two looked like a whole new ball game.

Larry was furious but remained silent. When you have the faster boat you never separate. You never give the other boat the leverage to make a big gain because of a shift in the wind direction. When you have the faster boat, you try to take the weather conditions and luck out of the equation. They had made a big mistake, but they had time to recover.

During the second half of the upwind leg, *USA-17* consistently sailed a knot or two faster than *Alinghi-5*; the Americans closed in on the Swiss as the two boats approached the top mark. "We're getting close to the lay-line here, guys, we're going to tack in a couple of lengths," JK said. "Ready—tacking." Jimmy swung the trimaran onto port tack, accelerated, and brought the boat up on the wind. They were aiming right at the top mark. They had hit the lay-line perfectly. "Looks good, JK," Jimmy said. "Nice call."

"Alinghi's tacking, guys," Larry said. "They're headed our way. It's going to be close. They're going to cross clear in front, but not by that much—one hundred meters at most. Here they come." Alinghi crossed *USA-17*'s bow, sailed another couple more boat-lengths, and then began a tack onto port. Commentators called Alinghi's critical tack "painfully slow." After Alinghi finally completed its tack and began to accelerate, the huge trimaran—with its wing sail towering above Alinghi's mast—sailed right through the catamaran's wind shadow and reclaimed the lead. *Ohmygod, we just sailed right through their lee,* Larry thought to himself. *We didn't even slow down.*

USA-17 rounded the top mark, eased the wing and jib, and pointed directly at the next corner of the triangular course, the jibing mark, thirteen miles away. The Swiss boat rounded only twenty-eight seconds behind the American team. In race two, unlike race one, Alinghi was sailing very well. They had recovered from their terrible start, and with Peyron at the helm, they crossed in front of *USA-17* not once but twice during the first upwind leg of the race. And it was still very close as both boats began the second leg of the race.

There were no maneuvers required on leg two of race two. To get to the next mark, all you had to do was drive straight. It was a thirteen-mile sprint—the ultimate test of boat speed.

USA-17's wing was thirty feet taller than Alinghi's mainsail, and the rigid wing could be trimmed much more precisely than Alinghi's soft sails. The combined advantages of size plus aerodynamic precision meant that the wing alone produced more than twice the forward thrust of Alinghi's two soft sails combined. And the heavier trimaran's big advantage in righting moment enabled her to translate the enormous power input of the wing into an output of raw, pure boat speed.

Leg two was like a drag race between a beautiful gray-and-red Mercedes-Benz convertible and a supercharged matte-black Indy car. The much faster trimaran left the catamaran in its wake. *USA-17* jibed around the second mark two minutes and forty-four seconds—more than a mile—in front. On the third and final leg to the finish, Jimmy, standing alone on the steering platform like a science-fiction star voyager, knew they had a huge lead. But disaster could still strike. The only time *USA-17* had held together perfectly—save for the faulty winch—was day one of the America's Cup. He looked at the massive wing and studied the instruments. They were hitting speeds of over thirty-three knots. He turned and looked over his shoulder. The Alinghi catamaran looked small, and was now more than two miles behind them. All Jimmy needed to do was get the trimaran safely across the finish line. As they drew closer, Jimmy began to think: *We are probably going to do this.* He let himself glance at the guys, and saw Larry nod and give him a thumbs-up.

The horn sounded and shouts rang out across the harbor as Oracle Racing's winged trimaran crossed the finish line. The American team had won the 33rd America's Cup. Jimmy, the youngest skipper to ever win the Auld Mug, gave *USA-17* a pat—and then another—right in front of her steering wheel.

The commentators gushed: "After two and a half years of controversy, finally, the America's Cup has been decided on the water. These giant multihulls have taken sailing to a place it's never been. Today, February 14th, 2010, in Valencia, Spain, after a fifteen-year absence—the America's Cup is America's again. And BMW Oracle, with their trimaran, returns it to the Golden Gate Yacht Club of San Francisco."

As cheers continued to ring out, Larry's first reaction was, *It's over, it's finally over.* It was a sigh of relief that he had not lost again. The joy of winning, the exultation of winning, would come a few sober moments later when he made his way across the large boat and gave Jimmy a hug. He congratulated and thanked everyone on the crew.

Shortly after they crossed the finish line, an Oracle Racing chase boat slid up next to the black trimaran and Russell Coutts jumped on board and joined his teammates—every one of them handpicked by the great sailor himself. Russell immediately started shouting,

"Everyone shut up! Shut up! I've got a question to ask, just one question: Where's our fucking Cup? Where's our fucking Cup?" Jimmy lunged for Russell and grabbed him, and the two of them staggered around on the winning boat hugging each other. Larry raised his fist in triumph, cut in on Jimmy, hugged Russell, and joined in the celebration.

When it was time to take the trimaran back to the harbor, Jimmy turned the helm over to Larry, who sailed her home. He sailed her for the last time anyone would ever sail her. She had done her job well. She survived stormy seas, claimed the sacred silver chalice, and brought everyone safely home. She was a giant. The water would never see the likes of her again.

Larry was alone and filled with emotion as he drove USA-17 back to Valencia. The last time he had a feeling anything like this was years earlier, when he drove USA-76 in a race against Alinghi in Newport, Rhode Island. Right after the start of the race in Newport, he could hear the people on land chanting, "Go USA, go USA." At that moment it became very clear that they were *not* BMW Oracle Racing—they were the American team.

It was dark when they arrived back at the harbor. Everyone on the crew jumped off the trimaran into chase boats, and headed toward the dock. During the slow chase boat ride, Larry turned and took one long last look at his triumphant pterodactyl—then he jumped onto the pier and ran as fast as he could. Russell, Jimmy, and others were being thrown right off the pier and into the frigid water. That was something he wanted to avoid, tradition be damned. He ran straight to his BMW and locked himself inside. He had spent more than ten hours out on the water, and he was so cold he could not feel his face. A freezing bath was a really bad idea.

Tugsy was at the docks, having watched the final race from a chase boat. He also had held his breath, hoping that USA-17 would hold together. For the builders and designers it had been a campaign like no other as they raced to a deadline that continued to move, having created a boat that had never before been built. He knew every bit of work that went into USA-17. She was conceptualized through creative and analytical genius and built with grit and determination by a crew that had to dig themselves out of plenty of holes. As he talked with the shore crew about getting the boat packed up and put away one last time—and getting the skyscraper of a wing safely onto the pier—Tugsy's tough exterior and poker face briefly melted away. The sailing team headed to the press event and party but he and his guys had a job to do. He couldn't help thinking of his very first boat, the seven-foot Sabot given to him by his father. He'd sailed it at the local Keri Keri Cruising Club. That boat was also lucky number 17.

"Before the press conference, I want to be able to move my face," Larry said, leaning his face into the heater. "I am hypothermic." They drove around like this until the ceremony was about to begin.

Inside the hall, Larry stood below the stage surrounded by revelers. When he turned around there was Norbert. The two hugged and looked at each other in sheer wonder.

"Commodore, we did it," Larry said. Norbert had never seen Larry this happy.

The program began and, as they started to head up the stairs, Larry directed Norbert to walk in front of him. Nearing the top of the podium, Larry placed his hands on Norbert's shoulders and whispered conspiratorially in his ear, "So what do your neighbors think of you now?"

Norbert laughed out loud. He knew the races were being closely followed in San Francisco, especially by his neighbors at the St. Francis Yacht Club.

Onstage, the old silver trophy, out of reach for so long, was handed to the new Cup defender, Larry Ellison.

Tens of thousands of people had gathered to watch the ceremony. Larry walked over to the microphone and said "Valencia, *muchas gracias!*" to cheers that refused to die down. He then took the precious 160-year-old America's Cup in both hands, raised it over his head, and pumped it up and down as the crowd continued to roar. Then he passed the Cup to Russell and Jimmy as the rest of the sailing team joined him onstage. It seemed that the cheers and applause would go on forever. Fireworks and confetti were launched, and magnums of champagne were sprayed. Then the esteemed Cup itself was filled with champagne and passed around, so the victors could drink from the oldest trophy in sports.

25

Valencia to San Francisco

February 2010

NORBERT WAS PACKED UP to leave Valencia for San Francisco when Judy Sim called. Larry wanted the commodore to bring the America's Cup home. Norbert would fly with the team and the trophy in first class.

"You mean I don't get to bring it back in coach?" Norbert said, thinking back to the dream of a decade earlier, on the night he'd connected his boating club to sailing's marquee event.

On the morning of February 19, Norbert and the Oracle Racing team, silver ewer in tow, began a journey that would take them from Valencia to Madrid to Frankfurt and then to San Francisco. The Auld Mug traveled with its own security and was packed like a Monet on loan from the Metropolitan Museum of Art, carefully, with gloved hands, and—in this case—sealed in a custom-made Louis Vuitton trunk.

Norbert walked into the first-class cabin with Russell, Melinda Erkelens, Jimmy, and a few of the other sailors and team administrators. The trophy, resting in its huge case, took up three seats in first class, across the aisle. Norbert thought it was the ideal seatmate: silent and beautiful.

Getting it from one flight to the next, though, was an ordeal, only slightly worse than lugging Madeleine's enormous suitcases around. Norbert always wondered how his tiny wife, who was five-foot-two and weighed under a hundred pounds, could have so much luggage. At every security stop, the Louis Vuitton trunk had to be opened and inspected and agents asked to have their picture taken with the trophy. As passengers found their seats for the next leg of the flight, some of the sailors helped the flight attendants angle and secure the Louis Vuitton trunk with rope, seat belts, and bungee cords.

A flight attendant, looking at the bowline and slipknots, joked that the sailors knew their way around a knot.

Norbert, who had a bag full of white BMW Oracle Racing hats, offered a cap to all of the flight attendants. As soon as they were in the air, the captain announced that team members from Oracle Racing were on board, along with the historic trophy. "We're bringing it back to the United States," the pilot said, "for the first time in fifteen years!" Cheers and applause broke out from the front of first class to the last seat in coach, and the flight attendants had a new addition to their uniforms—Oracle Racing hats.

Throughout the journey the case was opened so passengers could gawk. Norbert had to admit that next to his mother's 1978 Cadillac Seville, which he had in his garage and kept for its sentimental value, this was the nicest piece of metal he had ever seen. The Golden Gate was only the sixth trustee in the history of the Cup. The New York Yacht Club had held the trophy from 1851 to 1983, until it was won by the Royal Perth Yacht Club in Australia, which held it from 1983 to 1987. Then it was held by the San Diego Yacht Club from 1987 to 1995, followed by the Royal New Zealand Yacht Squadron from 1995 to 2003, and then Société Nautique de Genève from 2003 to 2010.

Tom Ehman, Oracle Racing's behind-the-scenes guy who did the job of twenty people and would be responsible for getting the Cup engraved, had told Norbert that the forty-five-pound trophy was going to get taller under Larry's watch. The boatbuilding team had orders to add a new carbon base and run a bolt from the bottom of the trophy to the throat. Ehman had chuckled when he noticed that Alinghi was the only team in the history of the Cup to choose a bigger font size for its engraving. A decision had been made among the Oracle ranks to return to the traditional font size but to spin around the bottom sterling-silver tier of the trophy so that Oracle would be on the front and Alinghi on the back.

Two hours before landing in San Francisco Norbert headed to the bathroom. He didn't want to look as exhausted as he felt when he stepped off the plane. He shaved, changed his clothes, smoothed his hair, and put on aftershave. The first plan had been for Russell and Norbert to carry the trophy out of customs, where a large crowd and loads of press were expected. On the plane, though, Russell said it should be Jimmy and Norbert who carried the trophy. Russell would follow.

When they passed through customs and the glass doors slid open, cameras flashed and cheers rang out. Norbert carried the trophy from the left side and Jimmy held it on the right side. After a short press conference, Norbert and the team headed to curbside and everyone jumped into waiting cars. The Cup had its own police escort. Their destination was the Golden Gate Yacht Club, where a bigger press conference was scheduled. Norbert, seeing that all of the reserved black cars were taken, approached a police car waiting to leave. He showed the policemen his ID from his officer days in Rohnert Park and thought to himself, *Once a cop always a cop.*

"I'm the commodore of the Golden Gate," Norbert said. "Can I grab a ride with you guys?"

The officers told Norbert to hop in. Arriving at the Golden Gate, Norbert jumped out of the back of the squad car and invited the officers to drop by the club anytime. The Cup had already been taken inside and Larry was said to be on his way. Oracle had built a tent outside and the place had been spruced up with new flowers and shrubbery. Inside was standing room only.

The press conference began in the main upstairs room—with its worn blue carpet, doors with portholes for windows, and ceilings with curved wooden beams like the bottom of a boat—and Larry gave a rousing talk about the responsibility of representing his country, the rewards of being part of a team, and the virtue of perseverance—never giving up. He talked about *USA-17* as a "stunning piece of engineering," and the "limit of what is technologically possible at the dawn of the twenty-first century." As Larry spoke, Norbert found a quiet place at the bar and ordered a cold beer.

He had been approached again recently by the head of the St. Francis with the idea of merging. This overture had happened before race one in Valencia, when he was sitting at the bar of the Holiday Inn. Peter Stoneberg, the St. Francis's incoming commodore, took a seat next to him. A lifelong sailor, Stoneberg congratulated Norbert on the trimaran and asked if he'd been able to get out on it. Norbert laughed and said he'd been out on it and had been terrified. "On the netting, you're thirty feet above the water, just when you set up," Norbert said. "When you fly a hull, you feel like you're sideways in the hands of King Kong. I walked off of it and my legs were shaking. I had to pretend that it was great, no problem, tough like John Wayne. But I was dying."

Stoneberg laughed and got to his point. When he said, "This could be a win-win situation," Norbert knew what was coming. The club that at one time would not give the Golden Gate the time of day wanted to merge—again.

"Here you are, within reach of the Cup, of bringing it back to San Francisco," Stoneberg had said at the bar in Valencia. "We should really talk about merging our clubs."

Norbert looked at Stoneberg and said, "You know, I've been talking with some of the guys at your club about this off and on for years. I'm all in favor but, again, I'd have to run it by my folks, and by Russell and Larry."

Afterward, when Norbert had mentioned the merger idea to Russell, Russell looked at him as if he was nuts. "Why would you want to do that? You've got the Cup! No. Don't even think about it," Russell said. And when Larry heard of the idea, he said, surely joking, "Okay with me, so long as they agree to trade buildings with us."

Norbert looked down the shoreline at the St. Francis. The Cup had passed right by its front door.

26

Rancho Mirage, California

March 2010

As THE AMERICA'S CUP TROPHY went on a national tour, Larry headed to Southern California. His romance with sailing had turned into an obsession with the sport's greatest prize. Finally, he had figured out how to build the best team and the fastest boat possible. As the defender, he needed to plan for the next Cup. But first he needed a break. He wanted to focus on another sport, the one that had consoled him during the turmoil after the 2003 America's Cup, when he said, "Fuck sailing! I'm going to take tennis lessons."

At around the same time he was winning the America's Cup, he had bought one of the world's great tennis tournaments, the BNP Paribas Open, for $100 million. He arrived in Indian Wells, near Palm Springs, in March—just a month after his America's Cup victory—for a benefit he spearheaded called "Hit for Haiti," bringing together superstars including Roger Federer and Pete Sampras playing Rafael Nadal and Andre Agassi to raise $1 million for relief for Haiti. Larry bought the tournament because he thought he could make it better, and also because he didn't want to see it move overseas. There was talk of it going to China.

He had thought of buying a basketball team—and looked at the Golden State Warriors—as he loved to play, and one of his all-time heroes was fourteen-time all-star Jerry West. He also looked into bringing a football team to Los Angeles. Tennis won out because he liked the guys who played, and it had become his latest passion. He had become a strong clay court player, and had deep and accurate ground strokes, but had to be dragged to the net and needed to up the pace on his first serve. He played five or six days a week at his house with Sandy Mayer, a Stanford alum who was a former Wimbledon and French Open doubles champion and had been the seventh-ranked singles player in the world.

In the same way his sailing had taken him from nearly capsizing on the San Francisco Bay in his Lido 14, which reminded him of the blue Tupperware box one might use to store teriyaki chicken in, to driving in professional match racing regattas and commanding Team USA in the America's Cup, Larry had graduated from taking sixty-minute lessons to rallying with his friends Roger Federer, Tommy Haas, and Rafael Nadal, who tried to convert him to a two-handed backhand.

The only thing he didn't love about owning the tournament was the commute. The tournament was ten days long, and every day he piloted his jet back and forth between his homes in Malibu and the tennis in Palm Springs. Not one to stay in hotels, he quickly realized that since he had bought the tournament, he needed a house to go with it—much as his wife, Melanie, might conclude that since she had the tobacco-brown Hermès Kelly bag, she now needed new shoes to go with it.

He told his realtor that he needed a house with lots of bedrooms. He wanted room for his family and friends, plus he planned to invite some of the players to stay at his house during the tournament. They'd have great dinners together, and he'd have formidable sparring partners.

The realtor told Larry that he could get a six-bedroom house or buy two adjacent houses.

Larry said he needed a house with at least eighteen bedrooms.

The realtor tried to explain to Larry that there were no houses in the Palm Springs area with eighteen bedrooms, but there was an estate for sale with a seven-bedroom main house plus twelve more bedrooms in eight separate guesthouses, in Rancho Mirage. It was on 250 spectacular acres and had a nineteen-hole golf course rated the thirteenth-best course in the country.

Larry didn't play golf—years ago when he had tried it, there had been profanity and thrown clubs—but he told the realtor, "The golf course doesn't matter."

Larry arrived at the property, walked into the main house, and commented on the decor: "Turkish brothel."

Then he corrected himself: "Turkish brothel—but not a high-end Turkish brothel."

He made his way through the house, which was called the Porcupine Creek Estate. Reaching the in-house movie theater he stopped. Things were going from bad to worse. On the back wall was an enormous mural showing the owner of the house seated between Kim Novak and Marilyn Monroe. The owner's wife was also in the mural, next to Einstein.

Moving on, Larry made note of the floating angels in the cloud frescoes on the ceilings, the Tiffany glass skylights, and the French marble fireplaces—not exactly his preferred clean, elegant, minimalist style.

"They tried to reproduce the Sistine Chapel here in the desert," Larry said. "But instead of hiring Michelangelo, they got confused and hired Michael and Angelo instead." Heading for the door, he said, "Horrendous. Worse than anything in Las Vegas."

Larry and his realtor left the property to look at other houses. After hours of searching and finding nothing big enough, Larry said, "Take me back to the brothel."

Larry bought the place from the creditors—the couple had divorced and filed for bankruptcy—for $43 million.

Larry's first call was to Glenn McPherson, who managed all of his properties. Larry told him the brothel needed transforming into something normal and that it needed to be done quickly, before his guests arrived.

"There are seven thousand pine trees on the golf course—*pine trees* in Palm Springs?" Larry said incredulously. "Some are dead and the rest are dying. We're going to have to replace them with palm trees. The house is horrible. Just paint over everything—the angels, Marilyn Monroe—everything. Paint all the plaster walls and ceilings our standard cream white. We've got to get the entire place landscaped, painted, and refurnished in five weeks." McPherson immediately got on the phone with Pottery Barn and placed his order to a stupefied-sounding rep. He needed thirty-five cream-colored couches, seventy easy chairs, and one hundred ottomans, for starters. The sales rep said that they did not have thirty-five cream-colored couches in inventory. McPherson then said, "I'll take what you've got, and give me the rest in light gray."

Larry had also just bought another property, the Astor estate in Newport, Rhode Island, which Melanie had spotted in 2004 when they were there for the UBS Cup. It was the Beechwood mansion, which he bought, having never seen the inside, for just under $11 million. Melanie was fixing up another house in Santa Barbara and thought it would be fun to work on the Astor estate, the former summer home of the Astor family, which in recent years had been rented out for weddings. Larry also owned ten houses on Malibu's Carbon Beach, and another Malibu house on twenty-two acres on Cross Creek that he was turning into a botanical garden and museum. He brought in more than one thousand species of orchids. He had two houses close to each other in Kyoto, Japan, including one on the temple grounds in Nanzenji, and also his house in San Francisco. He briefly considered buying a dairy farm on New Zealand's Bay of Islands, as he loved the Kiwis. And he had his eye on a few other major properties but was waiting for the right moment to snatch them up, in particular a tropical piece of land.

For decades, Larry had built up his Japanese art collection, and he planned one day to turn his home in Nanzenji into a museum. In recent years, he had been buying deco, surrealist, and impressionist pieces. He loved the paintings of Tamara de Lempicka, Paul Delvaux, and René Magritte but wasn't a fan of Salvador Dalí.

He had been buying works by Monet, Degas, Gauguin, and the French academic painter William Bouguereau. When he told his friend David Geffen, an acclaimed collector of abstract expressionists, that he had just bought two Bouguereaus, Geffen rolled his eyes and said, "Why?" Larry responded, "Because they're pretty. I don't collect the angels. I collect the French peasant girls." When Geffen continued to stare at him with a mix of horror, disbelief, and agony, Larry felt obligated to defend himself. "I bought a Bouguereau, I didn't have sex with a goat. I didn't do anything twisted. Okay, okay, I admit it. I like art that's beautifully rendered. At least I didn't spend millions on a Damien Hirst dead fish in a transparent plastic box." That was something both he and Geffen could agree on. Larry had a rule that he never bought art that he could have made himself over the weekend. His most recent buy was by his favorite artist, Vincent Van Gogh. It was a magnificent landscape with a price tag of $40 million. Until that, the most he had paid for a painting was $15 million. He found much of contemporary art to be fraudulent, but couldn't help being impressed with the profits generated when Damien Hirst and his entrepreneurial art dealer coconspirator sold a dead shark floating in formaldehyde for millions of dollars. Larry looked forward to receiving contemporary art auction catalogs from Christie's and Sotheby's because they always made him laugh. He would read the pretentious description of a plain white canvas aloud before turning out the lights.

Within no time McPherson, who had over one hundred painters working on the Rancho Mirage house at one point, had the Turkish brothel transformed. Even Larry's closet was fitted to order. In each of his houses, he had the same wardrobe: ten pairs of charcoal-gray wool slacks, ten cotton khaki pants, ten charcoal-gray cashmere sweaters, and ten gray cotton T-shirts, all from J. Crew. He also had khaki tennis shorts and *Sayonara* and Oracle Racing cotton shirts. He never wore jeans, as he found them uncomfortable. He still had his share of Brioni and Attolini suits, Charvet ties, and Edward Green shoes, but he had grown weary of the work required, especially with sleeves, cuff links, buttons, and ties. A few years earlier, Larry had been pictured in *Playboy* along with Will Smith, Michael Douglas, and San Francisco mayor Willie Brown as among America's ten best-dressed men. These days he liked to have a uniform that didn't require thinking.

Settled into his Rancho Mirage house, Larry had dinner one night with Roger Federer, and he mentioned a conversation he'd had earlier with another tennis great, Jimmy Connors. Larry had told Connors that sometimes he went out and "just hit" without really focusing on anything in particular.

Connors looked at Larry and said, "Oh, *you don't want to do that*." Larry recounted how Connors had given him a look "like I'd just told my rabbi that I was converting to Catholicism!" Larry was intrigued by Connors's reaction. To Connors, the idea of going out and hitting without being focused on improving your game was sacrilege.

Larry had come to understand the "charmed, tormented life" of athletes, that fitting subtitle of Jerry West's autobiography. Whereas Larry found a brutal but welcome clarity in sports, he had seen how professional athletes—including his dinner mate Federer—were defined by minutes or even seconds of competition. West wrote in his book: "Can you imagine what it's like to feel like you have a game won, and then you don't? One shot, one play, one call? What I do know is that it hurts, it really hurts." The athletes Larry knew were obsessed with the game they played. They were like his friend Steve Jobs, who worried about the color of the screws inside a computer, who wanted one switch and not two to control the doors in his plane. They reminded Larry of a line from *Tombstone*: Wyatt Earp asks Doc Holliday, "What makes a man like Ringo, Doc? What makes him do the things he does?" Doc replies, "A man like Ringo has got a great big hole, right in the middle of him. He can never kill enough, or steal enough, or inflict enough pain to ever fill it."

For better and worse, Larry had the same hole, and he tried to fill it by winning. But as soon as he closed in on one of his goals, he immediately set another difficult and distant goal. In that way, he kept moving the finish line just out of reach.

By the summer of 2010 Larry needed to focus his attention back on the Cup. He would think about not only how to defend but *where* to defend the Cup.

As it turned out, deciding on the host venue—Larry had committed to making an announcement by the end of 2010—was more complicated than he thought. San Francisco was an obvious choice, for it had the Golden Gate Yacht Club and it was where Larry had a home, the spectacular white, modern mansion with dead-on views of the bay. But the Eternal City of Rome had made an offer too grand to ignore. The Italian government's complex proposal could potentially net Oracle Racing hundreds of millions of euros to host the next America's Cup in the waters off the coast of central Italy, where the Tyrrhenian Sea meets the Mediterranean.

In the early summer of 2010 Larry flew to the Italian capital to meet with Prime Minister Silvio Berlusconi. The two men greeted each other and, setting negotiations aside, Berlusconi cheerfully and warmly said, "Ah, Larry, we have the same boat, the Perini Navi." The prime minister had bought his Perini Navi, a 184-foot super yacht named *Morning Glory,* from their friend Rupert Murdoch.

"But," Berlusconi added with a mischievous smile, "my Perini Navi is better than your Perini Navi."

"Oh?" Larry asked, standing in Berlusconi's elegant office, while ministers stood silently as if at attention. Old-world oil portraits dotted the walls and flags jutted out.

"So, Silvio, why is your Perini Navi better than mine?" Larry asked.

"Because," Berlusconi said, delighted by the question, "I have an *all-female crew,* except for the captain." The energetic prime minister raised his hand, excused himself, and promptly headed out of the room, returning moments later with a photo. Berlusconi handed

Larry an eight-by-ten-inch photo of his captain and crew aboard his boat. No one said a word, ministers remained at attention, and Berlusconi watched eagerly. Larry studied the photo, wondered what he could possibly say in response, and handed the photo back to the prime minister. Berlusconi laughed and nodded. The photo showed his crew of a dozen women—all young, all beautiful—standing on deck and lifting their shirts to expose their breasts.

"Why, yes, Silvio," Larry said, choosing his words carefully, "I see your yacht *is* better than mine."

Larry knew of the sex scandals and allegations of corruption that swirled around the controversial seventy-four-year-old Italian billionaire, who had dominated his country more than anyone else since Mussolini. Larry couldn't help but like him. His comments about his boat and crew were stunning in their political incorrectness, but they were made with an adolescent joy and innocence. Larry appreciated people who pursued their dreams and said what they thought—men like Howard Hughes, who raced planes, pioneered modern air travel, and invented myriad things, including the underwire bra. When Hughes shot *The Outlaw* with Jane Russell, he felt that the movie was not presenting Jane's breasts optimally, so he went to Hughes Aircraft and he and three other engineers wrote a long and detailed memo on the design of an underwire bra and what they were trying to accomplish to get proper décolletage.

Over the years, Larry had seen his share of fakes, and to him, Berlusconi was not one of them. Larry found it humorous how the actor George Clooney, who attended some of Berlusconi's wilder parties, claimed he only went to the parties to raise money for his charitable foundation. Clooney had choreographed his public image to be that of a morally enlightened person, but Larry preferred a forthright Berlusconi to the Clooney charade any day, though he expected *everybody* to abide by the law.

After Berlusconi returned the photo of his prized crew to a safe place, he came back into the ornate office so that he and Larry could get down to business. Larry loved Rome, and the Italians were crazy for the America's Cup. The country had three teams in the 32nd Cup, there was long-standing interest from Prada head Patrizio Bertelli, and Oracle's Challenger of Record was Vincenzo Onorato's Mascalzone Latino syndicate, sponsored by Club Nautico di Roma, located in the ancient port of Ostia.

The Italian plan was to hold the event in a newly developed port in the town of Fiumicino, home to the Leonardo da Vinci–Fiumicino Airport. The model for the deal would be the *dársena* in Valencia, the site of the 32nd and 33rd America's Cups. The Valencia port had been transformed from an industrial site into a working marina that would host the America's Cup, and later it would be turned over to private interests. Sixty cities had bid on being the host and venue for the 32nd Cup after Bertarelli won in 2003 and brought the trophy for the first time ever to Europe. The two finalists were Lisbon and Valencia, and Valencia had won out by offering the most. It would spend hundreds of millions of dollars to transform the port, and officials would pay around 90 million euros in cash and another 30 million euros in guaranteed sponsorships for the right to stage the event.

But the frenzy to host the 2007 Cup took place before the mortgage crisis in the United States, and before the sovereign-debt dilemma in Europe. Oracle Racing was now dealing with a different economic reality: huge governmental bailouts, crashing stock markets, and consumer pullbacks. Larry had received overtures from a handful of cities, with the most lavish and enthusiastic coming from Italy. Others had come from San Diego, California; Long Beach, California; Newport, Rhode Island; Valencia; and San Francisco.

Larry still loved the idea of San Francisco but he was more than a little wary of the city's politics and its penchant for lawsuits over everything from soccer fields in parks to shadows cast by skyscrapers. When the Olympic torch came through San Francisco in 2008, the torchbearer had to be routed away from thousands of people demonstrating against China's policies toward Tibet, and the flame had disappeared from view with no police escort for periods of the race, infuriating the Olympic committee. It was a city where a dozen different agencies, each represented by its own body of elected officials, often worked at cross-purposes, and where the mayor and the city's board of supervisors would be more his adversaries than his allies.

The meeting between Larry and the Italian prime minister ended with a handshake. Berlusconi was confident a deal could be reached, and Larry was pleased at the prospect of hosting the next Cup in the cornerstone of civilization, the great city of Julius Caesar and Augustus, with all of its pageantry and drama. *What better place for the America's Cup?*

To honor Oracle Racing for winning the America's Cup, on February 14, San Francisco mayor Gavin Newsom hosted the team at a victory party at City Hall. The sailors strode down the red-carpeted stairs—the gleaming trophy was front and center—and Larry spoke evocatively about sailing in San Francisco Bay.

Newsom listened as Larry talked with humor about his early days sailing out to the Golden Gate Bridge in his Lido 14 and described the waters of the bay as a spectacular "natural amphitheater." Larry made it clear that the host and venue for the Cup would be a competition and that San Francisco would need to "step up" in a significant way. Newsom handed Larry a key to the city and Larry handed Newsom an Oracle Racing jacket, which the mayor promptly put on.

In the weeks and months that followed, Newsom and his staff put together a proposal and started regular discussions with Stephen Barclay, the tightly wound chief operating officer of Oracle Racing, who served as chief negotiator. Newsom, who was thirty-six years old when he was elected mayor in 2003, was gathering as much information as he could on cities in contention, signing up for sailing blogs, and calling on friends and past donors to feed him information on the behind-the-scenes negotiations in other parts of the world.

Newsom understood that Rome was sincere, but he was also aware that Italy was becoming mired in its own economic woes.

Newsom and his economic development director Jennifer Matz had told Barclay from the start that, given the state of the economy, they were in no position to offer the team cash. Newsom told Barclay, "If the city can't write a check, we can do what we've done with the Exploratorium and others with long-term leases, and that is to either reduce the rent or give free rent." The city had done hundreds of deals with the Port of San Francisco using similar strategies, where private corporations put up money for development and received rent credits in return.

Newsom, who ran a successful wine business before entering politics, was amused by Barclay's intensity. He didn't blame Barclay for asking the city for more than it had ever done, but Newsom needed the heavily accented Kiwi to understand that San Francisco was a city that "prides itself on process and transparency." It was a city where the America's Cup waterfront deal would need approval from his office, the board of supervisors, port officials, the elected representatives from the San Francisco Bay Conservation and Development Commission, San Francisco Recreation and Parks, and the U.S. National Park Service, the federal agency that oversees Crissy Field and the Presidio.

Newsom offered Barclay long-term development rights to Pier 50, Piers 30–32, and Seawall lot 330. Pier 50, just south of the San Francisco Giants' ballpark, was twenty-two acres of prime land, situated in an area that had become home to a new hospital, a teaching center, and various start-up and global biotech companies. Larry would need to spend some $12 million to upgrade the twenty-two acres. Piers 30–32, under the Bay Bridge, made up twelve acres of dilapidated and red-tagged land being used as parking lots. Larry would need to spend $55 million to get them ready for the America's Cup and long-term use. Seawall 330 was across the Embarcadero from 30–32 and it needed immediate work. It was considered strategically important to the conjoined pier.

The deal Newsom offered stated that whatever Larry spent, Larry would receive back in free rent credits. As Newsom described it, "If they give they get, if they don't give they don't get." Barclay took it as a straightforward land transaction: the city couldn't give cash so it was giving land. If Larry spent $50 million to develop a property for the races, he would receive the same figure in rent credits from the city.

As negotiations progressed with San Francisco, the parallel talks with Rome had begun to unravel. When Barclay and Russell held a meeting with Claudio Gorelli, a stout, distinguished-looking, silver-haired administrator put in charge of the deal by Berlusconi—Gorelli was commodore of Club Nautico di Roma—Barclay asked for the terms to be put in writing. Gorelli scoffed and berated Barclay, saying with great passion that he didn't know "how things work in Italy."

By late fall San Francisco was the lead candidate and Barclay was feeling cautiously optimistic about the deal. However, around this time, word leaked out that the deal in Italy was crumbling as fast as the country's economy, and Berlusconi was dealing with the latest in a string of long-standing corruption charges. Larry was now just two months away from needing to announce the host and venue city.

Then, on December 1, Barclay, in Dubai for a race, received an e-mail saying the deal between San Francisco and Oracle Racing had been redrawn. The coveted Pier 50 and associated development rights were out (the Giants baseball team, which had just won the World Series, had its eyes on Pier 50). Offered in their place were Piers 27–29, the site of a long-proposed but stalled cruise ship terminal. Larry would use the terminal site, which the city would now be forced to invest in, for the America's Cup events and then hand the property back to the city.

Barclay couldn't believe what he was reading. All of a sudden, the development potential of the deal had been halved. Within a week of studying the new deal, he saw that in addition to the cut in development rights, the city would now cover in rent credits only the estimated costs of the redevelopment, not the actual costs. The Port of San Francisco, too, had added terms that placed taxes of one percent on any future condominium sales and fifteen percent on any lease assignments, thus reducing the value of any development that would take place there down the line. As a backup, Tom Ehman, Russell, and Barclay raced to Newport to see if a deal could be reached there. And in San Francisco, Barclay informed the famously fractious city board of supervisors, scheduled to vote on the deal on December 20, that if the deal as written went through Oracle Racing would "pull the plug" and the event would move elsewhere. Nevertheless, the redrawn plan was approved by the board, with a vote of eleven to zero.

The next day, Larry stepped in. He told Barclay that under no circumstances would he get into a battle with the city of San Francisco. Barclay was not to issue the strongly worded press release he had drafted and sent to Larry.

Calm but firm, Larry said, "Stephen, we're out of options and we're out of time. The next America's Cup is going to be in San Francisco even if I have to pay for it myself. I'll call the mayor and try to get a better deal, but I'm not optimistic."

Larry then got on the phone with Mayor Newsom and asked for some of the earlier language to be restored. Newsom, watching as City Hall emptied out for the holidays, said, "Let's not have all of these other people involved. How do you and I figure this out?" He found Larry as personable and forthright as anyone he'd ever met. Larry told Newsom that he wanted to hold the next Cup in San Francisco so long as they could agree on terms for the waterfront real estate where the team bases would be built. Newsom, who was leaving City Hall to be California's lieutenant governor, had a list of ten to fifteen items he wanted to accomplish before checking out of San Francisco. Landing the America's Cup was his number one priority.

Over a seventy-two-hour period Barclay and Russell—with Barclay working behind the scenes, telling people only half jokingly that he'd had hair before the process began—reframed half a dozen parts of the deal, the biggest being the elimination of the taxes the city was trying to place on condo sales and leases, and also the city's reimbursement of actual costs in lieu of estimated costs.

By New Year's Eve day Newsom and Russell, who was then off with his family on a vacation in the French Alps, had agreed to all of the terms, but the final paperwork needed to be sent to Larry, who was in the Caribbean with his family.

Newsom was at dinner in Cabo San Lucas with his wife, Jennifer Siebel Newsom, and Senator Dianne Feinstein and her husband, Dick Blum, when he got the call from Russell. The deal was done: San Francisco had won the rights to host the 34th America's Cup.

A few days later, back in San Francisco, Newsom said that the City by the Bay was the best place on earth to host an event of this stature, "and we could not be more proud to be the city that brings the America's Cup back home to the United States." He noted it was a "big deal for San Francisco, California, and the United States" and predicted it would pump more than $1 billion and some eight thousand jobs into the region.

There would be a spectacular new America's Cup village built along old, dilapidated piers, news cheered by developers and residents who had wanted something done about the decaying piers for decades. A course was drawn up along the waterfront and out to the Golden Gate Bridge, with the expectation that millions of people would watch from the shore. For the first time in the Cup's history the action would be free and accessible to all. Viewers could take in the race from landmarks including the Embarcadero, Crissy Field, the Marin Headlands, Angel Island, and the Golden Gate Bridge.

Successive America's Cup world series regattas would be staged across the globe, starting in August 2011 in Cascais, Portugal, and ending in San Francisco in September 2012. Then the Cup would head to Italy in the spring before returning home for the start of the Louis Vuitton Cup in early July 2013. The French fashion house had come back in and was committed to a great event in San Francisco, with 2013 marking the thirtieth anniversary of Louis Vuitton's first Cup event. And for the first time in more than two decades the races, including the world series and qualifying regattas, would be covered live by NBC and on-demand worldwide as well as on YouTube. The world series boats would be fast and agile AC45s, 44-foot catamarans, with a mast height of 70 feet (extendable to 83 feet), a displacement of 3,086 pounds, and a crew of five. The Louis Vuitton Cup and America's Cup would be contested in AC72s, 72-foot catamarans with a displacement of 13,000 pounds, and a stunning mast height of just over 131 feet. The boats would go dangerously fast, up to forty miles an hour. All of it would be covered live on international television. The reimagining of the 160-year-old America's Cup was under way and Larry wasn't just out to win the Cup—he was out to win everyone over.

27

Moscone Center, San Francisco

Fall 2011

"GOOD AFTERNOON, MY name is Sting," the musician said as he walked onstage at Oracle OpenWorld in his faded gray jeans and cream-colored T-shirt. "I'm excited to be at the largest technology conference in the world and perform for you tonight on Treasure Island. I'm impressed by the great technology used by this company, and I'm impressed by how the company is running this conference as sustainably as possible." With that, Sting raised his fist, said, "Have a great time," and exited the stage as quickly as he appeared, leaving conferencegoers starstruck and still holding up their phones like lighters.

The stage turned dark before the concert-size screens came to life with an MTV-style video of Oracle Racing's new AC45 catamarans sailing in the San Francisco Bay. The video, set to high-adrenaline music, showed the young, fit crew members as they sped from under the Golden Gate Bridge and over to Alcatraz Island. In one shot that elicited *oohs* and *aahs* from the crowd, a catamaran helmed by Russell Coutts pitchpoled, flipping end over end and sending crew members into the water and Russell flying straight through the sail.

The lights came back on and a woman's voice announced: "And now, Larry Ellison."

Larry, in a black mock turtleneck and caramel-brown suit, walked onstage. Sitting in front row center were Mark Hurd, his newly hired president; Safra Catz, Oracle's other president; and chief marketing officer Judy Sim. Filling up the entire front row of the adjacent section were members of the Oracle Racing team, along with Tom Ehman and some of the engineers and designers—all in racing shirts. Norbert was there every day as a part of the Oracle Racing presentations.

The twenty-ninth annual conference attracted a crowd of more than forty thousand people over five days. One of the anticipated topics was cloud computing, and Larry was expected to introduce Oracle's newest applications for the cloud, something critics said he was late in bringing to the game. Larry responded that he "could not have been late to the cloud" because he "invented the cloud" in 1998, when he founded NetSuite, which offered the cloud-based Software-as-a-Service (SAAS) for business management. NetSuite was started six months before Salesforce.com was founded in 1999 by Marc Benioff, a former Oracle employee. NetSuite was the second-biggest cloud company in the world, trailing Salesforce, but Larry vowed, "In a few years Oracle will be number one in the cloud." He also noted that "Salesforce.com has been around for more than ten years, but didn't call themselves a cloud computing company until six months ago. Now they claim to be 'the force behind the cloud.'" Larry considered Benioff, a former friend, neither friend nor foe. He looked at Benioff as just another CEO of another company he wanted to destroy.

Larry began his keynote address by talking about why Oracle had made a six-year effort to move to the next generation of technology that had been built around cloud computing.

"Six years ago, it wasn't called the cloud, it was called SAAS," Larry said. "The term 'cloud' was popularized by Amazon.com's Elastic Compute Cloud; then the term was opportunistically adopted by a raft of SAAS providers that were miraculously born again as cloud companies."

After a good hour of walking the audience through the service, Larry wrapped up his speech by saying, "We started this by working with our applications customers, with PeopleSoft and Seibel customers, with Oracle E-Business Suite customers, with Hyperion customers. We asked what they wanted in the next generation of technology. This was a six-year journey of rewriting all of our applications to meet the needs of our most demanding customers. It was a gigantic effort. Over one hundred Fusion application modules—all rewritten on top of modern Java middleware technology—available today, in the Oracle Cloud. It took us six years, but I think it was worth the wait."

As Larry thanked the crowd and turned to walk offstage, Safra Catz darted from her front-row seat and ducked down as she rushed backstage.

Reaching Larry, she held his arm. Her expression was alarming. "I'm so sorry," she said. "Steve just died."

Larry had seen his best friend over the weekend, when Steve decided to stop all medications, but Larry never imagined he would go so fast. Larry, who was supposed to do an interview with CNBC, instead got into his waiting car and headed back to Woodside. Apple released a statement saying that Jobs, who was fifty-six years old and battling pancreatic cancer, had died "peacefully at home with his family."

Larry sent an e-mail to Laurene, Steve's wife of twenty years, saying, "If you need me to do anything, tell me."

With his iPad on his lap, Larry blinked through tears. He thought of a walk he and Steve had taken in Castle Rock State Park. They used to take long hikes, but in recent times—as the cancer worsened—the hikes got shorter and shorter, until the two kept their walks close to home. The walks in Castle Rock were where Larry learned the details of what Steve was working on. It was on a walk sometime in 2005 that Steve first talked to Larry about his idea for the iPhone. The iPod had been released to great success but Larry was concerned with the iPhone idea. He knew that an iPod had a small amount of software but a telephone was loaded with applications and had a huge amount of system software, making it thousands of times more complicated.

"Microsoft started from scratch and totally fucked it up," Larry said.

Steve looked at Larry and said, "That's why we're taking the Mac OS and moving it over to the phone." Steve explained that everything that had been developed at NeXT Computer, and everything learned about graphical user interface for the Macintosh, was being applied to the iPhone.

Larry responded, "Good answer. That just might work."

More recently, Larry and Steve had talked about Steve's yacht being completed in Holland. Her name was now *Venus*, not *Aqua*. The two had spent years working on her, having started the process by studying the clean lines of a Wally 50m sailboat. *Venus* was magnificent, with forty-foot-long glass walls, reminding Larry of a floating Apple store. Steve had been looking forward to finishing the boat and taking his family out on her maiden voyage.

Back home, standing by the lake where he and Steve had debated things great and small, Larry was certain that decades from now there would be two guys walking somewhere, talking about their icons. Steve would be mentioned. He would be one of those "misfits, rebels, troublemakers, the round pegs in square holes, the ones who see things differently," words popularized in Apple's "Think Different" ad campaign. Steve would be remembered as one of those with "no respect for the status quo." As he said, "The people who think they are crazy enough to change the world are the ones who do."

Larry looked across the lake where he and Melanie had been married. They had divorced a year earlier. As he had predicted marriage changed things. The fights had begun and he wasn't a fighter, at least at home. He reserved his combat for work or sports. Now Steve was gone, and Tom Lantos, his father figure, also was gone, having died in 2008. Larry lived by the Japanese saying "Your garden is not complete until there's nothing more you can take out of it." But now things were being taken that he wished were still there.

28

Alouis Radiators, San Francisco

Fall 2011

Back in the radiator shop for another day of business, Norbert was in good spirits. The America's Cup would be coming to San Francisco. Business had picked up again after the recession and the banking and mortgage mess. He had meetings scheduled on the Golden Gate Yacht Club's hosting duties. In no time, the world's eyes would be on the San Francisco waterfront and his club would be front and center.

Norbert was whistling to himself when his father walked in. It was 1 p.m. on a Wednesday and he hadn't expected to see his dad that day.

"Hiya, Dad, how are you?"

Jozo looked at his son and said he had some news of his own.

"I'm selling the building," Jozo said.

Jozo had hinted at Norbert's daughter's birthday lunch a month earlier that he might sell the building, but Norbert thought it was a joke, or perhaps a thinly veiled threat.

"The most recent appraisal was two and a half million," Jozo said, noting that he would give Norbert first right of refusal. "I want to use the money to help the family, and to give some of it away."

"First right of refusal?" Norbert said, dumbfounded. He didn't exactly have an extra $2.5 million sitting around. Norbert pulled his dad aside so his employees wouldn't hear the discussion.

"Dad, I'm going to need some time on this," Norbert said in shock. He had employees who had been here for decades and the business was strong. *Where would he move to if the building was sold out from under him by his own father?*

Madeleine wasn't surprised when she heard the news. The America's Cup was Jozo's latest excuse to be unhappy with Norbert. "He always wanted you to focus on the shop, on *his* shop," she said. What probably pushed him over the edge, she speculated, was that Oracle Racing had won the Cup and that the Golden Gate and Norbert were being treated as vanquishing heroes.

"It's hard to take," Norbert said, "but in the end it is his building."

Madeleine asked if he would consider resigning as commodore to please his dad and keep the business.

"I've thought of that," Norbert said, standing in the bar of their Larkspur home, a framed photograph of John Wayne on the wall behind him. *If he quit the America's Cup, would it repair his relationship with his father? Would it be the right thing to do?* He needed time to think about it. He was fifty-six years old. *What should he do?* He felt as if he had an angel on one shoulder and a devil on the other. The angel was telling him one thing and the devil was urging him to cave in to his dad so he could keep the business, worth millions. It was his nest egg and his livelihood.

Driving to work, stuck in traffic on the Golden Gate Bridge, Norbert was reflective. His father was a mystery to him. When he was a young boy, he and his dad had been out securing a boat with bungee cords, Jozo on one side, barking orders at him, and Norbert on the other. The taut bungee line slipped and flew back, and the heavy metal hook hit Norbert hard in the head. Norbert opened his eyes and saw his father staring down at him, tears in his eyes, terrified he had killed his only son.

As Norbert watched the burned-orange span of the Golden Gate Bridge turn into the world's most beautiful parking lot, traffic coming to a stop, he realized something important. Had his mother, Gertrude, been alive, she would have talked sense into Jozo. She would have been proud of what her son had done and looked forward to the history that would be made in San Francisco, and at the Golden Gate, where she and Jozo had shared happy times.

Norbert gazed out to the right, to the soft gray sea and rocky coastlines of San Francisco and Marin, and over to the San Francisco waterfront. A tanker was heading in and sailboats were heading out from the docks. The light gray fog mixed with the morning's pale yellow. Along the shoreline, not far from the Golden Gate Yacht Club, windsurfers sliced through the waves. They looked free and unencumbered, so sure they could handle the wind and sea.

The decade had brought the unexpected to Norbert's life. He and Madeleine had traveled to great spots and made close friends, including Larry. Norbert had saved a yacht club and was now preparing to host one of the world's biggest sporting events. But it was the ironies, the *what ifs,* that played in his mind. Had his mom not died unexpectedly, his father would not have joined the Golden Gate Yacht Club and he would not have become commodore. Had he not become commodore, there would surely not be a Golden Gate Yacht Club today. Had he not reached out on that afternoon in 2000, Oracle Racing would probably be sailing out of Southern California or even linked to a yacht club on the East Coast. And had he not taken that fork in the road, the America's Cup would probably not be coming to San Francisco.

It was the same for his father. If Jozo's brother had gotten on the boat that fled Yugoslavia, Jozo would have stayed behind in his native land. He would not have met Gertrude, and he would not have come to the United States and opened a successful radiator shop. That escape in the dark of night from Hodilje was Jozo's fork in the road. He had taken it, creating a legacy that had made his family proud. The radiator shop was his father's to keep or to sell. His father had told him that he would be able to run the shop for the next two years. After that, maybe he would take a different fork in the road. The 34th America's Cup would be over and another in the works. He would be okay. As traffic picked up, and he took the exit for Marina Boulevard, Norbert knew he was leaving *his* mark. His father had brought the family to America, arriving on February 14, 1957. Norbert had been part of winning a trophy for America exactly fifty-three years later, on February 14, 2010. He and his dad had both found the American dream.

29

Stanford University, California

Fall 2011

INSIDE THE MEMORIAL CHURCH on the Stanford campus, Larry was seated between the folksinger Joan Baez and U2 front man Bono for a private, invitation-only memorial service to honor his best friend, Steve Jobs. The walkway in front of the chapel was lined with small white lights, and security was tight. Bill Clinton, Al Gore, and George Shultz were there, and Yo-Yo Ma played the cello.

Larry chatted quietly with Baez, whom Steve had dated when he was in his twenties. He laughed, recalling Steve's story of when he was at Baez's house and happened to answer the phone. "Joanie isn't here right now," Steve said. "Okay," the caller replied. "Please tell Joannie that this is Bob—Bob Dylan." Steve was unable to speak. He revered Dylan as an artistic genius—his lyrics had been a source of inspiration and insight during Steve's formative years.

Larry said to Baez, "Bob Dylan was probably the only person who ever intimidated Steve and left him speechless."

Larry knew Bono well, having had him as a guest on *Rising Sun*. Bono was one of the few people Larry had met in the entertainment industry whom he found entirely genuine. One afternoon on the yacht, when they were talking and playing music, Bono gave Larry his famous green guitar. Both Baez and Bono performed at the service. Steve's sister, children, and wife, Laurene, spoke. Jonathan Ive, Apple's head of product design, was the sole representative from the company to address the gathering. The only other person to speak was Larry. He had written his eulogy on his iPad a few nights before. It came to him easily, as had the speech he wrote for his son's wedding two weeks earlier. He just sat in bed and typed what came to mind, finishing in two hours.

Sitting in the ornate chapel—an interdenominational church built by Jane Stanford as a memorial to her husband, Leland—and listening to the encomiums, Larry sighed. Baez reached over and patted his arm. "It's going to be okay," she said.

Larry left the wooden pew and headed to the altar.

The title of his eulogy was "Steve: Irreplaceable."

Larry began, "They say that no one is irreplaceable. I don't believe that, not anymore. Steve Jobs is irreplaceable. The irreplaceable, creative genius of our generation. Our Edison. Our Picasso. We watch, listen to, and use the products of his mind every day and everywhere. He was unique—at once a sublimely inspired philosopher, artist, and inventor. A relentlessly determined entrepreneur, engineer, and leader. An intensely focused singularity that translated ideas into things that worked. In doing so, he reinvented entire industries: computing and communications, music and movies. All done in one, too short, lifetime."

Larry paused to survey the five hundred guests seated in the Chapel. "But that's not all he did," Larry went on.

That's just the visible-light portion of Steve's spectrum. He played other, less visible roles: father, husband, and my best friend. In each and every one of those roles, he is irreplaceable.

My twenty-five-year friendship with Steve was made up of a thousand walks. If there was something he wanted to talk about, and there always was, we'd go for a walk. We'd climb to the top of Windy Hill, hike around Castle Rock, or through the sand on the beach at Kona Village. More recently, our walks grew shorter: north on Waverly for a few blocks, then back home again.

Over the years, one particular walk stands out. We had a lot to talk about on that day, so we jumped in the car, put the top down, and headed out to Castle Rock State Park in the Santa Cruz Mountains. It was back in mid-1995. Steve was finishing up *Toy Story* at Pixar and running NeXT, the computer company he founded after he left Apple. Apple was in severe distress. It had gone steadily downhill during the ten years of Steve's absence. The problems were now so serious people were wondering if Apple would survive. It was too painful to watch and stand by and do nothing. So the purpose of that particular hike through the Santa Cruz Mountains on that particular day was to discuss taking control of Apple. My idea was simple: *buy* Apple and immediately make Steve CEO.

I knew we could borrow the money. Apple wasn't worth much back then. All Steve had to do was say yes. Steve favored a very different approach: persuade Apple to buy NeXT Computer. He'd join the Apple board, and over time, the board would recognize that Steve was the right guy to lead the company.

I said, "Okay, that might work. But Steve, if we don't buy Apple, how are we going to *make any money?*" Steve suddenly stopped walking and turned toward me until we were facing each other. He put his left hand on my right shoulder and his right hand on my left shoulder and stared unblinkingly into my eyes. "Larry," he said, "this is why it's so important that I'm your friend. You don't *need* any more money."

I said, "Yeah, I know, but we don't have to keep it. We could give it away."

Steve just shook his head and said; "I'm not doing this for money. I don't want to get paid. If I do this, I need to do this standing on the moral high ground."

"That moral high ground," I said, "well, that just might be the most expensive real estate on the planet." But I knew I had lost the argument. Steve had made up his mind, right there and then, at Castle Rock in the summer of 1995, to save Apple his way. At the end of the hike, right before we got into the car, I said, "Steve, you created Apple, it's your call. I'll do whatever you want me to do." The rest, as they say, is history: The iMac—sorry, no beige, iPod, iTunes—a thousand songs in your pocket, Think Different, the iPhone, iPad, and—for a moment—the most valuable company on earth. While it made Steve proud, it wasn't even one of his goals. Like the ancient Greeks during the age of Pericles, Steve pursued truth and beauty and an impossible perfection in what he built and how he lived.

One last story. Steve had this peculiar, delightful sense of humor and a trademarked, muffled laugh to go along with it. After work, we'd often go out to our favorite local Japanese or Indian restaurant. And sometimes we'd go away together on holiday to Kona Village on the big Island of Hawaii. All four of us would be there in Kona: Steve, Laurene, me—and *whomever* I was married to or dating at the time. We'd be in the middle of a dinner conversation, and suddenly there'd be this quiet laughter coming from Steve. The three of us would stop talking, turn, and look at him. Eventually, one of us would ask him, "What's so funny, Steve?" He would try to tell us, but each time he tried to speak, he could only get out a couple of words before he'd slowly look down at the table and start laughing again. This would happen over and over again until we all started to laugh and laugh, never having the slightest idea what Steve found so funny in the first place. Believe it or not, this happened a lot. Those moments are my most cherished and enduring memories of my time with Steve. The four of us sitting together at Kona, eating papayas, and laughing for no reason at all.

Larry folded his notes. "I'll miss those times," he said. "Goodbye, Steve."

After the memorial service, Larry went to the reception held in Stanford's Rodin Sculpture Garden, a two-minute walk from the church. Larry was there to support Laurene and try to guard her as much as he could. He found her surrounded, with everyone sharing stories of Steve. Then something else happened—everyone turned to talk to him. He was unable to respond; he excused himself and went for a walk around the campus, returning when the crowd was thinning. He found Laurene and told her he was heading home. He needed solitude and silence, or at least the sounds that soothed him. Normally, he drove himself, but he had a driver today, given the security in and out of the area around the chapel.

He arrived home and went to his bedroom. Opening the glass doors facing the lake, he let in the cool misty air and took in the sounds of moving water. It was the sound of life, the sound that sustained him. Larry sat on his bed and looked at the reflections dancing on the water. He worshipped nature but knew of nature's cruelty. He was at the place in life where friends were dying, and something fundamental was changing as the people around were going, never to be replaced.

He had read Walter Isaacson's biography of Steve and thought that it failed to capture the man he loved and respected. Larry felt that Isaacson, instead of finding Steve hardworking and brilliant, had shaped an argument that the Apple chief was ruthless and that it was the bad part of Steve that gave him his edge. Larry wondered why Isaacson wouldn't let Steve be a hero, why he wouldn't let him be the Edison of our time, as Larry saw him. The author made Steve *replaceable* and, in Larry's mind, fed into a culture based on a homogenized egalitarian ethos where everyone was the same, where there are no winners and no losers, and where there are no more heroes.

Larry looked at the one trophy he had in his bedroom. It was a trophy for the Cagliari Cup, the first time he'd won a regatta driving against the world's top pros, against the young gods of sailing. He kept the trophy because he had been judged by one thing: how well he sailed. The other trophy he had held on to was from the 1998 Sydney-to-Hobart race; he kept that trophy on his powerboat *Musashi*. Thirteen years had passed since he and the crew of *Sayonara* sailed at daybreak into the calm of the Derwent River. He could still hear the somber sounds of the bagpipes, feel the soft breeze, and marvel at the colors of the flowers on the riverbanks. The trophy reminded him—if there was ever a time when he forgot—of the glory of each new day. It reminded him that heroes exist. He had seen them on *Sayonara*. His maxi yacht was now housed in a temperature-controlled warehouse, and he would never sell her. In his mind, it wouldn't be fair to have her compete against more modern boats, and he couldn't stand to see her lose. And *USA-17,* his beautiful behemoth, also would never be sailed again for the simple reason that it would cost millions of dollars just to get her ready for the water. She was a $40 million wonder sailed in two races. Larry wanted the record-setting wing sail to end up at a museum.

Sometimes Larry would look around his Woodside house, as beautiful and serene and spectacularly landscaped as any place on the planet, or he would go down to his garage and look at the cars—his all-aluminum AC Cobra, his McLaren F1, his LFA Toyota, his Bugatti—and think, *How did this happen?* And there were times when he would walk into Oracle headquarters in Redwood Shores and look up at the huge cylindrical glass buildings and say to himself, *How do we pay all of these people?* Of course he knew, but the size of his life sometimes stunned him. He was a kid, he liked to say, born with all of the disadvantages needed to succeed.

Heading down a set of stairs into his movie-screening room, he ordered a late dinner. He had chefs on rotation, and a printed menu was offered to him with entrée selections. Turning on his television, he searched for tennis, listened to a bit of the news, had a quick bite, and decided to call it a night.

On his way out, he was surprised to see the America's Cup trophy. The 160-year-old Cup, which men had spent their lives and their fortunes pursuing, which had riveted nations and spurred new technologies, was here in his screening room. It came and went, out for appearances or over to the Golden Gate, then back to rest with him in Woodside. It was secure here. Some days he stopped to look at it; on other days he paid it no attention. There were times, such as now, when his mind was filled with other things, and he was startled even to see it there, jolted as if by someone's sudden presence in a room. Dimming the lights, Larry lingered for a moment to look at the glistening silver ewer. He had made friendships for life, including the commodore and a cast of characters—sailors, engineers, builders—who had all worked hard and realized their dreams. The America's Cup had been returned to America, and he and his team would defend it on the glorious natural amphitheater of the San Francisco Bay.

Larry knew that, in the end, the America's Cup was just a boat race, Wimbledon was just a tennis match, and the Super Bowl was just another football game. As Muhammad Ali once said, "It's just a job. Grass grows, birds fly, waves pound the sand. I beat people up." No one was going to live or die on the basis of these things. But contests were his best teachers. At some point, one person gets measured against another. They find out who wins and who doesn't, and along the way they learn something about themselves.

Larry had learned that he loved the striving, the facing of setbacks, and the trying again. It was what his friend Rafael Nadal said about savoring the fight and the winning would come.

Everest, it turned out, was never more beautiful than looking up from below.

PART IV

"It ain't over 'til it's over."
—Yogi Berra

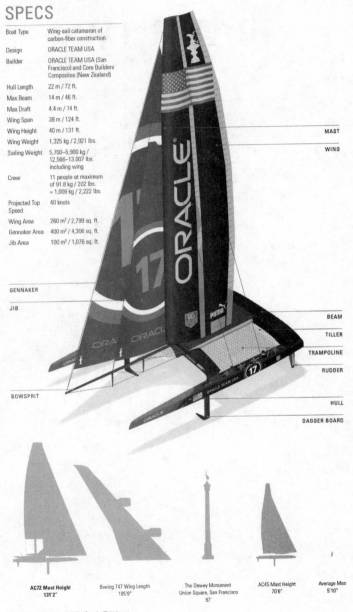

THE AC72

SPECS

Boat Type	Wing-sail catamaran of carbon-fiber construction
Design	ORACLE TEAM USA
Builder	ORACLE TEAM USA (San Francisco) and Core Builders Composites (New Zealand)
Hull Length	22 m / 72 ft.
Max Beam	14 m / 46 ft.
Max Draft	4.4 m / 14 ft.
Wing Span	38 m / 124 ft.
Wing Height	40 m / 131 ft.
Wing Weight	1,325 kg / 2,921 lbs.
Sailing Weight	5,700–5,900 kg / 12,566–13,007 lbs. including wing
Crew	11 people at maximum of 91.8 kg / 202 lbs. = 1,009 kg / 2,222 lbs.
Projected Top Speed	40 knots
Wing Area	260 m² / 2,799 sq. ft.
Gennaker Area	400 m² / 4,306 sq. ft.
Jib Area	100 m² / 1,076 sq. ft.

MAST

WING

GENNAKER

JIB

BEAM

TILLER

TRAMPOLINE

RUDDER

BOWSPRIT

HULL

DAGGER BOARD

AC72 Mast Height
131'2"

Boeing 747 Wing Length
105'9"

The Dewey Monument
Union Square, San Francisco
97'

AC45 Mast Height
70'6"

Average Man
5'10"

Oracle Team USA's AC72.

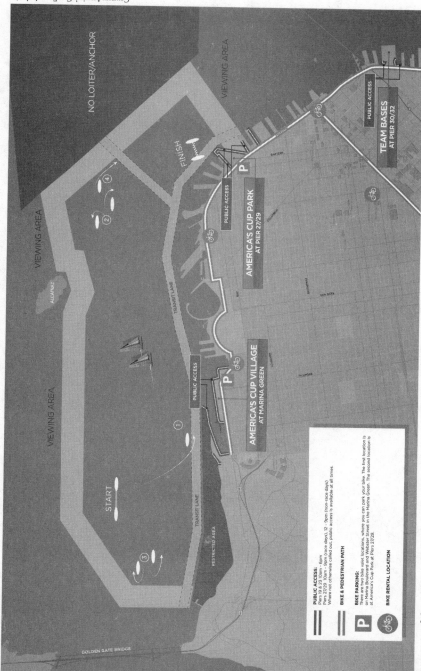

Course map of the 34th America's Cup.

30

San Francisco Bay

Summer 2012 to Summer 2013

EARLY ON THE MORNING of August 30, 2012, Oracle Team USA's new black catamaran was wheeled for the first time from the cool dark build shed at Pier 80 in San Francisco into the bright sunshine. The seventy-two-foot long hulls, painted gloss black, gleamed in perfection, smooth like glass, as graceful a combination of curves and angles as the stealthy F22 Raptor jet fighter.

The new class of America's Cup boat, the AC72, had taken nearly fifty thousand man-hours to build. Its three-dimensional hard wingsail, standing at thirteen stories—131 feet—was longer and larger in area than the largest jumbo jetliner wing. As the $11 million boat, emblazoned with the team's lucky number 17 and the American flag, was moved toward the water's edge, sailors stood by in hard hats, smiling at the nautical wonder. The wing, sealed in black aeronautical film skin, was slowly, carefully lifted by a giant crane. The stillness of the moment was broken by the sounds of seagulls and by cheers ringing out along the docks. The AC72 represented the most complex piece of engineering ever attempted for an America's Cup boat, mixing marine hydrodynamics, structural mechanics, aerodynamics, and optimization theory. The class of boat had been dreamed up to captivate a new generation of sailors, and was a move away from the heavy monohulls that made their way around the course at ten miles per hour to machines that sailed over fifty miles an hour and up to three times the speed of the wind.

"This is the first time the boat sees sunlight," said team engineer Dirk Kramers, who had been involved in the America's Cup since 1977, when aluminum was the cutting-edge material used for the 12-meter boats of the day. Kramers, admiring the black beauty, added, "She's been in the shed for the whole building process. Hopefully she behaves without any vices." Not far away was Mark "Tugsy" Turner, the watchful cohead of boatbuilding for Team USA. The launch of the AC72 was late by nearly two months, delayed by design and material modifications, and Turner was anxious to get the enormous cat into the water.

It had been a trying and exhausting process to get this behemoth built. But on this day, there was only pride and a sense of promise. The team, led by owner Larry Ellison, had imagined an extreme version of the America's Cup, racing close to shore for the first time in the regatta's 162-year history; in boats that flew above the water on hydrofoils at breathtaking speeds; and with unprecedented television coverage enhanced by onboard cameras, sensors, a GPS, and computer-generated graphics to make sailing understandable and accessible to the masses. All that, plus an expected windfall of more than $1 billion to the city of San Francisco generated by activities and tourism around the 34th America's Cup.

Starting a year earlier, in Cascais, Portugal, Oracle Team USA had competed in world series regattas held in spectacular venues across the globe, drawing huge crowds in Plymouth, England; San Diego, California; Naples, Italy; Newport, Rhode Island; and Venice, Italy. Over the summer, tens of thousands of people had turned out for more of the regattas in San Francisco, races that offered a preview of the Louis Vuitton Challenger Series that would start in July 2013 and the main event, the America's Cup, to begin September 7, 2013. The Golden Gate Yacht Club, with its mechanic Norbert back as commodore, played host to the world series events. The clubhouse, decks, and front lot were mobbed from morning to late at night. Larry stopped by the yacht club before the regattas to see the clubhouse and visit with Norbert. Up the road, the St. Francis Yacht Club also reaped the benefits of the racing, holding its own hot-ticket America's Cup parties. Competitors in the world series events included Oracle Team USA; Artemis Racing, Sweden; Luna Rossa Challenge, Italy; J.P. Morgan BAR (Ben Ainslie Racing), England; China Team; Emirates Team New Zealand; Energy Team, France; and Team Korea. The teams were competing on one-design forty-four-foot wing-sailed catamarans (AC45s), which clocked up to thirty-five knots (around forty miles per hour). There were close calls, crashes, and pitchpoling, and the strategy of adding speed and danger paid off. A video showing Oracle Racing CEO Russell Coutts and his crew capsizing an AC45 in San Francisco Bay quickly attracted more than two million views on YouTube.

Team USA was now just a year out from the start of the 34th America's Cup, and their iconoclastic owner was intent on turning sailing into an exhilarating sport. While Larry appreciated the gilded image of the Kennedys out sailing at Cape Cod, he wanted to move sailing into the twenty-first-century world of the X Games. He wanted kids to look at sailing and think it was as cool as skateboarding, as exhilarating as kite surfing.

As the morning sunshine warmed the old pier on San Francisco's industrial shoreline at this coming-out party for Team USA's AC72, the shiny carbon catamaran—embodying daring ingenuity and painstaking precision—was christened with a bottle of champagne. Glasses were raised and a toast given, wishing all of those who sailed on her "fair winds and good fortune."

Six weeks later, eleven sailors from Team USA headed out at 11:30 a.m. from Pier 80 for their eighth training session aboard the strapping AC72. It was October 16, and the team had already faced problems with the boat, including breaking one of their

L-shaped daggerboard-hydrofoils on the very first day of sailing, something that sent the hobbled cat limping back into the shed and revealed structural problems with the other daggerboards that had already been made.

The forecast for the day was ten to fifteen knots of breeze. Skipper Jimmy Spithill, considered Russell Coutts' choice to drive in the America's Cup, and crew headed out in the direction of Alcatraz with the idea of doing a series of training laps between the island and the Golden Gate Bridge. They would practice tacks and jibes and work on getting the AC72 up on the two hydrofoils that lifted the seven-ton boat out of the water, a mode of sailing called foiling. Because it dramatically reduced drag, with only the horizontal hydrofoil portions of the two daggerboards and the two rudders remaining in the water, foiling doubled the speed of the catamaran. It was the fastest way to sail an AC72 catamaran, and Jimmy and the rest of the crew were eager to learn how to do it.

As they practiced, the forecast wind speed of ten to fifteen knots proved wrong. It was now blowing at over twenty knots close to Alcatraz, and thirty knots near the bridge. The fresh breeze colluded with the ebb tide to churn the bay a frothy white, and the choppy waves were getting bigger, steeper, and closer together.

"Shit, we got a bit on," Jimmy said. "The wind is going nuclear on us." Jimmy and his crew were experienced racing together in catamarans, coming in first in the AC45 world series regattas. But the AC72 was new to them, bigger and incomparably more powerful than the AC45. As they turned toward the lee of Alcatraz and tucked in behind Treasure Island, they found some protection from the weather—the breeze calmed a bit. Now, three hours into their training session, Jimmy wondered if they should head to the quieter south bay.

"Let's do one more lap," he said.

As they sailed toward the Golden Gate Bridge, the wind was whipping at peaks of thirty-five knots. Conditions continued to worsen, making it clear to everyone on board that they were sailing on the edge, getting close to losing control of their boat. The call was made to head back to the base. That meant that Jimmy and crew had to turn *USA-17* from sailing upwind toward the Golden Gate Bridge to downwind toward Alcatraz Island. The maneuver is called a bear-away. When sailing a catamaran in strong winds, bearing away is both difficult and dangerous. As a catamaran turns away from sailing upwind and transitions to sailing downwind, the boat passes through a wind angle called the "death zone."

Sailing upwind on starboard tack, Jimmy began a left turn away from the bridge and toward the San Francisco city front. As the boat turned and the wind angle got wider, the catamaran transitioned from upwind to downwind, causing the huge wing sail to generate more and more power. The big cat suddenly surged forward and accelerated, like hitting the KERS button on a Formula One car. Efforts to trim and depower the wing failed. The AC72 continued building speed until both bows dug into a wave and the two hulls of the catamaran pitched downward and dove underwater like two submarines submerging side by side. As the front of *USA-17* dove deeper, the back end of the boat lifted into the air until the stern was pointing straight up. The AC72 continued its slow-motion tumble, and Jimmy—seeing that a terrible crash was now inevitable—screamed out: "We're going *now*! Watch out for your mates."

Trimmer and grinder Kyle Langford was on the leeward side and scampered as far forward as he could. Murray Jones, an America's Cup Hall of Famer who had won four consecutive America's Cup matches, had been uneasy sailing in such strong winds and wanted to return the boat to dock an hour earlier. Watching the bow go under, Jones—called "Cap" or "Captain" by the crew—knew it was going to be bad. He had gotten himself into one of the leeward cockpits, considered a relatively safe place to be. As the boat pitched forward past ninety degrees, Jones got lower in the cockpit and held on. Under the heavy groaning and screeching of parts, the catamaran suddenly stopped its somersault before completing its capsize.

The top of the wing slapped onto the surface of the water, but didn't break or submerge. The buoyant wing sail was keeping the fifteen-thousand-pound catamaran from turning completely upside down on top of the crew. Jones listened to the sounds the wing was making, fearing its main structural element, the wing-spar, might snap at any point. When he didn't hear the telltale sounds of cracking carbon fiber, he began to look around. Langford had been sitting on the trampoline about ten feet from him when the bows dug in, and he was now hanging vertically from the trampoline by his fingertips. Jones began talking to him, and managed to pull the wing sheet across his back, hoping Langford could grab it and climb down. But if the twenty-three-year-old Aussie let go of one hand to reach for the sheet, he was going to drop; it was all he could do to hold on with two hands. Jones then cleared the sheet and reassured Langford that nothing was in his way.

"You are going to have to drop," Jones told Langford, who eyed the rough water thirty feet below. Langford dropped and Jones held his breath. Thankfully, seconds later, Langford popped to the surface. Jones then worked his way to the forward cockpit and focused on what he could do to save the boat.

Tactician Tom Slingsby, who had been right behind Jimmy before the pitchpole, had watched in shock as the catamaran slowly rotated forward until the massive wing sail hit the water like the tail of a whale. Slingsby had thought they would be fine out of the bear-away. Now, with the wing horizontal and the hull vertical, a head count was taken. With a sense of urgency, the sailors jumped one at a time into the water and climbed aboard three different chase boats, fearing that the rough seas could at any moment break the wing-spar, causing the catamaran to finish its rotation and turn completely upside down.

Jimmy took another head count from his chase boat. Ten guys. Someone was missing.

"Where is Murray?" Jimmy screamed, feeling a terror he had never known. Jones was not on any of the chase boats.

As the men searched, Jimmy kept yelling, "Where is Murray!" The waves pounded the boat, making it difficult to hear. Finally, he spotted Jones—still aboard the AC72.

Jimmy exhaled. "Hey, Cap," he said. "You wanna come off there, mate?"

Over the next ten hours, the once-gleaming *USA-17* was pummeled by waves as the shore crew affixed ropes and lines to try to tow her back to base. They were in a battle against Mother Nature, and in a race against the setting sun. That evening, earth, moon, and sun lined up perfectly, creating the strongest ebb tide on San Francisco Bay all year. As the Oracle chase boats pulled the capsized boat one way, the five-knot gravitational force of the tide pulled the other. The crew was losing the tug-of-war; the strongly ebbing tide gradually sucked the high-tech catamaran underneath the Golden Gate Bridge.

The rig team manager stated the obvious: "We're in quite a situation." By 10:30 p.m., the catamaran had completed its capsize and both hulls were floating upside down. The wing sail, a $2 million marvel that took twenty thousand hours to build and had a control system more advanced than any used before on a boat, eventually succumbed to the pounding sea and broke apart. Some parts of the complex structure sank to the bottom of the Pacific Ocean. The wreckage was eerily illuminated by the chase boat lights and by lights from the bridge, which cast a burnt orange sheen over the oil-black water.

Finally, at close to 2 a.m., a waning tide allowed the salvage team to drag what was left of the boat back underneath the bridge, along the city front, and eventually to their base at Pier 80. Jimmy, cold and soaked like everyone else, was relieved that the entire boat hadn't been lost to the tide. Designer Dirk Kramers eyed the wreckage. "This is a time when we have to prove ourselves as a team," he said. "How we come out of this will prove whether we can win the America's Cup."

Mark Turner surveyed the wreckage and said little. A rebuild would take months, and had to be done at the same time they were finishing building their second AC72. His crew managed to save the spine off *USA-17* and recover both headsails: the jib and the Code 0. The next step would be to get flotation devices under the main structure of the boat, pump the water out of the two hulls, and then lift the boat onto the dock.

By 9 in the morning, Jimmy—who had gone to bed at around 4 a.m.—was back at Pier 80. He was heartened that the structure of the boat looked as good as it did, all things considered.

As he walked through the base, he was half expecting the shore crew guys to confront him for severely damaging their laboriously crafted boat. He knew he was responsible. He had made a terrible judgment call about sailing in such strong winds and going for *one more lap*. Jimmy was a fan of pushing past his comfort zone, but what he did was reckless and unnecessary, like trying to sprint before he could walk. The broken wing was laid out in pieces on the ground and looked like a carved-up carcass, with nerves and bones exposed. Wires could be seen inside the wing, under tightly compressed and nearly weightless layers of carbon fiber. The scene reminded Jimmy of an aircraft crash investigation. He knew he'd be getting a call from the boss.

When the call came in, Jimmy held up a hand by way of an apology. He immediately said, "It was very bad risk management. We weren't at that level to be out in those conditions. I'm fully responsible."

Larry thought testing their new ultrahigh-performance catamaran by sailing it near mid-span of the Golden Gate Bridge in thirty-plus knots of wind and a five-knot ebb tide was "recklessness bordering on insanity." He ignored Jimmy's apology. After a long pause, Larry said, "Good job getting everyone back safely. We could have easily lost someone out there. But we didn't . . . you didn't. Nothing else really matters." Then he added, "We'll recover from this. I know what we're doing is on the edge. You always learn more from adversity than success. If it doesn't kill you, it makes you stronger." The two talked for a few more minutes. Hanging up, Jimmy knew he had let himself down, let Larry down, let the entire team down. But talking to Larry was like having a switch turned back on. A new refrain was playing in his mind: *We'll get stronger from this.*

In the weeks that followed, chunks of the wing sail were found floating in the bay, and pieces ended up in people's homes and offices, displayed like trophies. Russell Coutts called the crash a "significant setback." Time on the water was critical. Standing near the wrecked wing, Coutts said, "We just lost three months, and this comes right at a time when you are making decisions on future components on your boat, on wings, on daggerboards, and so on. So you've lost the capability to experiment and test some of those components in a real way."

The crash and near destruction of the AC72 was only one of the challenges facing the 34th America's Cup. Earlier in 2012, Larry had pulled the plug on plans to rehabilitate and develop Piers 30–32, the twelve acres of dilapidated and red-tagged land that the city had used for parking. The original estimate of $55 million to shore up the pier and turn it into a base for racing teams had reached $110 million, and city officials were continuing to add restrictions on how Larry might get his money back, to the point where it appeared he wouldn't get his money back. Larry also relinquished Seawall 330, the three-acre parcel of land across the San Francisco Embarcadero, as it was tied to the deal on Piers 30–32. Any development of 30–32 would have involved the three acres. Adding to Oracle Racing's headache over its ever-changing negotiations with the city was a lawsuit filed by a former San Francisco city supervisor who insisted that another environmental impact study be done before any rehabilitation could take place. (A major independent environmental study had already been completed, at a cost of more than $1 million to Oracle Racing. It had been signed off on by city and federal agencies.)

Larry believed that members of the board of supervisors were doing what they considered was in the best interest of the city, but the overall process was complex, uncertain, and time-consuming. The negotiations, public hearings, permissions, and litigation had run out the clock. "We were out of time," Larry said of the development deal. "We could not complete the massive pier renovations we had planned in time for the start of the America's Cup. It was always, from the very beginning, an aggressive schedule for a large and ambitious project. I was disappointed, but not surprised, that we were unable to get it done. The political process moves more slowly in San Francisco than in Valencia, and that's probably a good thing. It would have been unprecedented for us to get a huge waterfront development deal like this approved and built in three years. With the benefit of hindsight, I think we were more than a little naive to ever believe we could get over all those hurdles and still get it done on time."

The biggest personal disappointment in the falling-out over the land deal was that Larry no longer had the "perfect place to build a private high school," one of his long-standing pet projects. He had thought he would build a new school on the waterfront site he was going to get from the city, then partner on the education project with Laurene Powell Jobs, Steve's widow.

"For a long time, I've wanted to build a private college preparatory academy," Larry said. "It's very hard to find enough space in a big city to build a high school and its associated athletic facilities. Then it occurred to me that the land we were getting from the city as a part of the America's Cup deal would be an incredibly cool location for a high school. Laurene and I talked about it, and she was all in. She said she would help me find the right people to hire, and help me run it. She's already devoted many years of her life to working with children at risk, helping them get on track and be prepared for a college education. She knows the right people and how to get things done. My education foundation has opened a lot of schools in India, but that's a lot different from opening a school in San Francisco. Think of a high school that's two-thirds Stanford and one-third Naval Academy. It would have been a private school, but with eighty percent of the kids on full scholarship, a student recruiting program to ensure high academic and athletic standards plus diversity, a student orchestra that would make Juilliard proud, and a superb athletic program—the kind that wins state championships. The kids would wear uniforms, and of course, everyone would learn how to sail. We'd go out and find talented kids, get them taught, coached, mentored, and off to college."

Larry added, "Maybe the city thought I was going to build a hotel. Even that isn't a *bad* thing; a hotel employs people and pays taxes. But what they thought doesn't make any difference. I had no interest in building a hotel. I wanted to build a great high school. I wanted to go to their basketball games and maybe teach a sailing class. That would have been fun. I was quite excited about building the school. I'm still excited about it. I'm just going to have to find another place to build it."

Six months after Oracle's AC72 broke apart, on May 9, Larry and his son, the filmmaker David Ellison, were about an hour into lunch with former president Bill Clinton when Larry noticed his team practicing out on the bay with the Swedish syndicate, Artemis Racing. Team USA had gotten its broken AC72 back in the water in February and were playing catch-up, having missed four critical months of on-the-water training. Mark Turner and his team spent nearly fourteen thousand hours rebuilding the AC72, even cannibalizing parts from *USA-17,* their prized trimaran that won the Cup in 2010.

The three men were seated in the living room of Larry's sleek and modern home on Upper Broadway in San Francisco, filled with art deco and surrealist paintings. The floor-to-ceiling windows offered expansive views of the bay, from the Golden Gate Bridge to the left, across to Marin and Alcatraz, and over to the Bay Bridge to the right. As the former president answered questions about a range of issues, from Iran's nuclear weapons program to the state of the global economy, Larry couldn't help but notice what was playing out on the bay.

On the water, Oracle and Artemis—owned by Torbjörn Törnqvist, a Swede who made his money in Russian oil, and managed by San Francisco's own Paul Cayard—had just finished a practice race and were getting ready to go again. The boats were close to Treasure Island on the Bay Bridge side, and Artemis was bearing away in moderate winds of around eighteen knots. In the midst of the turn downwind, the Swedish cat's forward crossbeam suddenly, violently broke, causing the port hull to yaw inboard until it snapped into two separate pieces. As the boat broke apart, Artemis rolled upside down with the still intact starboard hull coming to rest on top of the wing sail, while the wing sail itself sat on top of the large portion of the port hull that had sheared off from the main structure.

It was 1:03 p.m., and eight chase boats—four from Artemis, four from Oracle—were on the scene within seconds of the capsize. Crew members were transferred off the upside-down red catamaran one by one. A head count was taken. To everyone's horror, a sailor came up missing. The divers from the chase boats searched the water. Seven slow minutes later, the divers located the missing man, trapped between the folded-up wreckage. It took an additional three minutes to cut him loose from the torn remnants of the trampoline.

Boats from the San Francisco Fire Department were dispatched from the Marina Green and from a slip near Pier 23 along the Embarcadero; Coast Guard boats arrived and helicopters buzzed above. The missing sailor was Andrew "Bart" Simpson, an Olympic gold and silver medalist who had recently been hired as strategist and jib trimmer for Artemis. Simpson, a Brit, was close friends with sailing superstars Ben Ainslie—helming the Oracle boat this day—and Artemis' Iain Percy. It was Simpson's third day on the Artemis boat, which had a history of problems with the carbon fiber in the two crossbeam girders holding the hulls together. The boat was scheduled to go back into the shed after the day's practice.

Ainslie, the four-time Olympic gold medalist, watched in shock as medics alternated in compressing his friend's chest. Simpson was soon transferred to a chase boat and rushed to shore, arriving in the harbor behind the St. Francis Yacht Club. He was carried off the boat and laid on the dock. Medics continued pumping his chest, but at 1:50 p.m., Simpson's body was covered in a blanket. A makeshift tent was set up for privacy. Simpson was thirty-six years old. He left behind a wife, Leah, and two sons: Freddie, a towheaded three-year-old, and Hamish, six months old.

In the moments after Bill Clinton left Larry's house on Broadway in a flash of black SUVs, Larry's executive assistant, Mamei Sun, delivered the news that the capsize on the bay had resulted in the death of an Artemis sailor. Larry had seen only a boat in distress. In all of the possible scenarios of what could go wrong, he had never considered that someone would die in the America's Cup, with its relatively safe history.

One of the reasons he had sworn off open ocean racing after the Sydney-to-Hobart race of 1998 in favor of around-the-buoys regattas was that six people had died in that Hobart race. Larry said after that race, "There is no joy to be had competing in a sporting event where some of the competitors die." Larry canceled his afternoon meetings. He needed to understand exactly what had happened on the Artemis boat.

In the days and weeks that followed, an exhaustive investigation of the crash took place. The local and national headlines turned scathing: "IS THE AC72 THE BOAT THAT COULD SINK THE AMERICA'S CUP?"; "WHEN DID SAILING GET SO DANGEROUS?"; "WILL LARRY ELLISON'S EGO CAPSIZE THE AMERICA'S CUP?" Critics said Ellison had "overreached with the boats," something that was "killing a 160-year tradition." On-the-water training for all the teams was called to a halt, and a committee convened in response to the crash released a sweeping set of safety recommendations. Many of the thirty-seven recommendations were aimed at boosting the personal safety of the sailors, from improved helmets and underwater breathing devices to crew locators. The recommendations also called for reducing wind limits during the racing and making some structural changes, including requiring deeper rudders with larger winglets—the horizontal part of the rudder—to give the crews more control.

As Larry studied detailed information about the accident, including photographs and videos, he came to believe that Simpson's death was a "one-in-a-million-freak accident." There were divers in the water within thirty seconds of the capsize, yet Simpson wasn't found for seven minutes because his body was hidden in the wreckage and trapped by the folded-up trampoline netting of the boat. A cascade of structural failures, first the forward crossbeam and then the port-side hull, caused the accident, not the bear-away maneuver, and not a sailing crew error. His own team's capsize after a similar bear-away in far worse weather conditions ended with no serious injuries. And *USA-17*'s hulls and platform had held together even after hours of pounding in the waves. While stunned and saddened by Simpson's death, Larry remained convinced that the AC72 was the right boat for the 34th America's Cup.

The tragedy stayed with Larry, but the torrent of negative stories about the 34th America's Cup and the hits on him personally didn't bother him very much—because he didn't read them. Larry stopped reading most of the press years ago when Bill Clinton told him that reading too much criticism made it harder to do your job. Ever since, Larry had become very selective, reading only the *Economist*, the *Wall Street Journal*, and various science and technology publications. Another friend, the Australian media mogul Rupert Murdoch, told Larry that he "never talked to the press." Larry responded incredulously, "But Rupert, you *are* the press." Murdock nodded but didn't say a word. Larry decided that Rupert was right; most newspaper articles were negative, so the odds were stacked against you whenever you spoke to the press. Larry thanked Rupert for the advice and said, "I wish you had told me sooner."

Ever since, Larry stopped spending much time explaining himself to the media and simply got on with doing his job. He preferred that people judge him based on what he did rather than what he said. He thought President Teddy Roosevelt summed it up pretty well when he said: "It is not the critic who counts; not the man who points out how the strong man stumbles. The credit belongs to the man who is in the arena. If he fails, at least [he] fails while daring greatly."

But Larry had an increasing number of detractors. Only three teams were going to compete in the Louis Vuitton Challenger Series, compared with the sixteen originally promised. Oracle Team USA's original Challenger of Record, shipping magnate Vincenzo Onorato's Mascalzone Latino, bowed out in early 2011, in part because plans to host the Cup in Italy fell apart and also as a consequence of the country's underlying political and economic problems. Artemis Racing then stepped in as Oracle's Challenger of Record. Törnqvist, a lifelong sailor who'd only recently got into competitive sailing—in part thanks to encouragement from Russell Coutts—said that one of the draws of the 34th America's Cup was the push to make sailing more accessible and understandable. "If you look at football [soccer], its genius is the game's simplicity," Törnqvist said. "Everyone can connect to it. It's easy to watch and know who's winning. Formula One racing is also great to watch, and it's understandable. Sailing is not simple. The new format for the America's Cup is about reaching nonsailing audiences, making the boats distinctive and cooler-looking, with shorter and narrower racecourses and bringing the audience closer to the event." The French sailing team Aleph Equipe de France dropped out in 2012, also citing economic difficulties. Philippe Ligot, the team's CEO, explained, "France has, without a doubt, all the sporting, technical, and managerial talent to win the Cup, but the current economic environment makes funding a commercial team extremely difficult."

Longtime Cup backer Patrizio Bertelli from Italy, with two boats in contention, *Luna Rossa Piranha* and *Luna Rossa Swordfish*, raised the issue of the expense of mounting a campaign in the fall of 2012, just as his team's new AC72 was being launched in Auckland, New Zealand. Bertelli criticized the AC72s as too complex and too expensive to build, and believed the 34th Cup would be the "first

and last America's Cup in which we will see racing in the AC72."
He explained, "They are certainly fascinating boats, because they
are so extreme. But it has gone too far and the costs, even human,
have become too high and difficult to afford. The original thought
was to introduce a class of boats easy to manage, affordable, and
'human.' But something went wrong. The crew onboard has been
reduced, but now you need some forty people every time you
launch or lift the boat, and costs have risen."

Bertelli, who started sailing on small yachts of about 7 meters
(around 22 feet), eventually began to compete and do well in international regattas around the Mediterranean. His interest in racing
was matched by his love of innovation in design, and his quest for
the America's Cup began in 1997. Bertelli was in the studio of the
young and talented yacht designer German Frers, and the discussion
landed on a possible challenge for the Cup. Bertelli liked the idea "not
just because I have been passionate about the sea, yachts, and racing
ever since I was a young man, but because I thought this challenge
was a communication project absolutely consistent with Prada's key
values: uncompromising quality in every single detail and innovation
combined with a century-old heritage, technological research, and
pushing the stakes higher and higher." Bertelli also liked the idea of
being challenged to manage a complex project "over a number of
years in a field completely different from what I knew."

Even Team USA's own Russell Coutts, a key proponent of the
AC72s as the new choice of boat for the America's Cup, was starting
to see the AC45s as closer to the right size than its bigger brother.

"When we were thinking about the boats for the 34th America's
Cup, we agreed that we didn't want the America's Cup boat to be
slower than other boats," Coutts said. "The Volvo Ocean Race was
raced in seventy-two-footers. We didn't want our boats to be less
high-tech, and less grand, than those boats. So we thought seventy-
two feet was the smallest we could go and still look reasonable in
terms of scale on television. But when the AC45s came along, they
looked pretty good, something we realized after two or three events.
There is a number where you look too small on TV, but the 45s

ended up looking great. So that was what we were dealing with: on the visual side of things, the boats have to look spectacular and be big enough for people to say, 'Yes, this is the America's Cup catamaran.' But in the future, we need to come up with a more cost-effective cat."

The Louis Vuitton series, to determine who would go up against defender Oracle Team USA, began on July 4, less than two months after the tragedy of Andrew Simpson's death. The opening ceremony was billed as an "extravaganza," but was reviewed as "more fizzle than sizzle." Three days later, the round robin of the Louis Vuitton Challenger Series began with the three contenders but only one boat racing. The Artemis crash meant that the Swedish team would enter the series late so they could finish building their second AC72. Beginning with the first race, spectators appeared bored by the turnout on the water; thirty-year sponsor Louis Vuitton began to grumble about the event and threaten it would be their last; and some ticket holders were offered refunds.

The challengers to Oracle included Emirates Team New Zealand, Luna Rossa Challenge, and Artemis. The Italian team sat the first week out, awaiting a ruling from a jury of the world governing body for the sport of sailing, the International Sailing Federation (ISAF), on whether changes to the rudders—one of the new safety recommendations—were indeed required. The Italians protested, saying the changes were more about performance than safety, and that their boats were designed under the old rules and they wouldn't have time to build new rudders. So for the first week, New Zealand raced alone on San Francisco Bay. Larry thought the first race was a Zen riddle asking: "Who can win when one boat's racing?" He answered his own question, "Not NBC Sports, or any of our sponsors. That's for sure."

The first day of two-boat racing didn't come until Saturday, July 13, when Team New Zealand took to the ten-nautical-mile course and dominated Luna Rossa from start to finish. Coutts, watching Luna Rossa from a chase boat just off the course, called the Italian sailing team "hopeless" but agreed that they had the best-looking uniforms—gunmetal gray with chrome vests and red accents—and a strikingly beautiful boat and sail to match. It was a look to rival anything Prada had dreamed up for the runways of Paris and Milan.

Meanwhile, Oracle was doing everything it could to prepare for the racing without actually being in the competition. The team's two-boat, in-house racing—with Jimmy going up against Ainslie—was great, but not the same as the real thing. General manager Grant Simmer described it as like "dancing with your sister." Searching for a way to simulate the pressure of competition, Jimmy decided that extreme training was perfect preparation to ready the team for extreme sailing.

At 6:30 on the morning of July 18, members of the sailing team arrived at Pier 80 not knowing what to expect. Dressed in team shorts, T-shirts, and running shoes, the guys were divided into three groups and given vests in red, orange, or green. Bowman Brad Webb studied the liability release everyone was asked to sign warning of "serious risk and injury."

The team headed outside, where Pete Naschak, a high-performance trainer with Red Bull—the extreme sports promoter and sponsor of the Cup's first youth sailing event, to be held in early September, right before the start of the main event—told them, "This is all on you, guys. It lasts as long as you make it last. It will continue to go until you get it done."

Standing on the edge of the pier next to old pilings, Andy Walshe, Red Bull's director of high performance, ordered through a bull-horn: "Everyone in the water, in the water. Get in the water." The guys jumped into the frigid bay, and climbed back out. "Everyone, fifty push-ups. Now back in the water."

The drenched crew was then divided up into smaller teams, with each team given a rope nearly as big around and as long as a fire hose. They used the heavy ropes to scale shipping containers and traverse an obstacle course. Next came a drill where a sailor was placed in a tub of ice water while one of his teammates was given thirty seconds to look at and memorize the position of a handful of miscellaneous objects—pens, paper clips, sunglasses, and erasers—carefully arranged on a black cloth on the ground. Then all the objects were dumped into a bucket. The guy who had been trying to memorize the arrangement of objects then had to run to another teammate twenty-five yards away and tell him what the objects were, what order they were in, and their orientation. That guy then had to run back, select the right objects from the bucket, and arrange them exactly as they had been. Then and only then could the third guy be released from the ice. Sometimes it took several tries to get it right. Walshe explained that the goal was to get the group to think clearly and communicate effectively while under pressure.

About midday, the team headed to Treasure Island, just across the Bay Bridge, this time for training with some former Navy SEALs. They were given white coveralls, protective masks, and black paintball guns with scopes and were told they would go through simulated hostage situations where they would be hit with hostile fire.

"They are going to come into a hostile environment," Red Bull's Walshe said. "It raises their anxiety. We want them to keep their judgment under pressure and make it work. It's one thing to be tired and exhausted, and another to be tired and exhausted and have to make decisions that could be lifesaving."

Standing outside the training house on Treasure Island, Jimmy said that one of the biggest lessons of the day was "Slow can be fast. Be slow and smooth and methodical and pay attention. Cover for your buddy. Pay attention to the details." He added, "It's such a fantastic opportunity for us as we prepare for the upcoming Cup."

After the death of Simpson, Oracle Team USA had implemented a host of safety-oriented changes. One of the first involved replacing the black skin of the wing sail with a transparent Clysar film, so that if anyone were to be caught under the wing he would be easier to find or could more easily find his way out. The builders fitted parts of the boat's platform with lights that illuminated when submerged. And the team went through another SEALs training course—this one a week long—that involved first aid and CPR, plus training in how to extract sailors from the water and swim with heavy weights. They trained at the Stanford pool in jumping safely into the water from a 10-meter high dive. In addition, there were new analyses done of the wing, aimed at reducing the wing sail's power during certain maneuvers so they could brake into a turn and accelerate out like a Formula One driver.

The biggest risk with this new class of boat was its extreme speed. In the 2007 America's Cup in Valencia, Spain, boats clocked around nine knots upwind. The AC72 catamarans were already sailing about three times faster, going twenty-six knots upwind and over forty downwind. And the AC72 had the potential to reach even greater speeds—approaching fifty knots (just under sixty miles an hour) as their crews learned how to push the big catamarans to the limit. Oracle Racing's engineers and builders stiffened the boat's platform to add stability to the hull and crossbeam structure to reduce the likelihood of the bows digging in. Even the sailors' gear changed. They were now equipped with knives, oxygen canisters for use underwater, and harnesses to climb down from the rigging or the trampoline after a capsize. Neon lights were being made for their uniforms that would shine with intensity when submerged after ten seconds.

As the sailors saw it, driving an AC72 on San Francisco Bay was something like trying to climb K2, one of the world's highest peaks. Things could go terribly wrong in an instant. They couldn't eliminate the risks, but they could prepare for the worst. The sailors—adrenaline junkies all—were doing what they loved. Jimmy wanted his guys to be ready for the inevitable surprises that would be thrown their way, and to do so they needed to train under extreme circumstances. One of Jimmy's heroes was Charles Upman, the New Zealander who was twice awarded the Victoria Cross—comparable to the Medal of Honor in the United States—for bravery during World War II. It was written of Upman, "He showed superb coolness, great skill and dash, and complete disregard of danger. His conduct and leadership inspired his whole platoon to fight magnificently."

Jimmy loved the notion of guys who would do anything for their mates, who would make sure to never let them down. The consequences of what they were doing were markedly different

from Upman's, he knew. But some of the values—of pulling together as a team, of being an unbreakable unit—were the same.

On a Friday night in late July, Mark Turner was getting ready to
leave Pier 80 after another grueling week when he was stopped
by Oracle Team USA's rules adviser, Richard Slater, and told they
had a problem. The team's two AC45s—the smaller one-design
class of catamarans used in the world series regattas—had been
handed over to the America's Cup race management for use in the
Red Bull Youth America's Cup, to start September 1 and feature
nationality-based teams of young sailors. At least one of Team
USA's AC45 yachts was reportedly found by a measurer to have
lead weights in its forward king post, which helps brace the load
taken by the mast. The modification is illegal under the rules of
the regatta. The weights were said to have been there for several
of the eight world series regattas held in 2011 and 2012, promotional events sailed in different cities around the world to hone
the skills of the teams and generate interest in the main event.

Turner prided himself on never skipping a step and being ob-
sessive about precisely following every design measurement rule.
Putting weights in the king post—also called the dolphin striker—
was certainly not allowed, because the AC45 is a *one-design* class
of boat; in a one-design class, all of the boats are supposed to be
exactly the same. At home that night, Turner tossed and turned. If
what was discussed proved true, it *was* cheating. *Really dumb and
pointless cheating*, as the weight difference was too small to affect
the boat's performance.

The next morning, back at Pier 80, Turner went directly to Andrew Walker, the shore team member he had tasked with managing
the boats during segments of the world series. Turner had needed
to stay in the United States to focus on building the AC72s and
had his guys, including Walker, run the shore program on the road.
He wanted them to build their skills of getting the boats to the
races and getting them race-ready.

"You need to tell me if there is anything else," Turner said to Walker, a New Zealander.

Walker confirmed that 2.2 kilos (less than 5 pounds) of lead weight had been placed in at least one of the boats. Bryce Ruthenberg, a thirty-four-year-old Australian rigger who had joined Oracle in 2005, then told Turner that Walker had instructed him on the lead placement. Walker denied it, leaving Turner uncertain about what had happened and who was behind it.

As news of the emerging problem spread around the base, Jimmy's first reaction was that they'd been set up. He told Grant Simmer: "We gave the boats to the race management and someone has set us up here." He simply couldn't believe what he was hearing. And it couldn't be coming at a worse time, now just five weeks out from the start of the America's Cup.

Russell Coutts started an internal investigation that led him to believe that some team members had in fact violated the rules by adding the weights to one of their AC45 boats. Shortly thereafter, Team USA announced that they would cooperate fully with an external investigation of the incident to be conducted by a jury appointed by the International Sailing Federation. The five-person jury included Chairman David Tillett of Australia, Graham McKenzie of New Zealand, Josje Hofland of the Netherlands, and Bryan Willis and John Doerr, both of Great Britain. There were no Americans on the jury, and calls to have the New Zealander recuse himself went unheeded. The press jumped on the scandal, labeling the American team cheaters. A columnist for the *New Zealand Herald* wrote that the jury should "boot Oracle out of their own regatta. . . . Ethically, that's what should happen. It was cheating. Deliberate or accidental; institutional or the act of rogue elements—it doesn't matter. It's cheating."

In the weeks that followed—as Emirates Team New Zealand dominated in the Louis Vuitton Cup finals and looked set to win and challenge Oracle—members of Team USA were questioned by two of the jurors, New Zealander McKenzie and Willis of Great Britain. The two then reported their findings and conclusions to the other members of the jury, prompting Turner to remark, "The investigators are serving as the jurors." Team USA's two-boat sailing and testing came to a halt, as too many sailors were in closed-door sessions with jurors and there simply weren't enough crew members for both boats. Speculation abounded that Oracle could be forced to forfeit one or more races in the best-of-seventeen America's Cup finals, that Jimmy or other key sailors could be removed from their sailing team, or that the defender could be booted from the Cup altogether, throwing the whole event into chaos.

As the ISAF jury continued its investigation, Coutts issued a press release stating that Team USA was voluntarily forfeiting their wins in four of the world series regattas plus their two overall AC45 season championships. Larry agreed that Russell's decision to forfeit the past regattas was absolutely proper, but he remained utterly bewildered as to why anybody would add five pounds of lead to an AC45 when it wouldn't improve the boat's performance.

Larry was worried that key members of the sailing team might be suspended. He talked with Russell about the possibility of losing *both* of their wing trimmers, America's Cup veteran Dirk de Ridder and the talented but inexperienced Kyle Langford.

Larry asked Russell what the backup plan was if the jury kicked both of the wing trimmers off the team.

Russell replied, "We have Ben Ainslie."

Larry thought for a moment and said, "Well, Ben's a great sailor, and he has a lot of experience trimming the Finn [a single-handed Olympic-class boat designed back in the 1940s]. Is he willing to do it?"

Russell responded, "Yeah, he's kind of keen on it."

Larry came back, "Seriously, trimming the sail on a Finn dinghy and trimming the wing of an AC72 is not exactly the same thing, you know."

"No kidding," Russell responded with a laugh. "But you'll never believe what Ainslie said when I asked him to trim the wing."

"Okay. So, what did he say?" Larry asked.

"He said, 'Sure, how hard can it be?'"

Larry laughed. Sailors at this level were a rare blend of brainy engineers and guys with way too much testosterone. "Great," Larry said. "Glenn Ashby has three years of practice trimming the wing on the Kiwis' AC45 and AC72. Ben will have a few days of practice. *How hard can it be?*"

The ISAF jury ruling, expected to be rendered quickly, dragged on for weeks. It was issued to the team one week before the start of the America's Cup, and made public three days before the first race. By now, Team New Zealand had defeated Luna Rossa seven races to one in the finals to win the Louis Vuitton Cup. The international jury ruled that five Team USA employees had a role in the illegal placement of weights on the boat in the AC45 world series: The team's main wing trimmer, Dirk de Ridder, was suspended for the entire America's Cup, and sailor Matt Mitchell was banned for four races. Shore crew members Bryce Ruthenberg and Andrew Walker were excluded from the Cup. Langford was given a warning but not sanctioned. The jury fined the team $250,000 for failing "to discharge corporate responsibility." And in what left some Cup followers speechless, the ruling ordered that Oracle Team USA would have to start the finals in the 34th America's Cup two races down. They would now have to win eleven races, while New Zealand needed to win only nine.

Larry was in disbelief. The team was being penalized for an infraction that occurred during racing that had taken place a year earlier, in different boats, in a promotional event that was not a part of the America's Cup. He likened it to suspending a baseball player and penalizing his team two games in the World Series because the player tested positive for steroids a year earlier. Larry also couldn't believe the jury's explanation as to why the entire team would be penalized: because "procedures should have been in place" to prevent such misconduct.

Russell, too, was astounded by the verdict and called the penalties "outrageous" and "way out of proportion" for the infraction. He blamed the International Sailing Federation for "working behind the scenes" to lobby the jury against Oracle. "They were lobbying for their own reasons, to attack Oracle because they felt the event was all wrong." Russell added, "They're a political body. Nothing ISAF has done has been fantastically successful."

Larry put it even more strongly, saying, "Key members of the jury were heavily biased. There were no Americans on the jury. The juror from New Zealand most certainly should have recused himself; instead he tirelessly lobbied for us to be assessed penalties unprecedented in their severity."

Oracle Racing attorney Sidney Luscutoff said his clients were accused in a process that was "completely unfair." Two members of the jury conducted the investigations, placing themselves as prosecutors before helping to decide the case themselves. "It's utterly bizarre," he said.

Jimmy took time to absorb the news. Then he said, "Two points? It's not enough, mate. They fucked up. It's not enough. We're going to win anyway."

Like everyone else on the team, Jimmy had grown weary of the criticism of the Cup and the relentless attacks on Larry. He had told people who dismissed the Louis Vuitton races for having too few contenders, "Stay tuned—it's always been about two boats in the finals." They had gone through the capsize of their AC72 in October. They had faced the death of their friend Andrew Simpson, a tragedy that happened right in front of them. Now the cheating scandal had taken their attention and practice time away in the final crucial weeks leading to the 34th America's Cup.

In a meeting before the start of racing, Jimmy told the team, "We know that sometimes life can be bloody unfair. But the thing you know about sport, whether boxing or rugby or sailing, is that as soon as the bell sounds, all the bullshit stops, and it comes down to the guy who has worked the hardest and wants it the most. That's why we love sport. All the bullshit is about to stop."

31

The 34th America's Cup—
A Very Rough Start

September 2013

O N THE DAY before the first race of the 34th America's Cup, the computer models developed by Team USA's engineers spit out performance predictions for the upcoming regatta: the American catamaran was even with Team New Zealand when reaching or sailing downwind, but *USA-17* was faster upwind, especially in eighteen knots of breeze or more. The predictions coming from Russell Coutts and the members of Team USA's all-star afterguard had Jimmy Spithill beating New Zealand skipper Dean Barker in *most* of the starts—the start being the most critical part of the race. So there was a consensus in the American camp: *USA-17* would take the lead at the start, defend the lead on the reaching and downwind legs, extend the lead upwind—and sail away to victory. The people and the computers agreed that Team USA had an edge, albeit a small one.

A few weeks earlier, things had not looked so rosy.

As soon as Team New Zealand launched its catamaran for the Louis Vuitton series, Team USA made a study of the boat's visible design parameters. Those parameters were input into Team

USA's computers, enabling the American engineers to build a detailed mathematical model of New Zealand's AC72 and compare it with *USA-17*. Based on the fact that the two boats had different designs—different hull shapes, different platforms, and different structural supports—the computer predicted different performance outcomes for each of the boats under various wind conditions. But the computer models could not tell the whole story; the computers could model the *boats,* but not the *people* on the boats. The computers had no way of factoring in the impact of better helming or better crew work or overall performance.

As Russell and Larry watched Team New Zealand begin racing in the Louis Vuitton Cup, it was immediately apparent that the Kiwi crew work was far superior to their own. New Zealand's carefully choreographed crew constantly improved and innovated, eventually perfecting the foiling jibe—staying above the water while jibing—in their AC72. In fact, the New Zealand boat had gotten to the point where it hardly slowed down at all during a jibe. Team USA also feared that the Kiwis might be slightly faster when reaching and sailing downwind. Team USA had a lot of work to do, and not much time to do it.

During the weeks when Team New Zealand was busy crushing the competition in the Louis Vuitton Cup, Team USA was focused on catching up to the Kiwis in three areas: foiling jibes, reaching speed, and downwind speed. Team USA's design engineers changed the shape of their hydrofoils, which improved *USA-17*'s reaching and downwind speeds to the point where they were at least as fast as New Zealand's AC72. And every day, Jimmy and the crew practiced and improved their foiling jibes. The problem was, the Kiwis were just about perfect.

Now, the thinking from Team USA going into the first day of the America's Cup was that they had overcome their weaknesses while retaining their advantages. They expected to win the starts, race evenly reaching and downwind, and then pull away upwind. They *felt* like the favorites. But were they right?

The 34th America's Cup would have two races a day, four days a week—Saturdays, Sundays, Tuesdays, and Thursdays, weather permitting. With a possible nineteen races in all (the winner being first to win nine, with Oracle starting two points down and thus needing eleven to win), the regatta would tentatively wrap up by September 21. The course of ten nautical miles would be the same for all races, with five legs. It would take around thirty minutes. After Andrew Simpson's death months earlier, wind-speed limits of twenty-three knots had been imposed. But racing could also be called off if winds were too light or too far from the desired direction of 230 degrees, just west of southwest.

Team USA coach and former champion match racing helmsman Philippe Presti, a tall, silver-haired French sailor known for microanalyzing the strengths and weaknesses of the opponent as well as of his own team, told Jimmy and crew that Barker had "predictable patterns" when sailing the start of the race. Barker had helped win the Cup for New Zealand in 2000 after skipper Russell Coutts gave him the helm for the final race. Barker then lost the Cup in 2003 to the Swiss team Alinghi, helmed by Coutts. In 2007, Barker won the finals of the Louis Vuitton Challenger Series, only to be defeated again by Alinghi in the America's Cup. As Presti saw it, Barker "had holes in his game." Presti knew that every helmsman, even the great Coutts, sailed in patterns, and those patterns always had holes—which appeared in a moment, then disappeared just as quickly. When Barker gave him an opening, Presti wanted Jimmy to be aggressive—no hesitation—sail USA-17 right through that opening, and grab the advantage.

Jimmy, who had arrived at Pier 80 early on the morning of the first race to get in a workout with his boxing trainer, was prepared for the toughest competition of his life. He had seen Team New Zealand sailing at speeds their boat struggled to reach; the Kiwis' foiling jibes were still smoother; and his opponent was hungry to grab the Auld Mug and return it to the Royal Yacht Squadron of New Zealand after more than a decade away. The government of New Zealand had put an estimated $40 million into their team's overall $100 million effort, and an entire country was rooting for them.

Before docking out from Pier 80, the sailing team had breakfast together, with many of the guys eating multiple omelets. Team meteorologist Juan Vila, one of the world's top navigators, delivered the forecast for the afternoon: a strong flood tide with wind speeds predicted to be around sixteen knots from 250 degrees at the start of the first race, then building to over twenty knots by the start of the second race.

Presti went over the strategy for the race. The flood tide meant that there would be a strong current sweeping in underneath the Golden Gate Bridge and heading east toward Treasure Island. When racing in San Francisco Bay in a flood tide, the standard playbook calls for sailing downwind right in the middle of the racecourse to take maximum advantage of the current when it's going the same direction you are, then turning left onto port tack at the leeward gate (the two buoys marking the end of the downwind leg) and heading out behind Alcatraz as you sail upwind against the current. Alcatraz Island forms a barrier that blocks the flood tide and reduces the speed of the current, making the route behind Alcatraz the fastest way to sail back upwind toward the Golden Gate Bridge. Once you get to the island, you tack onto starboard and sail all the way over to the southern boundary of the racecourse along the city front. Then you have the option of playing the left side of the racecourse from Aquatic Park to the Golden Gate Yacht Club or minimizing maneuvers by sailing all the way across the course to the northern boundary.

Either way, you then have to set up on port tack for the final approach to the windward gate so you can make a right turn and bear away into the middle of the bay to once again take advantage of the favorable flood tide current at the beginning of the second downwind leg of the race. That's what the playbook says. Doing it is pretty easy if you're leading the race, next to impossible if you're behind.*

---

* If you try to follow, the boat in front blocks your wind and slows you down in the upwind leg.

At 10:15 a.m., sailors climbed aboard *USA-17* at Pier 80 and headed to America's Cup Park at Pier 27-29, trailed by the performance team and shore guys in chase boats. Once at the pier, packed on this opening day with thousands of spectators, the team spent an hour in their private lounge before the "dock-out show" at 11:45. The show offered prerace interviews and a chance for fans to snag photos and autographs. As team members headed from the pier to the boats, fans got high-fives and waved American and New Zealand flags. The first race was scheduled for a 1:15 start, and they would be out practicing by noon.

Talking to a commentator, Jimmy said, "We're ready to go. We've worked hard for this. It's time to put it all together on the water. If it were easy, it wouldn't be worth doing."

Dean Barker, the leader of the New Zealand crew, whose work had been described by commentators as "poetry in motion," said, "I'm really proud of the way the guys have come together. Obviously this is a big occasion for the team. We can only believe in what we've done. Will it be enough? One team is going to be faster. We hope it's us."

Coutts, asked for his prediction on the racing ahead, said, "I don't know who will win this. I'd put it at fifty-fifty."

On the bay, Larry, along with his family and longtime girlfriend, Nikita Kahn, transferred from his superyacht *Musashi* onto one of the team's forty-two-foot-long Protector chase boats. He was even more nervous than in 2003, when he drove *USA-76* in the first race of the Louis Vuitton Cup and had a hard time keeping his legs from shaking. Driving was stressful; watching was worse.

Also watching from the sidelines was Norbert, commodore of the beautifully refurbished Golden Gate Yacht Club. The little club, only the sixth winner and trustee in America's Cup history, was sold out for races, with hundreds of guests packing the first and second floors, and the bleachers out front were full. Norbert had been through all of the tumult over the preceding months, and was now inside the clubhouse in an area roped off as "the commodore's corner." He was too nervous to talk to anyone. The Golden Gate

Yacht Club had grown to 450 members, and as Norbert liked to sing, paraphrasing Tony Bennett, had "gone from rags to riches." Larry had orchestrated the clubhouse's major new face-lift, and the upstairs and downstairs now looked like a five-star resort, with hardwood floors, new fixtures, all new furniture—in Larry's favorite shades of sand, cream, and beige—as well as state-of-the-art audio and visual systems. Up the road, the St. Francis was also packed inside and out, with rooms booked months in advance for members of visiting yacht clubs.

Finally, after the lawsuits, scandals, tragedy, and disappointments, the first race of the 34th America's Cup was about to begin. The rules of the 34th America's Cup allowed the boat on port tack to enter the starting box—situated between the Golden Gate Bridge and Alcatraz—with two minutes and ten seconds to go before the start of a race. The boat on starboard tack had to wait an additional ten seconds before it was allowed to enter the starting area. The starting "box," which is irregularly shaped, is an area of around one-third of a mile long and a quarter mile wide—close in size to the island of Alcatraz. The boat that enters the box first has an immediate advantage.

Race one began on time. With two minutes, ten seconds to go, Team New Zealand was up on their foils and sailing on port tack as they flew past the bow of the race committee boat, turned down slightly, and sailed past the buoy marking the port-side entry to the starting area. Immediately after entering, the Kiwi boat accelerated to forty-two knots and sailed far behind the starting line. Ten seconds later, Team USA angled past the starboard entry buoy and entered the starting area. Jimmy sailed *USA-17* for about fifteen seconds, then jibed onto port and followed directly behind the Kiwi boat. With about a minute and thirty seconds to go, Barker tacked to windward—the Golden Gate Bridge side—of *USA-17* and started sailing slowly back toward the starting line. Jimmy waited a few seconds, then jibed directly below Barker. There was a fairly big gap between the two boats as they slowly sailed, side by side, getting closer and closer to the starting line.

With ten seconds to go before the start, Barker screamed, "Now—full speed!" The Kiwis' Glenn Ashby trimmed on the wing sail and the New Zealand catamaran accelerated toward the line. About a second later, Jimmy pulled the trigger onboard *USA-17,* and the American catamaran began to accelerate. But Barker got the timing right; the Kiwis hit the middle of the starting line first, going thirty-one knots as the gun went off. Jimmy was uncharacteristically late to cross the line, sailing at only twenty-eight knots. The huge catamarans were flying on their foils, side by side, pointing south toward San Francisco. The Kiwis were ahead by half a boat-length as both boats continued to accelerate to over forty knots.

Despite being late to the line and slightly behind, *USA-17* was still in a pretty good position. Team USA was the leeward boat, so they had the right-of-way. If they could maintain their overlap with the Kiwis, if they could hold their position, *USA-17* would take the lead when they rounded the first mark. But New Zealand, the windward boat, had the faster sailing angle to the mark. The Kiwis constantly increased their lead until they broke the overlap and rolled right over the top of Team USA. Barker had deftly exploited and extended the lead he'd earned at the start. The Kiwis were more than a boat-length in front of Team USA as they rounded the first mark of the first race of the 34th America's Cup. First blood—New Zealand.

The two boats sailed single file along the city front with the Kiwis in front. Then Barker and crew executed a perfect foiling jibe and headed out toward Alcatraz Island. Jimmy waited a few seconds, then jibed and followed. It was a good jibe—but not as good as New Zealand's. Then Barker jibed back onto starboard and the two boats sailed directly toward each other. New Zealand crossed 50 meters in front of Team USA. Both boats were sailing downwind at just under forty knots, with very little difference in speed between the two. The next time the two boats came together, Team New Zealand crossed in front by less than a boat-length.

It was a *very close* race. *USA-17* was never more than a few boat-lengths behind New Zealand. Both boats approached the leeward gate on port tack, setting themselves up to make a left turn around the left-hand buoy and head out behind Alcatraz Island to get relief from the flood tide current. Both teams were sailing according to the playbook—the same playbook. One of the television commentators remarked, "It's shaping up to be really good racing coming into the bottom mark. We've seen a smooth Team New Zealand and an aggressive Team USA."

Barker approached the left-hand buoy with a 70-meter lead, but New Zealand started their left-hand turn at too low an angle and finished at too high an angle, slowing them down dramatically. Jimmy made a beautiful rounding, holding his speed, overtaking Barker, and overlapping him to leeward. The Kiwis were forced to make a very slow tack onto starboard to avoid getting a penalty. *USA-17* had its first lead in the 34th America's Cup. At the Golden Gate Yacht Club, Norbert cheered. Out on the chase boat, Larry yelled to be heard over the engines, challenged to keep up with the big racing catamarans: "Horrible rounding by Barker. He totally fucked that up. Lots of pressure out there today."

The two AC72s were headed upwind in different directions. New Zealand sailed toward San Francisco while *USA-17* went offshore and ducked in behind Alcatraz Island. The Kiwis were battling against the flood tide current while the Americans were finding relief in the cone behind the island. *USA-17* got to the northern boundary of the racecourse and tacked back toward the center of the bay. Then New Zealand arrived at the southern boundary of the San Francisco city front and tacked. When the two boats came together, *USA-17* crossed clear in front of New Zealand, then headed toward the city front. A minute later, the two boats converged again. It looked like the giant catamarans were playing a dangerous game of chicken. *USA-17* crossed in front again, this time by inches.

The Kiwis were steadily making inroads into Team USA's lead. On the third upwind cross, *USA-17* was in front by less than a boat-length. Halfway through the upwind leg, the two boats were dead even. On the next cross, New Zealand had starboard right-of-way, so *USA-17* was forced to dip, and New Zealand recaptured the lead. After New Zealand tacked, the two boats sailed side by side, back out into the center of the racecourse. The boats were right next to each other, sailing in identical wind conditions, and sailing in the identical current. It was a perfectly controlled test of boat speed—a moment of truth. Which boat would win the upwind drag race? *Which boat was faster?*

The Kiwi catamaran slid right by the Americans. "Oh my God," Larry said. "They're faster than us upwind. That's *not* possible." When *USA-17* tacked back onto starboard, New Zealand tacked simultaneously, directly in front of the Americans, blocking their wind. Jimmy had no choice: he had to tack away, back into the center of the racecourse, back into the strong current going the wrong direction. New Zealand had taken total control of the first race.

It was a stunning moment, with the two America's Cup contestants viewable from shore for the first time in the history of the storied event. After all of the drama and attacks, the battlefield was now San Francisco Bay. About two thirds of the way up the leg, and after the two-minute drag race, New Zealand sped away toward the city front at more than twenty-five knots, sailed to about four boat-lengths of the boundary, and tacked back to port. To the anguish of Team USA fans—shocked by their team's inauspicious start—New Zealand had steadily increased its lead to over 150 meters as they sailed upwind toward the weather gate.

Both boats held on starboard until they got to the lay-line, tacked onto port, and set up for a bear-away around the right-hand buoy. New Zealand rounded the weather mark twenty-five seconds in front of Team USA. As both boats powered their way downwind, the Kiwis' lead only continued to grow. By the time they went through the leeward gate and made a right-hand turn onto the last reach toward the finish, Team New Zealand was ahead by thirty-four seconds. By the time they crossed the finish line, the Kiwi were 760 meters—around half a mile—in front of Team USA.

When *USA-17* had unexpectedly lost the side-by-side upwind drag race, Larry was stunned into focus. That was not supposed to happen. He had watched the rest of the race in expressionless silence. When the race was over, two things were apparent: Team New Zealand had a significant speed advantage upwind, and Team New Zealand had made gains in every tack. Larry thought, *Either our computer models are wrong, or we're not sailing our boat properly—or both. We've got a big problem.*

After the race, with the skippers wired for race recap, Barker said, "What we saw out there was one hell of a yacht race. We're happy with the way we sailed. We did a lot better upwind. As long as we keep the boats apart, we'll be good."

Jimmy's take was that the two boats were similar in performance. "It was a great little battle, and I look forward to the next one."

When the commentator asked what he was thinking of doing differently in the second race, Jimmy shot back, "Winning it."

At the start of the second race on Saturday, it was Team USA's turn to have the early port entry advantage. Jimmy entered the starting box, then sped away behind the line. Ten seconds later, Barker entered, then jibed and followed. At a minute and twenty-five seconds to go, Jimmy tacked onto starboard and headed back toward the starting line, Barker tacked directly to leeward of *USA-17*. Jimmy responded by reaching right over New Zealand's bow, grabbing the leeward right-of-way position back with one minute to go. Then Barker started making a series of S-turns, trying to prevent Jimmy from gaining a leeward overlap while avoiding getting too close to the line. It was a classic match-race prestart *pas de deux*. With twenty seconds to go, despite all his efforts, Barker got pushed too close to the line, and he had to slow down. Jimmy yelled, "I'm going for the hook," and he got it. Now Jimmy had a controlling leeward overlap that forced Barker to turn high into the wind to avoid contact, slowing the Kiwi cat down even further. Jimmy was in complete control with less than ten seconds to go.

Then the utterly unexplainable happened: *nothing!* Jimmy just sat there. As the time counted down, Barker was the first to turn down toward the line, first to accelerate, and first to cross the starting line.

Larry, sitting in his chase boat right above the starting line, stood up, threw his arms into the air, and screamed, "What the fuck—we were late to the line—*again*. What the hell is going on!" Larry's son David looked at his father and asked the same question: "What happened, Dad?" Larry slowly shook his head. "I *don't* know. Jimmy had complete control of the start, he forced Barker to sail high and slow . . . and then . . . and then he just sat there . . . lost track of the time . . . and he let Barker beat him to the line again."

In a virtual repeat of the first leg of the first race, Team New Zealand used the lead they won at the start to roll right over the top of *USA-17* and round mark one in front by a couple of seconds.

During the first downwind leg, the racing remained tight, with the Kiwis leading by a little more or less than a hundred meters all the way down the track. Every time *USA-17* jibed, New Zealand jibed to leeward and in front—a very strong tactical position. The two boats were glued together, doing about forty knots, as they approached the leeward gate. The Kiwis turned right and headed upwind toward the city front. *USA-17* followed, only six seconds behind.

With the Kiwis directly in front of them, Jimmy and crew worked hard to sail *USA-17* in a high mode, trying to keep their air clear. Barker also sailed high, trying to block Team USA's wind and slow them down. Barker was winning the battle. As they approached the city front boundary, Jimmy asked his tactician, John Kostecki, "JK, do we want to tack first here?" Kostecki looked around for a moment to assess the situation.

Too late—the Kiwis had reached the boundary and tacked first, leaving Team USA no option but to keep going and look for a lane of clear air above Team New Zealand. But there wasn't one. When *USA-17* tacked, they were following right behind the Kiwis. Team USA was eating Team New Zealand's dirty, disturbed air, and it was slowing them down. New Zealand tactician Ray Davies told Barker, "We're gaining all the time." Larry melodramatically slumped forward, closed his eyes, put his face in his hands, and mumbled, "We had to tack first there. Big tactical mistake. We're so screwed."

Jimmy was forced to tack *USA-17* to get out of the Kiwis' dirty air. Barker tacked at the same time. A classic tacking duel had begun. Both boats worked their way windward, toward the weather gate. But Team New Zealand was tacking better, and sailing faster. The Kiwis were finishing their tacks perfectly, immediately popping their windward hull out of the water to reduce drag and increase acceleration. And New Zealand had an upwind mode where they sailed at lower, more powerful wind angles. This enabled them to partially lift up on their foils and go very fast. The Americans had nothing in their arsenal that could match the Kiwis' low-fast upwind mode.

Throughout the beat to the weather gate, the Kiwis continuously extended their lead: 200 meters, 300 meters, 400 meters. The classic tacking duel was deteriorating into a classic beat-down. And because Larry wanted to sail the 34th America's Cup close to shore, tens of thousands of people got a live look at the scrappy Kiwis drubbing and pummeling the Americans' costly catamaran with the big Oracle logo on its wing sail.

The performance was painful for Russell and Larry to watch. It was clear to both of them that the Kiwis had made a lot of progress between the end of the Louis Vuitton series and today's racing. It was apparent that Jimmy and crew were losing more than 20 meters to Team New Zealand with every tack. *USA-17*'s speed during a tack bottomed out at eight or nine knots, while most of the Kiwis' tacks hit a low of between twelve and fourteen knots.

Team New Zealand rounded mark 3 an astounding forty-nine seconds in front of Team USA. The second run down to mark 4 saw the Kiwis sailing away—as if in a one-boat parade—850 meters out front. When the Kiwis crossed the finish line, they were 1,100 meters—more than a kilometer—in front of Team USA. It was a shocker.

Shortly after crossing the finish line, a subdued Jimmy Spithill turned to his crew and said, "Bad luck, guys." But luck had nothing to do with any of the things that had gone wrong on day one. Some of the things that had gone wrong Larry understood; some things he didn't. He understood how Jimmy could have an off day starting the boat—that could happen to anybody. He understood how the Kiwis could have developed a better technique for tacking their boat—that was fixable. All Team USA needed to do was watch New Zealand during the tacks and learn from them. After all, going to school on the Kiwis' crew work was how Team USA had improved their own foiling jibes over the weeks running up to the Cup. But one thing—one very big thing—Larry could not understand, and that was why the Kiwis' cat was so much faster than *USA-17* when sailing upwind. That was the exact opposite of what all their computer models had predicted.

Years of experience had taught Larry to trust computers and mathematics to accurately model the aerodynamics and hydrodynamics of sailboats. It wasn't an enormously complex problem like trying to model climate change and then predict the weather. Sailboats are relatively simple objects traveling through fluids—air and water—with well-understood properties. Computational Fluid Dynamics (CFD) is a tried-and-true technology—calculating forces and moments to simulate the interaction of those fluids with the surfaces of the sailboat. Larry and everyone else on Team USA relied on CFD to compute and accurately predict the speed of the two AC72 catamarans going upwind. But somehow, somewhere, something went wrong? Numbers never ever lied—*or did they?*

On the way back to *Musashi*, Larry talked with his nephew, Judge Jimmy Linn, who was his next-door neighbor when the two were growing up in the South Side of Chicago. Larry tried to explain: "We thought we'd be faster than the Kiwis upwind. We were competitive downwind, but *they* were faster upwind. What we predicted was wrong, and I don't understand why." He added, "When the two AC72s were racing upwind, side by side, in the same current and the same breeze, *that* told the story. When two boats sail right next to each other, *then you know* which boat is faster."

When they got to *Musashi*, Larry jumped on the phone with Russell. The two agreed that what they had seen on the water didn't jibe with what they believed their boat and team were capable of.

Russell said, "It doesn't make any sense. We *should* be faster than they are upwind. It doesn't make any sense to me at all. It must be the way they're sailing their boat." Larry replied, "Maybe. Or they could have something on their boat that we don't know about, something that's not in our computer models."

"Like what?" Russell said.

"Like their hydrofoils," Larry said. "Hell, I don't know."

Russell said, "I'm telling you, it's the way they are sailing their boat."

Larry let out a long sigh. "I hope you're right. That we can fix."

Back at the pier, the shore crew got the catamaran off the water and into her cradle. Every inch of the cat would be cleaned and examined for anything structural. Even seemingly superficial issues like worn paint would be carefully gone over and detailed in reports. In another part of the building, the sailors and managers met, and the engineers and designers analyzed video and data.

Philippe Presti, intent on "debugging" every situation, showed a video of Team New Zealand foiling upwind in what he called their "skimming" mode, where they were about 65 percent on the foils and the rest on the hulls. "Their skimming mode was around twenty-five to twenty-seven knots," Presti said in his thick French accent. "They are sailing lower and faster than we are. We have to try sailing the same low angles upwind as Team New Zealand." Presti also noted that Jimmy's positioning throughout the starts had been good but that right at the end, in both races, he was late accelerating to the starting line.

The problem wasn't Jimmy. The problem was Team USA's onboard starting software, which calculates the exact moment the skipper should "pull the trigger" and accelerate toward the starting line. For example, the computer will tell Jimmy that *USA-17* is ten seconds behind the line with fifteen seconds to go before the start. Jimmy then knows that he is five seconds *early*, so he has to slow down and *kill* those five seconds to avoid crossing the starting line before the gun goes off. Ideally, the helmsman wants to hit the starting line in front of and going faster than the other boat. An AC72 can accelerate rapidly and travels one boat-length (seventy-two feet) every second when going at full speed, so calculating time and distance from the starting line in your head can be tricky. For more than a decade, America's Cup helmsmen have relied on onboard computers to help them decide when it's time to accelerate toward the starting line.

Before the first race, Jimmy had gone through a number of practice starts on the water to calibrate the starting software and check the readouts on the PDA on his arm. During the prestart of each of the first two races, Jimmy looked at the start line and wanted to pull the trigger and accelerate, but the software told him to wait another second or two. Both times, the software got him late to the line. "We were missing the last, most important part of the start—pulling the trigger," Jimmy said. "We'd get into a good position and then we'd let them get a jump on us right at the end. The software was telling me I've got two or three seconds to kill and I'd say, 'Fuck, it doesn't look like that.'"

The starting software, developed in-house by the Spaniard Jose Luis Vela, known for creating some of the best performance measurement tools in America's Cup racing, had been put on hold in the final and crucial weeks leading to the start of the Cup because of the jury investigation into the team's alleged cheating. They hadn't had the time they needed to fully test all the software on the water—in different wind speeds, current conditions, wind angles, and starting situations. They had one or two more iterations to go with the programming. Late that night, after everyone else had gone home, Vela, along with Ian "Fresh" Burns, an engineer and team coordinator, sat in front of a panel of computers and went to work. They pored over recordings of every start the team had made over a four-week period, including the day's two races against Team New Zealand. They worked through the night, adjusting the parameters of the program, which calculated distance behind the line in seconds, based on the AC72's ability to accelerate at different wind angles and wind speeds. They had to fix the all-important acceleration calculation part of the program. Then, once they had an improved program, which could take several days, Jimmy would need to trust the data again, like getting back into a relationship once burned.

The next day of racing, Sunday, September 8, started promptly at 1:15, with wind conditions of eighteen knots and swinging through a ten-degree arc between 240 and 250 degrees. The early morning fog had lifted, and temperatures were expected to reach into the mid-eighties, which meant that wind speed would build throughout the afternoon. Team USA had the favored early port entry in the first race of the day.

Larry was back on his chase boat, and Norbert was in his upstairs corner at the Golden Gate Yacht Club. For the third race in a row Jimmy started to the left of Barker in the leeward position, but this time Jimmy pushed Barker very close to the starting line with several seconds to go. Barker was early to the line and had to slow down. As Barker slowed, Jimmy accelerated. *USA-17* hit the line first and with more speed than the Kiwis. Winning the start enabled Jimmy to maintain his controlling leeward overlap all the way to the first mark. As both boats began their left turn, Jimmy suddenly reversed direction and turned right instead, using his leeward right-of-way position to stop the Kiwis' turn and force them to go right to avoid a penalty or worse—a collision.

The maneuver is called a luff, and when done in catamarans going over forty knots, it can be dangerous. Barker was way too slow to react and the two boats almost collided. Penalty—Team New Zealand! The first penalty in the 34th America's Cup. The TV commentator, Olympic gold medalist and Artemis AC72 helmsman Nathan Outteridge, described Jimmy as "superaggressive at mark one." When the blue penalty light illuminated on the Kiwi catamaran, Larry yelled, "Great start. Crazy luff. That's the Jimmy Spithill I know." Race three could not have begun better for Team USA.

Oracle blazed downwind with a hundred-meter lead, which stretched to over 200 meters, or eighteen seconds, at the leeward gate. The two boats split at the bottom of the course, with *USA-17* heading toward the city and the Kiwis heading offshore behind Alcatraz Island. Right at the start of the upwind leg New Zealand showed better pace, going twenty-four knots compared with USA's twenty-two. The two boats engaged in a tacking duel as they worked their way up toward the Golden Gate Bridge. Jimmy was tacking the boat better than the day before, popping the windward hull right out of the water. But as the boats crossed, and crossed again, and again, Team New Zealand was continuously eating into Team USA's lead.

By the time both boats had reached Alcatraz the lead was diminished by more than half, to less than a hundred meters. New Zealand was consistently sailing lower, faster angles, going into their tacks faster, and coming out of their tacks faster. When New Zealand reached the city front boundary, they tacked onto port, and Jimmy tacked right in front of them, trying to block the Kiwis' wind. It didn't work. Barker ducked to leeward of *USA-17*, got the overlap, and forced Jimmy to tack back toward the city front. When *USA-17* tacked again to avoid the northern boundary, Barker tacked right in front of them. Now it was Jimmy's turn to duck to leeward and force the Kiwis to tack back toward the city. It was incredibly tight racing, a series of close-quarters, boat-on-boat maneuvers, as both teams fought hard for the slightest advantage.

When the Kiwis tacked at the boundary, Team USA tacked to leeward and was slightly in front, but the Americans' tack was painfully slow and the Kiwis got up to speed first and sailed right by *USA-17*. With both of the boats sailing on port, the tacking duel was over and the drag race began. As they sailed side by side, *USA-17* was simply unable to keep up with the Kiwi catamaran. It wasn't much of a drag race. Team New Zealand effortlessly glided farther and farther in front of the slow-moving Team USA. The Kiwis' upwind speed advantage was decisive.

Four-time America's Cup winning tactician Brad Butterworth described Team New Zealand's upwind boat speed as "dominant."

He summarized the Kiwis' comeback in race three in a few easy-to-understand words: "You can't beat that." Larry quietly turned to his son and said much the same thing: "They're a lot faster upwind than we are. Nobody understands why. If we don't figure it out soon, we're going to lose."

Barker and crew sailed the rest of race three in *delivery mode*: don't take any chances, don't make mistakes, keep the tactics simple, stay between your opponent and the next mark. *Don't lose a race you've already won.* The Kiwis had turned an eighteen-second deficit at the leeward gate into a twenty-nine-second advantage at the windward gate. All Team New Zealand had to do now was sail safely and conservatively to hold on to their big lead through the second downwind leg and the reach to the finish. That was the smart thing to do, and that's exactly what they did. Team USA had a perfect start, got a penalty on New Zealand at the first mark, had a solid lead at the end of the first run downwind, and still managed to lose the race by twenty-eight seconds. "Bad luck, boys," Jimmy said as they crossed the finish line. It was the second time he'd said it, and nobody believed it. It was a devastating defeat, the third in a row.

In between races, as the shore crew jumped onboard to check the boat, Presti climbed on to go over video of the race. Using his iPad and a program developed in-house, Presti isolated different parts of the race to analyze with Jimmy.

With spectators lining the shore of Crissy Field and the Marina Green and over to the Embarcadero, the next race—the fourth—began at 2:15. As the sun heated the land and lifted the air over Oakland and Berkeley in the east bay, the sea breeze steadily increased to more than twenty knots. The computer models predicted that the higher wind speeds would favor Team USA. Of course, those were the same computer models that had predicted that *USA-17* would be faster upwind than the Kiwis' boat. Maybe the computers were wrong about everything. Larry announced to his girlfriend, Nikita, to Oracle chief marketing officer Judy Sim, son David, and nephew Jimmy, "The wind conditions are absolutely perfect for us. We've got to win this race."

Team New Zealand entered on port and ran deep behind the line. Ten seconds later, *USA-17* entered, then jibed and followed. With a minute and thirty seconds to go, Barker tacked onto starboard. Jimmy then sailed across Barker's stern and tacked above and three boat-lengths behind him. With twenty-five seconds to go, Jimmy put the bow down and accelerated to leeward of Team New Zealand. A moment later, Barker responded and accelerated. Both boats sped toward the starting line, but Jimmy had accelerated first, so *USA-17* hit the line first and with more speed, almost forty knots. Team USA was tucked in tight to leeward and going faster than Team New Zealand. Jimmy had won the start again, and he was in complete control with a leeward overlap as both boats approached the first mark. Then Jimmy turned up aggressively, luffed the Kiwis, turned down hard, and made a left turn around mark 1. *USA-17* had accelerated downwind to over forty-five knots and built up a lead of more than a hundred meters before Barker could recover.

At the Golden Gate Yacht Club, Norbert and wife Madeleine cheered wildly. On the chase boat, Larry said, "Two great starts by Jimmy today. He did a much better job on time and distance to the line than yesterday. The boys worked all night to fix our starting software. It looks like that's one problem we can put behind us."

On the run downwind, New Zealand was first to jibe. Team USA went straight and increased their lead to 130 meters. *USA-17* was able to maintain that lead all the way over to the northern boundary near Alcatraz Island, and then down to the bottom of the racecourse. But when *USA-17* jibed onto the final approach to the leeward gate, the crew deployed the port hydrofoil at the wrong angle and the American cat suddenly pitched forward and dug in both bows. *USA-17* slowed down drastically, as if someone had hit the brakes. It was a huge boat handling error, and it cost Team USA most of its lead. By the time Jimmy turned right at the leeward gate, Barker was right on his transom, only five seconds behind.

As both boats headed upwind toward the thrilled spectators lining the city front, Jimmy and crew had to find a way to protect their slim lead on the upwind leg of the race, the leg where the Kiwis had been dominant in the previous three races. Things looked grim as Barker closed the gap to only one boat-length behind. Jimmy was sailing *USA-17* in a high slow mode, trying to position the back end of the American cat's starboard hull just to leeward of the Kiwis' port bow. It worked. *USA-17* got into a perfect lee bow position, blocked the Kiwis' wind, and Barker was forced to tack away onto port and head back into the middle of the racecourse. That's as close as New Zealand got to Team USA during the entire rest of the upwind leg. With the wind howling at twenty-four knots, *USA-17* had no trouble holding on to the lead throughout the tacking duel and all the way to the weather gate.

"Well, both boats are about the same speed upwind in twenty-four knots of breeze," Larry observed. "Unfortunately, there are two problems here: first, twenty-four knots is right at the upper end of the wind limits, so we won't be sailing in twenty-four knots very often, and second, the models say we're supposed to be *a lot faster* than they are in these conditions. And we're not. It's totally baffling." Jimmy Linn suggested, "Maybe you should hire smarter models." Larry shrugged and smirked, "There's an idea, Judge. And all ideas are welcome at this point—even that one. I have no clue why we're not faster than they are upwind."

As Team USA turned right at the weather gate, they were sixteen seconds and more than 200 meters in front of Team New Zealand. The Kiwis were able to close the gap on the downwind leg, but not enough. For the first time, Barker and crew watched from behind as Team USA cruised home with their first win in the 34th America's Cup. The score was three to minus one.

After a long debrief at the team base, Larry and Russell talked late that night. The Team USA CEO stubbornly insisted that the speed of their catamaran was "just fine." The way they were sailing it was not. The two men systematically went over what they knew. The Kiwis were sailing lower, faster angles, and sometimes fully foiling upwind at twenty-seven or twenty-eight knots. Because New Zealand was sailing faster upwind, they would go into their tacks at higher speeds and come out of the tacks at higher speeds, resulting in big gains with every tack. And Barker was quicker at popping the weather hull out of the water, enabling his boat to accelerate faster after the tack was complete.

They came up with a plan. Jimmy and the crew would lower their upwind sailing angles, increase their upwind speed targets, and adopt the Kiwis' tacking technique. The boys had all day Monday to relearn how to sail their AC72 upwind.

As planned, Jimmy and the team spent the day practicing sailing upwind and tacking like the Kiwis. They didn't stop practicing until the late summer sunset forced them back to the base. The Kiwis already knew how to tack and sail upwind, so they kept their boat in the shed and took the day off.

On Tuesday, September 10, both boats hit the water for race five of the America's Cup. The wind was blowing at sixteen to twenty knots, with a flood tide current of 1.9 miles per hour. New Zealand general manager Grant Dalton, his team now six wins away from winning the America's Cup, smiled on his way to docking out and said, "Oh yeah, I'd like to take the trophy back to New Zealand."

Team USA tactician and San Francisco native John Kostecki, heralded for knowing the tricky conditions of the bay better than anyone else, acknowledged that their win on Sunday was a big psychological boost for the team. "It was great to come back to the base and see the confidence," Kostecki said. "Today is going to be a pivotal day."

Race five began well for the Americans. Jimmy won his third straight start, and rolled right over the top of Barker during the first reaching leg. *USA-17* rounded the first mark with a three-second lead. As they sailed along the city front, Team USA increased its lead to nearly 150 meters, jibed first, and stretched out the lead to around 200 meters. As the American boat approached the leeward gate, the lead was back down to some 150 meters, but overall, things were looking better. The problematic starting software was working properly now, and Jimmy was winning start after start, as had been predicted before the regatta began. *USA-17*'s speed reaching and downwind was every bit as good as Team New Zealand's. Only one big question remained: had Team USA improved their upwind sailing technique enough to keep the Kiwis from passing them on the third leg of the race? Heading into the leeward gate with a nice lead, they were about to find out. Tactician Kostecki made the call: "It's going to be a foiling tack. Right mark foiling tack."

As Team USA approached the mark, they attempted a two-hundred-degree teardrop-shaped right turn around the buoy while staying up on their foils. The ill-conceived maneuver failed spectacularly—both of *USA-17*'s hulls crashed down into the water and dug in. The big black American catamaran shuddered, decelerated, and almost stopped. Team USA's staggering drunken pirouette around the buoy cost them all of their lead, before the upwind leg had even begun.

Television commentator Ken Read, sounding puzzled, said, "We've never seen anyone doing a foiling tack. I saw them *try* to do one yesterday during practice and I wondered if it was a mistake, thinking maybe they broke something." Read concluded, "I don't see a toolbox on deck for the confidence repair required." And Brad Butterworth, the four-time America's Cup winner, described Team USA's tactics as "the inmates running the asylum."

Watching the "foiling tack" from his chase boat, Larry went apoplectic. "What the fuck! Why did we tack right at the mark when we're in front? We needed to go straight there, at least for a few lengths. That was a massive tactical blunder. Oh yeah, and *there's no such thing as a foiling tack.* That's delusional sailing, a video game fantasy maneuver."

The race was over long before the Kiwis crossed the finish line a staggering 1,100 meters—one minute and five seconds—ahead. The Kiwis not only capitalized on the Americans' "foiling tack" debacle, but they tore away from Team USA upwind. Team New Zealand completed the three-nautical-mile upwind leg of the race a full eighty-five seconds faster than Team USA.

Immediately after the race, Russell, in a performance boat, pulled alongside USA-17 and Jimmy jumped onboard. The race was a tactical disaster, but even worse was the huge speed advantage the Kiwis continued to enjoy upwind. New Zealand now led the series four races to negative one. Jimmy said, "Right now, with this performance difference, they're going to get us." Russell called Larry on the chase boat and the two men agreed it was time to use their one and only "postponement card"—each team had one card to use during the regatta. They needed time to find an answer to as why USA-17 was so much slower upwind. The announcement was made that race six would be postponed until Thursday.

At the press conference after the loss, Jimmy was asked whether Kostecki would be on the boat on Thursday. "It's too early to make a decision right now," he said. "It's part of the reason why we played the card. We need some time to assess our program and the boat and get it heading in the right direction. Fortunately we've got some time and a lot of races left."

Asked if his own position was guaranteed on the boat, Jimmy said, "I can't guarantee anything. I probably can't guarantee I'll be there." Then he smiled and shared a line told to him by a mentor, the Australian Syd Fisher. "Syd used to say to me when something was going good, 'Be careful, because you can be a rooster one day and a feather duster the next.'"

After the team debrief, Russell talked with Larry. The two agreed that Kostecki was not having his best week, and discussed taking him off the boat. Larry pressed Russell. He wanted to change tacticians.

"A change like this in the afterguard has never worked," Russell said. "I honestly can't think of a single example where it improved the performance of the team."

Larry replied, "You're right. But I still want to change tacticians."

After a very long pause, Russell slowly said, "Okay, there's one guy who can do the job . . . Ben Ainslie."

"Actually there are two guys," Larry said. "But you already have a job, Russell. You've got to figure out why we're so damn slow upwind. Or, said another way, why is New Zealand so fast? What are they doing that we're not?"

Russell spent the next several hours weighing the pros and cons before committing to the change. The more he thought about it, the more enthusiastic he got about reconfiguring Team USA's afterguard. When he discussed it with teammate and close friend Murray Jones, Russell said, "That combination is pretty compelling," referring to America's Cup champion helmsman Jimmy Spithill, four-time Olympic gold medalist Sir Ben Ainslie, and strategist Tom Slingsby, another gold medalist.

Meanwhile, over at Pier 80, the shore crew guys got USA-17 out of the water and onto her cradle. The daytime crew would work until 7:30 or 8 p.m., when the eight-member night crew arrived to work until the next morning. Inside the conference room, the team analyzed race video. Their downwind speed was good, and they'd had a strong start, hitting the line just right. The start software was improved and Jimmy was more confident with the data he was getting. But tactics were a problem, and the boat was not moded right when sailing upwind.

Team USA needed to know exactly how their opponent was configuring their boat when sailing upwind. While everyone watched race video, Presti again went over what they already knew. "New Zealand is sailing low and fast with the hulls sixty-five percent out of the water," he said. "As soon as they sail in their quick skimming mode they are much faster than we are upwind." But USA-17 had failed to partially lift up and go into that skimming mode when Jimmy sailed at the same low angles as the Kiwis. Clearly the Kiwis were doing more than simply sailing upwind at low angles. But what?

While trying to solve the upwind mystery, Team USA's designers came up with a variety of ideas to speed up their AC72 in other ways. They were making a lot of small changes they hoped would add up. The rudder angle on USA-17 was changed from a negative angle to neutral. The shore crew had been constantly repainting the bottom of the rudders because of cavitation—the speed of the rudder going through the water caused the water to bubble or boil, inducing vibration and increasing drag. The cavitation started when they hit around forty-three knots downwind. To reduce and delay the start of cavitation, Paul Bieker, the team's appendage design engineer, made the two AC72 rudders thinner while keeping the radius of the curved control surfaces the same. Joseph Ozanne, the young engineer who had helped build the gigantic 23-story wing sail for the original *USA-17* trimaran, obsessed over the angles of the AC72 sail. The rudder change gave *USA-17* a bit more speed downwind, but did nothing for its upwind speed.

Over the next two days, Kostecki, officially off the boat, and Presti worked with Ainslie to make sure he knew all of the on-board systems.

Jimmy, meanwhile, told the team, "We've been through worse than this." He had seen the shore crew work through the winter without a day off to get the boat he had capsized back on the water. While building new parts, the crew had salvaged capsized parts for reuse and taken other parts from their massive trimaran that had won the America's Cup in 2010. Jimmy had expected the shore crew to blame him for the crash. Instead, the builders told Jimmy not to worry: "We'll get you back out there soon." Jimmy hadn't forgotten, either, how Larry's support had been unwavering, and it still was. Larry was absolutely positive that Jimmy would get the job done if Russell and the design team could figure out the answer to the upwind speed riddle.

"We can win races," Jimmy told the team, over and over again.

The reconfigured Team USA lost the next two races, the first by forty-seven seconds and the second by over a minute. A *New York Times* story with the headline "CUP TURNING INTO ROUT AS KIWIS WIN TWICE MORE" painted a bleak picture for Team USA and said the crew shake-up did nothing to change Oracle's fortunes, as "yachting's biggest event has become a romp for Emirates New Zealand." The story went on, "The Kiwis, winners of six of the first seven races, including both on Thursday, need three more victories in the best-of-17 series to wrest the trophy from Golden Gate Yacht Club and Oracle. With two races scheduled Saturday, and two more on Sunday, the trophy and plans for the next competition in three or four years could be headed to the southern hemisphere before the weekend ends."

But for Team USA fans, there were signs of progress. There appeared to be better communication between Ainslie, Slingsby, and Jimmy, and there were no huge tactical mistakes. The change in the afterguard, the so-called thinking part of the boat, could just need time to gel.

Back at Pier 80 for the debrief, Presti complimented the team on better tactics and tacking. As he talked, though, he noticed that some of the guys looked lost in thought. For the first time, he was hearing team members talk of *losing* the Cup. There was a universal desire to win a few more races for Larry, but also a sense that the end was near. Presti and Ian Burns focused on parts of the race where the team had excelled, and talked in detail about what had gone right. They went over some stats of the closer first race. With a wind speed average of 11.6 knots and a peak of 13.4 knots, the teams had sailed exactly the same distance (12.3 nautical miles) and were close in average speed (the Kiwis at twenty-seven miles per hour and Oracle at twenty-six). But Team USA had reached a higher top speed, forty-six miles per hour to New Zealand's forty-four.

Wanting to boost spirits and also take the pressure off, Presti landed on an idea. "*Forget the Cup,*" he told the team. "*Just forget the Cup.* Focus instead on small pieces of the puzzle. Eventually we're going to put all of those pieces together."

On days when they weren't racing, the team had been trying out new daggerboard hydrofoils, the retractable appendages that make the hulls levitate out of the water and begin to fly over the surface. Under Cup rules, a team is allowed to make no more than five pairs of daggerboards. Each AC72 operated with two daggerboards and two rudders. The breakage of a daggerboard on the team's very first day of practice had revealed a design flaw in daggerboards one and two, the first pair. The team was now sailing with daggerboards nine and ten; on Monday, the sailing team had tried out daggerboard five on the starboard side, but the crew came back from practice and said the heavier number five daggerboard didn't help upwind, and that nine and ten were faster downwind.

Downwind speed was not the problem; upwind speed was the problem. If Team USA's AC72 catamaran continued to be slow and vulnerable upwind, if they remained a couple of knots slower than Team New Zealand, they were all but certain to lose the Auld Mug. The situation was desperate. Team USA needed a breakthrough, and they needed it soon.

Better downwind speed meant absolutely nothing if Team USA's AC72 catamaran continued to be slow and vulnerable upwind. If they remained a couple of knots slower, they were all but certain to lose the Auld Mug. The situation was desperate. Team USA needed a breakthrough, and they needed it soon.

That evening, Russell and the design team reviewed video taken from helicopters during the day's racing. One of the aerial shots, looking directly down on the wing of New Zealand's AC72, caught their attention. The intriguing video was stopped and slowly backed up, and then one frame was frozen on the screen. Everyone in the room focused on the angle of the Kiwis' wing flap. One of the team's senior designers broke the silence. "Holly shit! It looks like they're sailing upwind with a lot more camber in their wing than we are."

They carefully measured the frozen image. It was a revelation: the Kiwi's wing flap was set at a *forty-degree* angle to the wing's main element. That was in stark contrast to *USA-17*. The American catamaran raced upwind with its flap set at *thirty degrees*. "That's got to be it," said Russell, shooting up from his chair. "Nothing has made any sense up until now. The computer models say our boat is faster than they are upwind, but the models assume the wings have the same camber and trim. They're sailing with radically more camber in their wing than we are. More camber, more lift—more lift, more power upwind. We thought going beyond thirty degrees of camber would create too much drag. Obviously we were wrong."

With Team USA down six races to negative one, and less than forty hours to go before the start of race eight of the America's Cup on September 14, Team USA's engineers and designers believed they had finally discovered the secret to Team New Zealand's superior speed upwind. They were sure they had their breakthrough. Now they were in a different race against a different enemy—*time*.

Over the next few hours the engineering and design team, including Ozanne, designed a series of related modifications that increased the camber of the wing, lowered the center of effort, and moved the overall loading back to better balance the boat. The team's boatbuilders had to physically modify the structure of their catamaran so the wing flap could be bent beyond thirty degrees, all the way to forty degrees—and even more. The builders would be working all night for the next couple of nights. Once the modifications to the boat were made, the upwind performance of *USA-17* would no doubt be dramatically improved. They were energized. They had thirty-six hours to rebuild several critical parts of the world's most complex sailboat. If they finished in time, they would test their changes in race eight of the America's Cup.

The designer of the wing's control systems—the equivalent of a car's gearbox—was a Frenchman named Dimitri Despierres, a mechanical engineer and America's Cup sailor who had worked with Oracle racing since 2003. Despierres knew the wing like a parent knows his child. It had three elements: the "main element" in front; the "middle element," called the tab; and the "flap element" in the back, consisting of four flaps. In order to increase the load on the bottom flap, they had to decrease its twist. Once the twist was removed, the flap became more loaded.

To accomplish this, they had to go back and "tune" their control system. As Despierres noted, the real breakthrough in innovation on *USA-17's* wing was not the wing itself but the way it was controlled. Instead of using cylinders and a complex system of pulleys and blocks, he and his colleagues had created a mechanism that had never been used before on a boat. It was composed of chains, including conveyor chains and high-end bicycle chains, all commercially available. The conveyor chains, which were stronger, were used for flap one and two, which had more loading and were capable of controlling about twelve thousand pounds, whereas the lighter bicycle chains on flaps three and four were able to handle around two thousand pounds.

The control system created for the AC72 was compact enough that it could go *inside* the wing, not outside like New Zealand's wing control system. *USA-17*'s control system was far more versatile in adapting to new configurations, twists, and requirements of the crew, usually without requiring modifications to the structure of the boat. However, increasing the camber all the way to forty degrees and beyond did require significant structural changes to *USA-17*. Team USA's chief boatbuilder, Mark Turner, had delivered miracles in the past, and everyone believed he could do it again.

The question remained, though: were the changes coming too late?

Fifteen minutes before the start of race eight, the wind was blowing at 18 knots coming out of 260 to 265 degrees. Today would be the first time the teams would race in an ebb tide. The strong current sweeping out toward the Golden Gate Bridge was churning up bigger waves on the racecourse. The wind limits were 21.7 knots for the first race and 22.6 knots for the second.

During a TV interview on his way to dock-out, Jimmy said, "We've taken the spine off [the bowsprit used in light winds to attach *USA-17*'s large Code 0 headsail], so no option for the Code 0 today. We'll save some weight there, and we've made other changes to the boat." Those "other changes" were closely guarded secrets, certainly not to be discussed on TV. "We've been very aggressive," Jimmy offered, "but we need to be."

Team New Zealand entered the starting box on port, sailed a long way behind the line, then jibed just above the layline. The day's ebb tide heavily favored the leeward boat, and Barker was fighting hard for the leeward position. As Barker led Jimmy back toward the starting line, Jimmy went for a hook, a leeward overlap, with only ten seconds to go. But Jimmy was going too slow, Barker stayed clear in front, and then he timed his acceleration to the starting line perfectly. All Jimmy could do was follow the Kiwis as they sprinted toward the city, rounded mark 1 in front, and then headed downwind. The Kiwis held a slim lead, around 140 meters, as they arrived at the leeward gate. It was a close race. Team New Zealand turned right at the gate, Team USA turned left. The two boats split the course as they began the three-nautical-mile beat upwind that had been the downfall for Team USA since the start of racing. This was the do-or-die moment.

Right away, you could see the difference. *USA-17* was hitting speeds of twenty-eight knots upwind, slightly faster than the Kiwis. As the two boats worked their way up toward the windward gate, the Kiwis' lead began to shrink: 140 meters, 100 meters, 80 meters. As the boats crossed, and crossed again, the Kiwis' lead continued to get smaller: 70 meters, 50 meters, 30 meters. Halfway up the third leg of race eight, the Kiwis' lead had almost vanished. Gary Jobson was the first to comment: "Oracle Team USA is actually sailing through the water faster than Emirates Team New Zealand. That's the first time we've seen that." Ken Read had to agree: "It just looks like they're going quicker through the water all the time. Their changes have made a difference here—bottom line." Kiwi tactician Ray Davies, sounding concerned, noted of Jimmy: "He's going pretty well down there."

Larry, taking it all in from his chase boat, said, "We're catching them. They're not faster than us upwind anymore. What we have here is a whole new ball game."

As the two boats converged in the middle of the racecourse, New Zealand tacked onto port directly to leeward and slightly in front of *USA-17*'s bow. Barker's lee bow tack forced Jimmy to tack away back onto starboard. But the Kiwis' lead was less than a boat-length. The next time the two boats came together, New Zealand crossed clear ahead but continued toward the city front, while the Americans headed offshore. The Kiwis had *surrendered their starboard advantage*. The next time the two boats converged, *USA-17* would have the right-of-way.

As Team USA approached the northern boundary of the race-course, Jimmy tacked onto starboard and pointed his bows directly at the Kiwi catamaran sailing on port. Rather than crossing, Team New Zealand decided to tack onto starboard, in front and to lee-ward of the fast-oncoming Team USA. The boats were on a collision course. Then, right in the middle of their rushed attempt to do a lee bow tack, the Kiwis' wing sail failed to reverse camber—fold the other way—causing the thirteen-story catamaran to become unstable. *It began to tip over.* The starboard hull rose slowly, higher and higher, out of the water, with the camber still stubbornly re-fusing to reverse.* With their weather hull more than thirty feet above the water, wing trimmer Glenn Ashby screamed, "Hydro hydro—keep it going—hydro." On the verge of disaster, the guys onboard Team Zealand kept grinding to feed the hydraulics. No one could believe what they were seeing.

Inside the clubhouse of the Golden Gate Yacht Club, all was quiet. Across town at Oracle's VIP lounge, Club 72 at Piers 27–29, hands were held to mouths. Even the blasé bartenders stopped what they were doing to stare at the flat-screen TVs. Tom Ehman shook his head. It was his 11th America's Cup, and it was by far the most nerve-racking. He knew the boats and sailors were travel-ing at highway speeds, under high-pressure loads and severe stress. Seeing it all unfold, after three decades of being involved in the

---

* Looking from directly above the wing sail of a catamaran sailing on starboard tack, the wing sail should look like this: <

When sailing on port tack the wing sail should look like this: >

When tacking from port onto starboard the wing sail is supposed to reverse camber, going from this shape: > to this shape: <

During the near capsize, the New Zealand wing sail did not reverse camber; it kept this shape: > before, during, and after the tack.

Cup, and three years trying to defend it for the Golden Gate Yacht Club—where he was vice commodore—the stoical Ehman could only watch and hope. As the Kiwis fought to right the boat, Ehman flashed to the dramatic moment in a 1995 Louis Vuitton race when the monohull *One Australia* broke in two and was literally sucked underwater and disappeared, all in the span of a minute. Ehman didn't want this America's Cup to end in catastrophe.

The massive boat from New Zealand, its starboard hull high in the air like a gymnast doing the splits, was now within half a degree of tipping. Whether hydraulic failure or human, the wing remained popped the wrong way. The hopes of a nation waited five long seconds to see if the boat would come back down. Three sailors were on the starboard hull, high in the air. The other eight, including Barker, were on the port hull.

Jimmy, within feet of the endangered Kiwi boat, executed a last-minute crash tack to avoid a collision. Then, in a moment that few watching would soon forget, the Kiwi boat somehow, miraculously, began to right itself, and its starboard hull came down, splashing hard onto the water. All of the sailors were still onboard.

Larry, watching from the racecourse, said quietly, "I'd rather lose every single race than have another capsize. We don't need any more AC72 crashes in this regatta."

Because Team USA was on starboard tack during the near capsize and collision, Team New Zealand was penalized, and the rattled Kiwis—happy to be in one piece—struggled to recover. Team USA grabbed a lead of twenty-eight seconds at the weather gate. The Kiwis didn't put up much of a fight for the rest of the race. The American defenders increased their lead to over 700 meters on the downwind leg, and finished the race 900 meters, or 54 seconds, ahead of the challengers from New Zealand.

The next race, race nine, was abandoned shortly after the start, with the Kiwis in the lead. The wind had exceeded the 22.6-knot limit for the day.

At the afternoon press conference, Jimmy, looking energized by his team's win, said, "Mate, it is on. This is the turning point.

We've been saying it all along, that we can win races. It really felt the last few days that the Kiwis have been thinking about where to put the trophy and I can tell you we're going to fight the whole way." As Presti listened to Jimmy, he couldn't help but smile. There were a lot of good things happening on the water. Among other things, the day's racing represented the first time *USA-17* was fully foiling upwind—going around thirty knots, faster than the Kiwis' best-ever upwind foiling speed of twenty-eight knots.

Jimmy was greatly relieved that the Kiwi boat hadn't gone over. "It was close to being a huge pileup," he said. "It would have been serious if I weren't able to bail out. You never like to see that. I've got a lot of mates on that team. I was looking at my mate Glenn Ashby up there and was thinking, Oh God, I hope those guys are going to be all right. For us, we were glad they didn't go over."

Barker said the crew had rushed a tack in front of Team USA. Then, trying to explain how they recovered, Barker paused. "I think we had someone looking down on us giving us a little help," he said. "I think that's as close as you can ever possibly get before it would have ended up over on its side."

Barker added, "We're at the top end of wind range today and you've got to make sure you are error-free around the course. We made one mistake and it cost us the race, but it also came very, very close to costing us a lot more than that." Team New Zealand didn't have a second boat.

Team USA ended the day with its second victory of the series, which now erased the two-point penalty. Going into races nine and ten, scheduled for Sunday, New Zealand had won six races and had six points; Team USA had won two races but had zero points.

Over the next several days, crowds continued to pour into America's Cup Park, the newly built cruise ship terminal and pier with restaurants, bars, shops, an amphitheater for musical performances—by the likes of Sting, Train, Journey, and more— huge outdoor flat screens and an AstroTurf Puma yard with beanbag chairs and games for the family. Fans were also staking out positions along the waterfront, whether in the ticketed bleacher seats or along the beaches and Marina Green. Private parties were held in homes overlooking the bay, and out in boats and superyachts. And private chalets were available for $25,000 a day. The Golden Gate Yacht Club was booked with parties and member events from breakfast through dinner.

After a day of postponement, race nine, now moved to September 15, began in winds of 19 knots and a strong 2.2-knot ebb tide. Jimmy entered on port, sailed very low in the box, got tight to leeward of Barker, and totally controlled him during the remainder of the start. British tactician Ben Ainslie offered a comment of "lovely work" as Jimmy luffed Barker and slowed him down. Moments later *USA-17* took off toward San Francisco with the Kiwis well behind. Team USA rounded the first mark four seconds in front.

Team USA sailed faster than the Kiwis all the way down the downwind leg. When *USA-17* turned right at the leeward gate, they had an eighteen-second lead. That lead continued to build on the upwind leg. Team USA was now tacking beautifully, and fully foiling upwind, sailing away from the Kiwis. Team USA rounded the third mark with a thirty-three-second lead, the fourth mark with a forty-seven-second lead, and finished the race with a decisive forty-seven-second victory.

Larry was ecstatic. They were still down, 6 to 1, on the scoreboard, but his team had won the last two races convincingly. *USA-17* was sailing well downwind *and* upwind. Team New Zealand had asked some hard questions, and Team USA had responded with some pretty good answers.

Larry was *almost* confident as the second race of the day began. Team New Zealand entered on port tack, sailed deep into the starting box, and then jibed right onto the low layline, the left edge of the starting box. Team USA entered on starboard, and jibed above and behind the Kiwis. As Barker headed toward the starting line, he actually dipped below the layline, overprotecting his leeward position. Barker now had to sail high and slow to get back up to the layline. This gave Jimmy the opportunity to pull the trigger and accelerate first.

As both boats crossed the starting line, USA-17 was going twenty-six knots while the Kiwis were hitting only nineteen. It looked like Jimmy had won another start, but he still had to break the overlap and get around Barker before they reached mark 1. *It was so close.* USA-17 came within about a meter of breaking the overlap and rolling over the top of the Kiwis. But close doesn't count, except in horseshoes. Barker did his job well; he held on and rounded mark 1 in front.

The Kiwis managed to maintain a small lead all the way to the leeward gate, then Barker turned right and headed toward the city, and Jimmy split left, eleven seconds behind. At the first cross, New Zealand's lead was 140 meters, but USA-17 was consistently going faster upwind. Halfway up the beat, the Kiwis lead was down to 90 meters. After the next cross, the lead had shrunk to 30 meters, a little more than a boat-length. As the two catamarans converged once again, Team USA had starboard right-of-way, and New Zealand was forced to dip and go behind it. The Americans had taken the lead in race ten. On the next cross, Team New Zealand had starboard advantage and turned the tables on the Americans, grabbing the lead back. It was lead change after lead change, something that had never happened before in the long history of the America's Cup. Gary Jobson described it as "match racing on steroids."

After one more cross, the two boats split at the weather mark and raced downwind—*dead even.* The Kiwis' 140-meter lead had been entirely erased during the upwind leg, so when the two boats came together for their first downwind cross, they were bow to bow. The two catamarans were on a collision course, foiling toward each other at the breathtaking closing speed of over *ninety miles an hour.* New Zealand was on starboard and had the right-of-way. Rather than jibing before they got to the Kiwis, the Americans made a split-second decision to slow down and go behind them. But slowing down and reaccelerating, a catamaran going over fifty miles an hour is a 10 out of 10 on sailing's degree-of-difficulty scale. *USA-17* slowed too much, and then accelerated too slowly. Team USA utterly botched a maneuver too difficult to have been attempted in the first place. In a matter of seconds, Team USA went from dead even with the Kiwis to 200 meters *behind*. It was a fatal mistake. Team New Zealand's lead was never seriously threatened again. Barker and company sailed away to a seventeen-second victory in race ten of the America's Cup.

Larry was not happy. "Stupid self-inflicted wound!" he said, incredulous. "We needed to jibe there, not go behind. The boys did such a great job coming all the way back on the upwind leg, then we threw the race away on that crazy high-speed downwind dip. We just can't afford many more big mistakes. We started with nine lives and we've used up seven of them."

If Team New Zealand were to win the next two races, the Cup would be theirs.

Race eleven, canceled on Tuesday, was now being held on Wednesday, September 18. It started in seventeen knots of breeze and a strong two-knot ebb tide. Barker entered first on port, sailed behind the line, and then jibed two boat-lengths below the layline marking the left edge of the starting box, the same exact position he grabbed for himself in race ten. It made it virtually impossible for Jimmy to get to leeward of the Kiwis. All Jimmy could do was jibe and follow. Barker *owned* the leeward position, and used it to maintain control. As the two boats crossed the starting line, Barker luffed Jimmy and slowed him down. It was a brilliant job by Barker, who won his second start in a row. The Kiwis rounded the first mark 3 seconds in front of the Americans.

The racing downwind was close, less than a hundred meters separating the two boats all the way to the leeward gate. The Kiwis turned left, and then the Americans turned right, only six seconds behind. As the two boats worked their way upwind, the Kiwis crossed in front of the Americans again, and again, and again. By the time they reached the windward gate, Team New Zealand had increased its lead to seventeen seconds.

The boats raced downwind with the Kiwis in front. The mood on the Kiwi boat was calm and confident. "Very nice, boys, going beautifully," said tactician Ray Davies as their lead increased from 200 to 350 meters. Then the Americans made a late charge toward the leeward gate, cutting the Kiwis' lead to less than 100 meters. But it was too little and too late. New Zealand held on and won the race by fifteen seconds.

Larry, his chase boat filled with family and friends, shook his head. "We almost caught them upwind," he said. "We almost caught them downwind. We're a little bit faster than they are, but there is no way we're going to pass them every race; they're just too good to let that happen. If Barker keeps winning the starts, the odds are long against us." Jonathan Dubin, a close family friend and FBI SWAT team leader from Larry's hometown of Chicago, paused for a moment, thought about what Larry had said, then uttered emphatically, "Jimmy's going to win the next start, and we're going to win the next race. It's one race at a time from here on out—one race at a time."

The score was now eight to one. The Kiwis were on match point, needing to win only *one more race* to bring the oldest trophy in international sports home. As everyone knew, there was no second place in the America's Cup.

32

The Comeback

September 19 to September 25

PLANS WERE UNDER WAY for the Auld Mug's return to New Zealand. Emirates Airlines sent a Boeing 777 to San Francisco to fly the victors and their glistening silver ewer home. In Auckland, ballrooms were booked for celebrations; in San Francisco, Kiwi sailors checked out of hotel rooms. With four races scheduled for the weekend, Team New Zealand was preparing for a Monday departure. General manager Grant Dalton talked about adopting a nationality rule that would require America's Cup sailors to be citizens of the country they were representing. The "new rule" was aimed directly at four-time America's Cup winner Russell Coutts, the Kiwi sailing superstar who twice won the Cup for New Zealanders—then broke their hearts and took it away.

Norbert consoled himself by thinking about how far the little Golden Gate had come from the brink of bankruptcy. "We had a great run," he said to his wife Madeleine. One of the wiser things he had done in recent times was to arrange for his father, Jozo, to not only be out of town during the America's Cup, but to be out of the country at the family's home in Hodilje. Jozo wasn't scheduled to return until after it was all over.

Now, with the Kiwis at match point, Norbert had prepared a short concessionary speech for when he had to hand over the Auld Mug to the Royal New Zealand Yacht Squadron. He planned to say, "Sometimes you win, and sometimes you lose," words inspired by John Wayne, and to end with: "Remember the name of the trophy. It's the *America's Cup*, so take good care of her, 'cause we'll be back!"

Ian Burns, the engineer and team manager who had been with Oracle Racing since the beginning, looked at the situation with the Kiwis on match point and thought of the statistical improbability of winning, of coming back from this far behind. There was no room for a single mistake. They'd had constant issues with the boats in the months leading up to the finals, and they had never strung more than a week together without something failing onboard.

One of his jobs over the past months had been to keep track of what they called "race losers." Whenever the sailors were out practicing on the water, Burns logged what went wrong. Hydraulics were a "problem child," but there were other persistent issues. Many days saw multiple failures, failures that if not rectified would have cost them the race. They had rarely strung two days of on-the-water practice together without some kind of problem. He would hear the optimists talking about a comeback and he would think, *Okay, now the statisticians have left the room.* And there was no shortage of statisticians in the sports betting parlors of Las Vegas; their bookmakers put the odds of Team USA successfully defending the America's Cup at 700 to 1.

Larry was not happy when he heard that speeches were being written and plans being made for the handover of the Cup, but he ignored it all until he was asked to settle an argument over *who* was going to give the concession speech during the handover. "Let me get this straight: people are fighting over who gets to give the concession speech? I don't give a fuck who gives the concession speech. If we lose, everyone who wants to give a concession speech can give a concession speech. But we haven't lost yet. Why don't we focus on winning the next fucking race, rather than concession speeches."

Larry added, "Team New Zealand didn't come here to put on a good show. No one *gives* you this stuff. They came here to take the Cup home. These guys are good. They did a lot of work. They came *very* prepared."

Larry, a licensed commercial pilot with thousands of hours flying jets, likened their situation to a plane in distress. When pilots have a serious emergency, they immediately go into problem-solving mode, and they stay in that mode until the problem is solved—or until just before impact. In that final moment, the aircraft's cockpit voice recorder captures the pilot's brief concession speech. There are two versions of the speech, one secular, one not: "Oh God" and "Oh shit." Larry, who had survived so many storms and crises over the years, had not yet reached his "Oh God" or "Oh shit" moment. Down 8 points to 1, he remained in problem-solving mode.

Reflecting on the situation, it was clear to him that Team New Zealand had arrived in San Francisco better prepared than Team USA. During the first several races the Kiwis were sailing their catamaran close to its maximum potential speed, while Team USA was sailing *USA-17* at nowhere near its potential. Fortunately, Team USA's learning curve sailing this new class of catamaran was a vertical line. They were making improvements every race. The speed was better. Ainslie was making good tactical calls. Slingsby was doing an expert job of picking the marks and breeze. And Langford—the youngest man on the cat, now controlling the boat's engine, the source of power—was trimming more skillfully. Days earlier, when Oracle Team USA had only trailed 6 to negative 1, a reporter had asked Jimmy if he was under pressure. Jimmy responded, "I think the question is, imagine if these guys [Team New Zealand] lost from here, what an upset that would be."

But most important, the engineering changes to the American catamaran had dramatically improved its upwind speed. "We've made a lot of progress," Larry said. "We're learning to foil upwind at speeds of over thirty knots, faster than the Kiwis. We just have to do it more consistently. We're going into the tacks with more speed than the Kiwis, so we're coming out of the tacks with more speed than the Kiwis. Their tacking advantage is gone." Larry had laughed when Jimmy, after executing a beautiful series of "roll tacks" during race eight, started to explain the details of his newly learned technique for quickly popping the weather hull out of the water to fellow helmsman-turned-tactician Ben Ainslie. Ainslie quickly cut him off: "Lovely tack, Jimmy, lovely tack. Now please shut the fuck up and drive the boat . . . you can tell me all about it later."

"If the America's Cup was starting over tomorrow, I'm confident we'd win," Russell told Larry. "We've learned a lot, and we have some more changes we want to make to the boat that should speed us up even more. I just hope it's not too late. We're *at least* as fast as they are now. Jimmy just has to go out there and win some starts. If he can do that, if he can keep us in it, we'll give him a faster boat every day."

Jimmy, for his part, kept thinking about something his friends in the Navy SEALs told him: that the guys who failed to make it through the brutal SEAL training course were the ones who *looked ahead* and realized there was no way they could take three more days of torture. The ones who made it only thought about their *present task* and told themselves "I've just got to finish this run" or "I've just got to get this rubber boat through the waves one more time." Jimmy told himself, *I've just got to go out and win one more race. That's all I've got to do.*

Jimmy arrived at Pier 80 at around 6:30 on the morning of September 19—the day of races twelve and thirteen, if necessary. The score was 8 to 1 (Oracle had three wins). Again, the strong winds had played havoc on the schedule, forcing the cancellation of races the day before. Jimmy's routine was to get in workouts before the rest of the guys arrived. He warmed up on this chilly morning with a run around the pier. Their massive trimaran *USA-17,* Larry's "black pterodactyl" that won the Cup for the team in

2010, was out front and served as a kind of welcome and warning to visitors. Larry's beloved maxi yacht, *Sayonara*, was stored off to a side of the pier, looking elegant but outmatched, Chris Evert next to Serena Williams.

Jimmy always wanted to do more than the other guy. Earlier in the year, the team had a grinding contest, which Jimmy almost won. He wanted the team to know he was willing to go through as much pain as they went through for him on the water. In everything he did, Jimmy wanted to be the first in the trenches, first on the line.

After his run, he headed inside to spar and hit the pads with his boxing trainer, Brent Humphries. Jimmy jokingly told Humphries that he should put on a Dean Barker mask. "No way," Humphries said. "You'll knock me out." Midway through the workout, Humphries said to Jimmy, "Do you think Dean Barker is up doing this? No way." Jimmy loved his boxing workouts with Humphries and Tom Slingsby. The three men, all redheads, called their workouts "red mist" as they went after each other with brutal force. Jimmy carried with him two sayings from his days as a young boxer: "Only the fit are fearless," and "The harder you work, the luckier you get."

As Jimmy pushed himself, he visualized the day's race. He was focused on what he needed to do to win. The boat was getting faster every day, and the team was coming together. Kyle Langford had stepped into the job days before the start of the America's Cup. In the first days of racing, Langford would come off the water and be hit with all kinds of ideas as to what he could do differently with the wing. After a few days of this, it was decided that Langford would take direction from one person only—Kevin Borrows, who was in charge of the daily sail and wing report. Presti asked all of the designers in charge of the wing who wanted to give input to report to Borrows.

At around 10:30 that morning, the sailors climbed aboard their black cat. Jimmy told colleagues and invited guests: "We'll see you back here tomorrow, mates."

Once at America's Cup Park, the team settled into their private lounge. Just before it was time for the dock-out show, the team had a visit from Christy Walton of the Wal-Mart family, who had become friends with Jimmy and had been out sailing with him on the AC72. Walton, America's richest woman, held a kids'-style *Avengers* bag. "I have a present for you," she said, revealing the contents of the bag: dozens of kiwis.

"Boys," she said, "here's what you're eating today!"

The room filled with laughter and the sailors had fun devouring the fruit. The moment of levity stayed with the sailors as they boarded the AC72.

Meanwhile, TV commentators were all business, posing the question: "Is this the day the America's Cup goes to New Zealand?" On his way to the boat, Jimmy said he was "excited" and looking forward to "coming back and proving everybody wrong." Ken Read observed that "with the boats so evenly matched, you can make the case that the boat that wins the start will go on to win the race."

Out on the course, the wind was peaking at nearly seventeen knots and coming out of 235 to 240 degrees. The first race of the day was scheduled to begin at slack tide, so there was no current in the starting area. Team USA had port entry for the prestart for both of the day's scheduled races.

Jimmy entered on port and sailed away from the line at over 40 knots. Barker entered ten seconds later, crossed close behind the American catamaran, then jibed and followed *USA-17*, right on Jimmy's tail. With a minute and thirty seconds to go, the two boats jibed simultaneously with Barker to leeward and in front. But Barker got too close to the starting line; he had to slow down. With fifty seconds to go and Barker going slow, Jimmy put *USA-17*'s bow down, dipped to leeward of the Kiwi catamaran, and accelerated until his starboard hull was fifty percent overlapped with the Kiwi's port side hull. It was a *dominant hook*. Jimmy had leeward right of way and total control. He immediately turned up, forcing Barker to turn up and tack away onto port—and slowly sail *away* from the starting line. With Barker going in the wrong direction, Jimmy turned down for the line, accelerated, and crossed the starting line several boat-lengths in front of Barker.

Ken Read summed up Jimmy's start with a "Wow!" Match racers call it a *kill start*, meaning the race is over before it begins. Barring a major mishap, Jimmy's kill start on Barker would probably give Team USA a big enough lead to allow them to hold on and sail to victory in race twelve. And that's what they did. Team USA led coast-to-coast, thrilling fans and crossing the finish line thirty-one seconds ahead.

As the big black cat did a flyby in front of America's Cup Park to AC/DC's "Back in Black," Larry high-fived Jonathan Dubin, the only one left sharing his chase boat and watching the races with him. Most of his family and friends had gone back home, to work in Chicago and LA. The few friends that remained—tennis player Tommy Haas and Nobu restaurant owner Meir Teper—were on another chase boat, giving Larry the room he needed to obsess and brood about the racing. He even managed to get into a fight with his girlfriend, Nikita, who was doing her best to support him through the long series of stressful races. The only one who seemed unruffled by Larry's mood was Dubin, who said his job and training had prepared him to "deal with difficult guys" and dangerous situations. Johnny and Larry watched the races without talking much. When Larry jumped into the chase boat at the beginning of a race day, Johnny would greet him by saying, "Fuck, I'm totally stressed." Larry would respond, "One race at a time, baby." Johnny would say, "One race at a time." That was about it.

The next race of the day, race thirteen, was postponed with less than two minutes to the start. The wind exceeded the prescribed limit of twenty knots.

At the afternoon press conference, Jimmy, asked how he liked seeing the Kiwis squirm, smiled and said, "I'm loving every minute of it. We can win seven more races."

Barker, known to show little emotion, said his team would continue to do what they were doing, minus the mistakes. "Today I just made a meal of the start," he said. "I was on the back foot, and these guys are sailing well enough that you're not going to get a chance to get past them. We're certainly very pleased with the way the boat's going and everything else, and we know that if we sail properly, we'll give them a decent run."

Jimmy noted the strong performance of the team and the boat, including their newfound strength in foiling upwind. "Now we're very competitive around the racetrack and the guys sailing the boat believe we can win it. We've been changing everything. We're doing it constantly. We're learning so much about our boat. The only way to learn it is when you get really pushed, and we're getting pushed. You've got two of the best teams in the world, and that's the ultimate way to improve your performance. So every single day we're changing something."

Heading into race thirteen, on September 20, Team USA was again at match point, down eight races to two on the scoreboard.

Wind conditions were extremely light and the question of the day was whether the boats could make it around the course in under the imposed time limit of forty minutes. If not, the race would be abandoned. The race was billed as another do-or-die situation for Team USA. The Kiwis were just one victory away from claiming the 34th America's Cup. Before dock-out, Barker said of his opponents, "There's no question the Oracle guys are going a lot better than they were two weeks ago. We think it's pretty even between the boats. There are areas where we're strong and we will play to our strength and minimize our weaknesses." Jimmy paused on the way to the boat and said, "We've got this never-give-up attitude. The boys are very very hungry. The fact that we're at match point has excited the team. We're confident in our boat now. We believe we can win this."

The start of race thirteen was delayed because of extremely light winds and a hovering fog. When the race finally did start, the Kiwis entered first, unrolled their massive Code 0 gennaker headsail, and used it to barely get across *USA-17*'s bow as the two boats crossed close together in the starting box. The winds were so light that Jimmy did not jibe and follow Barker; instead he turned directly for the starting line. Barker then turned and followed Jimmy. Everything was happening in *slow motion*. The two boats glided toward the starting line in the fog. When they crossed the starting line, *USA-17* was to leeward and in front. The short first leg of the race took forever. Jimmy luffed Barker, and held him high above mark 1 for what seemed like an eternity. Eventually, Jimmy turned Barker loose, pointed *USA-17*'s bows downwind, and slowly drifted around mark 1, a meaningless ten seconds in front of the Kiwis.

"I hate conditions like this," Larry said to Johnny. "There are holes [spots where there is no wind] all over the racecourse. One boat is going to be in the right place at the right time, get into the breeze first, and win this race by two miles. You might as well toss a coin. It has nothing to do with how well we sail or how fast our boat is."

The Americans led the Kiwis in a long, slow slide downwind. When the two boats jibed onto starboard and sailed back toward the city, each struggled to accelerate past fourteen knots. Then it happened. Team New Zealand got into a puff of breeze—a gift from the wind gods—accelerated to twenty knots, and rolled over the helpless Team USA, which mustered only thirteen knots. The Kiwis opened up a commanding 500-meter lead in less than a minute. Gary Jobson quickly cautioned those viewing the races on NBC, "Remember, New Zealand has two competitors here, Team USA and the time limit." The rules of the 34th America's Cup specified that races had to be completed in less than forty minutes or the race would be abandoned.

The Kiwis led all the way downwind, and led all the way back upwind. When New Zealand hit the halfway point on the second downwind leg they had opened up more than a thousand-meter lead on Team USA. Now their sole remaining competitor was the clock. They had to finish the race within the forty-minute time limit. If the wind picked up, if the Kiwis found dark water and good air, the Cup was theirs. New Zealand had a massive lead. Three years of training, tens of millions of dollars, the hope of a nation, and only one nautical mile to go.

Standing up in his chase boat, Larry stared at the bright light being reflected off the glassy surface of the water around the leeward gate and the reach to the finish. He glanced at his watch, "There's less than six knots of wind down there. They're not going to make it."

Johnny jumped up. "Are you sure?"

Larry nodded and smiled. "I'm sure."

"We're still alive," Johnny said as he hugged him.

As the Kiwis slowly sailed to within a mile of the finish line, the VHF radios onboard both catamarans crackled, "This is race committee. The time limit has expired. This race has been abandoned." The time limit had been put into the rules to prevent races being won and lost in light and variable wind conditions like they were sailing in today—conditions where luck, the favor of the wind gods, trumped both sailing skill and boat speed.

Onboard Team USA, Jimmy looked at his guys and smiled. "I told you it wasn't over," he said. Jimmy had never stopped telling the team that the tide would turn and they had to keep fighting. After their first two wins, grinder Jonathan "Jono" Macbeth, a highly competitive endurance athlete before becoming an America's Cup sailor, came to Jimmy and said, "We're still in the corner." After another win, he came to Jimmy and said, "We just got out of the corner and need to land a couple more." Now Macbeth said, "Okay, time for the knockout."

Television commentator Ken Read said of the abandoned race, "I'm speechless. I can't feel worse for these guys. The good news is they're still up eight to two."

Johnny asked Larry, "Is Ken Read from New Zealand?"

"No, he's an American. But he *loves* the Kiwis," Larry replied. "I think he puts on his Team New Zealand jacket before he goes to sleep every night."

Later that afternoon, the second attempt at race thirteen began in twelve knots of breeze and an ebbing tide. Dean Barker shouted, "Full pace, full pace!" as the Kiwis sprinted toward their port entry into the starting box. Jimmy entered on starboard, jibed, and followed Barker. With a minute and thirty seconds to go, Barker jibed low in the box, Jimmy tacked well above him, and both boats began to make their way back to the starting line. With thirty seconds to go, Jimmy put the bow down, dove to leeward, and went for the hook. Barker fended him off brilliantly, crossed the starting line in front, and rounded mark 1 with a lead of three seconds.

The Kiwis stretched out their lead to 150 meters at the very beginning of the downwind leg. But Team USA found more breeze on the north side of the racecourse. For the next two minutes, *USA-17* was going an astounding six knots faster than the Kiwis. Team USA went from 150 meters behind to 150 meters ahead. It was a tricky day on San Francisco Bay, and Ainslie and Slingsby were doing a better job of locating the breeze than Kiwi tactician Ray Davies.

Everything continued to go wrong for Team New Zealand. They got a penalty for not giving way when the two boats came together on their first downwind cross. Then, right before the leeward gate, they made two very slow jibes, one right after the other, followed by a terrible mark rounding.

Team USA started the upwind leg a hundred meters in front, and with the help of a lucky left-hand wind shift, they finished the upwind leg 400 meters in front. By the time they finished the second downwind leg their lead had grown to 700 meters. When the race finally ended, Team New Zealand was a stunning one minute and twenty-four seconds behind Team USA.

It was a brutal day for the Kiwis, filled with bad luck and bad errors. Barker, asked about the abandoned race, said, "Luck is something you never walk away from. It's a case of executing a race. We have a lot of confidence that we can go out and race to win."

Jimmy said, "We believe we can win; it's as simple as that. With these boats on that racecourse, you can dodge all sorts of bullets out there. At the start of regatta it felt like everything was going against us. Now it feels like it's starting to turn."

In race wins, New Zealand was at eight and Team USA at five. On the scoreboard, the Kiwis held at eight points to Team USA's three. Races fourteen and fifteen were scheduled for Saturday, September 21, but were held the next day—again due to the changing wind conditions of San Francisco Bay, conditions that offered too much wind one day and little breeze the next.

With Team USA on a three-race winning streak, people turned to good luck rituals and talismans. Larry had his routines, and he wasn't changing the clothing he wore on race days. He wore a shirt by the Italian company Slam, which sponsored the team in 2007, a *USA 76* vest from the 2003 campaign, and the team's new Puma jacket with his name on the back. He had a black Team USA hat, a pair of five-year-old Maui Jim sunglasses, Adidas waterproof nylon pants, and Adidas black and white tennis shoes. Hygiene demanded that he change his socks and underwear daily, but that was it. He made sure none of his other clothes were taken away to be washed. Some race days he and his family stayed on *Musashi*, some days he drove himself to his Japanese home in Woodside. Driving gave him an opportunity to decompress and think. He never stayed in his elegant art deco home five minutes from the San Francisco waterfront because he found it uncomfortable and unfamiliar. He was comfortable on the water, he was comfortable in his Japanese garden, but he was never comfortable in the city.

At Oracle's VIP lounge at America's Cup Park, Norbert—who always said a quiet prayer for the team at dock-out—wore his lucky American flag shirt, sometimes with his black Stetson. Jimmy's wife, Jennifer, from San Diego, wore American-flag-patterned leggings. Elizabeth Murphy, a producer for Oracle Corporation known to insiders as the "Trophy Wife" because she is charged with the safety and schedule of the Cup, waved a small American flag over the crowd just as racing began. Tom Ehman, Team USA's director of external affairs, who had been involved in the America's Cup for thirty years, was poker-faced and spoke to no one during the race.

"Today is another big day for the Cup," Kyle Langford said. "We're really enjoying the challenge of stopping the Kiwis. The more wins we can take off them, the more pressure we can put on them. We're focusing on one race at a time."

The fog had rolled in, there was a flood tide, and the wind was averaging 11.4 knots and peaking at 14.9 knots. With the race about to begin, Slingsby said to the team, "Have a good one, bro" as if they were heading out for a casual run on the beach. Team USA practiced its starts a half-dozen times before the Kiwis arrived on the course.

Jimmy entered first on port. Ten seconds later, Barker entered on starboard, jibed, and tried to follow. But as soon as Barker jibed, Jimmy tacked and headed back toward the starting line. Barker tacked and again tried to follow, but this time Jimmy wiggled left, then right, and positioned *USA-17* directly to leeward of the Kiwi catamaran. The two boats crossed the starting line at the same time and raced side by side toward the first mark. But halfway along the reach, Jimmy turned right, luffed Barker, and slowed him down. By the time Jimmy turned down and rounded mark 1, all Barker could do was follow, six seconds behind.

As the downwind leg began, *USA-17* consistently sailed slightly faster than the Kiwi catamaran. And Team USA's crew was jibing better than Team New Zealand's. It was a dramatic turnaround. Every day the American boat got faster; every day the American crew sailed her better. By the time they turned left at the leeward gate, *USA-17* had a lead of 300 meters.

Team USA sailed toward the cone behind Alcatraz Island, looking for about a knot and a half of relief from the flood tide current that was slowing up both boats as they beat their way upwind. The American boat tacked when they got to Alcatraz and sailed all the way across the racecourse right into light breeze along the San Francisco shore. That gave the Kiwis the opportunity they needed to a mount a comeback, closing to less than a hundred meters behind the Americans. Ainslie advised Jimmy to sail at a lower, faster angle upwind: "We need to speed up a bit. They're really coming into us." Then Ainslie made the call to do *two tacks*, to position *USA-17* to make a right turn at the windward gate so they could start their second downwind leg offshore. The Kiwis were already set up to do only *one tack,* and head inshore toward San Francisco. Calling for the extra tack was a controversial move, but he and Slingsby saw more breeze offshore. Shortly after their turn downwind, Team USA's lead shot back up to 300 meters. Ainslie's critical call made the difference. "And that's why you have a four-time Olympic gold medalist as your tactician," noted Ken Read.

The American boat held off multiple Kiwi charges on leg three and again on leg four. When *USA-17* turned right at the leeward gate, they got up on their foils and flew across the finish line at close to thirty-six knots, twenty-three seconds ahead of the Kiwis.

Ainslie said of the high-pressure race, filled with wind shifts and leads extended and diminished: "You're trying to sail the boat as fast as you can but it's getting lighter. The guys did a good job of sailing. We managed to hold on and make the right decisions. But there were a few nervous moments."

The TV commentators reminded viewers that the pressure remained squarely on the American team. "Team USA's tactician, Ben Ainslie, had all the right answers in the first race. Will he get it right in the day's second race? Because if he doesn't, the Cup is on its way to New Zealand."

The second race of the day, race fifteen, began with Jimmy entering the starting box on port going almost forty knots. Barker entered on starboard, then jibed and followed. Jimmy tacked, passed very close to windward of Barker, then immediately dipped low in the box and got to leeward of the Kiwis. The boats sailed side by side and crossed the starting line at the same time, but Jimmy had the leeward position, and he used it to maintain control throughout the first leg of the race. *USA-17* rounded mark 1 in front of the Kiwis.

On the first downwind leg, Team USA sailed much faster than the Kiwis, and amassed a huge lead. By the time they turned right at the leeward gate, they were a full minute in front of Team New Zealand. As the two catamarans sailed toward the Golden Gate Bridge, the Americans started fully foiling upwind at over thirty-two knots, surging farther and farther ahead of the Kiwis. Gary Jobson, who had been the winning tactician on Ted Turner's America's Cup boat, was impressed. "Look at the difference in speed here, guys," he enthused.

Then he asked America's Cup helmsman Ken Read a question: "So, Ken, it looks like Oracle is going to win this one. They need to win four more and NZ needs one. Which boat would you take? The faster boat?" Read didn't bite, unable to conceive of or consider the possibility of his beloved Kiwis losing eight races in a row. But when *USA-17* crossed the finish line of race fifteen, the American team proved they could win four races in a row. Could they win the next four? To Jobson's experienced eye, Team USA now had the faster boat. He was the first of the expert commentators to say it out loud. He clearly believed that Team USA now had better than a 50-50 chance of coming all the way back, and holding on to the Cup that everyone else thought they were certain to lose.

After the day's races, Larry called Russell to tell him he was "a genius" for putting Ainslie on the boat as tactician. They both laughed and agreed that Sir Ben had done a great job in very tricky conditions during the first race. "On a day like today, it's so easy to make a bad tactical call and lose a race," Russell said. "But Ben got all the important calls right. He was the key guy out there today, and he did a great job for us."

Still, Russell always asked for more. Back at the base that evening, after the debrief, Russell cornered Ben and told him, "One of the things you might want to think about is doing a better job on the laylines to the marks. You might be giving away a bit of distance." Ainslie, the knighted star from Great Britain, stared at Russell, the knighted legend from New Zealand, narrowed his gaze, and slowly shook his head, as if to say, *Give me a fucking break*. Russell walked away smiling, aware he'd made the decorated Ainslie mad as hell.

That same Sunday evening, after the racing was over, Larry went to his house in San Francisco, put on a suit, and headed over to Oracle OpenWorld, his company's conference that annually drew some sixty thousand attendees to San Francisco's Moscone Center. Everyone had assumed that the America's Cup would have ended before Oracle OpenWorld started, but it hadn't, so Larry would juggle time spent with the team and time spent preparing for and giving presentations to tens of thousands of conference attendees.

Larry was scheduled to give the first keynote speech of the conference's opening night. When he came in and sat down in the first row of the main hall, filled with fifteen thousand people, he felt slightly light-headed and dizzy, which he attributed to the accumulated stress of racing day after day at match point. While he waited to be called onstage, he asked Judy Sim for a Coke, took a few sips, and then imagined himself getting up onstage and fainting. *That would not be good for the stock price*, he told himself. *And Safra will think I just dropped dead.* He looked at his watch. He had five minutes. *Drink your Coke. Close your eyes. Relax. Breathe slowly. When they call your name, go up onstage—and do your job.*

When his name was called, he slowly rose and took his time greeting members of Team USA, who filled the first two rows on the left side of the hall. One by one, he shook their hands and said, "Nice job, boys." He gave Jimmy a hug and said, "Hey, skipper, you're winning *all* the starts these days. You must have missed the *Sesame Street* episode on sharing."

Over the next ninety minutes, he delivered his keynote, speaking a little slower than he normally would have. He was fine until the last fifteen minutes, when he felt drained, like a spring slowly winding down. When he got to his waiting car and the driver asked, "Sir, would you like to drive?" Larry responded, "No chance. I'm going to have a hard time just staying awake while you drive." He got into the back of his politically correct silver Lexus 600H hybrid sedan and closed his eyes. The next thing he remembered was the car stopping in front of the garage in Woodside.

It had taken him a decade to win the Cup and three years preparing to defend it. The stress was getting to him. Down match point, there was no margin for error. They could not afford a single tactical error, or any kind of equipment failure. They had to win eight races in a row. They were halfway there.

At 1:15 on Monday, September 23, the gun went off and the sixteenth race of the 34th America's Cup began. The two boats sailed across the starting line at exactly the same time, and Barker had the favored leeward position, but Jimmy hit the line with more speed—a lot more speed. He used that speed to roll right over the top of the Kiwis and round mark 1 in front.

Team USA held on to their lead during the first run downwind, back up the beat to the windward gate, and all the way back downwind again. Team USA sailed an error-free race. Ainslie clamped a tight cover on the Kiwis, calling for Jimmy to tack or jibe so that *USA-17* was always positioned between Team New Zealand and the next mark. There were no passing lanes, no openings, no opportunities for Barker and company to get back into the race. When Team USA crossed the finish line thirty-three seconds in front, they had won their fifth race in a row.

There were no more scheduled days off—every day was a race day. Wind conditions permitting, there would be two races per day until the Cup was decided. Race seventeen on Monday was pushed to Tuesday, due to light winds this time. The Kiwis had three more chances. It had been six days since Emirates Team New Zealand had won a race. Each day, the pressure was building on Barker.

Races seventeen and eighteen were now scheduled for Tuesday, September 24. The breeze was blowing at 18 knots out of the west, and the 1.6-knot flood tide brought the current relief cone behind Alcatraz Island back into play.

Jimmy entered the starting area on port and sped away from the starting line at almost forty-two knots. Ten seconds later, Barker entered on starboard, crossed Jimmy's track, then jibed and followed. With one minute and thirty seconds to go, Jimmy jibed to leeward of the oncoming Barker, who tacked well to weather of *USA-17*. Both boats were headed back toward the starting line, sailing side by side, going less than half-speed, about seventeen knots. With fifty seconds to go, Barker put the bow down, closed the gap, and rolled over the top of *USA-17*.

It was *not* a good move. Barker had positioned the Kiwi cat right in front of *USA-17*. But there was still thirty-five seconds to go, and Barker was only twenty-five seconds behind the starting line. He had to slow down and somehow kill ten seconds. With Jimmy right behind him, pushing him, that was *impossible*. As Barker slowed down, Jimmy accelerated, ducked to leeward, and overlapped the Kiwi catamaran by half a boat-length. It was a dominant hook: Barker was trapped above him. Jimmy gradually turned up, and closed the gap between the two boats, forcing Barker to turn up to avoid contact and the penalty that went with it. When Barker turned up, slightly past head-to-wind, he created a few meters of space between the two boats. Then, with the boats still overlapped and the Kiwi catamaran almost stopped, Barker turned his wheel to the *left* and tried to accelerate. Jimmy responded by slowly turning his wheel to the *right*, and *USA-17*'s starboard bow gently tapped the Kiwis' port-side hull. *Contact—penalty Team New Zealand!*

After the collision, *USA-17* glided farther forward until the two boats were in perfect formation, side by side, a couple of meters apart. Barker turned his wheel ever so slightly back to the right, desperately trying to create more separation between the two boats—but if he turned too far to the right, his stern would swing out and he would cause a second collision. With the boats so close together, Barker was helpless, trapped to windward; all he could do now was point straight up, head-to-wind. That caused the Kiwis to slow down and stop. They were dead-in-the-water, but not for long. They began to drift to leeward toward *USA-17*. As their boat drifted closer and closer, Ben Ainslie started waving his arms and screaming at the Kiwi crew, "We've got to bear away, com'on—COM'ON." *Bang.* The Kiwis port bow hit the starboard hull of the American catamaran. *Collision—penalty Team New Zealand! Again.*

There was no damage to either boat. The same could not be said about the Kiwis' confidence. As *USA-17* pulled away from Team New Zealand's motionless catamaran, Ainslie glared at the Kiwi crew, shouted something unpleasant, then threw his right arm up in the air in a British version of an Italian "up yours" gesture. Then the Olympic gold medalist turned his back on Barker and congratulated his team's skipper and helmsman: "Nice work, Jimmy." Jimmy had had a *kill start* a few races ago, but this time, he was even more lethal. He shot Barker, and then he drove a stake right through his heart.

By the time the Kiwis finally got to mark 1, they were eighteen seconds and 400 meters behind Team USA. Throughout the rest of the race—downwind, upwind, downwind, reach to the finish—they never got close. Team New Zealand lost race seventeen before it started. When they crossed the finish line twenty-seven seconds behind the Americans, it was just a formality.

Team USA did not wait around to watch the Kiwis finish the race. Right after *USA-17* crossed the finish line, the giant thirteen-story catamaran made a graceful right-hand U-turn and cruised close by thousands of cheering American flag-waving fans crowding the piers and lining the shore. Then they sailed right up next to the boss. Larry's chase boat was overflowing with family and friends. They had surprised him by flying in that morning. Jimmy brought the huge catamaran within a couple of feet of the chase boat, smiled, and waved. Larry kissed Nikita and hugged his son David. Excitement was building. Confidence was building. Belief was building. The Americans had momentum.

Larry, who had been scheduled to give his second keynote address at Oracle OpenWorld that afternoon, had made the decision to instead stay on the water. He knew the decision would be criticized. It took him ten years to finally win the Cup. It could take just one more race to lose it. Win or lose, he wanted to be with the team.

Team USA had now won six races in a row, and *a total of nine races* overall. The Kiwis had won only eight. Without the infamous two-point penalty for cheating, the America's Cup would have been over: the team representing the once near-bankrupt Golden Gate Yacht Club would have defended successfully, and the team representing the Royal New Zealand Yacht Squadron would be heading home empty-handed. But Team USA's nine wins on the water translated to seven points on the scoreboard, one less than the Kiwis, who were not planning on going home just yet. What had once looked like a certain and decisive victory for the challengers was beginning to take on the shape and shadow of the greatest collapse in sports history. Barker had the weight of a nation on his shoulders.

Before the racing, Presti, who was matter-of-fact and hardly superstitious, had a certain feeling that he wouldn't dare articulate. Presti could see that Barker was shaken. He saw it in his body language, in the forward posture of his shoulders. He had studied Barker for a long time, and had sailed against him years earlier. He knew what the Kiwi skipper would do in various scenarios; Presti had told the team that Barker was "steady" and "predictable." The losses were getting to him, as was Jimmy's unblinking bravado during the press conferences.

Presti also could see that his guys had developed a rare chemistry to go with their undeniable momentum. The crew members were hardly the best of friends—Ainslie and Jimmy had been fierce competitors in the in-house racing, trying to destroy each other on the water. But now, Ainslie was providing Jimmy with more than just tactical help. He was evaluating gains and losses on the water, was clear on optimal modes, had great communication with Slingsby, and shared some of the leadership responsibilities. Presti was also amused by Sir Ben's communication. After a particularly good start, Ainslie would say in his crisp British way: "Oh, lovely start!" And Langford, who had spent the week before the beginning of the America's Cup being interviewed by a jury over the cheating scandal, with no time on the water, had stepped into his role with courage and skill.

Before the start of race eighteen, Presti continued to remind the guys to *forget the Cup*. "One race at a time," he said. "One start. One jibe. One upwind. Be what you do. Don't look too far ahead."

As the teams got their boats into position under clear, sunny skies, Larry wondered aloud whether Barker could erase the psychological damage done by the devastating defeat in the start of the first race. He had seen a lot of sports legends crumble, including his own former helmsman Chris Dickson. And, Barker had won just *one* of the last seven starts. This recent kill-start wound was only an hour old, leaving little time for healing. To make matters worse, the wind had picked up and was now blowing at around twenty knots, conditions that favored Oracle Team USA. But Barker had the early port entry, which was a big advantage. If Barker could grab an early lead in the next race, Team New Zealand had a good chance of winning the 34th America's Cup.

With two minutes and ten seconds to go, the Kiwi catamaran accelerated to over thirty-seven knots; then Barker turned the wheel slightly to the right and the red-winged sailboat from the future flew into the starting area. Barker was on port tack, headed away from and behind the starting line. Ten seconds later, *USA-17* entered on starboard, sailed to just above the Kiwis' track, jibed onto port, and followed behind and to weather of Team New Zealand. With a minute and twenty-five seconds to go, Barker jibed and pointed toward the starting line. Jimmy jibed at exactly the same time, positioning *USA-17* right in front of Barker. It was the opposite situation as the last race. This time it was Barker's turn to push Jimmy and to go for the overlap. *Barker got the hook.* But only for a moment. Jimmy accelerated just in time and broke the overlap. So close—but disaster averted.

There were five seconds to go as both boats turned down and accelerated for the starting line. They crossed the line dead even, but Barker had the controlling leeward position. Team USA would have to break the overlap and roll the Kiwis to get around mark 1 in front. But Barker held on and maintained his overlap all the way to mark 1. Then he luffed Jimmy hard. *It was payback time.* Jimmy had to turn sharply to the right to avoid the collision and avoid the penalty. As he suddenly changed direction, both of *USA-17*'s foiling hulls leapt even higher above the water. Then the big catamaran nose-dived back into the bay. As both bows dug in, two rooster tails of water splashed high into the air. The American catamaran slowed down. Barker turned left around mark 1 and sped away downwind, 70 meters ahead of Jimmy.

Barker had not folded under pressure. Instead, he rose to the occasion and did his job brilliantly. You could hear the cheers coming all the way from Auckland.

For days, TV commentator Ken Read had continued to say with confidence, "Just win a start, the rest comes easy." And Read repeatedly told the NBC audience "the Kiwi boat is fast enough" to hold off the Americans and win a race if they could just grab the lead. Now Barker had won the start of race eighteen.

Early on the run downwind, Team USA had a bad jibe and the Kiwis' advantage grew to 200 meters. But Team USA was consistently going faster and faster, eating into that lead. Midway down the run, the Kiwis' lead had been cut in half. Ken Read described *USA-17* as "flying downwind," then wondered aloud if the "Kiwis' boat was fast enough."

Leading into the leeward gate, the Kiwis had the option of turning left or right. *USA-17* would likely take the split and go the opposite way. In a flood tide on San Francisco Bay, the standard sailboat racing playbook says to make the *left turn* and head into the cone behind Alcatraz Island for relief from the unfavorable current. That's usually the right thing to do—*but not always*. New Zealand tactician Ray Davies positioned the Kiwi catamaran for the left turn at the leeward gate, and then Barker turned left. It turned out to be a terrible tactical mistake. The wind had shifted since the start of the race, so the right turning mark was at least a boat-length closer than the left turning mark. Worse yet, the boat that turned right would be sailing into more wind. Team USA took the split and turned right, now only seven seconds behind the Kiwis.

Team USA sailed toward the city front for about a minute, then tacked onto port and headed back toward the center of the race-course. They were sailing in more wind and going faster than the Kiwis. A minute later, Team New Zealand tacked onto starboard. The two boats were converging, and the Kiwis had a 50-meter lead and starboard advantage. Barker said, "Nice tack, boys," and asked his tactician, "What are you thinking?" Ray Davies responded, "I think we hit 'em"—meaning the Kiwis planned to do a lee bow tack in front of *USA-17* to block their wind.

The Kiwis then tacked to leeward and in front of Team USA, but they were too far to leeward, and not far enough in front. They *did not* tack in the right spot. They *did not* block *USA-17*'s wind. Instead of being forced to tack away, *USA-17* was able to keep on coming, fully foiling upwind at thirty-two knots. The Americans rolled over the Kiwis and took the lead. When the Kiwis tacked on the boundary, Team USA tacked right in front of them, blocking their wind. The Kiwis had to tack away. *USA-17* continued in its fully foiling upwind mode, building a lead of 150 meters in a couple of minutes. "What's shocking to me is how quickly it all happened," said Ken Read. Gary Jobson summed it up: "Right now, Oracle Team USA is a faster boat going upwind."

But that wasn't the whole story. Kiwi tactician Ray Davies had made two serious tactical errors during the critical race. He turned left at the leeward gate and sent the Kiwi boat into less breeze than if he had turned right. And he had called for a lee bow tack with only a 50-meter lead, a difficult-to-impossible maneuver to pull off in AC72 catamarans. Tactical blunders had plagued the American team during the early races of the 34th America's Cup. Now New Zealand was making tactical mistakes when they could least afford them.

Oracle Team USA astounded race viewers with its foiling speed upwind. Their lead grew to over 300 meters as they got to the windward gate nearly a minute before the Kiwis. *USA-17* was faster downwind too. When they got to the leeward gate and turned right toward the finish, the Americans' lead had grown to over a kilometer. When they crossed the finish line, the comeback was complete.

The teams were now even at eight points each. The Americans had won their seventh straight race, and in the words of one TV commentator, "For Dean Barker and Emirates Team New Zealand, the nightmare continues."

But from Larry's perspective, Barker had handled the pressure well. He used his port entry to win the start and get his team the lead. Then Davies got it wrong and Ainslie got it right at the leeward mark. But the big difference was boat speed upwind. Every day the Americans were going faster. In races seventeen and eighteen, they cambered their wing at more than forty degrees, a more acute angle than the Kiwis were using. *USA-17* was consistently foiling *upwind* at thirty-two knots. At the beginning of the Louis Vuitton Cup, the AC72s were foiling *downwind* at thirty-two knots.

At this point, the American team had a faster boat: faster downwind, faster reaching, and much faster upwind—just like the original computer models had predicted. The computer models had been right—with the parameters given—and Russell had been right. Team USA had not been getting anywhere near the maximum potential speed out of their boat because they hadn't known the right way to trim the wing, set up the loads, and balance the rudder. But now they did. They had studied and copied the Kiwis, and then they'd improved upon what they'd learned.

Russell was now feeling pretty good about how the team had performed under pressure. With one race to go, he couldn't help himself. He knew when to give the guys space, and when to lighten the mood. When Russell spotted Ainslie at the base, he went up to him and said, "Hey those laylines still need some work." Fortunately, the best Olympic sailor of all time now smiled back.

The teams were heading into a winner-takes-all race for the 34th America's Cup. In the 162-year history of the America's Cup, that had happened twice before. In 1920 the New York defender won. In 1983, the Australian challenger did.

On Wednesday morning, on the final day of the America's Cup, Jimmy woke early but couldn't get out of bed. He and several guys on the team had come down with the flu. He had felt lousy for days, but couldn't take any medication because of drug testing. He wasn't going to be hobbled by the flu, but he certainly wasn't going to make it to his early morning training and boxing session.

By noontime, the boats were out on the racecourse, and the wind was around nineteen knots, blowing from 265 to 270 degrees. The countdown was beginning. On the nineteenth day, after eighteen races, the America's Cup would be decided in one thirty-minute race scheduled to start at 1:15 p.m. The score was even at eight points each and the race was being called "one of the most improbable and inspiring days in the history of sailing."

San Francisco office workers planned late lunch breaks so they could catch the races, and a steady stream of locals and tourists poured into the city's waterfront viewing areas. Workers stuck in meetings planned to watch what they could on the free America's Cup app, offering racing and commentary in real time. Many parents took their kids out of school for the historic race, and even the scathing local press had come around. The *San Francisco Chronicle,* which had written off the event as a debacle, now wrote, "Just when you thought it was safe to leave the water, the America's Cup has blossomed into a fantastic affair. It's really a remarkable turn of events when you think about it. The America's Cup was the event everyone loved to hate. The participants were painted as bickering billionaires, intent on sinking their sport's greatest event in a tidal wave of cheating and tragedy and acrimonious squabbles. The economic impact was suspect. The overall interest was minimal. Then, the tide changed course. Instead of petering out in a lopsided blowout, the finals have become thrilling."

Larry was in his usual spot, bobbing around in his Protector chase boat, near the port entry to the starting box. His family and friends were onboard. There were hugs and handshakes all around. He sat down between his girlfriend, Nikita, and his FBI pal, Johnny. The two men said in unison, "One race at a time, baby, one race at a time."

The wind had dropped to around sixteen knots with a moderate flood tide current and relatively smooth water.

In a prerace interview, Barker, looking calm, said, "I have complete belief in our team, our guys, and I know we can win the race. It's obviously a big ask the way the Oracle guys have been sailing. They've improved a huge amount, but they're not unbeatable." Then he smiled slightly and added, "A lot has been made about today. It's a monumental occasion for the America's Cup. It will be remembered for a long, long time. We have to go about making sure *we* remember it for the right reasons."

Jimmy said, "We're not going to leave anything in the tank. The boys every single day find another level. I'm going to ask for everything."

With less than thirty minutes to go before the start of the "race of the century," Larry spotted something going on with the wing of his catamaran. He didn't like what he saw. His trusted builder Mark Turner was on the platform with the sailors, and a rigger was on a halyard making his way up the sail.

Larry quickly got word that a carbon component in the main control element had come apart. It was being glued back together by rigger Jeff Causey.

"*Glued* back together!" Larry shouted into his iPhone.

David tried to reassure his father, saying, "Its fast-drying resin infused with carbon—very strung stuff, Dad."

"I got it," Larry shot back. "It's good glue, fucking awesome glue. Wonderful. *How could anything possibly go wrong when we've got really good glue?*" Larry let out a big sigh and sat down.

A moment later, Meir Teper of Nobu, a close friend and neighbor of Larry's in Malibu, climbed onboard.

"What's wrong?" Teper asked, seeing Larry's expression.

"The good news is we have a faster boat than they do," Larry said in a monotone. "The bad news is it's broken."

"What if we can't race?" Teper asked.

"Well, then we lose the America's Cup," Larry said.

Teper stared at Larry in disbelief, then turned and looked at his wife, Katya. Neither one of them knew what to think.

On the boat, the rigger Causey was applying methyl acrylic, a quick-setting adhesive in a tube, to the top part of flap two, which was less than halfway up the sail. The part that held a pin for the control arm had broken. The $2 million wing sail wouldn't work without it.

Turner watched from below, thinking, *This is happening minutes before the start of the most important race in Cup history?*

Causey rappelled back down. He and Turner got back into their chase boat, and Jimmy and crew sailed away.

"Okay, they're sailing," Larry said, not convinced the glue would hold.

Team New Zealand once again had the advantage of the early port entry in the winner-takes-all race. The wind was blowing at 17 knots, and a flood tide of 1.4 knots was keeping the waves small. Barker entered the box with two minutes and ten seconds to go before the start. He then sped away behind the line at nearly 40 knots. Ten seconds later, Jimmy came in on starboard, sailed down to Barker's line, then jibed and followed. With a minute and a half to go, Barker began his jibe low in the starting box, just above the layline. Jimmy then tacked well to weather of the Kiwis, and the two boats sailed side by side.

With a minute to go, both boats were sailing toward the starting line, a big gap between them. With forty-five seconds to go, Jimmy put the bow down, going for the hook. Barker defended by putting his bow down too. Jimmy never got close to Barker. He broke off the attack, and turned back toward the starting line. Barker turned up and paralleled *USA-17* with twenty-five seconds to go.

Then, as time counted down, Barker turned up a bit and closed the gap between the two boats, using his leeward right-of-way position to force Jimmy to sail high and stay clear. With only ten seconds to go, it was all time and distance to the line. With six seconds to go, Barker turned down and accelerated. A second later, Jimmy did the same. The boats crossed the starting line at the same time, going the same speed, with Barker in a controlling tight-to-leeward position. It was another great start by Barker, two in a row.

Jimmy had to gain at least a boat-length on the short reaching leg toward the city or Barker was going to round mark 1 in front. He couldn't do it. Barker maintained the controlling overlap all the way to the first mark. When Jimmy started his left turn onto the downwind leg, Barker turned right and luffed him hard. Jimmy responded to the luff by snapping *USA-17* back to the right. The big AC72 catamaran didn't like being thrown around like a dinghy. She stuffed both of her bows deep under the water in protest, resulting in a huge amount of white water being thrown up in the air. It looked like a couple of depth charges had just gone off right in front of *USA-17*. Then the American AC72 shuddered, and slowed.

Larry gasped as *USA-17*'s two bows dove and submerged. He held his breath and watched and waited. He slowly exhaled as *USA-17* recovered, curled around mark 1, and accelerated downwind in hot pursuit of Team New Zealand. "Well, if that didn't break the control arm, maybe the glue will hold her together after all," he said.

Barker had done his job well. He used his early port entry to win the start and get the lead. *Would it be enough? USA-17* was first to jibe onto port, then the Kiwis jibed. It was a side-by-side downwind drag race with both boats going over forty knots. New Zealand was only 40 meters in front. With the wind blowing between eighteen and nineteen knots, the downwind speed of the boats was very even. As they approached the northern boundary, the boats simultaneously jibed onto starboard. The Kiwi cat was now positioned directly in front of *USA-17*, less than a boat-length separating the leader's stern from the follower's bow. Once again, the two catamarans jibed at the same time as the Kiwis reached the port layline to the leeward gate. With a slender 60-meter lead, Barker went through the gate, turned left, and headed for current relief behind Alcatraz, while Jimmy turned right to get the split.

So far, it was almost an exact replica of race eighteen—except this time, it was even closer. As both boats headed upwind, the Americans were only three seconds behind.

Team New Zealand was first to tack on the upwind leg. Then Team USA tacked. As both boats converged in the middle of the racecourse they were dead even, bow to bow—but the Kiwis had starboard advantage. Jimmy was forced to put the bow down and dip and cross behind Team New Zealand. After the first cross, the Americans headed offshore and the Kiwis sailed toward the city. Then both boats tacked and converged a second time. But this time, Team USA had starboard advantage. The TV commentators described it as "a moment of truth"—and it was. *USA-17* passed clear ahead of Team New Zealand on the second cross. Gary Jobson noted, "We're going to learn a lot here in the next couple of minutes. If USA continues to gain, their boat is a lot faster." On the third cross, the starboard advantage went back to the Kiwis, but it didn't help. *USA-17* crossed clear in front again, with an even larger lead than at the last cross.

The spectacle on San Francisco Bay was breathtaking, and the regatta that began in 1851 with elegant monohulls viewable only as dots on the horizon now involved space-age catamarans flying on hydrofoils above the water just offshore. Suburban moms cheered with captivated kids, Financial District types paused next to bike messengers, and even Americans and Kiwis rooting for their own teams could appreciate the scene, with the iconic Golden Gate Bridge, the stunning cats, and the fierce competition.

Witnessing the continuous gains being made by the Americans on the upwind leg, Ken Read finally conceded to Gary Jobson, "Boat speed, boat speed, boat speed—a tactician's best friend." Until the previous day Read had maintained his "win the start, win the race" mantra. But Barker had won the last two starts, only to get passed upwind.

Team USA increased its lead to 160 meters as they raced toward the weather gate, but they took nothing for granted. Facing another cross, Ainslie told the boys, "This is it, this is it, work your asses off." Team USA was *continuously foiling upwind.* The very last set of engineering changes to *USA-17* had enabled that mode, and it was proving decisive over the final two days of the 34th America's Cup. "Pull away here, Jimmy," Ainslie said, as the lead grew to 260 meters. "Great gains guys; great gains, guys," Ainslie said. Seconds later, looking toward the stronger wind ahead, the Brit cautioned, "Higher load, higher load." Team USA rounded the right mark of the weather gate twenty-six seconds ahead of the Kiwis.

Mark Turner watched and wondered if the glue joint on the wing sail control arm would hold together.

As Team USA raced downwind, their lead grew and grew until it reached almost 700 meters. The American boat was foiling along at around forty knots on its final approach to the last turning mark in the race when Jimmy cracked a smile as huge as his lead. Suspecting the crime of premature celebration, Ken Read cautioned, "Don't smile *yet,* Jimmy."

But Jimmy wasn't smiling about the lead. He was smiling because Kyle Langford had slipped backward and lost control of the wing sheet, the rope controlling the trim angle of the wing. Reflexively, Langford reached out and somehow—at the last possible second—grabbed the loose sheet with one hand, regaining control and averting disaster. In that split second, with the finish line just ahead and years of work and struggle behind, the boat could have capsized. Jimmy realized that the angel of death had passed over them. His smile was one of relief. Jimmy patted Langford on the back, and said, "Nice one, mate. Hang in there, we're almost home."

USA-17 turned right around the fourth and final mark of race nineteen. The finish line was in sight. The television audience following on NBC and on the America's Cup app saw the stars and stripes of the American flag virtually superimposed on the water. It was not the day for New Zealand's blue flag with its Southern Cross of four stars. Less than a minute later, when the Americans crossed the final finish line in the 34th America's Cup regatta, the Kiwis still had 760 more meters to go. It was over. Team USA had won its eighth race in a row, completing what many heralded as the greatest comeback in the history of sports.

As the crowds went wild, as horns blared and phones were held high and aimed at the water, as the team's "Back in Black" theme song was blasted, Jimmy had a brief moment that felt strangely quiet. He took in the afternoon light, the pulsating crowds, and looked at his teammates. He gave the massive black catamaran—which he'd taken to calling "the old girl"—a gentle pat on her side. He smiled when he saw grinder Simeon Tienpont lean down and kiss the winning machine. He watched these hulking men, who in the weeks before had looked like nothing could break them. Now they were jumping and hugging and lifting one another up. He knew of the pain, the sacrifices, and the work that had gone into this moment. Jimmy wanted to carry *this* moment always.

Larry was soon onboard and caught up in his own joy. He hugged Jimmy, Ben, Tom Slingsby, Joey Newton, each of the massive grinders, everyone. Then he shouted, "Hey, guys, do you know what you did? You just won eight races in a row. You just won the America's Cup!"

And as *USA-17* headed back to Pier 80, foiling along at forty-two knots, Jimmy turned to Larry and said, "Hey, mate, you're not wearing a helmet." Larry put his hand on Jimmy's shoulder and shouted, "Boats have tried to kill me before, but I'm feeling lucky today. Let's go faster."

Later that afternoon, back at the pier, Larry credited the engineers and builders who stayed up night after night designing and building the modifications to their AC72. He credited the guys who went out every day and relearned how to sail the boat, employing new steering and trimming techniques to exploit every modification. And he credited Russell Coutts, now a five-time America's Cup winner, for "figuring it all out." Larry talked about his team CEO as the indispensable man: "Russell never lost faith in the computer models that said we should be faster upwind. He studied the Kiwis, worked with the designers, until he learned and understood why we weren't. Then he orchestrated change after change to our boat until, by the end of the regatta, we were faster upwind—fast enough to win."

As for his own role, Larry paused and said, "I'm very proud of the guys. It was their victory, not mine. Russell, Jimmy, Ben, Tommy, Joey, Tugsy. All the guys on the team. I really think of this as something they did, not me. But I'm very proud to be a part of the overall effort—a part of the team."

Jimmy listened to Larry and nodded. Adjusting his cap, he said, "On your own, you're nothing. But when you've got a team like this, they make you look great."

All of the setbacks, curveballs, and criticism were actually *motivating*, the two-time America's Cup winner said. "The team looked down the barrel of a gun every day and never flinched," Jimmy said, flashing a grin. "There's nothing like going all in."

Epilogue

The 35th America's Cup

L ESS THAN A week after winning the America's Cup for the second time, Larry sat in the quiet living room of his Woodside home and talked about what comes next. He was still assimilating all that had gone wrong, and all that had gone right, to pull off an epic victory being called "the comeback of comebacks," a win that "made the Red Sox [down 0–3 to the Yankees in the 2004 American League Championship Series] look like they were playing mini golf."

Larry called the races of the 34th America's Cup "the most magnificent spectacle" he'd ever seen on the water and said he believes the regatta has "changed sailing forever."

His vision for the next America's Cup is a departure from anything done before.

"We're going to start with two years of globe-trotting, Formula One–style racing in AC45s," he said. "AC45s are inexpensive to build, transport, and sail. You can throw an AC45 and its support equipment and chase boats into a couple of containers and ship them to regattas all over the world: Shanghai, Tokyo Bay, Marseilles, the Port of Rome, anywhere."

Larry continued, "By using AC45s, we keep the costs to a manageable level, so we expect to have twelve teams entered in the 35th America's Cup. The teams will be divided up into two divisions: Atlantic and Pacific. The Atlantic Division will have teams from France, Germany, Great Britain, Italy, Sweden, and Switzerland. The Pacific Division will have teams from Australia, China, Japan, Korea, New Zealand, and San Francisco, USA."

Larry said the top four finishers in the AC45 races during 2015 and 2016, two from the Atlantic group and two from the Pacific, will qualify to race in their division championships in the spring of 2017. The division championships will be contested in the new AC60s, a lot bigger than the AC45s and just as spectacular and fast as the AC72s, but not as expensive. The Atlantic Division championship regatta will be in the Port of Rome; the Pacific Division championship will be in Shanghai. A couple of months later, the Atlantic and Pacific division winners will race their AC60s along the leeward coast of Maui, Hawaii, for the Louis Vuitton Cup. The Louis Vuitton winner will stay in Hawaii to race their AC60 against Oracle Team USA in the 35th America's Cup. To date, Larry has signed a number of key people, including Russell Coutts, Jimmy Spithill, and Tom Slingsby, to be a part of his next campaign.

Holding the Louis Vuitton Cup and the main event, the America's Cup, in Hawaii is part of another of Larry's long-standing dreams. In June 2012, he purchased the island of Lanai for $300 million. It was a far-fetched fantasy he had had since he was in his twenties, when he first flew over one of Hawaii's smallest inhabited islands in a Cessna 172 and was captivated by the thousands of acres of fragrant pineapple fields. Since becoming the owner of 98 percent of the 141-square-mile island, he has proposed or implemented an array of changes, from building an ultraluxury hotel on the pristine, white-sand beach facing Molokai and Maui to returning commercial agriculture to the clear-cut acres. He plans to endow a sustainability laboratory that will help make the island "the first economically viable one-hundred-percent-green community." Both of the Four Seasons hotels on the island will undergo major remodels. Larry and his team have met with experts in desalination and solar energy to change the way water and electricity are generated, collected, stored, and delivered on the island. The abiding goal, Larry said, "is to make the island better for everyone, especially the people who live there." Having the Louis Vuitton Cup on the waters between Maui and Lanai would be a boon to the island's tourism and visibility.

"That's the plan, anyway," Larry said. "We have a lot of work to do. We have to make deals with all the cities where we want to hold races. It's not going to be easy to pull this off. All that, plus we have to get an agreement with the Challenger of Record, the Hamilton Island Yacht Club of Australia." Hamilton Island is owned by Bob Oatley, who made his fortune as a coffee trader and a vintner. Oatley, who has a net worth of just under $1 billion, has said he is hoping to pull in corporate sponsorships and government help. Australia last challenged for the Cup in 2000, when the twenty-year-old Jimmy Spithill was skipper.

Larry said that the tradition of holding all the races in one city for the duration of the Louis Vuitton Cup and then the America's Cup doesn't make commercial sense.

"The previous practice of going to only one city, Auckland or San Francisco or Valencia, and being in the same location for months at a time is not the best way to get fans all over the world excited about our sport," he said. "It should be more like Formula One, where you have races all around the world and all of the races count toward the championship. People want to see Team China racing in Shanghai and Team Japan racing in Tokyo Bay. Now that's exciting. But we have to keep the costs down to make sure that there *is* a Team China and a Team Japan."

The key part of the next America's Cup will be lowering the costs, so more teams can participate. "To race an AC72 in San Francisco cost the teams at least a hundred million dollars," Larry said. "To race an AC45 all over the world in 2015 and 2016 plus an AC60 in 2017 will cost each team as little as thirty million dollars, all in. The AC45 is a one-design boat with a five-man crew—so it's easy to ship, set up, and race. And this time the AC45 racing will be more than a pretty preseason show leading up to the America's Cup. This time, points earned for each and every AC45 race, match races and fleet races, will determine whether or not you qualify to race for your division championship in AC60s in 2017. So the next America's Cup actually begins with the AC45 racing in 2015. Every race is important—just like Formula One."

He added, "We plan to have AC45 races in every country where we have a team: Auckland, New Zealand; Sydney, Australia; Shanghai, China; Venice, Italy—twelve cities in twelve different countries. The TV coverage should be stunning. Look at the AC45 regatta we held in Venice a couple of years ago. It was beautiful. Check it out on YouTube."

Larry also envisions creating a worldwide brand around the America's Cup. "Sailing is a cool international sport with a long history," he said. "Racing close to the shore has helped build our fan base. The computer-enhanced TV coverage has made the racing understandable to nonsailors. By racing all over the world, we can continue to build our international fan base. If we are successful in building up our TV and live audience, that will attract more and bigger sponsors."

Larry remains convinced he can transform sailing into an "exciting and popular professional sport." But to do that, he said, "a lot needs to change. We want to keep the best of the past and combine it with modern technology. We want to create a twenty-first-century sports business that will support sailing professionals and their families. Businesses that don't make money are not sustainable. Sports that don't make money are just hobbies for rich guys."

Larry has now put nearly fourteen years into the America's Cup, and he has learned a great deal about pursuing and defending sailing's Holy Grail. Little is easy when it comes to the America's Cup, he now knows. Not the engineering, building, sailing, or administration. He acknowledges that he had no idea when he made the decision in Antigua in April 2000 to go after the Cup that it would become a business, not a hobby. "The sum total of my experience was designing, building, and racing *Sayonara*," he said. "I didn't realize that recruiting and managing the one hundred and fifty people that make up an America's Cup team has a lot more in common with my job running Oracle than my experience racing *Sayonara*. You need engineering and design teams, build teams, shore teams, sales and marketing teams for sponsorships, accountants, and athletes that race the boat. You need a CEO and managers for every group. I didn't have a sense of the organization's size or complexity. Competing for the America's Cup is a job, not a hobby."

Larry noted that the painful parts of running a business also apply to running an America's Cup syndicate. "If you want to win, you have to be willing to make very hard personnel decisions," Larry said. "If you want to be the best, you have to hire the best, and you have to constantly be looking to upgrade your people. I had to lose twice before I finally came to terms with saying good-bye to the guys I sailed with on *Sayonara,* guys who weren't quite good enough to help us win the America's Cup. It was very hard for me to say good-bye to the friends I had sailed with and won with for years. But if you own a professional football team, you cannot let someone play quarterback just because he's your friend. Now, Russell has to make the hard decisions. He decides who can help win the next Cup and who's past his prime. It's a tough business."

Each Cup campaign has cost Larry between $100 million and $200 million. When asked about the exact cost, Larry said, "Sponsors paid a lot of the overall cost. How much did I spend? The truth is, I don't know, and I don't want to know." There are days when all of the work and expense feel worth it, and there are days when he wishes he had picked another goal. "I have asked myself, 'Why am I doing this?'" Larry said with a laugh. "I feel like the dog that caught the bus. If I had known what I was getting into, I would have done things very differently. I would have started with Russell Coutts. He's not just a great sailor—Chris Dickson is a great sailor too, though Russell is even better—but Russell is a guy who can run a very large and complex organization. He's an engineer, a manager, and even more important, a leader—that rare person other people will follow. For me, what started as a hobby gradually became an obsession. It took a while for me to understand how and why I made such a large emotional and financial commitment to winning a boat race."

He went on, "My life has been all about testing my limits and learning from failure. It's been a journey of discovery, of seeing how far I can go. I'm trapped in a never-ending cycle of competing and learning. Once I was successful with *Sayonara,* it was time to raise the bar, so I tried the America's Cup. I was unsuccessful at first—but I learned from it—and eventually we won. Now we're defending the America's Cup. So how do I get off this merry-go-round? How do I stop when I'm winning?" Larry paused and looked out at his man-made lake, framed by bluestone boulders from the Sierras. Finally, he said, "It's hard for me to quit when I'm losing—and it's hard for me to quit when I'm winning. It's just hard for me to quit. I'm addicted to competing."

Norbert, meanwhile, will serve as commodore of the Golden Gate Yacht Club through 2014, and will continue to be involved as long as Larry wants him there. "I've put a lot of years into the club," Norbert said. Looking ahead, the mechanic is searching for a new location in San Francisco for his auto shop, and he's going to try to "adapt with today's economy and the needs of the people." He'll focus on air-conditioning and full automotive services. Norbert holds no grudges against his father, though now there are two things the men don't discuss: the yacht club and the business. He chuckles thinking of the day when Jozo told him to stick to what he knew: radiators. When he opens his new shop, his bread and butter will be a thing of the past. He will no longer sell, distribute, or fix radiators. But he will carry on another family tradition: the name will remain Alouis.

Appendix

The America's Cup Races

AFTER THE FIRST international regatta was held in 1851, with the schooner *America* defeating the best that the British had to offer, the America's Cup was largely a race between two nations. That changed after 1983, when Australia wrested the Cup away from the New York Yacht Club, sending a message that the America's Cup—held by the United States for 132 years—was a true competition. Subsequent races saw entries from up to a dozen countries. Here is a list of the races waged and won following that first race around the Isle of Wight. (YC = Yacht Club. NYYC = New York Yacht Club.)

1. 1870	*Magic* NEW YORK YC	beat	*Cambria* ROYAL THAMES YC
2. 1871	*Columbia* and *Sappho* NYYC	beat	*Livonia* ROYAL HARWICH YC
3. 1876	*Madeleine* NYYC	beat	*Countess of Dufferin* ROYAL CANADIAN YC
4. 1881	*Mischief* NYYC	beat	*Atalanta* BAY OF QUINTE YC

5. 1885	*Puritan* NYYC	beat	*Genesta* ROYAL YACHT SQUADRON
6. 1886	*Mayflower* NYYC	beat	*Galatea* ROYAL NORTHERN YC
7. 1887	*Volunteer* NYYC	beat	*Thistle* ROYAL CLYDE YC
8. 1893	*Vigilant* NYYC	beat	*Valkyrie II* ROYAL ULSTER YC
9. 1895	*Defender* NYYC	beat	*Valkyrie III* ROYAL YACHT SQUADRON
10. 1899	*Columbia* NYYC	beat	*Shamrock I* ROYAL ULSTER YC
11. 1901	*Columbia* NYYC	beat	*Shamrock II* ROYAL ULSTER YC
12. 1903	*Reliance* NYYC	beat	*Shamrock III* ROYAL ULSTER YC
13. 1920	*Resolute* NYYC	beat	*Shamrock IV* ROYAL ULSTER YC
14. 1930	*Rainbow* NYYC	beat	*Shamrock V* ROYAL ULSTER YC
15. 1934	*Enterprise* NYYC	beat	*Endeavour* ROYAL YACHT SQUADRON
16. 1937	*Ranger* NYYC	beat	*Endeavour II* ROYAL YACHT SQUADRON
17. 1958	*Columbia* NYYC	beat	*Sceptre* ROYAL YACHT SQUADRON
18. 1962	*Weatherly* NYYC	beat	*Gretel* ROYAL SYDNEY YACHT SQUADRON
19. 1964	*Constellation* NYYC	beat	*Sovereign* ROYAL THAMES YC

20. 1967	*Intrepid* NYYC	beat	*Dame Pattie* ROYAL SYDNEY YACHT SQUADRON
21. 1970	*Intrepid* NYYC	beat	*Gretel II* ROYAL SYDNEY YACHT SQUADRON
22. 1974	*Courageous* NYYC	beat	*Southern Cross* ROYAL PERTH YC
23. 1977	*Courageous* NYYC	beat	*Australia* SUN CITY YC
24. 1980	*Freedom* NYYC	beat	*Australia* ROYAL PERTH YC
25. 1983	*Australia II* ROYAL PERTH YC	beat	*Liberty* NYYC
26. 1987	*Stars & Stripes* SAN DIEGO YC	beat	*Kookaburra III* ROYAL PERTH YC
27. 1988	*Stars & Stripes* SAN DIEGO YC	beat	*New Zealand* MERCURY BAY BOATING CLUB
28. 1992	*America³* SAN DIEGO YC	beat	*Il Moro di Venezia* YACHT CLUB OF VENICE
29. 1995	*Black Magic* ROYAL NEW ZEALAND YACHT SQUADRON	beat	*Young America* SAN DIEGO YC
30. 2000	*Team New Zealand* ROYAL NEW ZEALAND YACHT SQUADRON	beat	*Luna Rossa* YACHT CLUB PUNTA ALA
31. 2003	*Alinghi* SOCIÉTÉ NAUTIQUE DE GENÈVE	beat	*Team New Zealand* ROYAL NEW ZEALAND YACHT SQUADRON
32. 2007	*Alinghi* SOCIÉTÉ NAUTIQUE DE GENÈVE	beat	*Emirates Team New Zealand* ROYAL NEW ZEALAND YACHT SQUADRON

33. 2010   *USA-17*   beat   *Alinghi 5*
GOLDEN GATE YC   SOCIÉTÉ NAUTIQUE
DE GENÈVE

34. 2013   *USA-17*   beat   *Team New Zealand*
GOLDEN GATE YC   ROYAL NEW ZEALAND
YACHT SQUADRON

Author's Note

THE IDEA FOR THIS BOOK can be traced back more than a decade, to 2002, when I first learned from Larry Ellison that he was going to form a team to compete for the America's Cup. What made the story so compelling to me wasn't the Cup itself, for I wasn't yet a follower. I was intrigued by the back-story of how Larry had joined forces in his quest for the Cup with a blue-collar boating club situated along the San Francisco marina and not the blue-blooded St. Francis. When Larry told me the Golden Gate Yacht Club's commodore was a radiator repairman, I knew this was a story I wanted to tell. Larry said with conviction that he would win the Cup and bring back the oldest trophy in sports not only to America but to the waters of San Francisco Bay. I quickly made a call to the Golden Gate and met with the commodore, Norbert Bajurin, who impressed me with his earnestness, intelligence, and candor. I loved his story, and the story of his family coming to America for a better life, and finding a welcoming place in the Golden Gate Yacht Club. As I learned more of the story, I was intrigued and touched by how the race for the America's Cup altered not only the fate of the Golden Gate Yacht Club, but Norbert's life—for better and for worse. I followed Oracle Racing's losses in 2003 and 2007 and watched as Larry and Norbert and crew pulled off a victory on Valentine's Day in Valencia in 2010. The America's Cup itself, with all of its colorful history and technological daring, pulled me in. Even from afar, I felt I had a personal attachment to the victory, as I'd followed the dreams and defeats from day one. And when I watched the America's Cup world series races in San Francisco in the summer and fall of 2012 I was more than impressed. Larry's goal had become a reality. Norbert had helped make it happen. The boats were spectacular, the races were thrilling, and the crowd was won over. And, of course, the comeback by Team USA is something I will never forget.

Reporting for this book involved countless interviews with sailors, engineers, coaches, builders, and America's Cup historians. I spent months reviewing video, audio, and team notes from various races; reading sailing periodicals; and then talking time and again with Larry, Russell, Jimmy, Tugsy, Tom Ehman, and others about the races. I even took sailing lessons to better understand the terms and maneuvers, and to get a better sense of the sport's appeal.

One of the great days in reporting came when I was invited to sail with Jimmy Spithill on one of his team's two AC45 catamarans. Spithill drove one boat and Russell Coutts drove the other. We headed out toward the Golden Gate Bridge on a cold and foggy day for a practice session, and within about fifteen minutes Jimmy told me to move from my crouched position at the back of the boat—where you get drenched by waves—and make my way up on the trampoline and take a seat next to him. He instructed me to lean back over the hull and tuck my feet up and under the hiking strap made of seat belt–like material running along the netting. We were flying across the water when Jimmy handed me the tiller and told me to drive. We were heeling at around forty-five degrees and racing none other than Russell Coutts, whose boat was on a parallel track, a dozen feet away.

"You crash it, you own it," Jimmy laughed. In that moment, I could feel the adrenaline of the sport and I could see the technological wonder of the boat at hand as it reacted to the slightest touch, as it groaned and creaked and cut through the choppy sea.

What captivated me was being out in the elements of San Francisco Bay—the strong winds, big waves, and descending fog. It was all-enveloping, an environment you can react to, but can't control.

When Jimmy took the tiller back I looked at the stunning boat, fast-moving crew, and expanse of water and said, "You've got a pretty cool office." The Aussie with the wind-chafed face smiled.

I've come to learn that the America's Cup is the pinnacle of sailing, attracting millionaires and billionaires and the sport's greatest athletes, engineers, and builders. It produces boats that have never been seen before and is an event that still represents the technological innovations of nations. But another part of it—the part I relished on the San Francisco Bay—is older than the Cup itself. It is the allure of the sea, the thrill and risks of going up against Mother Nature, the reminder, as Eugene O'Neill wrote, that "the sea hates a coward."

Acknowledgments

FIRST I WANT to thank Larry Ellison for the time he gave me for this story. Over the course of two years, we met regularly, and talked for hours at a sitting. Although he is one of the most difficult people to schedule time with—I had my life turned upside down on a regular basis—Larry is entirely yours when you are finally seated next to him. He does not check his phone or e-mail and he doesn't take calls (except once, from Safra Catz, during Oracle's trial against Google, when he had exceedingly interesting and irreverent things to say about Larry Page).

I found him to be predictably brilliant, but also thoughtful, self-deprecating, and fall-out-of-your-chair funny. In other words, very different from how the public perceives the high-flying billionaire. I also found him to be inspiring. He has taken his near-death experiences (notably the hurricane of Sydney-to-Hobart) to heart, living each day as fully as he can, and setting new goals just as he achieves old ones.

Larry is an interesting mix of living large—buying islands, flying planes, dining with presidents and prime ministers, and running a company of 120,000 people—while cherishing the small and ephemeral moments. He will stop in mid-sentence to watch a merganser land on his lake. "That's my favorite duck," he'll say, before launching into a discussion about the bird and its history, patterns, and uniqueness. He finds profound meaning in the beauty and impermanence of nature. Larry's life—over-the-top experiences and all—has much to teach. I'm grateful for our conversations. I'm also grateful for the work he put into the book, and the expertise he brought to the sailing material.

Next, I want to thank Norbert, who let me deep into his life and shared with me his personal stories—sometimes joyous, sometimes extremely painful. Norbert is an everyday hero who lives a good, full, honest life and takes care of his family, friends, employees, and community. But he's also someone who found a way to change a slice of history. He went after something that others told him was out of his reach, out of his league. He is one of the classiest guys I know. I believe that the America's Cup would not have come to San Francisco if it weren't for him. I also appreciate his wife, Madeleine, who put up with all of my questions over the years, and never objected to my needing more time with Norbert.

For help from the Oracle Racing and corporation side, I want to especially thank Tom Ehman, the sailing team's director of external affairs, who is a walking encyclopedia of information on Cups past and present, and who responded thoughtfully to my relentless questions about everything from sailing terms to wind conditions during specific regattas. Thank you to Judy Sim, Mark "Tugsy" Turner, Bill Erkelens, Russell Coutts, Chris Dickson, Jimmy Spithill, and Joseph Ozanne. Also thank you to Lucy Jewett, a longtime Cup enthusiast who shared her stories with me, and to Bob Fisher, author of *An Absorbing Interest: The America's Cup*, who helped me with the Appendix. Thank you, too, to sailing aficionados Tom Webster and Peter Huston for sharing their knowledge.

On the publishing side, a special note of appreciation to my literary agent Joe Veltre, at the Gersh Agency in New York, who is there for me every important step of the way. To my skilled editor at Grove/Atlantic, Jamison Stoltz, who stayed calm even in some trying times and who gave me ideas, support, and direction; and to Grove's publisher, Morgan Entrekin, who loved the story from the start.

I also thank my wonderful family, starting with my brothers David and Kevin and their families. My late father, Wayne, a voracious reader—who came from behind, worked hard, and found success—would have been taken with this story. And a special and eternal note of gratitude to my best friend and mom, Connie. She has always supported me in this crazy, joyous, torturous, but ultimately incredible endeavor of being a writer.

Finally, to my young son, Roman, my smart, funny, and wildly creative boy. I know you got tired of hearing me say I still had to work after putting you to bed. You always made me smile when you wandered out in your pajamas, way past your bedtime, and saw me sitting at my computer. You came over and hugged me and asked, "How many more chapters, Mama?"

When you are older, I hope you will read this book and find inspiration to make your own dreams come true. Whatever they are, dream big.